Exam Ref AZ-303 Microsoft Azure Architect Technologies

Mike Pfeiffer
Derek Schauland
Gurvinder Singh
Nicole Stevens

Exam Ref AZ-303 Microsoft Azure Architect Technologies

Published with the authorization of Microsoft Corporation by:
Pearson Education, Inc.
Hoboken, NJ

ISBN-13: 978-013-680509-0
ISBN-10: 0-136-80509-4

Library of Congress Control Number: 2020947522

ScoutAutomatedPrintCode

TRADEMARKS

WARNING AND DISCLAIMER

SPECIAL SALES

For information about buying this title in bulk quantities, or for special sales opportunities (which may include electronic versions; custom cover designs; and content particular to your business, training goals, marketing focus, or branding interests), please contact our corporate sales department at corpsales@pearsoned.com or (800) 382-3419.

For government sales inquiries, please contact governmentsales@pearsoned.com.

For questions about sales outside the U.S., please contact intlcs@pearson.com.

CREDITS

EDITOR-IN-CHIEF
Brett Bartow

EXECUTIVE EDITOR
Loretta Yates

ASSISTANT SPONSORING EDITOR
Charvi Arora

DEVELOPMENT EDITOR
Rick Kughen

MANAGING EDITOR
Sandra Schroeder

SENIOR PROJECT EDITOR
Tracey Croom

COPY EDITOR
Rick Kughen

INDEXER
Timothy Wright

PROOFREADER
Abigail Bass

TECHNICAL EDITOR
Thomas Palathra

EDITORIAL ASSISTANT
Cindy Teeters

COVER DESIGNER
Twist Creative, Seattle

Contents at a glance

Contents

Acknowledgments

I am indebted to Microsoft Press for the opportunity to co-author this book, in association with Mike Pfeiffer, Derek Schauland, and Nicole Stevens. The co-authors hardly need any introduction, as they are well known for their professional prowess and their in-depth knowledge of the Microsoft Azure Platform.

A big thank you goes to reviewers Thomas Palathra and Rick Kughen for their well-coordinated efforts and due diligence, from conceptualization to publication of this book. I am indeed grateful to the entire Pearson Team, especially Ms. Loretta Yates and Ms. Charvi Arora, for their cooperation, support, and patience throughout this journey.

I am indeed grateful to my wife, Jaspreet Kaur, and, daughter Amritleen Kaur, for the tremendous encouragement that helped me walk the tightrope of schedules and deadlines.

Last but not least, I submit myself in reverence to Guru Nanak, the great spiritual Guru, whose blessings enabled an incredibly small and a nondescript individual like me with wisdom and opportunity.

—GURVINDER SINGH

About the Authors

MIKE PFEIFFER Mike Pfeiffer is a 20-year tech industry veteran who's worked for some of the largest technology companies in the world, including Microsoft and Amazon Web Services (AWS). He's the founder and chief technologist at CloudSkills.io, a cloud consulting and training firm. Mike is an author for Pluralsight, international conference speaker, Microsoft Azure MVP, and host of the CloudSkills.fm podcast.

DEREK SCHAULAND Derek Schauland is an IT professional with 20 years' experience. He currently specializes in cloud technologies. He spent 10 years of his career as a Microsoft MVP, first in file system storage and then in cloud and datacenter management. In addition to writing about cloud technologies, he has co-authored three other books and countless articles and blogs. Outside of the technology space, he enjoys barbecuing with family and friends.

GURVINDER SINGH Gurvinder Singh is a Microsoft Certified Azure Solutions Architect with 13 years of diversified software development experience. He has a strong programming background and hands-on experience on .NET and C#. Since the past few years, Gurvinder has been guiding large enterprises in the transformation of legacy applications into cloud-native architecture with a focus on migration to Microsoft Azure. He is extremely passionate about technology, especially with the Microsoft Azure platform (PaaS, IaaS, and Serverless).

NICOLE STEVENS Nicole Stevens is technical director of an independent software vendor (ISV) in the United Kingdom. Nicole has 20 years' experience in software development, starting out as an Oracle DBA troubleshooting performance, design, and integration issues for large enterprises across EMEA (Europe, Middle East, and Africa). Switching to an ISV start-up brought fresh challenges, with a role spanning IT pro, technical consultancy, and DevOps engineer. Nicole's current focus is architecting cloud native solutions whilst assisting in the refactor of legacy software solutions for customers in Azure.

Introduction

The purpose of the AZ-303 certification exam is to test your understanding of the Microsoft Azure solutions architecture. The exam validates your ability to recognize which Azure services comprise a particular solution, and it validates your knowledge of real-world design scenarios and architecting Microsoft Azure solutions. This book provides a broad understanding of Microsoft Azure that empowers small, medium, and large-scale enterprises who want to adopt comprehensive app innovation and modernization strategies using the tools and services of their choice.

While we've made every effort possible to make the information in this book accurate, Azure is rapidly evolving, and there's a chance that some of the screens in the Azure portal are slightly different now than they were when this book was written. It's also possible that other minor changes have taken place, such as name changes and so on.

Azure supports a wide range of programming languages, frameworks, databases, and services. Consequently, IT professionals must quickly learn a wide range of technical topics. An overabundance of instructional content is available, which makes finding the right material difficult. This book cuts through the extraneous content and provides the information you need to prepare for the exam.

This book covers every major topic area found on the exam, but it does not cover every exam question. Only the Microsoft exam team has access to the exam questions, and Microsoft regularly adds new questions to the exam, making it impossible to cover specific questions. We encourage you to consider this book a supplement to your relevant real-world experience and other study materials. If you encounter a topic in this book that you do not feel completely comfortable with, use the "Need more review?" links in the text to find more information and take the time to research and study the topic. Great information is available in the Microsoft Azure documentation (*https://docs.microsoft.com/azure*) and Microsoft Learn (*https://microsoft.com/learn*).

Organization of this book

This book is organized by the "Skills measured" list published for the exam. The "Skills measured" list is available for each exam on the Microsoft Learn website: *http://aka.ms/examlist*. Each chapter in this book corresponds to a major topic area in the list, and the technical tasks in each topic area determine a chapter's organization. If an exam covers six major topic areas, for example, the book will contain six chapters.

Preparing for the exam

Microsoft certification exams are a great way to build your resume and let the world know about your level of expertise. Certification exams validate your on-the-job experience and product knowledge. Although there is no substitute for on-the-job experience, preparation through study and hands-on practice can help you prepare for the exam. This book is *not* designed to teach you new skills.

We recommend that you augment your exam preparation plan by using a combination of available study materials and courses. For example, you might use the Exam Ref and another study guide for your "at home" preparation and take a Microsoft Official Curriculum course for the classroom experience. Choose the combination that you think works best for you. Learn more about available classroom training and find free online courses and live events at *http://microsoft.com/learn*. Microsoft Official Practice Tests are available for many exams at *http://aka.ms/practicetests*.

Note that this Exam Ref is based on publicly available information about the exam and the author's experience. To safeguard the integrity of the exam, authors do not have access to the live exam.

Microsoft certifications

Microsoft certifications distinguish you by proving your command of a broad set of skills and experience with current Microsoft products and technologies. The exams and corresponding certifications are developed to validate your mastery of critical competencies as you design and develop, or implement and support, solutions with Microsoft products and technologies both on-premises and in the cloud. Certification brings a variety of benefits to the individual and to employers and organizations.

MORE INFO **ALL MICROSOFT CERTIFICATIONS**

For information about Microsoft certifications, including a full list of available certifications, go to *http://www.microsoft.com/learn*.

Quick access to online references

Throughout this book are addresses to webpages that the author has recommended you visit for more information. Some of these links can be very long and painstaking to type, so we've shortened them for you to make them easier to visit. We've also compiled them into a single list that readers of the print edition can refer to while they read.

Download the list at *MicrosoftPressStore.com/ExamRefAZ303/downloads*

The URLs are organized by chapter and heading. Every time you come across a URL in the book, find the hyperlink in the list to go directly to the webpage.

Errata, updates, & book support

We've made every effort to ensure the accuracy of this book and its companion content. You can access updates to this book—in the form of a list of submitted errata and their related corrections—at:

MicrosoftPressStore.com/ExamRefAZ303/errata

If you discover an error that is not already listed, please submit it to us at the same page.

For additional book support and information, please visit *http://www.MicrosoftPressStore.com/Support.*

Please note that product support for Microsoft software and hardware is not offered through the previous addresses. For help with Microsoft software or hardware, go to *http://support.microsoft.com.*

Stay in touch

Let's keep the conversation going! We're on Twitter: *http://twitter.com/MicrosoftPress.*

CHAPTER 1

Implement and monitor an Azure Infrastructure

Working as a Microsoft Azure cloud solutions architect, you will be designing solutions and engaging with IT professionals who will implement your design. So, why does the AZ-303 certification exam require you to know how to deploy and configure resources? As an architect, you must understand how resources are linked to create a solution that meets your customers' requirements, while adhering to the pillars of great architecture:

- Cost optimization
- Operational excellence
- Performance efficiency
- Reliability
- Security

To achieve this requires a deep understanding of how each underlying resource is implemented and configured. The AZ-303 exam expects you to demonstrate this knowledge through hands-on labs, both through the Azure portal and on the command line.

Once your design is implemented and starts to move through the stages of development and testing, you need feedback to ensure that these pillars are maintained. There is little point having a solution in production that is expensive, consistently fails, and is insecure. Monitoring the infrastructure throughout development and testing and into production provides continuous feedback at every stage, and it ensures that your product does not fail or become insecure.

Each resource in Azure can be configured for monitoring to return feedback to centralized locations. The AZ-303 certification exam expects you to demonstrate a solid understanding of monitoring. You must know how to configure your resources for monitoring, how to collate the data, and how it can be visualized to pinpoint possible issues and faults.

The Azure Solution Architect certification is an expert-level title, so you are expected to have at least intermediate-level Azure configuration abilities. You are also expected to have basic scripting skills with the Azure CLI and the Azure PowerShell modules.

Skills covered in this chapter:

- Skill 1.1: Implement cloud infrastructure monitoring
- Skill 1.2: Implement storage accounts
- Skill 1.3: Implement VMs for Windows and Linux
- Skill 1.4: Automate deployment and configuration of resources
- Skill 1.5: Implement virtual networking
- Skill 1.6: Implement Azure Active Directory
- Skill 1.7: Implement and manage hybrid identities

Skill 1.1: Implement cloud infrastructure monitoring

Continuously monitoring applications and infrastructure will enable your customers to be timelier in their responses to issues and changes. Responses to alerts generated from a well-monitored system can be automated, meaning in some circumstances, an application can self-heal. There are many monitoring solutions within Azure, each with its own use cases and configurability. As a solution architect, you need an excellent understanding of which monitoring solution fits which use case. This skill looks at some of the monitoring options available to you, what they monitor, and how to configure them.

This skill covers how to:

- Monitor security
- Monitor performance
- Monitor health and availability
- Monitor cost
- Configure advanced logging
- Configure logging for workloads
- Initiate automated responses by using Action Groups
- Configure and manage advanced alerts

Monitor security

Your customers' reputation is linked with the security of their systems; therefore, as an architect, you must know how to design secure systems. This is only one part of the puzzle; you cannot assume that your design is bulletproof. You must also be able to instruct your customers how to monitor systems continuously for potential attacks and mitigate the threats before data becomes at risk.

There are multiple security examinations available for Azure, though for this exam, you need to know the options available to you to monitor security and their high-level use cases.

Azure Security Center

When architecting solutions in Azure, there is a shared responsibility between the customer and Azure to ensure the resources are kept safe. Azure Security Center is an infrastructure security management system designed to help mitigate the security challenges that moving workloads to the cloud brings:

- **Lack of security skills.** Your customers might not have the traditional in-house skills and capital needed to secure a complex infrastructure.
- **Increasing attack sophistication.** Attacks are becoming more sophisticated, whether your workloads are in the cloud, are on-premises, or are part of a hybrid cloud and on-premises setup.
- **Frequently changing infrastructure.** Because of the flexibility of the cloud, architecture can rapidly change, bringing ever-moving attack vectors.

Security center comes in two tiers: Free and Standard:

- **Free tier.** The free tier is enabled by default and provides security recommendations on Azure VMs and App services.
- **Standard tier.** The standard tier increases monitoring to any cloud VM and hybrid VM workloads. The standard tier also includes some of the most frequently utilized PaaS services, such as data, storage, and containers.

When you activate Security Center for either tier, a monitoring agent is required for most of the security assessments. You can configure Security Center to automatically deploy the Log Analytics Agent onto Azure virtual machines, though PaaS (Platform as a Service) services require no extra configuration. For on-premises and cloud VMs, the Log Analytics Agent must be manually installed. Once the agents are installed and configured, Security Center begins assessing the security state of all your VMs, networks, applications, and data. The Security Center analytics engine analyzes the data returned from the agents to provide a security summary, as displayed in Figure 1-1.

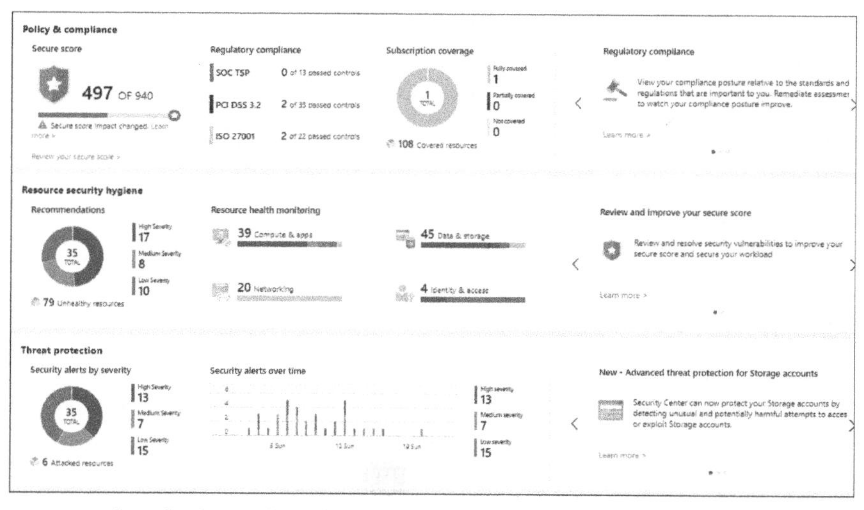

FIGURE 1-1 Security Center Overview blade

Figure 1-1 provides an excellent overview of the Security Center standard tier core features:

- **Policy & Compliance.** This section includes the Secure Score, which is a key indicator to how your infrastructure is secured. Security Center assesses resources across your subscriptions and organization for security issues. The Secure Score is an aggregation of identified security issues and their corresponding risk levels. The higher the Security Score, the lower the risk. The compliance section tracks whether regulations for standards such as ISO 27001 and PCI DSS are being followed.
- **Resource Security Hygiene.** This section provides resource and network recommendations. Drill through the menus to view recommendations and remediate them to improve your security posture and the Secure Score.
- **Threat Protection.** Logs from data and compute resources are passed through algorithms for behavioral analysis, anomaly detection, and integrated threat intelligence to look for possible threats. Alerts are created depending on severity.

The standard tier also includes just-in-time (JIT) access for Azure VMs. With JIT access enabled on a VM, an administrator can request access from an IP range for a specified length of time. If the administrator has the correct RBAC permissions, Azure creates a network rule, and the administrator is granted access. Once the specified time has passed, Azure removes the network rule to revoke access.

Azure Sentinel

Azure Sentinel is a security orchestrated automated response (SOAR) and security information and event management (SIEM) solution. Security Center is used to collect data and detect security vulnerabilities. Azure Sentinel extends beyond this by bringing in tools to help your customers hunt for threats, and then investigate and respond to them—all at enterprise scale:

- **Collects data at cloud scale.** Data collected includes other cloud, on-premises, Microsoft 365, and Advanced Threat Protection data.
- **Detect undetected threats.** Threats are detected using Microsoft analytics and threat intelligence.
- **Investigate threats with AI.** You can hunt for suspicious activities at scale.
- **Respond to incidents.** Azure Sentinel includes built-in orchestration and automation of common tasks.

Azure Sentinel requires a Log Analytics workspace when it is enabled and is billed based on the amount of data ingested from the workspace.

Monitor performance

Once the applications your customers have architected go into production, response time is likely to be one of the main KPIs your users are interested in. Performance needs to be monitored so that your customers know about potential issues before the application users do. This section looks at how to configure resources for performance monitoring and how Azure Monitor can use this data to look for performance issues.

Configure diagnostic settings on resources

Azure automatically generates audit and diagnostic information across the platform in the form of platform logs. Platform logs are invaluable to an architect because they contain information generated across different layers of Azure:

- **Activity Log.** All write operations `(PUT, POST, DELETE)` on a resource (the management plane). Tracked at the subscription level, this log contains who made the change, from where a change was made, and when a change was made.
- **Azure Active Directory Log.** This is a full audit train and tracking of sign-in activity for Azure Active Directory.
- **Resource Logs.** Resource logs are available for operations that were performed within a resource (the data plane). For example, a request on a WebApp or the number of times a logic app has run can both be logged. The resource log detail varies with resource type because each resource delivers a different service.

This information gives an architect a view of what is currently happening on their customers' application(s) and what happened previously.

Activity Log and Azure Active Directory Log are automatically available to view within the Azure portal. Resource logs must be configured at the resource level through diagnostic settings before they can be viewed. Configuring diagnostic settings has the same generic steps, regardless of the resource type.

PLATFORM AS A SERVICE (PAAS)

Follow these steps on a platform as a service (PaaS) resource to enable diagnostic settings:

1. Navigate to the menu blade for a PaaS resource in the Azure portal. Scroll down to **Monitoring** and click **Diagnostic Settings**. The **Diagnostic Settings** blade opens, which shows a list of settings that can be streamed to other destinations. Click **Add Diagnostic Setting** to configure data collection.
2. Clicking **Add** opens the **Diagnostics Setting Configuration** blade, as shown in Figure 1-2.
3. In the **Diagnostic Setting Name** field, add a unique name for this diagnostic setting at the resource.
4. Under **Category Details**, select all categories of data you want to collect:
   - **Log.** These are the resource logs. The categories of log will differ depending on the resource type chosen. This screenshot is from a Logic App.
   - **Metric.** Choosing this option will stream numerical metric data in a time series format about this resource.
5. Under **Destination Details**, select at least one destination for the chosen categories to stream to:
   - **Log Analytics.** Check this to stream data to a Log Analytics workspace. For more information about Log Analytics see "Configure a Log Analytics Workspace," later in this chapter. If **Log Analytics** is selected, it becomes mandatory to select the **Subscription** and **Log Analytics Workspace**, which will receive the data, as shown in Figure 1-2.

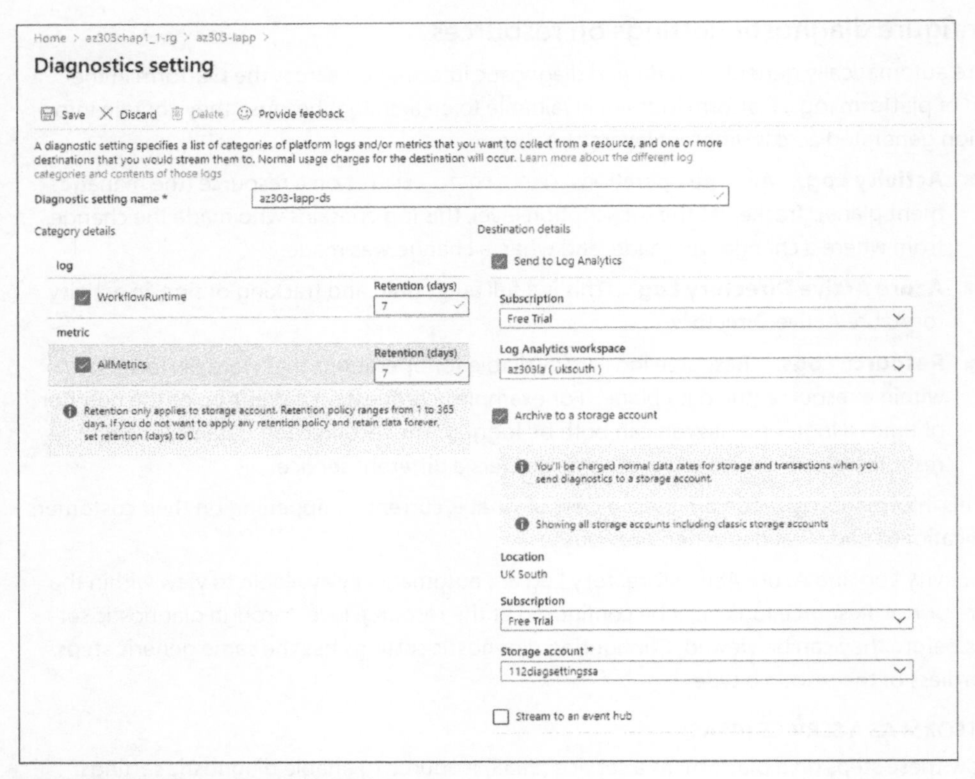

FIGURE 1-2 Configure diagnostic settings

- **Archive To A Storage Account.** Check this to archive your chosen categories into a storage account; this option is most useful if future auditing of the resource is required. Once you have chosen this option, the **Retention (Days)** entry point is enabled with a value of 0 for each selected category, as shown previously in Figure 1-2. Edit this number value to set the number of days each category should be retained. If you change this value later, it will only take effect on new logs and metrics stored. Old logs and metrics will continue to be retained for the original retention period. If **Archive to Storage Account** is selected, a **Subscription** and **Storage Account** must be selected from the respective drop-down menus, as shown previously in Figure 1-2.
- **Stream To An Event Hub.** Select this option to send diagnostics data to an Event Hub. Sending data to an Event Hub enables streaming of the data outside of Azure to third-party applications, such as security information and event management (SIEM) software. If **Stream To An Event Hub** is selected, the **Subscription** and **Event Hub Namespace** fields must be populated.

6. Once the diagnostic settings are chosen, click **Save** at the top left to save the choices. The categories and destinations selected are now displayed on the **Diagnostics Settings** blade, and data will automatically be sent to the chosen destinations.

Diagnostic settings also can be managed on the command line through PowerShell using the `Set-AzDiagnosticSetting` cmdlet or the `az monitor diagnostic-settings` Azure CLI command. For example, to enable specified log categories for an Azure SQL database, execute this command in PowerShell:

```
Set-AzDiagnosticSetting -Name sqldb112-diagsettings '
-ResourceId $dbResource.ResourceId '
-Category QueryStoreRuntimeStatistics, QueryStoreWaitStatistics, Errors,
 DatabaseWaitStatistics, Deadlocks -Enabled $true '
-StorageAccountId $storageResource.ResourceId '
-WorkspaceId $workspaceResource.ResourceId
```

AZURE VIRTUAL MACHINES

Azure VMs are not part of PaaS. Instead, they form part of Azure's Infrastructure as a Service (IaaS) offering, and you manage them. For an Azure VM to log data, the Azure diagnostics extension must be installed. Doing so sets up an Azure Monitor agent on the VM. The diagnostic extension is an Azure VM extension, meaning it can be installed via an ARM template or on the command line. It can also be installed through the Azure portal. The name of the extension differs between operating systems. For Windows, it is the Windows Azure diagnostics extension (WAD); for Linux, it is the Linux diagnostic extension (LAD). To install either extension through the Azure portal, navigate to the **Diagnostic Settings** menu item of any Azure virtual machine. You will have the option to choose **Enable Guest-Level Monitoring** if the diagnostic extension has not already been installed. Once installed, tabs for metrics and logging are enabled within the **Diagnostic Settings** blade. The number of tabs and their configurable contents depend on the operating system of the VM. For a Windows VM, these tabs are displayed:

- **Overview.** This is a summary page that shows the options selected in the other tabs.
- **Performance Counters.** Choose **Basic** to pick from groupings of counters to be collected, such as **CPU**, **Memory**, and **Disk**. Choose **Custom** to pick specific counters.
- **Logs.** Choose **Basic** to pick from groupings of **Application**, **Security**, and **System** logs to be collected, or choose **Custom** to select specific logs and levels using an XPath expression, IIS Logs, .Net application logs, and event tracing for Windows (ETW) logs can also be selected for collection.
- **Crash Dumps.** Collect full or mini dumps for selected processes.
- **Sinks.** Optionally, you can send data to Azure Monitor or Application Insights.
- **Agent.** If the diagnostics agent is malfunctioning, it can be removed from this tab and can then be reinstalled. You can also edit the **Log Level**, maximum local disk space (**Disk Quota**), and **Storage Account** for the agent.

If you have created a Linux VM, you will see the following tabs:

- **Overview.** This is a summary page that displays the options selected from the other tabs.
- **Metrics.** Choose **Basic** to pick from groupings of metrics to be collected, such as **Processor**, **Memory**, and **Network** and their sample rates. If you choose **Custom**, you

can then choose **Add New Metric** or **Delete** specific metrics, and you can set individual sample rates.

- **Syslog.** On this tab, you can choose which syslog facilities to collect and the severity level at which you want to collect them.
- **Agent.** If the diagnostics agent is malfunctioning, it can be removed from this tab, and can then be reinstalled. Also, you can **Pick A Storage Account** for the agent.

> ***NOTE*** **DIAGNOSTIC SETTINGS AND DIAGNOSTICS EXTENSION**
>
> **Not all the services have the Diagnostic Settings menu item in their menu blades. When the Diagnostic Settings option is missing, navigate to the resource group and click Diagnostic Settings. If Diagnostic Settings can be enabled for the service, it will be listed. For example, VPN gateways must be configured in this way. If you are planning to use the Log Analytics extension on a Linux VM, it must be installed before the diagnostic extension.**

Create a performance baseline for resources

Baselining resources gives your customers a view of what expected resource behavior looks like. When performance degradation occurs, your customers can use their resource baselines to aid in their analyses and fault resolution.

Azure Monitor collects two main types of data:

- **Metrics.** Timeseries and numerical-measured values or counts, such as CPU usage or waits
- **Logs.** Events and trace files

The metrics in Azure Monitor form the baseline, giving a timeseries view of your resources. You can see a metrics view for most single resources by choosing the **Metrics** menu against the resource itself. You can use this to build up a view of how your resource is performing. Here is an example for an Azure VM:

1. In the Azure portal, navigate to any virtual machine and click **Metrics** on the **Virtual Machine** menu blade.
2. You must now choose the metrics to add to the chart. The scope has already been selected for you—it is the VM. Select a metric from the **Metrics** menu and then select an aggregation from the **Aggregation** menu. Click away from the metric, and it will be added to the chart.
3. To add a new metric, click **Add Metric** and repeat step 2. Repeat this process until all metrics you require are present on the chart.

Figure 1-3 shows a metrics chart, with the CPU performance for the last 24 hours suggesting this VM might need to be scaled up.

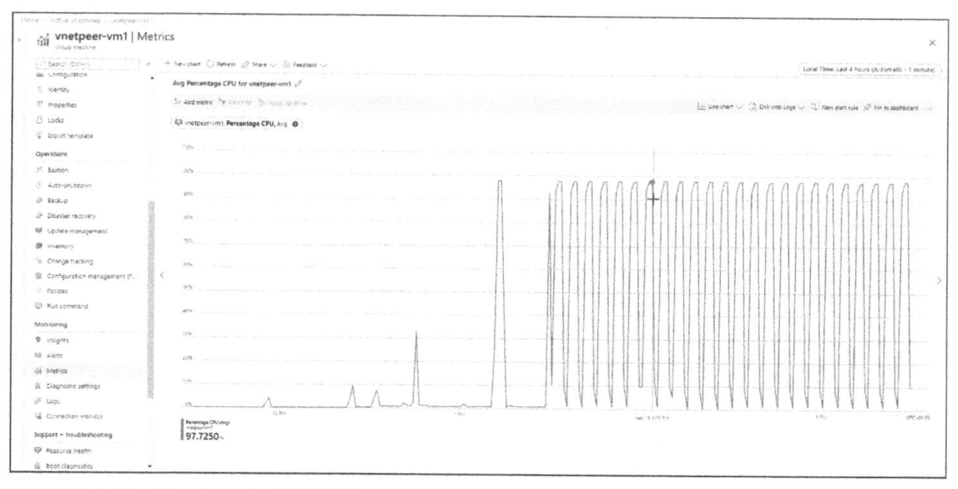

FIGURE 1-3 Metrics chart for VM CPU usage

4. Once completed, you can choose to add the chart to your Azure portal dashboard by clicking **Pin To Dashboard**. To navigate to a dashboard page, click the menu icon at the top left of any Azure page, click **Dashboard**, and choose the name of the dashboard to which you added the chart.

Monitor for unused resources

Because of the flexibility of Azure, it can be easy for your customers to have unused or under-utilized resources hidden within their subscriptions. With pay-by-the-minute or hourly billing, the cost of an unused resource could affect spending considerably. Azure Advisor contains cost recommendations that cover the following:

- **Under utilized VMs.** These are VMs that can be downsized or deallocated.
- **Right-sizing database sources.** Azure SQL, MySQL, or MariaDB can be downsized.
- **Idle network gateways.** These are VNet gateways that have not been used for 90 or more days and could be deleted
- **Reserved VM / PaaS instances.** You can buy capacity up front to save costs based on PaaS (Platform as a Service) and VM usage.

The Azure Advisor recommendations are free, and you can access Azure Advisor through the Azure portal:

1. Search for **Azure Advisor** in the search resources bar in the Azure portal. Select **Azure Advisor** in the drop-down menu that opens from the search bar as you type the resource name. The **Azure Advisor** overview page loads, as shown in Figure 1-4; the **Cost** summary is shown at the top left.

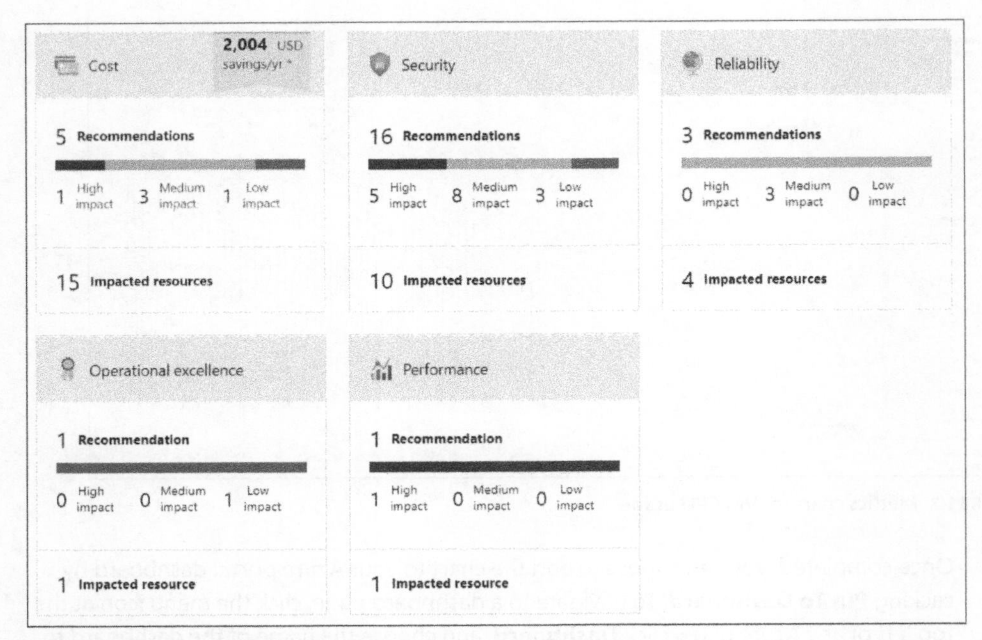

FIGURE 1-4 Azure Advisor Overview blade

2. Click the **Cost** square to drill into the recommendations. Each recommendation is shown as **High Impact**, **Medium Impact**, or **Low Impact**, and the number and type of **Impacted Resources** are shown at the bottom of each recommendation. Potential yearly cost savings are shown in the top right of the **Cost** square.

Monitor performance capacity

Azure Monitor can collate data from many different sources through a variety of agents. In a hybrid environment, your customers will need a single view across their organization. To deliver this functionality, your customers will need to combine on-premises workload metrics with those from Azure. The diagnostic agent for VMs will only collect data from Azure VMs; it does not support on-premises VMs.

The Log Analytics Agent will collect data from Azure VMs, on-premises VMs, and VMs managed by System Center Operations Manager (SCOM). The Log Analytics Agent is also referred to as "OMS Linux Agent" or "Microsoft Monitoring Agent (Windows)." The Log Analytics Agent can be installed on an Azure VM from the **Virtual Machines** section of a **Log Analytics** workspace. The installation on an on-premises machine requires the agent to be downloaded and installed from the command line.

The VM data collected by the Log Analytics Agent can be viewed in Azure Monitor Log. Azure Monitor Log uses KQL (Kusto Query Language) to create reports on the data using queries. Azure Monitor Log comes with built-in queries to help you get started. To view your data using these queries, log in to the Azure portal and follow these steps:

1. Search for **Monitor** in the search resources bar at the top of the Azure portal. (Note that Azure Monitor is listed in the Azure portal as **Monitor**.) Select **Monitor** in the drop-down menu that opens from the search bar as you type the resource name.
2. Choose **Logs** from left pane. Azure Monitor Logs opens with the **Example Queries** page. Scroll through the **All Queries** section, where you can see the list of Azure resources that have example queries.
3. Scroll to the bottom and choose **Other** > **Memory And CPU Usage**. The example KQL is loaded into the query pane. Click **Run** to execute the query and view results.
4. Click **Select Scope**, which is located to the left of **Run**. Here, you can choose the scope at which your query will run. Select a resource group that contains virtual machines that are sending data to Log Analytics. Click **Apply**; you are returned to the Query Editor, where the selected scope is now to the left of **Select Scope**. Click **Run**; the data returned is restricted to your selected scope, which is the resource group you just selected.
5. Now alter the KQL by editing it directly. In Figure 1-5, the KQL has been edited from the one selected in Step 3 above. The `TimeGenerated > ago(2h)` predicate filter has been set to 2 hours ago, and the summarization of values returned— `bin(TimeGenerated, 2m)`—is grouped to 2 minutes.

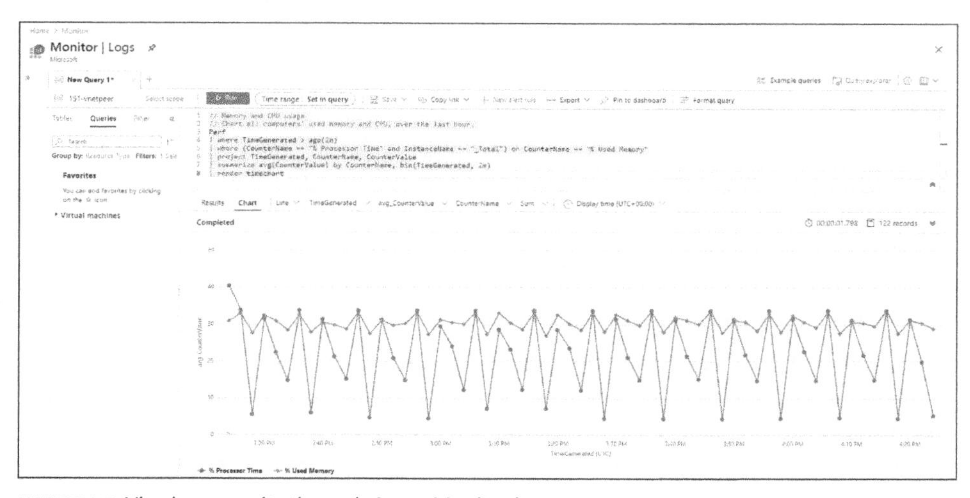

FIGURE 1-5 Viewing capacity through Azure Monitor logs

EXAM TIP KQL

It is important to have a basic understanding of the KQL language for the exam, though this can be difficult without access to the infrastructure that is creating data to query. Microsoft provides a tutorial database and a demo log analytics portal. These can be accessed for practice at *https://docs.microsoft.com/en-us/azure/data-explorer/kusto/query/tutorial* and *https://portal.loganalytics.io/demo*.

NEED MORE REVIEW? **AZURE MONITOR LOGS**

The example in Figure 1-5 shows a single use case for Azure Monitor Logs. To learn more about the vast number of services whose data can be mined through logs and metrics, visit *https://docs.microsoft.com/en-us/azure/azure-monitor/platform/data-platform-logs*.

Visualize diagnostics data using Azure Monitor

Azure Monitor can collate data from many different sources through a variety of agents. Your customers will find the vast amount of data almost impossible to analyze without a graphical representation of the data. You have already seen how Azure Monitor can pin charts to your dashboard, but you can have more visualization capabilities by using Azure Monitor workbooks, which read metrics and logs from Log Analytics to create visualizations of data across multiple sources. Azure Monitor comes pre-loaded with workbook templates, which allow your customers to view insights about their resources, such as identifying VMs with low memory or high-CPU usage or viewing the storage capacity of their storage accounts. All templates can report across a subscription. To view the Performance Analysis workbook template in Azure Monitor, follow these steps:

1. Search for **monitor** in the search resources bar at the top of the Azure portal. (Note that Azure Monitor is listed in the Azure portal as **Monitor**.) Select **Monitor** in the drop-down menu that opens from the search bar as you type the resource name.
2. In the Azure Monitor menu, click **Workbooks**, and from the **Gallery** under **Virtual Machines**, click **Key Metrics**.
3. Choose the subscription you want to view and the Log Analytics workspace to which your VMs are logging metrics. Choose a **Time Range** to further filter the data. The workbook visualization loads with the **Overview** tab selected. The **Overview** tab displays the CPU utilization for all VMs in the selected subscription.
4. Click the **Key Metrics** tab to view the key metrics of CPU, disk, and network usage in a tabular format, as shown in Figure 1-6.
5. Click through the other tabs. The **Regions** tab displays the highest CPU usage in each Azure region where the subscription contains a virtual machine. The **Resource Health** tab displays the health of each virtual machine in the subscription. Clicking the virtual machine in the **Resource Health** tab will drill through to the **Resource Health** blade of the virtual machine.
6. Return to the **Gallery** you navigated to in Step 2 and explore the other Workbooks available for virtual machines.

If your charts do not load, it is because VM insights have not been configured for the VMs. This is also indicated by a red exclamation mark and a **Not Onboarded** appearing to the right of the **Time Range** drop-down menu. To configure VM insights, see "Configure logging for workloads," later in this chapter. Go back to the **Gallery** to explore the other templates available to you.

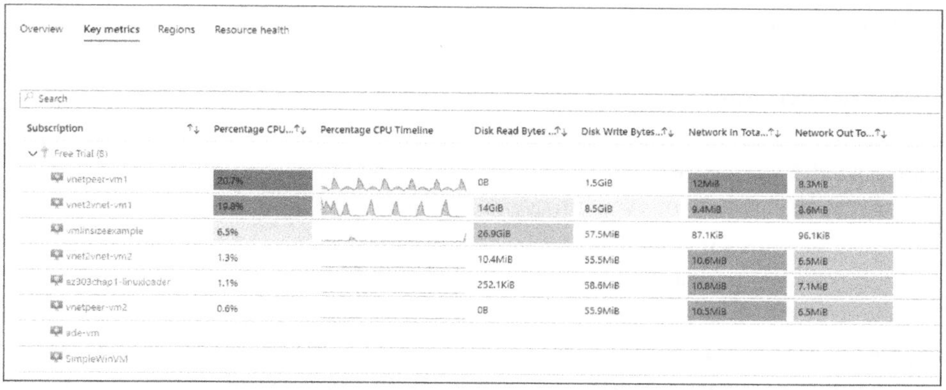

Overview Key metrics Regions Resource health

Search

Subscription ↑↓	Percentage CPU...↑↓	Percentage CPU Timeline	Disk Read Bytes ...↑↓	Disk Write Bytes...↑↓	Network In Tota...↑↓	Network Out To...↑↓
Free Trial (8)						
vnetpeer-vm1	20.7%		0B	1.5GiB	12MiB	8.3MiB
vnet2vnet-vm1	19.8%		14GiB	8.5GiB	9.4MiB	8.6MiB
vmlinsizeexample	6.5%		26.9GiB	57.5MiB	87.1KiB	96.1KiB
vnet2vnet-vm2	1.3%		10.4MiB	55.5MiB	10.6MiB	6.5MiB
az303chap1-linuxloader	1.1%		252.1KiB	58.6MiB	10.8MiB	7.1MiB
vnetpeer-vm2	0.6%		0B	55.9MiB	10.5MiB	6.5MiB
ade-vm						
SimpleWinVM						

FIGURE 1-6 Key Metrics workbook template showing the CPU, disk, and network usage for virtual machines

Azure Monitor can also send log and metric data to other sources for analysis, such as Power BI, where further sources of data can be combined to create business reporting. Operational dashboards can be created using Grafana. (You can do this by installing the Azure Monitor plugin from within Grafana.) Grafana is an open-source platform primarily used for detecting and triaging operations incidents.

Monitor health and availability

Understanding how to monitor the health of your customers' application infrastructure is key for detecting potential issues and reducing downtime. Because your customers' application infrastructure uses Azure services and these services can be affected by service-related downtime, your customers might require alerts if an underlying service becomes unavailable. This section looks at methods to do just that.

Monitor service health

Azure Service Health tracks the health of Azure services across the world, reporting the health of resources in the regions where you are using them. Azure Service Health is a free service that automatically tracks events that can affect resources.

To view Azure Service Health, log in to the Azure portal and search for **service health** in the search resources bar at the top of the portal. Select the **Service Health** menu option, which will be shown as an option in the drop-down menu as you type the resource name. The menu options on the left-hand side under **Active Events** correspond to the type of events, which are tracked in Azure Service Health:

- **Service Issues.** Azure services with current problems in your regions
- **Planned Maintenance.** Maintenance events that can affect your resources in the future

- **Health Advisories.** Notification of depreciation of features or upgrade requirements that you use
- **Security Advisories.** Security violations and notifications for Azure services that you are using

Choosing **Health History** from the **Service Health** menu lists all historical health events that have happened in the regions you use over a specified time period.

Selecting the **Resource Health** menu option lists resources by resource type and shows where service issues are affecting your resources. You can click the listed resource to drill down for the resource health history or to read more about a current issue affecting the resource.

Navigating back to the **Service Health** menu, you can create an alert for **Service Health** events in **Health Alerts**. **Health Alerts** monitors the activity log and sends an alert if Azure issues a **Service Health** notification. Therefore, diagnostic logs must be configured at the subscription level to include **Service Health**; otherwise, **Health Alerts** will not be configured.

Monitor networking

Monitoring network health for IaaS products is performed with Azure Network Watcher. Azure Network Watcher has tools to view metrics, enable logging, and diagnose and monitor resources attached to an Azure Virtual Network (VNet). Azure Network Watcher is automatically activated for a region as soon as a VNet is created in your subscription. To understand the monitoring capabilities of Azure Network Watcher, you need to explore three tools: Network Watcher Topology, Connection Monitor, and Network Performance Monitor.

TOPOLOGY

Azure Network Watcher topology gives an overview of all VNets and their connected resources within a resource group. To view a topology, open the Azure portal and search for **network watcher** in the search resources bar at the top of the page, select Network Watcher from the drop-down menu that is displayed as you type the resource name. **Topology** can be selected in the menu on the left side of the portal in the **Network Watcher** menu. Select a **Subscription** and **Resource Group** that contains at least one VNet. The topology will automatically load, as shown in Figure 1-7.

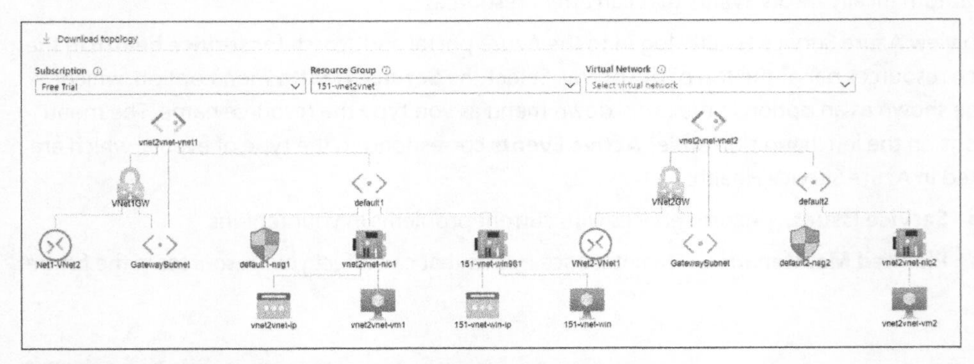

FIGURE 1-7 Network Watcher Topology for a specified resource group

Figure 1-7 shows two VNets: vnet2vnet-vnet1 and vnet2vnet-vnet2. This is the network topology of the infrastructure created in "Implement VNet-to-VNet connections," later in this chapter. An additional virtual machine (151-vnet-win) has also been added to the default1 subnet. You can see the mandatory gateway subnets, their VPN Gateways (VNetGW1, VNetGW2) and the connections for each VPN Gateway (VNet1-VNet2 andVNet2-Vnet1).

CONNECTION MONITOR

Connection Monitor is generally used to view latency; it can provide the minimum, average, and maximum latency observed over time or at a point in time. This data can be used to monitor whether moving Azure resources to new regions might decrease latency. **Connection Monitor** can also monitor for topology changes that can affect communication between a VM and an endpoint. If an endpoint becomes unreachable, the **Connection Troubleshoot** feature of **Network Watcher** can identify the reason as being DNS resolution, VM capacity, firewall, or routing issues.

NETWORK PERFORMANCE MONITOR

Network Performance Monitor (NPM) monitors network performance between points in your infrastructure. NPM detects network issues and can be configured to generate alerts based on thresholds set for a network link. NPM has the following capabilities:

- **Performance Monitor.** Detect network issues across your cloud and hybrid environments
- **Service Connectivity Monitor.** Identify bottlenecks and outages between your users and their services
- **ExpressRoute Monitor.** Monitor end-to-end connectivity over Azure ExpressRoute

To use Performance Monitor in Azure, at least one VM on your network will require the Log Analytics Agent to be installed. Network Performance Monitor is enabled in Network Watcher.

> ***NEED MORE REVIEW?*** **NETWORK WATCHER**
>
> **To learn more about monitoring IaaS networks using Network Watcher, see *https://docs.microsoft.com/en-us/azure/network-watcher/*.**

Monitor cost

Azure charges your customers for the resources and technologies they use and the data that flows between the resources and their users. In most cases, as soon as a resource is created, your customers will start being charged for the resource. Without controlling and monitoring spend, your customers could be in for a shocking bill at the end of the month! The cost management features of Azure Cost Management and Billing enable your customers to control costs by analyzing spend and receiving alerts based on spend thresholds.

Monitor spend

Azure Cost Management uses budgets to control costs and alert your customers when budgets are about to be breached. When a budget is about to be breached, Cost Management and Billing can raise an alert to enable your customers to act. To create a budget, use Cost Management in the Azure portal, and follow these steps:

1. Open the Azure portal and search for cost management in the search resources bar at the top of the Azure portal. Select **Cost Management + Billing** in the drop-down menu that opens as you start to type the resource name.
2. Select **Cost Management** in the left-hand menu. The **Cost Management** menu now loads. Choose **Budgets** from the **Cost Management** section of the **Cost Management** menu.
3. If you have any budgets, they will be listed on the **Budgets** blade which is now displayed. Click **Add** at the top left to add a budget.
4. The **Create Budget** tab is opened, which has the configuration sections in the following list. Once you have chosen your options, your budget should appear as shown in Figure 1-8.
   - **Scope.** You can set a budget at the management group, subscription, or resource group levels. For example, set the **Scope** to the subscription level.
   - **Filter.** This is often used to filter to a taxonomic tag, such as a department, to provide cross-organization budgetary views. For this example, do not add a filter.
   - **Name**. Enter a **Name** for your budget.
   - **Reset Period.** Choose the period over which your internal budget period resets. For this example, set the **Reset Period** to **Billing Month**.
   - **Creation Date.** This is the date to start the budget. You can choose options from the start of the current billing month or options that extend into the future. For this example, leave the default setting.
   - **Expiration Date.** This is when the budget will end. For this example, leave this as the default setting.
   - **Budget Amount.** The limit you require to be set for the budget. This will be in your subscription currency, which may differ from your local currency. Enter a value that is just above your current spend. Click **Next** at the bottom of the page.
5. The **Set Alerts** tab is now active, which is where you can configure an alert on your budget. For a budget alert, you have the following configuration options:
   - **Alert Conditions.** Enter the **% Of Budget** upon which you would like the alert to fire. Your customers will need to set this to a value that will give them time to remediate possible overspend before the limit is breached. For this example, choose **75%**. Leave **Action Group** empty, as you will explore action groups later in this chapter in "Initiate automated responses by using Action Groups."
   - **Alert Recipients.** Enter the email addresses of the person(s) who requires this report.
6. Click **Create**; the budget is created along with its corresponding alert.

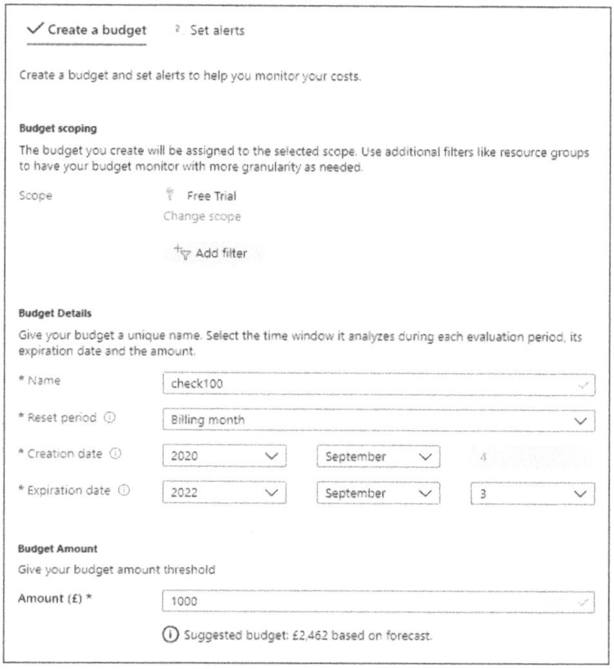

✓ Create a budget   2 Set alerts

Create a budget and set alerts to help you monitor your costs.

Budget scoping

The budget you create will be assigned to the selected scope. Use additional filters like resource groups to have your budget monitor with more granularity as needed.

Scope   Free Trial
Change scope

Add filter

Budget Details

Give your budget a unique name. Select the time window it analyzes during each evaluation period, its expiration date and the amount.

* Name   check100

* Reset period   Billing month

* Creation date   2020   September   4

* Expiration date   2022   September   3

Budget Amount

Give your budget amount threshold

Amount (£) *   1000

Suggested budget: £2,462 based on forecast.

FIGURE 1-8 Creating a budget in Cost Management

When a cost alert is triggered, the notifications are fired, and an active alert is created for the budget. The alerts can be viewed in the **Cost Alerts** menu option displayed on the left of **Cost Management**. In **Cost Alerts**, you have the option of dismissing the alerts or re-activating a dismissed alert.

Report on spend

Azure Cost Management is also the best place to report on spend. Navigate back to the **Cost Management** menu in the Azure portal and choose **Cost Analysis**. The **Cost Analysis** blade is preconfigured with a summary dashboard of your current and past spend, as shown in Figure 1-9.

Figure 1-9 shows the spend on the current billing month, with accumulated costs broken down into services, locations, and resource groups. You can change the scope to management group, subscription, or resource group. The ability to filter by tag is considered a best practice, and it is one of the key features of cost analysis. For example, if you tag by department, you can produce an analysis of each department's spend. Click **Download** at the top of the page to manually download the chart data or to schedule spend data for extraction to a storage account.

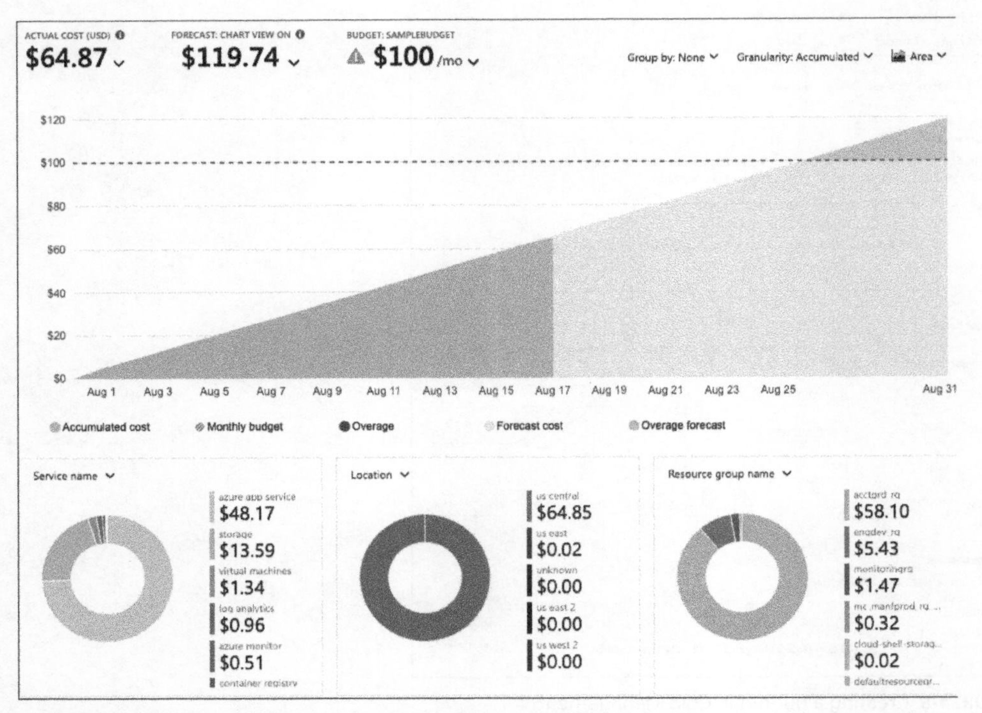

FIGURE 1-9 Cost analysis to report on spend in Azure Cost Management

Configure advanced logging

Advanced monitoring in Azure Monitor is done through Insights, which is part of Azure Monitor. Insights provides your customer with a specialized monitoring experience for their applications and services. Insights leverages Azure Monitor Logs which sit on a Log Analytics workspace. Therefore, before you explore Insights, you will need to create and configure a workspace.

Configure a Log Analytics workspace

To create a Log Analytics workspace in the portal, search for **log analytics** in the search resources bar at the top of the Azure portal. Select **Log Analytics Workspaces** in the drop-down menu that opens as you type in the resource name. To add and configure a workspace, follow these steps:

1. Click **Add** at the top-left of the **Workspaces** blade. Enter a name for the workspace, choose a resource group, and select the region where you need your workspace to reside. Click **Review + Create**, and then click **Create** to create the workspace.
2. Once created, your new workspace is listed. Click the workspace name to look at the configuration options.
3. In the left-hand menu under **Settings**, choose **Agents Management**. At the top of the page are **Windows Servers** and **Linux Servers** tabs. To manually onboard a VM to Log

Analytics, you will require the ID and keys from these tabs. You will explore on-boarding VMs in "Configure logging for workloads," later in this skill.

4. On the **Log Analytics Workspaces** menu, choose **Advanced Settings**. The **Data** section is where you can configure which counters and log files are collected for your resources. For example, click **Data** > **Windows Performance Counters**. The counters available are listed, but until you select **Add The Selected Performance Counters**, the data will not be collected for any Windows VM connected to this workspace. Once selected, the screen is updated, as shown in Figure 1-10.

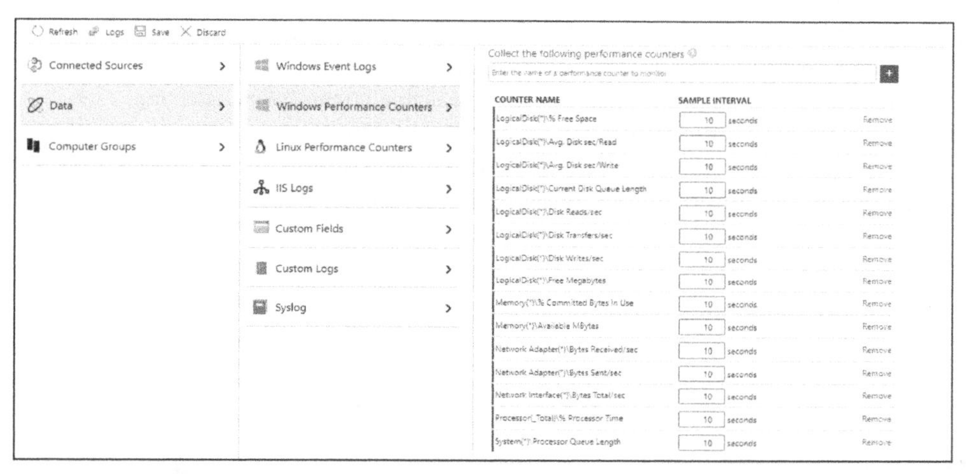

FIGURE 1-10 Configuring the Log Analytics workspace to collect Windows Performance Counters

When the VM Log Analytics Agents refresh their configurations, the agents pick up the new counter configurations and send the selected data back to the Log Analytics workspace.

5. You will need to repeat this exercise for event logs, Linux performance counters, and other data sources you require.

6. Staying in the Log Analytics workspace that you have just created, click **Virtual Machines** in the left-side menu. A table is displayed, which lists the VMs that could be connected to the Log Analytics workspace you have just created. The performance counter configuration you made in steps 3 through 5 will only affect VMs listed as **Connected** in this table.

Implement and configure Azure Monitor insights, including app insights, networks, and containers

Modern applications hosted within the cloud are often complex, combining multiple PaaS and IaaS services. Monitoring, maintaining, and diagnosing such applications can be an almost impossible task if tools to analyze application data and alert on key metrics are not implemented. Azure Monitor provides Insights, which brings full stack observability across applications and infrastructure, thus enabling deep alerting and diagnostic capabilities. This section looks at the Insights available for applications, networking, and containers in Azure Monitor.

APPLICATION INSIGHTS

Application insights is an Application Performance Management (APM) service for developers to monitor their live applications. Application insights will automatically detect anomalies across hybrid, on-premises, or public cloud applications where you need to

- Analyze and address issues and problems that affect your application's health
- Improve your application's development lifecycle
- Analyze users' activities to help understand them better

To integrate Application Insights with your applications, you must set up an **Application Insights** resource in the Azure portal. To do this, navigate to **Application Insights** in the portal and click **Add**. Choose a name, resource group, and region to create the resource. Once the resource is created, an **Instrumentation Key** is available on the **Overview** page. Your customers give this key to their developers. Developers use a software development kit (SDK) to add an instrumentation package to their applications. The instrumentation package uses the Application Insights instrumentation key to route telemetry to the Application Insights resource for analysis.

Once telemetry is flowing to Application Insights, there are built-in visualizations that allow you to analyze your environment. Figure 1-11 shows two of the visualizations: Application Map and Live Metrics.

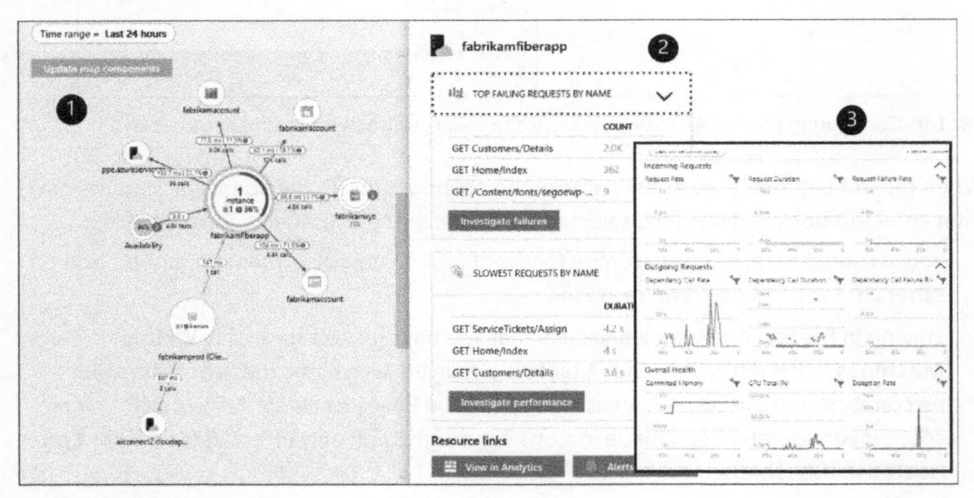

1. Application Map
2. Live Metrics
3. Live Metrics drill through

FIGURE 1-11 The Application Map and Live Metrics, which is part of Application Insights

Application Map displays an overview of your application, where each node is an application component. The links between nodes are the dependencies. The Application Map shows health KPI and alert statuses on each node, which you can drill into for detailed analyses.

Live Metrics provides a real-time view of your application without having to configure settings, which might affect availability. You can plot metric counters live, and you can drill through to failed requests and exceptions.

Two other commonly used insights are Availability and Failures; example output for both is shown in Figure 1-12.

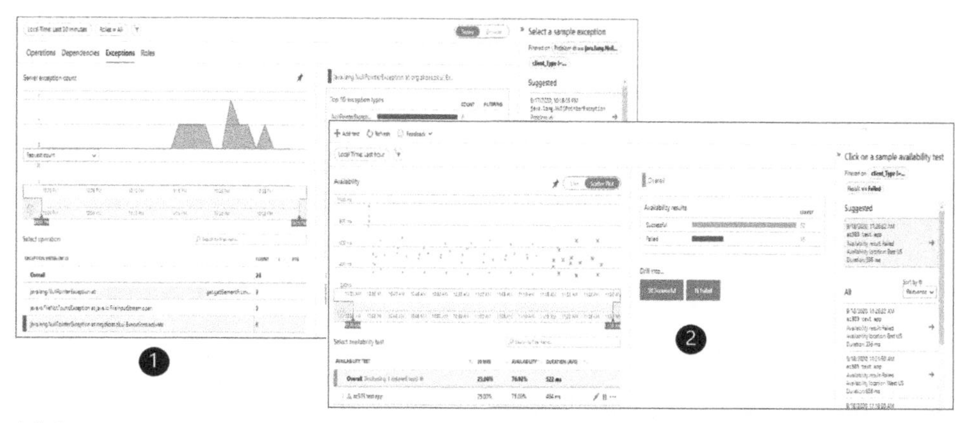

1. Failures
2. Availability

FIGURE 1-12 Failures and Availability insights

Failures are displayed in the top-left portion of Figure 1-12. Failures are plotted over a time range and are grouped by type. You can click the **Successful** and **Failed** buttons under **Drill Into** to investigate operation, dependency, and exceptions.

Availability must be configured by adding an availability test to the Availability page of Application Insights. You enter the URL of the endpoint you want to be monitored, and Azure tests availability from five different locations. You can also configure the availability test to check the response time for downloading page dependencies, such as images, style sheets, and scripts. Azure plots the responses on the availability page charts, which include latency. You can set up alerts from the availability tests for immediate notification of possible downtime.

NETWORK INSIGHTS

Network Insights provides a comprehensive overview of your network inventory without any configuration. You can view the health and metrics for all network resources and identify their dependencies. The following Insights are available through Network Insights:

- **Search And Filtering.** You might have thousands of network resources. Viewing the analysis data for a single resource can be tricky. With **Search And Filtering**, you can enter a single resource name, and the resource along with its dependencies will be returned.
- **Alerts.** This shows all alerts generated for the selected resources across all subscriptions.

- **Resource And Health Metric.** Grouped by resource type, this is a summary view of the selected components. The summaries are displayed as tiles.
- **Dependency View.** Drill through the health and metric tiles to view dependencies and metrics for the chosen resource type, as shown in Figure 1-13 for two VNet gateways in a VNet-to-VNet configuration.

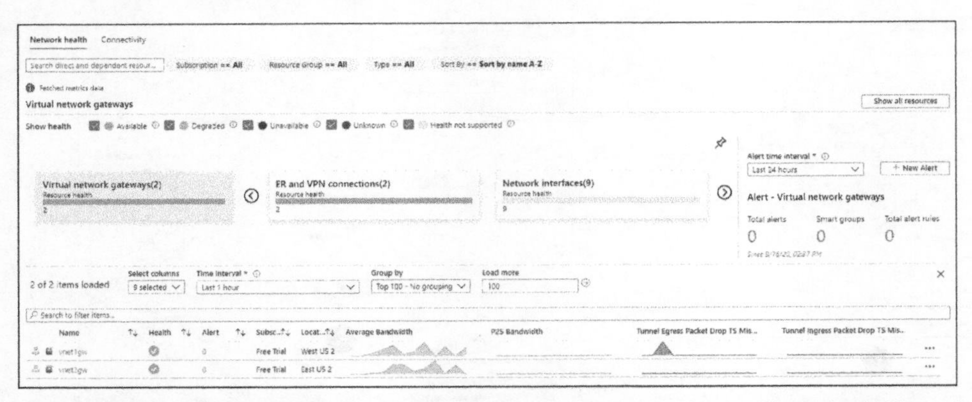

FIGURE 1-13 The dependency view of two VNet gateways in a VNet-to-VNet configuration in Network Insights

AZURE MONITOR FOR CONTAINERS

When you are architecting solutions with containers, monitoring them is critical. Azure Monitor for containers collects processor and memory metrics from container workloads. The workloads can be deployed on-premises to Kubernetes on Azure Stack, or they can be deployed on Azure Kubernetes Service (AKS), Azure Container Instances (ACI), or other Azure-based, third-party container orchestrators.

When enabled, the Kubernetes Metrics API sends metrics for controllers, nodes, and containers. Container logs are also collected. The metric and log data are sent to a Log Analytics workspace, which is a requirement for Azure Monitor for containers. The method for enabling Azure Monitor for containers differs depending on the service it is to be enabled on. Here is an example command to create an AKS cluster with Azure CLI:

```
az aks create --resource-group $resourceGroupName --name myAKSCluster --node-count 1
--enable-addons monitoring --generate-ssh-keys
```

The `--enable-addons monitoring` option enables Azure Monitor for containers. If you want to use an existing Log Analytics workspace, you must pass it the workspace ID with `–workspace-resource-id`; otherwise, a Log Analytics workspace will be created for you. You can also enable monitoring on an existing cluster using the following Azure CLI command:

```
az aks enable-addons --addons monitoring --name myAKSCluster --resource-group
$resourceGroupName
```

The `--workspace-resource-id` can be specified to use an existing workspace. Once the metrics and logs are being collected, you can access the data from the AKS cluster's **Insights** menu or through the Azure Monitor **Containers** menu. If you are using Azure Monitor, you will need to select the **Monitored Clusters** tab at the top of the window and then select the cluster you want to view. The **Cluster** view is a summary of counters for the cluster, as shown in Figure 1-14.

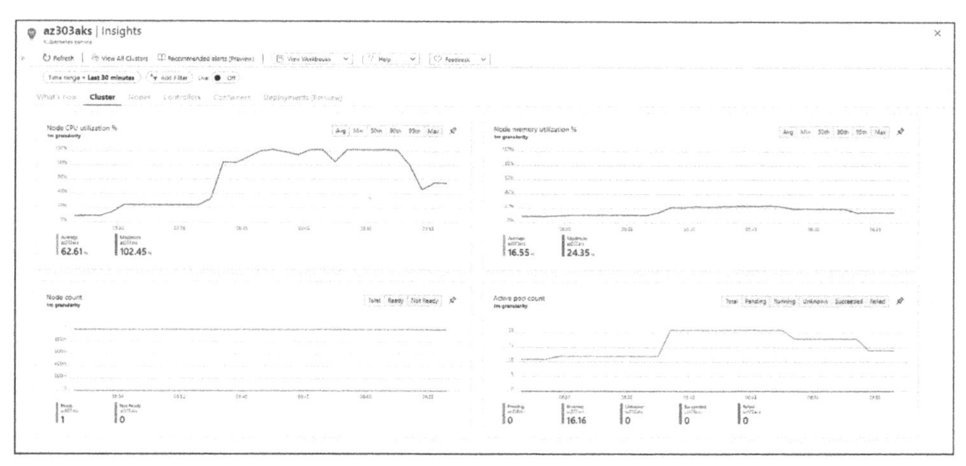

FIGURE 1-14 The Cluster summary view for AKS in Azure Monitor for containers

In Figure 1-14, the top-left chart shows the **Node CPU Utilization %** of the cluster. The application running on AKS in this example contains an HTML front end (azure-vote-front) with a Redis instance on the back end (azure-vote-back). To deploy this infrastructure follow the Azure quickstart: *https://docs.microsoft.com/en-us/azure/aks/kubernetes-walkthrough.* When the application is deployed there is one replica of azure-vote-front which is being stressed by multiple concurrent requests. Across the top of the window are six tabs: What's New, Cluster, Nodes, Controllers, Containers, and Deployments (Preview). In Figure 1-15, the **Nodes** tab has been selected. The top node listed in the table in Figure 1-15 is named azure-vote-front. The **Trend 95th %** column displays a single small green bar; eight red, full-height bars, which suggests a large increase in application traffic.

- The number of replicas for azure-vote-front is increased to ten. This can be seen from the nine listings of azure-vote-front underneath the original node. There is no data for these nodes while the top node in the table is at full capacity. The yellow bars for the new nodes and the original node show the load has been distributed equally between each of the 10 nodes. Looking back to Figure 1-14, the manual scale to 10 azure-vote-front nodes corresponds quite nicely to the bottom-right chart, **Active Pod Count**. You can also see the increased CPU demand of the 10 nodes displayed on the **Node CPU Utilization %** chart. Switching back to Figure 1-15, the number of azure-front-end nodes is scaled back to 7, and then shortly afterward, it is scaled to 3. This corresponds to the stop in data of the bottom 3 azure-vote-front nodes in the **Trend 95th %** column, and then it corresponds to the stop in data for all but the top three nodes. You can also see the increase in stress on the top 3 nodes as the **Trend 95th %** column bars increase in size and go from yellow to orange to red.

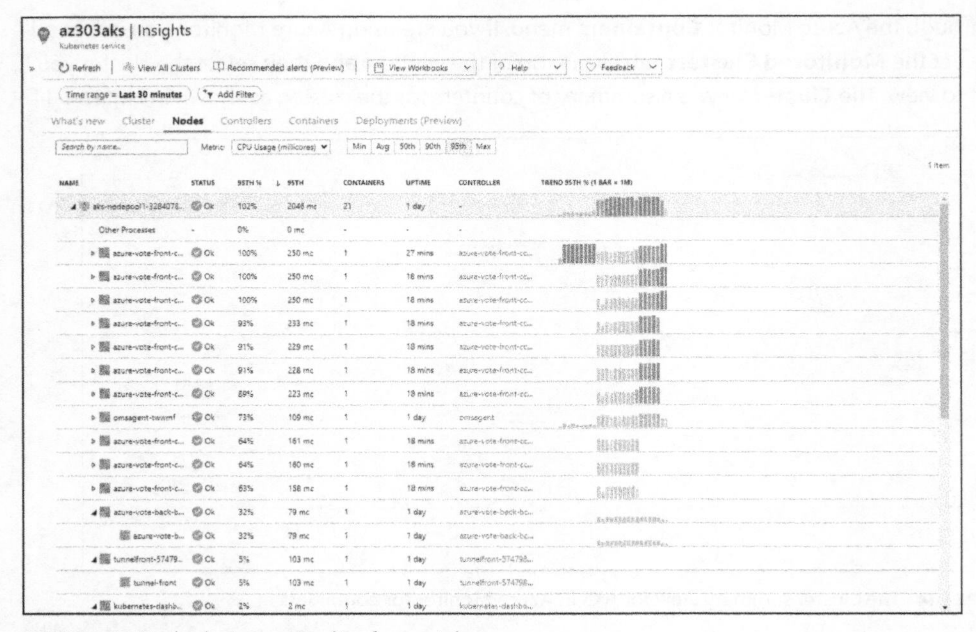

FIGURE 1-15 Nodes in Azure Monitor for containers

> ***NEED MORE REVIEW?*** **AZURE MONITOR INSIGHTS**
>
> **Insights is an immense tool; to learn more, visit *https://docs.microsoft.com/en-us/azure/azure-monitor/insights/insights-overview*.**

Configure logging for workloads

When architecting VMs at scale, monitoring their workloads and dependent resources has been historically complex. Azure Monitor for VMs is designed for scale, and it analyzes Windows and Linux VMs and VM scale sets through its health and performance metrics. Azure Monitor for VMs monitors the VMs and application dependencies on workloads that are in Azure, on-premises, or in other clouds.

On-boarding a VM in Azure can be performed one at a time in the Azure portal by navigating to a VM, scrolling down in the **Azure Monitor** menu to **Monitoring**, choosing **Insights**, and clicking **Enable**. The Azure portal sends a deployment request to the VM to install the Log Analytics and Dependency agents. The Dependency agent is required for mapping dependencies, and Log Analytics agent for collecting performance and log data. Azure Monitor for VMs is designed for monitoring workloads at scale, if you are deploying for hundreds of VMs you will need to automate the task. Azure Policy can be configured to deploy the agents, report on compliance, and remediate non-compliant VMs. For on-premises and other cloud VMs, the agents can be deployed manually or pushed out through a designed state-management tool.

Once the data is collected, it can be viewed in the **Insights** blade of a single VM, or for a rolled-up aggregated view at the subscription level from within Azure Monitor. To view the aggregated data and explore the output in the Azure portal, follow these steps:

1. Search for **azure monitor** in the search resources bar at the top of the Azure portal. Choose **Monitor** from the drop-down menu that is displayed once you start to type the resource name.
2. In the **Insights** menu, click **Virtual Machines**.
3. The **Getting Started** tab for VM Insights is displayed. From this tab, the following configuration options are shown:
   - **Monitored.** This option shows the machines being monitored by Azure Monitor for VMs. You can choose to view the data at subscription, resource group and single VM level by clicking on the listed names.
   - **Not Monitored.** This option lists VMs in your subscriptions that are not monitored. From here, you can enable the VMs.
   - **Workspace Configuration** From here, you can configure the Log Analytics workspaces that have been enabled for Azure Monitor for VMs.
4. Click the subscription name to view the performance of all enabled VMs. This view includes CPU, memory, network, and disk metrics. Just below the **Performance** tab are further analysis view tabs; click through these to view the aggregate charts and lists (see image A of Figure 1-16).
5. Go back to the **Get Started** tab and choose a resource group with multiple VMs. Next, click **Map** to view the dependencies for the application, as shown in the inset (B) portion of Figure 1-16.

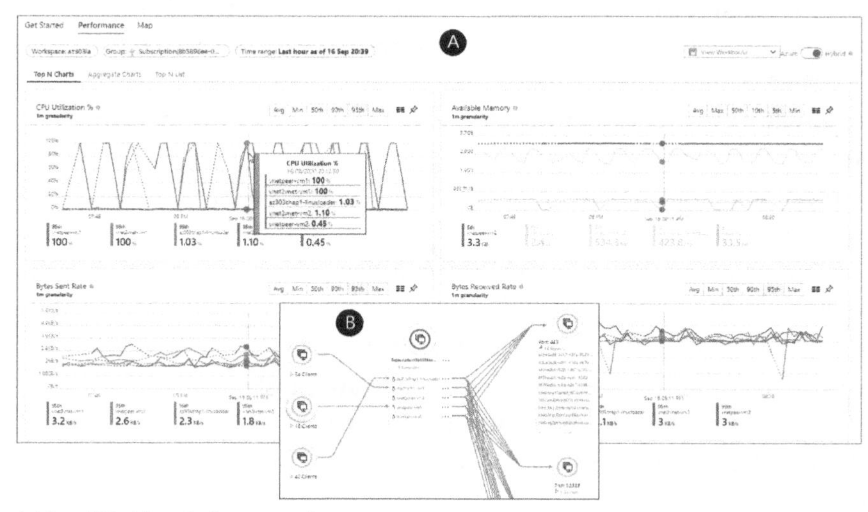

A. Virtual Machines Performance tab
B. Virtual Machines Map tab

FIGURE 1-16 Azure Monitor for VMs using the Performance and Map tabs

NEED MORE REVIEW? **AZURE MONITOR FOR VMS**

To learn more about monitoring workloads at scale, visit ***https://docs.microsoft.com/en-us/azure/azure-monitor/insights/vminsights-overview.***

Initiate automated responses by using Action Groups

Throughout this chapter, alerts have been referenced and set up by specifying single email accounts. For your customers deployments, it is highly unlikely that a single individual will be responsible for an alert or set of alerts. Also, an email might not guarantee a quick enough response to an issue. When you are looking to mitigate slow responses to an alert, you should recommend configuring action groups. An action group is a collection of notifications and automation tasks that are triggered when an alert is fired. You can set up multiple action groups that notify different groups or trigger different responses, depending on the alert. To examine the options available in an action group, follow these steps to create an action group in the Azure portal. Note action groups can also be created on the command line and with an ARM template.

1. Navigate to **azure monitor** using the search resources bar at the top of the Azure portal. Choose **Monitor** from the drop-down menu that is displayed once you start to type the resource name.
2. Click **Alerts** in the **Monitor** menu, and then click **Manage Actions** at the top of the **Alerts** blade. The **Managed Action** blade will open.
3. If you have any action groups, they will be listed in the **Manage Actions** blade. Click **Add Action Group** at the top-right to add a new action.
4. The **Create Action Group** configuration page is displayed with the **Basics** tab open. Click **Next: Notifications >** at the bottom of the page. Following are the options shown on the **Basics** tab:
   - **Subscription.** Choose the subscription into which you want to save the action group.
   - **Resource Group.** Choose a resource group from the subscription or create a new default resource group for action groups.
   - **Action Group Name.** This is the name for the action group, and it must be unique within the resource group.
   - **Display Name.** This is included in email and SMS messages.
5. The **Create Action Group** page switches to the **Notifications** tab. Here, you can configure how users are alerted if the **Action Group** is triggered:
   - **Notification Type.** This is the type of notification that will be sent to the receiver. You can choose from:
     - **Email Azure Resource Manager Role.** Choosing this option emails all subscription members of the role.

- **Email / SMS message / Push / Voice.** A push notification will be sent to the Azure app that is linked to an Azure AD account, Voice calls a number, including a land line. There are limits to these actions: 1 SMS every 5 minutes, 1 Voice every 5 minutes, and 100 emails an hour.

- **Name.** The name of the notification. It must be unique from other notification names and from action names.

6. Click **Next: Actions >** at the bottom of the page.
7. The **Create Action Group** page switches to the **Actions** tab. Here, you can configure automated actions if the **Action Group** is triggered:
   - **Action type.** This is the automated action that will be performed when the action group is triggered:
     - **ITSM.** Automatically log a ticket in a specified IT Service Management (ITSM) software.
     - **Logic App.** Create a logic flow to automate a response such as posting a message to Microsoft Teams.
     - **Secure Webhook / Webhook.** This option sends a JSON payload to an external REST API.
     - **Azure Automation Runbook.** Use this option to create a runbook to run code in response to an alert, such as stopping an Azure VM following a budget breach.
     - **Azure Function.** Use this option to invoke an Azure function to run in response to an alert, such as starting a VM that has been stopped.
   - **Name.** The name of the action. It must be unique from other action names and from Notification names.
   - **Configure.** This option is activated once the **Action Type** is chosen. Here, you enter the notification details, **Webhook URL**, **Logic App Name** or **Function App Name**. You can also enable the common alert schema, which provides the following functionality:
     - **SMS.** This creates a consistent template for all alerts.
     - **Email.** This creates a consistent email template for all alerts.
     - **JSON.** This creates a consistent JSON schema for integrations to webhooks, logic apps, Azure functions, and automation runbooks.
8. Once you are happy with the action group configuration, click **Review + Create** to add the action group.

Configure and manage advanced alerts

Throughout this skill, you have explored how to monitor resources for a wide range of issues and anomalies. The sheer scale of the data that can be produced while monitoring solutions architected in the public and hybrid cloud is vast. This means trying to sift through the data manually to detect problems will be almost impossible or take an unreasonable and expensive amount of labor. Creating alerts based on the underlying metric and log data will automate some of these tasks for your customers.

Collect alerts and metrics across multiple subscriptions

Azure Monitor alerts give you the ability to trigger alerts on resources for a subscription. The alerting experience is unified for the three types of alert: Metric, Log, and Activity Log. For example, you might want to know whenever a VM is stopped in your production subscription, so that you can try to restart it. Follow these directions to create the VM stopped example alert in the Azure portal:

1. Navigate to Azure Monitor, choose **Alerts** in the left-side menu. At the top of the page, click **New Alert Rule**.
2. The **Create Alert Rule** blade loads, which allows you to select a subscription, resource group, resource, or set of resources. Choose all virtual machines in your subscription by using the **Virtual Machines** filter and a single location.
3. Now, to select all the VMs in the same location, select the subscription (as shown in Figure 1-17). At the bottom right, you can see the available signal types, which are resources within the same location; Metric and Activity Log are both available.

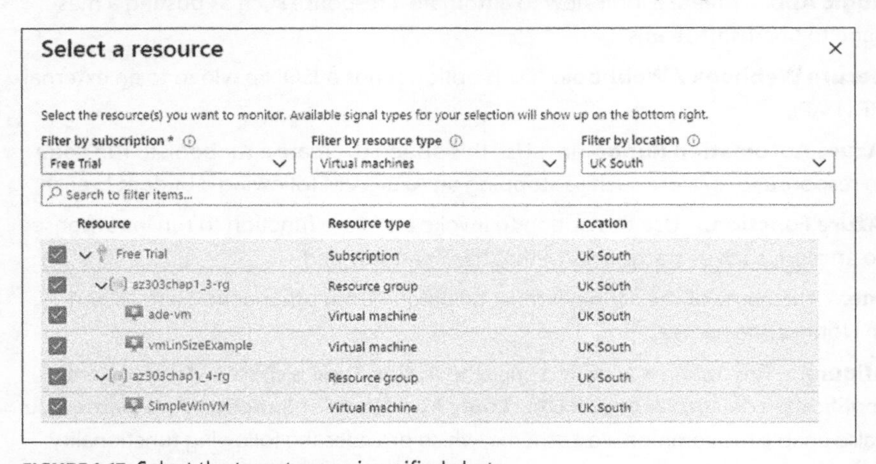

FIGURE 1-17 Select the target scope in unified alerts

4. Now, change the **Filter By Resource Type** and **Filter By Location** to **All** and select the subscription once more. Note the available signal types is now just **Activity Log** because **Metric** cannot be used for alerts across regions. Click **Done**.
5. Click **Select Condition**, which opens the **Configure Signal Logic** page. The signal types available will depend on the **Scope** selected in the previous step:
   a. **Log.** Create a KQL query for data in log analytics; if the query returns rows, then the alert is fired.
   b. **Metric.** Set a threshold value against a metric, such as "greater than an average of X." If the threshold is breached, the alert is fired.
   c. **Activity Log.** If a matching Activity Log type is created in the subscription's activity log, the alert is fired.

The signal type available at the Subscription level is Activity Log. Enter **virtual machine** in the search box to filter the data. Scroll down on the same blade and select **Deallocate Virtual Machine (Microsoft.ClassicCompute/virtualMachines)**. Leave **Alert Logic** set to **All**. Click **Done**.

6. Click **Action Group** to pick an action group. Recall from the previous section that this is a grouping of notifications and automated responses. For this example, create an action group that emails you.
7. Enter an **Alert Rule Name** and **Description**, and then select a **Resource Group** to save it to.
8. Click **Create Alert Rule** to create the alert rule.
9. Test the alert by stopping a virtual machine within your selected subscription.
10. If you need to collect alerts across multiple subscriptions, you can automate the process using ARM templates to deploy an alert configuration to each subscription.

View alerts in Azure Monitor Logs

All alerts that have been triggered, regardless of where they are set up, can be viewed in the unified alerts experience in Azure Monitor. To access this information, navigate to Azure Monitor and click **Alerts** in the left-hand menu. The **Alerts** blade is displayed listing all alerts for the last 24 hours. The alerts are grouped by severity. For example, all alerts of severity 0 are grouped into a severity line titled **Sev 0**. Clicking the line for a severity will drill down to the alerts that are contained within that severity rating. Choosing a specific alert in the detail view gives you the option to change the status of an alert to acknowledged.

A similar view of the data is available through **Azure Monitor Logs**, within **Workbooks**. From Azure Monitor, select **Workbooks** in the left-hand menu. Scroll down in the **Workbooks Gallery** and select the **Alerts** workbook template under **Azure Resources**. A similar view to that of the unified alerts experience is shown. You have the option to filter by **Subscriptions**, **Resource Groups**, **Resource Types**, **Resources**, **Time Range**, and **State**. Clicking a an alert in the **Alert Summary** list drills through to the **Alert Details**, as shown in Figure 1-18.

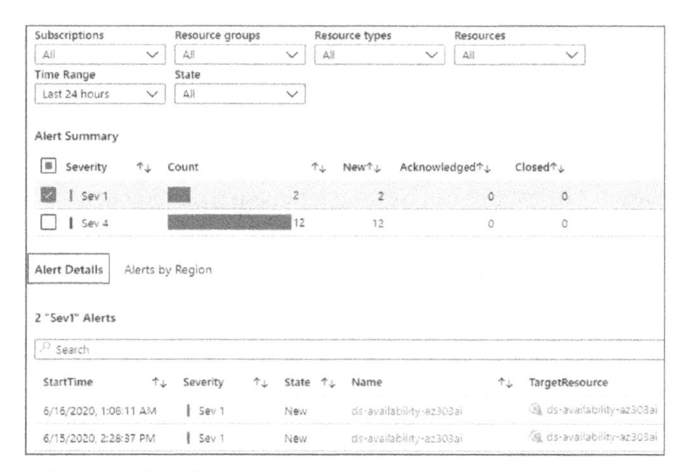

FIGURE 1-18 The Alerts Workbook template for Azure Monitor logs

Skill 1.2: Implement storage accounts

Azure Storage is a managed data store. It is secure, durable, massively scalable, and highly available out of the box. You can configure Azure Storage to withstand a local outage or natural disaster by using replication. Azure Storage can accommodate a vast variety of data use cases across its core services and is accessible worldwide. As an Azure architect, you need to know how a storage account and its core services can be configured to suit your customers' requirements.

This skill covers how to:

- Select storage account options based on a use case
- Configure Azure Files and Blob Storage
- Manage access keys
- Configure network access to the storage account
- Implement Shared Access Signatures and access policies
- Implement Azure AD authentication for storage
- Implement Azure Storage replication
- Implement Azure Storage account failover

Select storage account options based on a use case

Configuring a storage account during the creation process determines the features that are available for use. This configuration governs which core services, performance tiers, and access tiers are accessible after account creation. Therefore, when architecting storage for your applications, careful consideration must be given to the storage account options.

All storage accounts are encrypted at rest using Microsoft-managed encryption keys and Storage Service Encryption (SSE) for data at rest.

Core services

To explore storage accounts further, it is important to understand the core services available in an Azure Storage and how they can be used:

- **Azure Blobs.** Azure blobs are optimized for storing massive amounts of unstructured data—either binary or text based. Azure blobs can be used for images, documents, backup files, streaming video, and audio. Blobs come in three types:
  - **Block blobs.** Binary and test data, up to 4.7TB.
  - **Append blobs.** Block blobs that are optimized for appends and are good for logging.
  - **Page blobs.** Random read/write blobs used for VM VHD files or disks and can be up to 8TB.

- **Azure Files.** Server Message Block (SMB)–based fileshare service. Use as a replacement for a traditional on-premises fileshare or share configuration files between multiple Azure workloads. Azure Files can be synchronized to an on-premises server for hybrid fileshare scenarios.
- **Azure Queues.** Stores messages of up to 64K. Typically used for first-in first-out (FIFO) asynchronous processing scenarios.
- **Azure Tables.** A structured NoSQL data service. It is a key/value store that has a schema-less design, which can be used to hold large amounts of flexible data. (Azure Cosmos DB is recommended for all unstructured flexible data.)
- **Azure Disks.** Disks for virtual machines. Although listed as a core service, it is not configurable; instead, it is fully managed by Azure.

Storage account type

The core services available for use depend on the storage account type chosen. The default type for a storage account on creation is General-Purpose V2, which is the Microsoft-recommended storage account type and supports all core services listed in the previous section.

The following Azure CLI command creates a General-purpose V2 account called `az303defaultsa`.

```
az storage account create --name az303defaultsa --resource-group $resourceGroupName
```

To change the storage account type, add the `--kind` parameter, which has the following options:

- **StorageV2.** Also known as **General-purpose V2**, this is the default for a storage account and the Microsoft-recommended account type. Access to all core services and their associated performance tiers and access tiers is available.
- **Storage.** Also known as **General-purpose V1**, this is provided for legacy support of older deployments. Access to all core services and performance tiers is available but no access tiers are available for selection. It is possible to upgrade from V1 to V2 using the command line.
- **Blob Storage.** This is provided for legacy support of blobs. All access tiers are available, but only standard performance is available for selection. Use **General-purpose V2** instead of **Blob Storage** when possible.
- **BlockBlobStorage.** Low latency storage for blobs with high transaction rates, premium performance with no access tiers.
- **FileStorage** Files only, premium performance and no access tiers. This option can be specifically configured for file related performance enhancements such as IOPS bursting.

The following Azure CLI command creates a `BlockBlobStorage` account called `az303blockblob`:

```
az storage account create --name az303blockblob --resource-group $resourceGroupName
--kind BlockBlobStorage
```

Access tier

Blobs support three access tiers, Hot, Cool, and Archive. The access tiers are optimized for specific patterns of data usage. These patterns correspond to the frequency of access to the underlying data. This means by selecting your access tier carefully, you can reduce your costs. Examining this further:

- **Hot tier.** Highest storage costs, lowest access costs. Used for frequently accessed data and is the default tier.
- **Cool tier.** Lower storage costs than hot, higher access costs. Use for data that will be stored "as is" and not accessed for at least 30 days.
- **Archive tier.** This is at the blob level only. Lowest storage costs, highest access costs. Only use for data that will remain "as is" that will not be accessed for at least 180 days and can stand high retrieval latency of several hours. Great for long term backups and archival data.

```
az storage account create --name az303blobaccesstier --resource-group $resourceGroupName
-kind StorageV2 -access-tier hot
```

The Azure CLI command above creates a General-purpose V2 account called `az303blobaccesstier` with a Hot access tier.

```
az storage account create --name az303blobaccesstier --resource-group $resourceGroupName
--kind StorageV2 --access-tier hot
```

An access tier can be changed at any time using the command line or Azure portal. To change `az303blobaccesstier` to the Cool tier in Azure CLI, issue the following command:

```
az storage account update --name az303blobaccesstier --resource-group $resourceGroupName
--kind StorageV2 --access-tier cool
```

NOTE **EARLY DELETION PENALTY**

Changing the tier from Archive or Cool before the respective 180-day or 30-day periods will incur an early deletion penalty equivalent to the remaining days' cost of the storage.

EXAM TIP AZURE STORAGE CONFIGURATION

Understanding which core services, access tiers, and performance tiers are available for the storage account types is an important area for this certification. See *https://docs.microsoft.com/en-us/azure/storage/common/storage-account-overview#types-of-storage-accounts* for further review.

Configure Azure Files and Blob Storage

Once you have chosen your storage account options, you need to set up use case–specific "containers" for your data. These are the Azure Storage core services, as previously listed. The method of creating these containers changes depends on the core service you are configuring. The AZ-303 certification requires you to understand the configuration for Azure Files and Blob Storage.

Azure Files

Azure Files can be configured on the command line and within the Azure portal. Follow these steps to configure Azure Files by executing cmdlets in PowerShell:

1. Use these cmdlets to create a storage account:

```
$resourceGroupName = "12storage"
$location="northeurope"
$storageAccountName = "az303fsdemosa"
New-AzResourceGroup -Name $resourceGroupName -Location $location '
    -Tag @{department="development";env="dev"}
$sacc = New-AzStorageAccount '
    -ResourceGroupName $resourceGroupName '
    -Name $storageAccountName '
    -Location $location '
    -Kind StorageV2 '
    -SkuName Standard_LRS '
    -EnableLargeFileShare
```

   These PowerShell cmdlets create a storage account named `az303fsdemosa` that supports the Azure Files core service. If you compare these cmdlets to the Azure CLI command from the "Access tiers" section, it is somewhat similar except for the `-EnableLargeFileShare` cmdlet. This cmdlet instructs Azure to enable File shares of more than 5TB in this storage account. The storage account object is stored in a `$sacc` variable, which enables you to use the storage account context later in your configuration without having to retrieve it again. You will explore storage account contexts in "Manage access keys," later in this chapter.

2. Create a fileshare named `az303share` and set a max size of 1TB using `-QuotaGB` in this PowerShell cmdlet:

```
$shareName = "az303share"
New-AzRmStorageShare '
    -StorageAccount $sacc '
    -Name $shareName '
    -QuotaGiB 1024
```

NOTE CHANGING QUOTAS

Quotas can be changed with Update-AzRmStorageShare.

3. At this point, you could start uploading files to your share once you have created a folder structure that is called a "directory structure" in Azure Files. Execute the following commands in PowerShell to create a folder named `topLevelDir`:

```
$dirName = "topLevelDir"
New-AzStorageDirectory '
    -Context $sacc.Context '
    -ShareName $shareName '
    -Path $dirName
```

   PowerShell returns the URL for the directory, as shown in the following output:

```
-Directory: https://az303fsdemosa.file.core.windows.net/az303share

Type          Length     Name
Directory     0          topLevelDir
```

This URL can be used from inside an application to access the directory from anywhere, providing the application is authenticated and authorized to do so.

4. You should still have the storage account context in your PowerShell session. You can now use this instead of the directory URL to upload a file to your new directory. Execute this cmdlet to upload a file named `file.txt`:

```
"AZ-303 Azure Files share example" | out-file -FilePath "file.txt" -Force
Set-AzStorageFileContent '
    -Context $sacc.Context '
    -ShareName $shareName '
    -Source "file.txt" '
    -Path "$($dirName)\file.txt"
```

Use the Azure portal to explore the storage account fileshare and check for the file's existence.

Blob Storage

Blobs are stored in a container; you can think of a container as a grouping of blobs. A container works for blobs in much the same way a folder does for files. As previously discussed, an Azure Storage account can support multiple core services. Therefore, for this example, the `az303fsdemosa` storage account will be updated to enable blobs to be stored. Follow the steps below— executing the commands in PowerShell—to configure a blob container, upload a file, and further explore the blob configuration options. This example assumes you are continuing from step 4 in the previous section ("Azure Files") with the storage account context available in the `$sacc` object. If this is not the case, read the "Manage access keys" section later in this chapter to learn how to obtain the storage account context:

1. In PowerShell, execute the following cmdlet to create a blob container named `images`:

```
$containerName = "images"
New-AzStorageContainer '
     -Name $containerName '
     -Context $sacc.Context '
     -Permission blob
```

Note the parameter `-Permission`, which sets the public access level of the blob; there are three values for this parameter:

- **None.** This parameter means no public access is allowed; containers with this parameter are private. To use this container, a service must authenticate and be authorized to do so.
- **Blob.** This parameter grants read access to the blobs in the container when directly accessed. Container contents or other data cannot be accessed without authentication and authorization.
- **Container.** This parameter grants read access to the blobs and the container. The contents of the container can be listed.

2. You can now use the storage account context to upload files to the container. Execute the following commands in PowerShell to upload a file to the images container created above.

```
Set-AzStorageBlobContent -File "D:\az303files\uploadTest.jpg" '
  -Container $containerName '
```

```
    -Blob "uploadTest.jpg" '
    -Context $sacc.Context
```

NOTE EDIT THE CODE BLOCK

You will need to edit this code block to set the `-File` parameter to an image file that exists on your client. You might also want to change the `-Blob` parameter so that the file names match after upload.

3. Open the Azure portal and navigate to the `az303fsdemosa` storage account. In the **Storage Account** menu, under **Blob Service**, choose **Containers**. Click the **Images** container name to view the file stored within it.
4. On the **Storage Account** menu, click **Data Protection**. Here, you can configure **Blob Soft Delete**, which enables a mechanism for recovering accidentally deleted Blobs. The retention policy is between 7 to 365 days. **Blob Soft Delete** is a storage account–level property that affects all blob containers. To enable **Blob Soft Delete** using PowerShell, set a retention policy on the storage account object using the following command:

   ```
   $sacc | Enable-AzStorageDeleteRetentionPolicy -RetentionDays 7
   ```
5. Switch back to the Azure portal and click through the other blob service options to further examine them:
   - **Lifecycle Management.** This option allows you to set rules to automatically transition blobs through the Cool and Archive tiers to possible deletion after a specified number of days since modification.
   - **Custom Domain.** Blob storage can be configured to use custom domain names.
   - **Azure CDN.** This option provides integration to Azure CDN to give consistent latency for access anywhere in the world.
   - **Azure Search.** This option adds full text search to blobs using Azure Cognitive Search.

Manage access keys

When you create a storage account, Azure also creates two access keys, which can be used to programmatically access the account. For example, in the "Azure Files" section, "context" was mentioned on multiple occasions. An Azure PowerShell context object holds authentication information, which allows you to run PowerShell cmdlets against resources. In the "Azure Files" section, the context is a storage context, which allows you to run storage cmdlets on a storage account resource that requires a context. To retrieve the context for the account in PowerShell, you must first retrieve the access key for the storage account. The context is retrieved using the key. For example, on the `az303fsdemosa` account used in the "Azure Files" section, you would use this code:

```
$key1=(Get-AzStorageAccountKey '
    -name $storageAccountName '
    -ResourceGroupName $resourceGroupName '
    ).value[0]
```

```
$key1
$ctx = New-AzStorageContext '
-StorageAccountName $storageAccountName '
-StorageAccountKey $key1
```

`$key1` stores the primary access key, and the storage context is in `$ctx`. The context can be used to manage the storage account configuration and access the stored data.

Microsoft recommends that the access keys be regularly rotated. Rotating the keys helps to keep the storage accounts secure by invalidating old keys. To manually rotate the keys, the following process must be followed:

1. Alter service connections to use the secondary key.
2. Rotate the primary key in the Azure portal or on the command line. For example, to rotate `key1` for the `az303fsdemosa` storage account in PowerShell, execute the following commands:

```
New-AzStorageAccountKey '
  -ResourceGroupName $resourceGroupName '
  -Name $storageAccountName '
  -KeyName key1
```

3. Alter service connections to use the primary key again.
4. Rotate the secondary key using the same method as shown in step2.

The switch between primary and secondary in this process is why Microsoft recommends that only the primary or secondary keys are used by all services by default. Otherwise, connections to storage accounts will be lost when you rotate the keys.

> ***NEED MORE REVIEW?*** **MANAGE ACCESS KEYS**
>
> **To learn about using Azure Key Vault to manage access keys, see *https://docs.microsoft.com/en-us/azure/storage/common/storage-account-keys-manage*.**

Configure network access to the storage account

The configurable core services are bound endpoints, and each has a unique address based on a well-known URI:

- **Blob.** *http://<storage-account-name>.blob.core.windows.net*
- **File.** *http://< storage-account-name>.file.core.windows.net*
- **Table.** *http://< storage-account-name>.table.core.windows.net*
- **Queue.** *http://< storage-account-name>.queue.core.windows.net*

The endpoints are public, and by default, the storage account is configured to accept all traffic to the public endpoints, even traffic from the Internet. However, you cannot gain access to an endpoint without proper authorization through an access key, shared access signature (SAS) token, or via Azure AD. It is likely that your customers' use cases will require the public endpoint to be secured to a range of IP addresses or to a specific VNet. This is configured using storage firewalls and virtual networks. You may use the command line or the Azure portal to configure network access. To explore settings in the Azure portal, follow these steps:

1. Using the Azure portal, search for **storage account** in the search resources bar. Select **Storage Accounts** in the drop-down menu that is displayed as you type the resource name into the search. Select **12storage** from the storage account list. This step assumes you still have available the storage account you created earlier in this chapter. If not, pick any newly created storage account.
2. In the **Storage Account** menu, scroll down and click **Firewalls And Virtual Networks** to open the blade.
3. The default configuration of **All Networks** is selected. As discussed, this means all traffic, even Internet traffic, can access the endpoint. Choose **Selected Networks**. The configuration options for VNets and the storage account firewall are shown in Figure 1-19.

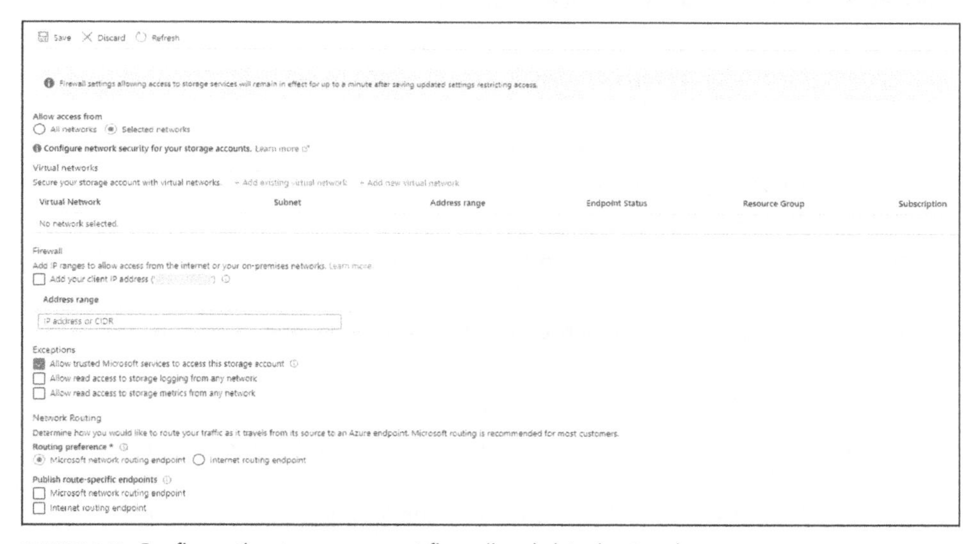

FIGURE 1-19 Configure the storage account firewall and virtual networks

4. By choosing **Selected Networks**, the network rule is now set to "deny," which means no traffic is allowed access to the storage account private endpoints by default. To allow access to your services, specific rules must be added in the **Firewall** or **Virtual Networks** sections of the **Firewalls And Virtual Networks** blade.
5. The **Firewall** section governs which public IP address ranges can be granted access to the storage account. You have the option to configure the following settings:
   - **Add Your Client IP Address.** The Azure portal picks up your public Internet-facing IP address from your browser. Choosing this option will add your client to the access list. For this demo, leave this option unchecked.
   - **Address Range.** Individual IP addresses, such as your customers' static public Internet-facing IP addresses or a range of addresses in CIDR notation, can be added.

6. Access to the storage account can be secured to specific subnets within a VNet, which further isolates access to your storage account. The VNet can be in a different subscription. From the **Virtual Networks** section on the same blade, you have the following options:
   - **Subscription.** This is where you choose the subscription in which your VNet resides.
   - **Virtual Networks.** This is where you choose a VNet, though only networks within the storage accounts regional pair will be listed.
   - **Subnets.** This is where you choose the subnets of the chosen VNet that require access.
7. Click **Enable.** This will create a service endpoint for storage in the VNet.
8. Click **Add.** This allows you to add the VNet and selected subnet for access to the storage account.
9. The options show in the **Exceptions** section cover access to Azure services that cannot be isolated through VNet or firewall access rules:
   - **Allow Trusted Microsoft Services To Access This Storage Account.** Leave this selected to allow logging, back-up services, and specific services granted access by a system managed identity.
   - **Allow Read Access To Storage Logging From Any Network.** Selecting this allows access logs and tables for storage analytics.
   - **Allow Read Access To Storage Metrics From Any Network.** Selecting this option allows access metrics for storage analytics.
10. Once the configuration is complete, click **Save**.
11. To test the updated configuration, switch back to PowerShell. Use the cmdlets from the "Manage access keys" section earlier in this chapter to retrieve the context. Now re-run the command to add a blob that we discussed in the "Configure Azure files and Blob Storage" section of this skill:

```
Set-AzStorageBlobContent -File " D:\az303files\uploadTest.jpg" '
-Container $containerName '
-Blob "uploadTest.png" '
-Context $ctx
Set-AzStorageBlobContent : This request is not authorized to perform this
operation. HTTP Status Code: 403 - HTTP Error Message: This request is not
authorized to perform this operation.
```

Your public-facing IP address is not part of the access list, so you will receive the 403 error above. Return to the Azure portal and select **Add Your Client IP Address** and follow the steps in step 4 above and click **Save**. Wait a short time—on average around a couple of minutes—and then rerun the cmdlet to add a blob. The blob will be added because your IP address is now on the allow list. Complete the same exercise from within a virtual machine that is part of the subnet added in step 5. You should be able to add the blob without error.

Private endpoint

Private endpoints are a relatively recent addition to the configuration options for storage account network access. Private endpoints give VMs on a VNet a private link to securely access the storage account. The traffic between the VM and storage account flows from the client into the VNet's private endpoint and across the Microsoft backbone to the storage account. This method of access has the following benefits:

- Block data exfiltration from the VNet by securing traffic to the private link
- Securely connect on-premises networks to a storage account by using a VPN gateway or ExpressRoute into to the VNet with the private link
- Configure the storage account firewall to disable all connection to the public endpoint

When you create the private endpoint, you must specify which storage account core service requires access. Azure then creates a private DNS zone that allows the original storage endpoint URL to resolve to the private endpoint address, which is aliased with a `privatelink` subdomain.

> ***NEED MORE REVIEW?*** **CONFIGURE NETWORK ACCESS TO THE STORAGE ACCOUNT**
>
> **To learn more about configuring network access to a storage account and private endpoints for azure storage, see *https://docs.microsoft.com/en-us/azure/storage/common/storage-network-security* and *https://docs.microsoft.com/en-us/azure/storage/common/storage-private-endpoints.***

Implement Shared Access Signatures and access policies

The access key of a storage account grants the holder authorization to all resources on the storage account. This method of authorization is unlikely to follow the principle of least privilege for your use cases. A shared access signature (SAS) for a storage account grants restricted-access, rights-specified services, enabling granular control over how the holder of a SAS can access the data. To explore how SAS is configured for a storage account and see how a SAS is used, follow these steps:

1. From the Azure portal, enter **storage account** in the search resources bar and choose **Storage Account** from the drop-down menu that is displayed as you type the resource name. From the list of storage accounts, select the `az303fsdemosa` storage account used in the previous sections from the list. If this does not exist, select any other storage account with a blob container and blob.
2. In the **Storage Account** menu at the left, select **Shared Access Signature** from **Settings**. The **Shared Access Signature** blade where the SAS can be configured opens to the right. Figure 1-20 shows an example configuration:

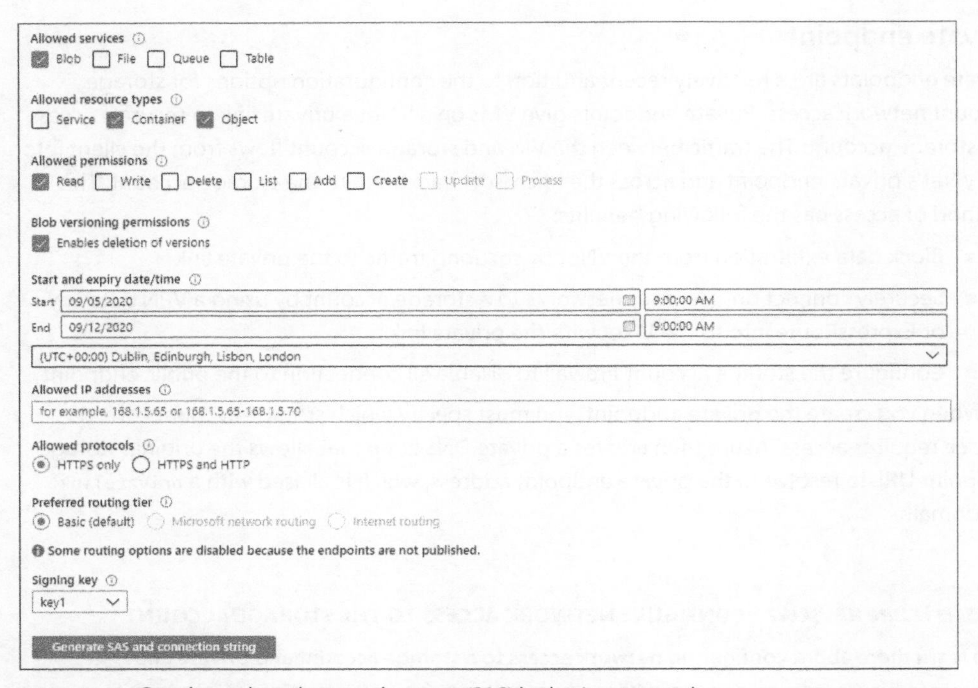

FIGURE 1-20 Creating a shared access signature (SAS) in the Azure portal

3. The configuration shown creates an SAS to access blob containers. Each configuration setting defines the granularity of the authorization:
   - **Allowed Services.** The core service(s) that the SAS can access.
   - **Allowed Resource Types.** Access to the API levels under the allowed service:
     - **Service.** Service-level APIs, such as list containers, queues, tables, or shares.
     - **Container.** Container-level APIs, such as APIs to create or delete containers, create or delete queues, create or delete tables, or create or delete shares.
     - **Object.** Object-level APIs, such as Put Blob, Query Entity, Get Messages, Create File, and so on.
   - **Allowed Permissions** The permissions defined by resource type.
     - **Read / Write.** Valid for all resource types.
     - **Delete.** Valid for Container and Object types.
     - **Other options.** All other options are valid for Object types.
   - **Enables Deletion Of Versions.** When allowed permission is set to delete (the bullet points above), the SAS grants permission to delete blob versions.
   - **Start And Expiry Date/Time.** The time boxing for the SAS, the SAS will not work outside of this data range.
   - **Allowed IP Addresses.** Single addresses or ranges in CIDR notation. Leave blank for any IP address.

- **Allowed protocols.** HTTPS or HTTPS and HTTP.
- **Preferred Routing Tier. Basic.** If endpoints have been specified in the firewalls and virtual networks configuration for the storage account, you can also select the routing types for the endpoints.
- **Signing Key.** The access key used to sign the SAS. Note, if you rotate your keys, your SAS must also be regenerated.

Using the above information and looking at Figure 1-20, you can deduce the access granted by this SAS to the storage account resources. It will grant access to the blob service at the container and object level. The read-level access allows listing of blobs stored in a container and reading of blobs within the container. The **Enables Deletion Of Versions** checkbox can be ignored because deletion at the object level is not a granted permission. The SAS will be valid from 9 AM on June 12 to 9 AM on June 19 and is accessible over HTTPS.

4. Click **Generate SAS And Connection String as Displayed** in Figure 1-20. The SAS token and URL are created and displayed below the **Generate SAS And Connection String** button. The format of the strings is displayed in Figure 1-21.

FIGURE 1-21 Generated SAS Connection String, SAS Token, and Blob Service SAS URL, as displayed in the Azure portal

If you look at the SAS Token and Blob Service SAS URL in Figure 1-21, the parameters directly after the `?` are the options chosen on the SAS creation screen. The large string after `&sig=` is the digital signature used verify and authorize the access requested.

SAS tokens, URLs, and connect strings can be used by many programming languages through their software development kits (SDKs) to access storage account data. To see this in action, here is the PowerShell output from the "Manage access keys" section from earlier in this chapter, which has been updated to use the SAS token generated from the Azure portal:

```
$resourceGroupName = "12storage"
$storageAccountName = "az303fsdemosa"
$SASToken = "?sv=2019-10-10&ss=b&srt=co&sp=rx&se=2020-06-19T08:00:00Z&st=2020-06-12T08:0
0:00Z&spr=https&sig=ceDhRXv2uu9370cRaCrtVdrHd1WDy8gLqNboZkqxwxM%3D"
$containerName = "images"

$ctx = New-AzStorageContext '
-StorageAccountName $storageAccountName '
-SasToken $SASToken
```

Execute the commands above in a PowerShell terminal to set the context using the SAS token passed to the `-SasToken` parameter. The SAS token grants read access, so it can be used to get a blob from a container. To get the blob, execute the following commands in PowerShell:

```
Get-AzStorageBlobContent '
    -Container $containerName '
    -Blob "uploadTest.png" '
    -Destination "d:\az303files\" '
    -Context $ctx
     Container Uri: https://az303fsdemosa.blob.core.windows.net/images

Name                             BlobType  Length          ContentType
LastModified                  AccessTier SnapshotTime         IsDeleted
uploadTest.png               BlockBlob 592021         image/png
2020-06-11 23:44:18Z Unknown                                      False
```

Do not forget to ensure that the client you are running the PowerShell from has network access to the storage account; otherwise, the above cmdlet will error!

If you now tried to execute the add blob cmdlet from the "Configure Azure Files and Blob Storage" section earlier in this chapter, it will error because the SAS token is creating a context that only has read access. To test this, execute the following commands in PowerShell:

```
Set-AzStorageBlobContent -File "D:\az303files\uploadTestSAS.png" '
-Container $containerName '
-Blob "uploadTestSAS.png" '
-Context $ctx
Set-AzStorageBlobContent : This request is not authorized to perform this operation
using this permission. HTTP Status Code: 403 - HTTP Error Message: This request is not
authorized to perform this operation using this permission.
ErrorCode: AuthorizationPermissionMismatch
ErrorMessage: This request is not authorized to perform this operation using this
permission.
```

Implement Azure AD authentication for storage

Azure Storage account access tokens and SAS tokens must be shared to be used. Although the shared tokens can be securely stored in Azure Key Vault to minimize risk, there is still the possibility that a token could be stored in source control or transmitted in an insecure manner. This is a possible security vulnerability, and as an Azure architect, it is part of your role to minimize potential security vulnerabilities.

Azure Active Directory (Azure AD) can be used to create a security principal in the form of a user, group, or application. The security principal can be granted permissions to Azure Storage blobs and queues using role-based access control (RBAC). In this model, the security principal is authenticated to Azure AD and an OAuth token is returned. The token is then used to authorize requests against Azure Storage. No credentials are shared with Azure AD authentication; for this reason, Microsoft recommends using Azure AD for authorization against a storage account whenever possible.

Using the example storage account `az303fsdemosa` that you have been exploring throughout this skill, you can test user principal access. If you no longer have this storage account, substitute the `$storageAccountName` and `$containerName` variables for ones that exist in your subscription. For this example, you will need to place a text file into the `$containerName` variable. The following code snippets use a text tile named `storage-az303demo.txt`.

Open a PowerShell terminal and log in as the user who created the storage account. Execute the following cmdlets to set the context using Azure AD and try to retrieve the test blob:

```
$resourceGroupName = "12storage"
$storageAccountName = "az303fsdemosa"
$containerName = "images"

$ctx = New-AzStorageContext '
-StorageAccountName $storageAccountName '
-UseConnectedAccount

Get-AzStorageBlobContent '
    -Container $containerName '
    -Blob "storage-az303demo.txt" '
    -Destination "d:\az303files\" '
    -Context $ctx
```

Note the `-UseConnectedAccount` parameter of `New-AzStorageContext` above. This instructs the cmdlet to use OAuth authentication to retrieve an access token for the logged in account. This OAuth token is then used to get the permissions to the storage account, which becomes part of the storage context.

The `Get-AzStorageBlobContent` cmdlet will fail with a 403 error—request not authorized. The account you are logged in with created the storage account; it was automatically given the owner role to the storage account. The owner role is for the "management plane" of an Azure resource, and the account has full access to manage the configuration of the storage account. The owner role has no permissions on the "data plane"; therefore, it cannot read, write, update, or delete data. The command line or Azure portal can be used to grant the required permissions through RBAC. Open the Azure portal and follow these steps to grant read permission to the Blob Storage:

1. In the search resources bar at the top of the portal, enter **storage account**, then choose **Storage Account** on the drop-down menu that is displayed as you type the resource name. From the list of storage accounts, select the `az303fsdemosa` storage account or the account used in the previous section from the list.
2. Click **Access Control (IAM)** in the menu. This is where permissions are assigned via RBAC. Click the **Role Assignments** tab. If you have been following along through this skill, you will see no users listed here. This tab shows all granted role assignments that affect this resource; these can be at the resource level or they can be inherited from a parent scope.
3. Click **Add** at the top and choose **Add Role Assignment**. In the top drop-down menu, choose **Storage Blob Data Reader**. This will grant read-only permission to the blob service of the storage account. Leave **Assign Access To** set as **Azure AD User, Group Or Service Principal**. You can now search for a user, group, or service principal. Find the user, which could not execute the previous PowerShell cmdlet and select it. The **Add Role Assignment** blade should look as shown in Figure 1-22.

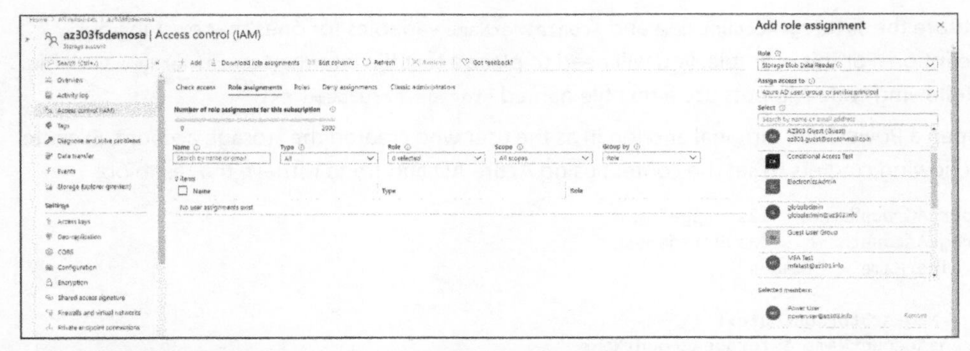

FIGURE 1-22 Assigning the Storage Blob Data Reader Role to an Azure AD user

Click **Save** at the bottom of the assignment to assign the permission, which will take you back to the **Role Assignments** list. If you scroll down to the bottom, the Storage Blob Data Reader role has been added.

4. Switch back to the PowerShell terminal and re-run the cmdlets from the beginning of this section. The `Get-AzStorageBlobContent` cmdlet no longer errors, and the blob is retrieved.

This example explains how to grant permissions to a user or group, but what about an application? It is more likely that, as an architect, you will be designing a solution where an application is accessing the storage resources. An application requires a service principal or managed identity, which are granted the permissions to access the resource. You can think of a service principal or managed identity as equivalent to a service account in an on-premises Active Directory. Microsoft recommends using a managed identity where possible. The steps below use a combination of Azure CLI and an Azure Function as an example:

1. Create an Azure function with an HTTP Trigger. For help with this see the "Implement Azure functions" in the "Implement solutions for apps" skill in Chapter 3.
2. In the Azure portal, search for **function app** in the search resources bar at the top. Select **Function App** and click the name of the function you created in step 1.
3. Select **Functions** in the left-hand menu and then choose **HttpTrigger1** from the function list in the **Functions** blade.
4. On the left side, choose **Code + Test**. Copy the code listed below and paste it into the PowerShell edit replacing the code displayed. Click **Save**.

```
using namespace System.Net
# Input bindings are passed in via param block.
param($Request, $TriggerMetadata)
# Write to the Azure Functions log stream.
Write-Host "PowerShell HTTP trigger function processed a request."
$resourceGroupName = "12storage"
$storageAccountName = "az303fsdemosa"
$containerName = "images"
$ctx = New-AzStorageContext '
-StorageAccountName $storageAccountName '
-UseConnectedAccount
$blob = Get-AzStorageBlobContent '
```

```
    -Container $containerName '
    -Blob "storage-az303demo.txt" '
    -Context $ctx '
    -Force

$body = $blob.ICloudBlob.DownloadText()
# Associate values to output bindings by calling 'Push-OutputBinding'.
Push-OutputBinding -Name Response -Value ([HttpResponseContext]@{
    StatusCode = [HttpStatusCode]::OK
    Body = $body
})
```

In the code snippet above, you will see that the middle section is almost identical to the cmdlets executed to read the blob with a user principal. The context is retrieved using `-UseConnectedAccount` and passed to `Get-StorageBlobContent`. The destination has been removed so that the Azure Function stores the file in `wwwroot`. `-Force` is added so that the file is overwritten each time the function is executed. The text from the blob is extracted to `$body`, and it is output to the function response. Note this example has been designed for use with a text file.

Click **Test/Run** > **Run** to execute the function. It will fail with the following output to the Function log, as shown in Figure 1-23. In this example, the function is not running under an Azure AD account, which means `-UseConnectedAccount` cannot authenticate and the context is null. A managed identity must be assigned to the Azure Function for authentication.

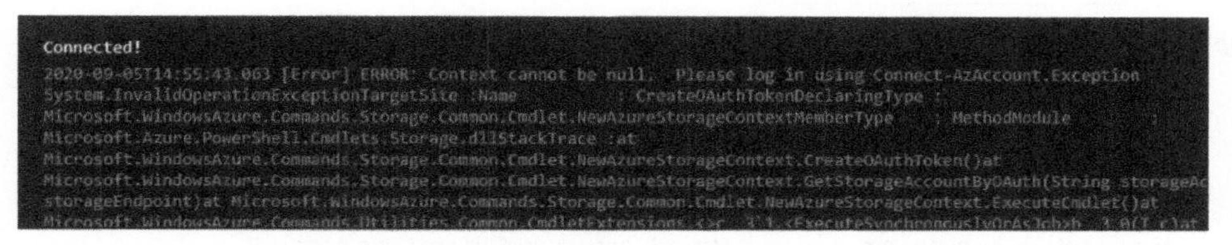

FIGURE 1-23 Function execution error from null context

5. To assign an identity, click the function name in the breadcrumb trail at the top of the Azure portal. Scroll down through the menu and click **Identity**. Leave the tab at **System Assigned** and change the **Status** to **On**. Click **Save**. The function now has a system-managed identity. A system-managed identity is an identity that follows the lifecycle of the resource it is assigned to; if the resource is deleted, so is the identity. When a managed identity is created on an Azure function, two environment variables are created: `MSI_ENDPOINT` and `MSI_SECRET`. Developers can use these within code to retrieve the OAuth token for the managed identity. It is then passed to the Azure resource as part of a request so that the request can be authorized. In this example, `Get-NewAzContext` wraps this process for you, so it does not have to be specifically coded.
6. Click **Functions** in the left menu, select **HttpTrigger1** > **Code + Test** and then run the function again. The error has changed to a 403—authorization error. The function is now retrieving the context of the managed identity, but the identity does not have permission to read the blob.

7. Assigning RBAC roles to a managed identity is almost identical to that of a user. Navigate to the storage account you are using for this walkthrough—`az303fsdemosa`. Click **Access Control (IAM)** in the left menu, and then click **Add** at the top. Click **Add Role Assignment**. Under **Role**, select **Storage Blob Data Reader**. Under **Assign Access**, click **Function App**, which is listed under **System Assigned Managed Identity**. The name of the function app you have been using for this walkthrough will be listed. Click the function app name; the role assignment blade will look as shown in Figure 1-24. Click **Save**.

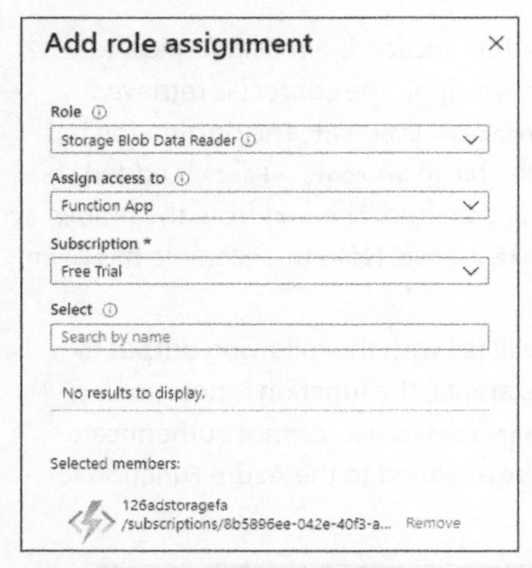

FIGURE 1-24 Assigning read access on a blob service to a system-managed identity

8. Navigate back to the function app and use the same process as described in step 7 to run the function app again. The code will now execute without error and the contents of the file are displayed in the output window. Note that you will still receive a 403 error if your function app does not have network access to the storage account.

Implement Azure Storage replication

Azure automatically replicates your storage data three times within the datacenter it is stored, protecting against underlying physical hardware failure. There are further high availability options for Azure Storage, each with its own use case:

- **Locally redundant storage (LRS).** Azure makes three copies of the storage account and distributes them throughout a single datacenter in your home region. Here, you have protection against the failure of a storage array.
- **Zone-redundant storage (ZRS).** Azure makes three copies of the storage account and distributes them across multiple datacenters in your home region. Here, you have protection against datacenter-level failures. Note that only General-Purpose V2 storage accounts can use the ZRS replication option.
- **Geo-redundant storage (GRS).** Azure makes three copies of the storage account in the home region, and three copies in a second, paired region. Paired regions are

geographically close enough to have high-speed connectivity to reduce or eliminate latency. Here, you have protection against regional failures.

- **Geo-zone-redundant storage (GZRS).** Azure creates copies within the availability zones of the primary region and then replicates the data to the secondary region. This is the Microsoft-recommended level of replication encompassing the highest levels of durability, availability, and performance.
- **Read-access geo-redundant storage (RA-GRS).** This is the same as GRS with the exception that you can access the storage account in the secondary region; the base URL path is *https://<account-name>-secondary.<service>.windows.net.*
- **Read-access geo-zone-redundant storage (RA-GZRS).** This is the same as RA-GRS, but Azure also copies data across the availability zones of the primary region.

You must also consider cost; the more the data is replicated, the higher the SLA and the higher the cost.

EXAM TIP* *STORAGE ACCOUNT SERVICE LEVEL AGREEMENTS

It can be beneficial to understand the SLAs for each redundancy type. See *https://docs.microsoft.com/en-us/azure/storage/common/storage-redundancy* for further review.

The replication type is specified when the storage account is created. In the "Select storage account options based on a use case" section of this chapter, you created a storage account with the Azure CLI. The `--sku` parameter was omitted; the `sku` parameter is where the replication type is selected. The `sku` consists of two parts: the performance level (Standard or Premium) and the replication type (LRS, ZRS, GRS, or RAGRS). Only LRS and ZRS may have a premium performance level. Execute the following command to create a read-access geo-redundant storage account in Azure CLI:

```
resourceGroupName="12storage"
storageAccountName="az303ragrs"
az storage account create \
    --name $storageAccountName \
    --resource-group $resourceGroupName \
    --kind StorageV2 \
    --sku Standard_RAGRS
```

The JSON returned by the cmdlet above contains this section:

```
"secondaryEndpoints": {
   "blob": "https://az303ragrs-secondary.blob.core.windows.net/",
   "dfs": "https://az303ragrs-secondary.dfs.core.windows.net/",
```

These are URLS (endpoints) for the secondary region.

NEED MORE REVIEW? **DATA REDUNDANCY**

To learn more about data redundancy for storage accounts, visit *https://docs.microsoft.com/en-us/azure/storage/common/storage-redundancy.*

Implement Azure Storage account failover

Storage accounts configured for geo-replication can be manually failed-over to the secondary endpoints if there is an outage at the primary. You should also recommend that your customers perform test failovers as part of their disaster recovery plans. To initiate a failover, you can use the command line or the Azure portal. Log in to the Azure portal and follow these steps. You will be using the geo-redundant storage account `az303ragrs` that you created in the previous section:

1. In the search resources bar at the top of the portal, enter **storage account** and then choose **Storage Account** from the drop-down menu that is displayed as you start to type the resource name. From the list of storage accounts, select the `az303ragrs` storage account or the account used in the previous section ("Implement Azure Storage replication").
2. The menu opens at the **Overview** blade. Look at the **Status** field which reads: "Primary: Available, Secondary: Available." The **Location** field will show the selected paired region. The primary is in the first location; the secondary is in the second.
3. Scroll down in the menu and click **Geo-Replication**. The map shows the location of your primary and secondary endpoints. Scroll down to the bottom of the map and click **Prepare For Failover**. The **Failover** blade states when the primary and secondary was last synced and that you will lose data after this point. Also, note the paragraph that states when the secondary becomes the primary, the new primary will be converted to locally redundant storage (LRS). You must update the storage account to get back to geo-redundant storage after the Failover. This can be performed using the Azure portal, Azure CLI or PowerShell. Type **yes** in the **Confirm Failover** box and click **Failover**.

NEED MORE REVIEW? **STORAGE ACCOUNT FAILOVER**

To learn more about disaster recovery and failover for storage accounts, visit *https://docs.microsoft.com/en-us/azure/storage/common/storage-disaster-recovery-guidance*.

Skill 1.3: Implement VMs for Windows and Linux

As an architect, it might seem unusual that a skill for the exam involves implementing and configuring virtual machines (VMs). However, lift-and-shift operations are often a cloud architect's bread and butter in a large enterprise. This skill will look at the configuration options for a VM and how to design for scale and availability.

This skill covers how to:

- Select virtual machine size
- Configure storage for VMs
- Configure Azure Disk Encryption
- Configure High Availability
- Deploy and configure scale sets
- Implement Azure Dedicated Hosts

This is an expert-level certification, so there is an expectation that your skill set will already include creating Linux and Windows virtual machines in the Azure portal. It is also expected that you possess basic scripting skills in Bash and PowerShell.

Select virtual machine size

It is highly likely that you will encounter many projects as an architect which will involve lifting and shifting on-premises virtual machines (VMs) into the cloud. An essential part of this task is assessing each on-premises VM's workload and sizing an appropriate VM in Azure. There are many VM sizes available in Azure, and all are optimized for specific workloads. You need to have a good grasp of these optimizations and where to apply them. See Table 1-1.

TABLE 1-1 Virtual machine types and sizes summary

VM Type	Sizes	Description and usage
General Purpose	A, B, D	Balanced CPU to Memory. Dev and test applications, medium sized database, and application servers
Compute optimized	F	High CPU-to-memory. Application servers, network appliances, and batch
Memory optimized	E, M, DSv2m Dv2	High memory-to-CPU. Database servers and large caching / in-memory processes
Storage optimized	L	High disk throughput. For big data, NoSQL and data warehouses
GPU	N	Heavy graphics rendering and machine learning
High-performance compute	H A8-11 (will be deprecated 3/2021)	The highest-power CPUs available. Some sizes can also have Random Direct Memory Access (RDMA) network interfaces.

The table above provides a broad overview of how the lettering at the start of a VM size denotes the VM's type. Each letter can have multiple configurations of CPU cores, memory sizes, and storage capacities.

To view the options in the portal, choose to add a virtual machine resource, scroll down to **Size**, and click **Change Size**. This will display the options available to you. The size options available to you alter between regions, and you can list the VM sizes available in each location using PowerShell or in this example with the Azure CLI:

```
az vm list-sizes --location uksouth --output table
```

The output of the command above lists all the VM sizes available for the given location, `-location uksouth`. You can use Bash or PowerShell operators to filter your results. For example, issue the following command in PowerShell to show all VMs available in a region with eight cores:

```
Get-AzVMSize -Location uksouth | Where NumberOfCores -EQ '8'
```

To create a virtual machine outside the portal, you must specify the size as part of the create command. The `Name` column from the output of the command above is the value that must be passed into the `create` command:

```
az vm create    --name vmLinSizeExample \
  --resource-group $resourceGroupName \
  --image UbuntuLTS \
  --size Standard_B1s \
 --generate-ssh-key
```

If the workload on a VM alters or if it was incorrectly sized on creation, you will need to resize your VM. You can resize a VM while still allocated, but you can only resize it to a size available on the cluster it was created. To check the sizes available to you, execute this command:

```
az vm list-vm-resize-options --resource-group $resourceGroupName --name vmLinSizeExample
--output table
```

If the size you require is not listed by `az vm list-vm-resize-options` but is listed for `az vm list-sizes`, you must deallocate the VM before resizing. Azure will then re-create the VM in a new cluster:

```
az vm resize --resource-group $resourceGroupName --name vmLinSizeExample --size
Standard_DS2_v2
```

NEED MORE REVIEW? **VIRTUAL MACHINE SIZING**

To learn about the options available for virtual machine sizing, visit the Microsoft Docs article "Sizes for Linux virtual machines in Azure" at *https://docs.microsoft.com/en-us/azure/virtual-machines/linux/sizes*. Make sure to explore the description of each type. This page also features a link to more information about Windows virtual machines.

Configure storage for VMs

Virtual machine storage can be managed or unmanaged, though the recommended mode is managed. With a managed disk, the storage account, underlying storage limits, and encryption are taken care of for you.

There are four disk types available in Azure, and each disk type has different limits and therefore, different specific use cases, as shown in Table 1-2.

TABLE 1-2 Disk type

Disk type	Use case	Max size	Max throughput	Max iops
Ultra disks	IO intensive Top-tier databases and transaction-heavy workloads	65G	2000MB/s	160,000
Premium SSD	Production applications Performance workloads	32G	900MB/s	20,000
Standard SSD	Dev and test servers Light-usage applications and web servers	32G	750MB/s	6,000
Standard HDD	Non-critical and backup	32G	500MB/s	2,000

The cost for each disk type rises as you move between the different disk types, with ultra disks having the highest cost.

Originally, all Azure VMs were created with unmanaged disks. You can convert the unmanaged disks to managed using the Azure portal or the command line. First, you must deallocate the VM and then convert it. For example, the following command shows how to deallocate a VM in Azure CLI:

```
az vm deallocate --resource-group $resourceGroupName --name vmLinSizeExample
az vm convert --resource-group $resourceGroupName --name vmLinSizeExample
az vm start --resource-group $resourceGroupName --name vmLinSizeExample
```

NEED MORE REVIEW? **MANAGED DISKS**

To learn about managed disks and disk types available to IaaS in Azure, visit the Microsoft Docs article "Introduction to Azure managed disks" at *https://docs.microsoft.com/en-us/azure/virtual-machines/linux/managed-disks-overview.* We recommend that you review all the Disk Storage Concepts sections and review the SELECT A DISK TYPE FOR IAAS VMS section.

A virtual machine uses disks in three roles: OS Disks, temporary disks, and data disks. OS disks store the files for the selected operating system when the VM was created. OS disks cannot use an ultra disk. However, if you are using ultra disks for your data disks, it is recommended that you use premium SSD for your OS disk. OS disks can also utilize an ephemeral OS disk. The data for ephemeral OS Disks is stored in the local VM's storage and not in Azure Storage. The local storage provides read and write operations at much lower latency and makes the imaging process faster. Storing the data locally to the host means ephemeral disks incur no cost; however, if an individual VM fails, it is likely that all data on the ephemeral disk will be lost. Ephemeral OS disks are great for stateless applications, where failure of a VM will not affect the application because traffic will be queued or re-routed. An Ephemeral OS disk is chosen in the Azure portal under the **Advanced** section of the **Disks** tab on creating a virtual machine in the Azure portal or on the command line. For example, in Azure CLI, use the `--ephemeral-os-disk true` flag:

```
az vm create \
 --resource-group $resourceGroupName \
 --name vmEphemOSDisk \
 --image UbuntuLTS \
 --ephemeral-os-disk true \
 --os-disk-caching ReadOnly \
 --admin-username azureadmin \
 --generate-ssh-keys
```

NEED MORE REVIEW? **EPHEMERAL OS DISKS**

To learn more about ephemeral OS disks, visit the Microsoft Docs article "Ephemeral OS disks for Azure VMs" at *https://docs.microsoft.com/en-us/azure/virtual-machines/windows/ephemeral-os-disks.*

Temporary disks contain data that can be lost during a maintenance event or the deallocation of a VM. Therefore, do not put critical data on a temporary disk. Data does, however, persist on a temporary disk following a normal re-boot.

Data disks contain data, web pages, or custom application code. Multiple data disks can be added to a VM; the maximum amount depends on the VM size. You saw the `MaxDataDiskCount` column when executing the `az vm list-sizes` command in the "Select a virtual machine size" section, earlier in this chapter. The max data disks figure was also listed in the Azure portal view. Data disks support all the Azure disk types.

It is not mandatory to create data disks when you create a VM unless you have chosen an image that requires data disks. You can add one or more data disks once a VM has been created. To add a data disk, you can use the Azure portal and command line. For example, use this code to attach a data disk in PowerShell:

```
$diskConfig = New-AzDiskConfig -SkuName Premium_LRS -Location uksouth
-CreateOption Empty -DiskSizeGB 128
$disk1 = New-AzDisk -DiskName dataDisk1 -Disk $diskConfig -ResourceGroupName
resourceGroupName
$vm = Get-AzVM -Name vmName -ResourceGroupName resourceGroupName
$vm = Add-AzVMDataDisk -VM $vm -Name dataDisk1 -CreateOption Attach
-ManagedDiskId $disk1.Id -Lun 1
Update-AzVM -VM $vm -ResourceGroupName resourceGroupName
```

Note the `-CreateOption Empty` parameter on the first line for `New-AzDiskConfig`. This parameter creates a new empty disk to attach to your VM. Empty disks need to be initialized once attached by using disk management on Windows or partition and mount commands on Linux. Custom script extensions can be used to automate this task on scale.

The `-CreateOption` parameter also takes `Upload` as an input. The `Upload` option is used to create a disk configuration in Azure Storage and then upload a VHD directly into it. Uploads can be for on-premises disks or for copying disks between regions. Note, VHDX files must be converted to VHD first. The final value for `-CreateOption` is `FromImage`. You build your custom VM, prepare it for generalization with sysprep, and then use the resultant image to create one or more Azure VMs.

> ***NEED MORE REVIEW?*** **ADDING DISKS**
>
> **To learn more about adding disks, visit the Microsoft Docs article "Add a disk to a Linux VM" at *https://docs.microsoft.com/en-us/azure/virtual-machines/linux/add-disk*. Also, we recommend that you review all pages from the Manage Storage section of the How-to guides in the Virtual Machine documentation.**

Configure Azure Disk Encryption

Azure protects customers from the unlikely event of an attacker gaining access to physical media by encrypting data at rest. By default, disks are encrypted at rest with server-side encryption (SSE) using Microsoft-managed keys. The automatic and transparent nature of the disk encryption means that no changes are required to the application code to make use of it. The encryption by SSE is FIPS 140-2–compliant; however, for some use cases, this might not fit your compliance and regulatory requirements. If a VHD is copied from the storage account it is in, it will be decrypted. The possibility of decryption outside the storage boundary is why Azure Security Center will flag VMs that have not had Azure Disk Encryption (ADE) enabled.

ADE is performed at the VM operating system level, which adds an extra layer of security for the VM. The BitLocker (Windows) and DM-Crypt (Linux) features of an operating system provide volume encryption of the OS and data disks. Because this is an operating system feature, not all operating system versions are supported. Azure Disk Encryption uses a Data Encryption Key (DEK) to encrypt the data; you then have the option of using a key encryption key (KEK) to encrypt the DEK for added security. Encrypting the DEK with a KEK is known as "envelope encryption." The DEK and the KEK must be stored in Azure Key Vault, which means the OS must have access to the key vault.

Azure Disk Encryption is performed on virtual machines that have already been created. Encryption can only be performed from the command line. Follow the steps below to encrypt the disks on an existing Windows VM `$vmName` using Azure CLI:

1. Perform a snapshot of the VM disks to be encrypted; this is done for restore purposes in case of an error during encryption. You can also run this command to verify Azure Disk Encryption is not enabled on the VM:

   ```
   resourceGroupName="az303chap1_3-rg"
   location="uksouth"
   vmName="ade-vm"
   vaultName="ade-vk"
   ```

```
keyName="ade-kek"

az vm encryption show --resource-group $resourceGroupName --name $vmName
Azure Disk Encryption is not enabled
```

2. Create a key vault using the following command . This key vault must be in the same region as the VMs you want to encrypt. Note the `-enabled-for-encryption` parameter, which enables the key vault for disk encryption; without this, the encryption in step 3 will fail.

   ```
   az vm encryption enable --resource-group $resourceGroupName --name $vmName
   --disk-encryption-keyvault $vaultName
   ```

3. Encrypt the VM using this command, which creates the DEK for you in the specified key vault set: `-disk-encryption-keyvault $vaultName`. Note the `-volume-type ALL` parameter. `ALL` instructs the encryption process to encrypt all OS and data disks. You can also replace `ALL` with `OS` or `DATA` to encrypt only those types.

   ```
   az vm encryption enable --resource-group $resourceGroupName --name $vmName
   --disk-encryption-keyvault $vaultName --volume-type ALL
   ```

4. Check the status of disk encryption on the VM once more. If you scroll through the JSON output from the following command, you can see the encryption status of each disk as `EncryptionState/encrypted` as displayed in Figure 1-25.

   ```
   az vm encryption show --resource-group $resourceGroupName --name $vmName
   ```

```
az303@Ubuntu: az vm encryption show --resource-group $resourceGroupName --name $vmName
{
  "disks": [
    {
      "encryptionSettings": [
        {
          "diskEncryptionKey": {
            "secretUrl": "https://ade-vk.vault.azure.net/secrets/0DF924D9-92A1-4267-BEE6-5610AE86DBDD/d2ab64ad775c4dc6a6
80e03d500ad1a9",
            "sourceVault": {
              "id": "/subscriptions/8b5896ee-042e-40f3-a274-e7bbec8133d7/resourceGroups/az303chap1_3-rg/providers/Micros
oft.KeyVault/vaults/ade-vk"
            }
          },
          "enabled": true,
          "keyEncryptionKey": null
        }
      ],
      "name": "ade-vm_disk1_823ef6ea0e004cc9853503c8867339a7",
      "statuses": [
        {
          "code": "EncryptionState/encrypted",
          "displayStatus": "Encryption is enabled on disk",
          "level": "Info",
          "message": null,
          "time": null
        }
      ]
    }
  ],
```

FIGURE 1-25 Verify disks are encrypted in Azure CLI

5. To check that the OS disk is encrypted from within the VM, RDP into the VM and open Windows Explorer. Click **This PC** in the left navigation pane. The padlocks on the `C:` and `D:` drive verify they are protected by BitLocker, as shown in Figure 1-26.

FIGURE 1-26 Verify disks are protected by BitLocker in Windows Explorer

The first three steps above are the minimum required to encrypt a VM with Azure Disk Encryption. To explore the encryption process in step 3 further, you can display all the secrets that are now stored in the keyvault `$vaultName` by using the following command in Azure CLI; the output is shown in Figure 1-27:

```
az keyvault secret list --vault-name $vaultName
```

```
az303@Ubuntu: az keyvault secret list --vault-name $vaultName
[
  {
    "attributes": {
      "created": "2020-09-05T16:04:08+00:00",
      "enabled": true,
      "expires": null,
      "notBefore": null,
      "recoveryLevel": "Recoverable+Purgeable",
      "updated": "2020-09-05T16:04:08+00:00"
    },
    "contentType": "BEK",
    "id": "https://ade-vk.vault.azure.net/secrets/0DF924D9-92A1-4267-BEE6-5610AE86DBDD",
    "managed": null,
    "name": "0DF924D9-92A1-4267-BEE6-5610AE86DBDD",
    "tags": {
      "DiskEncryptionKeyFileName": "0DF924D9-92A1-4267-BEE6-5610AE86DBDD.BEK",
      "MachineName": "ade-vm",
      "VolumeLabel": "Windows",
      "VolumeLetter": "C:\\"
    }
  }
]
az303@Ubuntu:
```

FIGURE 1-27 Azure Key Vault secret following disk encryption

If you look about halfway down in the output in Figure 1-27, you can see the line `"contentType":" "BEK"`. BEK stands for BitLocker encryption key. The BEK is the data encryption key (DEK), as described at the beginning of this section. When the encryption command was issued, Azure created the BEK automatically and stored the key in the key vault. If more than one volume existed for the VM, a BEK would have been created for each one.

If you must use your own encryption keys for regulatory purposes, you will need to encrypt the generated BEK with a key encryption key (KEK). To encrypt with your own KEK, you must import your key into the key vault and then re-issue the encryption command, as shown in this Azure CLI command:

```
az keyvault key import --name $keyName --vault-name $vaultName --pem-file ./keys/ade-
kek.pem --pem-password $password
az vm encryption enable --resource-group $resourceGroupName --name $vmName --disk-
encryption-keyvault $vaultName --volume-type ALL --key-encryption-key $keyName
```

Re-run the command from above Figure 1-25 to check the encryption status again:

```
az vm encryption show --resource-group $resourceGroupName --name $vmName
```

Note the addition of the `keyEncryptionKey` section, detailing where the KEK is stored.

NEED MORE REVIEW? **AZURE DISK ENCRYPTION**

To learn more about configuring Azure Disk Encryption, visit the Microsoft Docs article "Azure Disk Encryption for Virtual Machines" at *https://docs.microsoft.com/en-us/azure/security/fundamentals/azure-disk-encryption-vms-vmss.*

Configure High Availability

So far in this skill you have been exploring configurations on a single VM. A single VM in Azure carries an SLA of 99.9 percent but only when Premium SSD or ultra disks are used for all OS and data disks. If Premium SSDs are not used, the VM has no SLA. An SLA is a service-level agreement, which is the minimum amount of time that Microsoft guarantees a service will be available.

An SLA of 99.9 percent guarantees that the downtime on a single VM will be no more than 43 minutes a month. This may not seem like a lot of time, but what if it was during a customer's peak trading hour of the month? Using single VMs for an application introduces a single point of failure. There are three situations in which an Azure VM could be affected:

- **Planned maintenance.** VMs must be updated to ensure reliability, performance, and security. When updates require reboot of a VM, you are contacted to choose a maintenance window via Azure Planned Maintenance.
- **Unplanned hardware maintenance.** Azure predicts that underlying hardware is about to fail and live-migrates the affected VMs to healthy hardware. A live-migrate pauses the VM so network connections, memory, and file access are maintained, but performance is likely to be reduced at some point in the migration.
- **Unexpected downtime.** This is when hardware or physical infrastructure fails without warning. This can be network, disk, or other rack-level failure. When Azure detects unexpected downtime, Azure migrates the VM and reboots it to heal it; the reboot causes downtime. Downtime will also occur in the unlikely event of an entire datacenter outage.

As an architect, you must design to remove single points of failure, which can be achieved by architecting highly available (HA) solutions. To architect a highly available VM-based solution in Azure, you need to understand availability zones and availability sets.

Availability sets

Availability sets in Azure are used to mitigate the effects of a rack-level hardware failure and scheduled maintenance on VMs. When you place your VMs into an availability set,

Azure distributes the workload across multiple update domains and fault domains. An update domain is a logical group of underlying hardware that can be rebooted or undergo maintenance at the same time. When patches are rolled out, only one update domain will be affected at a time. A fault domain is a physical section of the datacenter; each section has its own network, power, and cooling infrastructure. If a hardware failure occurs on a fault domain, only some of the VMs in your availability set are affected. The logical and physical concepts of how fault and update domains enable high availability are displayed in Figure 1-28.

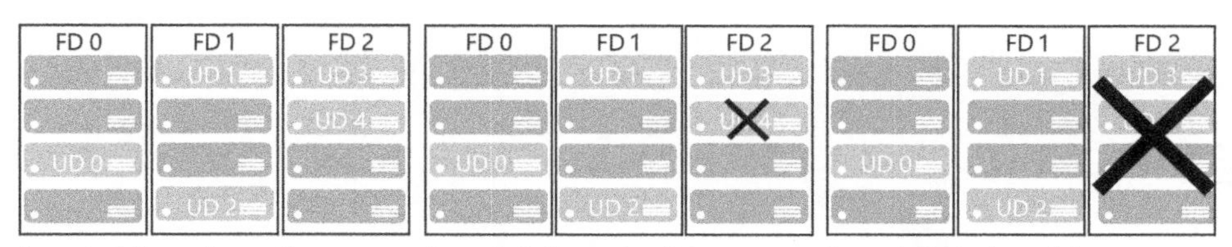

Example 1: Normal operation Example 2: Planned maintenance Example 3: Hardware failure

FIGURE 1-28 Availability set update and fault domain examples

Each of the three examples in Figure 1-28 represents an Azure datacenter distributed into update domains (UD) and across fault domains (FD) for an availability set. In Example 1, the operation is normal and the VMs are distributed into the default of three fault domains and five update domains. You may have a maximum of three fault domains, though update domains can be increased to 20. When the number of VMs in the set goes beyond five, Azure will sequentially increase the VMs in each update domain by one. UD 0 will increase to two VMs, UD 1 will increase to two VMs, and so on. For these examples, assume there is one VM in each of the five update domains.

Example 2 in Figure 1-28 represents a planned maintenance event. Azure starts the patching process by patching and rebooting UD 4. Azure repeats the patch and reboot process on each update domain in turn. If you have five VMs in your availability set, four VMs are available at every point in the patching process.

Example 3 in Figure 1-28 represents a hardware failure on FD 2. Update domains UD 3 and UD 4 go down, but UD 0, UD 1, and UD 2 are available, which is three VMs. If a planned maintenance event occurs while the VMs in UD 3 and UD 4 are moved and healed, two VMs are available.

Using availability sets ensures that at least one VM will be available during a planned or unplanned maintenance event. This increases the SLA for VMs within an availability set to 99.95 percent or about 22 minutes of downtime a month. To configure an availability set for VMs, you start by creating the availability set. In the portal, type **availability set** in the search resources bar at the top of the portal, choose **Availability Sets** when the drop-down menu is displayed as you type the resource name. Once the **Availability Sets** screen loads, click **Add**. Figure 1-29 shows an example of a completed **Create Availability Set** page.

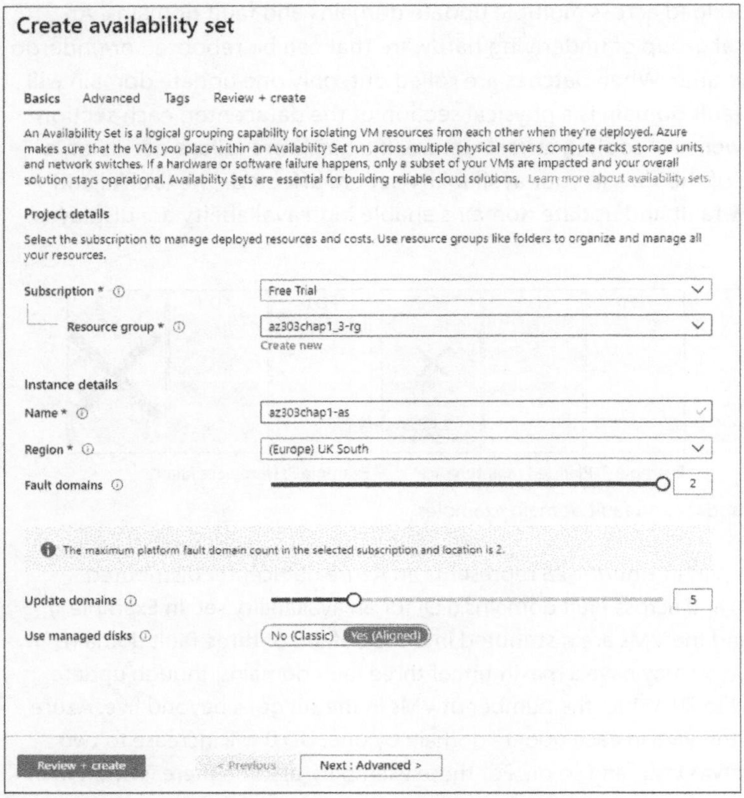

FIGURE 1-29 A completed availability set creation page

For a virtual machine to be added to an availability set, it must exist in the same region as the availability set. Looking at Figure 1-29 you can also see the warning reading: `The Maximum Platform Fault Domain Count In The Selected Subscription And Location Is 2`. This is caused because the region—UK South—only provides two fault domains. Changing this to another region, such as West Europe, would allow three domains. You can query the max fault domain count for a region from the command line. If you set the **Use Managed Disks** option to **Yes (Aligned)**, the VM disks will be distributed across storage fault domains, preventing single points of failure for your VM's disks. If you do not utilize managed disks, you will need to manually create a storage account for every VM in an availability set.

Once the availability set is created, you can assign VMs in the portal or on the command line; for example, in Azure CLI, you specify the `--availability-set` parameter, as shown below:

```
az vm create \
    --resource-group $resourceGroup \
    --name $vmNamei \
    --availability-set az303chap1-ag \
    --size Standard_DS1_v2  \
```

```
    --vnet-name $vnetName \
    --subnet $subnetName \
    --image UbuntuLTS \
    --admin-username azureuser \
    --generate-ssh-keys
```

You can only add a VM to an availability set on creation of the VM. If you need to assign a VM to an availability set after creation, the VM must be deleted and re-created. Once your availability set is created and VMs have been deployed, you add a load balancer to distribute traffic between available VMs.

If the solution you are creating is for a multi-tier application, you must create an availability set for each tier when architecting for high availability.

Availability zones

An availability zone is made up of one or more datacenters, each zone having its own networking, power, and cooling. The zones are physically separated, so using availability zones will protect you from datacenter failures. Each availability zone has a fault and update domain, and these work in the same way as described for availability sets. Note, you cannot combine availability sets and availability zones. Availability zones are not available in every region, and not every VM SKU is available in an availability zone. You can check what is available on the command line. For example, in Azure CLI, you would execute this command:

```
az vm list-skus -l uksouth --zone --output tsv
```

The `--zone` parameter on `az vm list-skus` will list VMs that are available for use in an availability zone. If you switched the location above to `uknorth`, no SKUs would be listed. At the time of this writing, `uknorth` has no availability zones. To add a VM to an availability zone, you specify the zone as part of the VM configuration; for example, you could execute this command in PowerShell with the `-Zone` parameter:

```
New-AzVMConfig -VMName $vmName -VMSize Standard_DS1_v2 -Zone 2
```

To achieve 99.99 percent SLA for an availability zone, you must also ensure that network connectivity and storage for the VM is within the same zone. If the add VM process is creating managed disks and the `-Zone` parameter is set, the storage will be automatically placed in the correct zone.

If your solution requires high availability across regions, availability zones will not be adequate. You will need to architect a multi-region solution with traffic being balanced across the regions. An example of a multi-region architecture is shown in Figure 1-30.

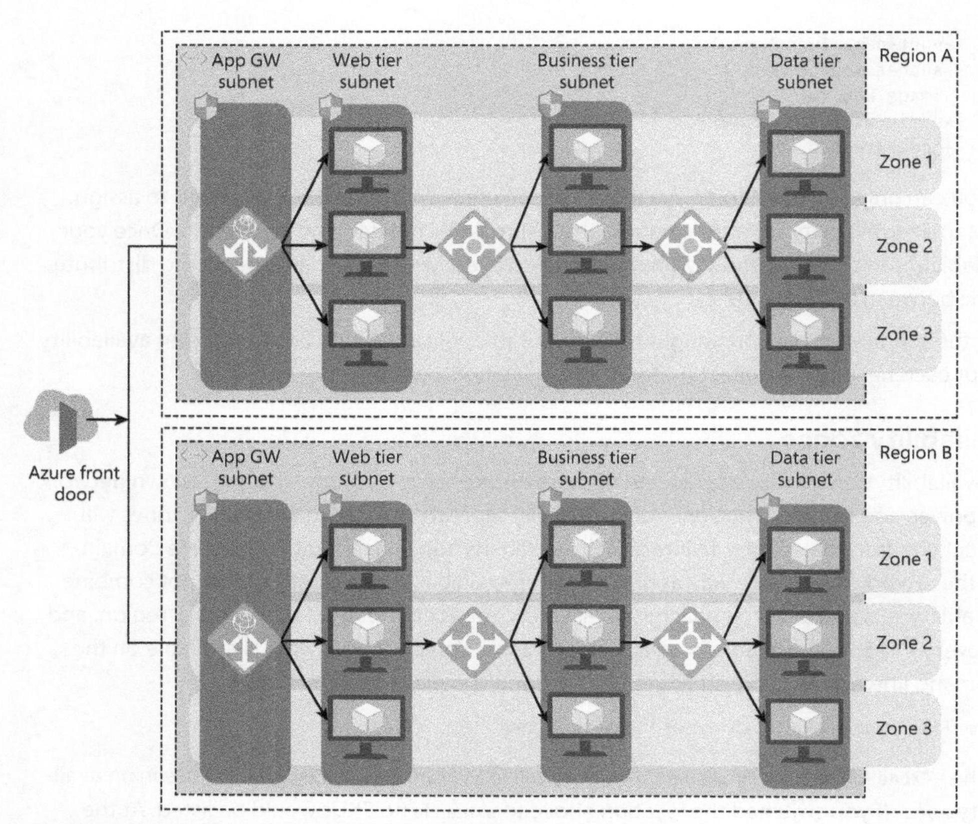

FIGURE 1-30 Multi-region high availability for IaaS with a web front end

EXAM TIP ***AZURE VM SLAS***

Have a good understanding of the SLA percentages for a single instance VM, VMs in an availability set and VMs across availability zones.

NEED MORE REVIEW? **HIGH AVAILABILITY FOR VIRTUAL MACHINES**

To learn about the availability configurations available to virtual machines, visit the Microsoft Docs article "Manage the availability of Windows virtual machines in Azure" at *https://docs.microsoft.com/en-gb/azure/virtual-machines/windows/manage-availability*.

Deploy and Configure Scale Sets

An historical issue with on-premises datacenter configuration is having to purchase hardware in advance to deal with future predicted load. A virtual machine scale set (VMSS) in Azure enables you to deploy a set of load-balanced and identical VMs. These VMs can be scaled vertically or horizontally to meet demand. The load balancer distributes the incoming workload across the scale set VMs. If the load balancer's health probe detects that a VM is not responding, the load balancer stops sending traffic to that VM. A scale set can bring a level of redundancy, and the distribution of the load might aid with application performance. To add a VM scale set, you can use the Azure portal or command line. For example, to add a scale set in Azure CLI, execute the following commands:

```
az vmss create \
  --resource-group $resourceGroupName \
  --name myScaleSet \
  --image UbuntuLTS \
  --upgrade-policy-mode automatic \
  --admin-username $adminUser \
  --generate-ssh-keys
```

The `az vmss create` command above adds a VM scale set for Ubuntu-based VMs. Note you can use the `--zones` parameter to place a scale set across a zone or zones to increase availability. You may also use custom images in a scale set; these must be VMs that are deallocated and generalized first.

Once you have added a scale set, you can use the Azure portal to explore the scale set settings. At the top of the portal, enter **scale set** in the resources search bar and press Enter. Select your scale set, click **Instances** in the menu blade, and notice there two instances have been created. An instance is a VM in a scale set. By default, the `az vmss create` command has two VMs and a load balancer. You can also specify an existing load balancer or application gateway when creating a scale set. In this example, the load balancer is created automatically with no routing rules, so you must add them. For example, in Azure CLI, this command will route HTTP traffic to the VMs:

```
az network lb rule create \
  --resource-group $resourceGroupName \
  --name myLoadBalancerRuleWeb \
  --lb-name myScaleSetLB \
  --backend-pool-name myScaleSetLBBEPool \
  --backend-port 80 \
  --frontend-ip-name loadBalancerFrontEnd \
  --frontend-port 80 \
  --protocol tcp
```

You must also add a health probe to the load balancer if you need to check the underlying VMs for availability.

Switch back to the Azure portal and open the **Instances** blade. Select an instance and look at the **Overview** blade. VMs in a scale set have no public IP address. If maintenance is required for an instance, a jumpbox must be configured to RDP or SSH into the instance. Go back to the scale set blade and click **Scaling**. The default setting for scaling is **Manual**, but in the Azure portal, you can drag the slider up or down to scale the number of instances in or out. To perform scaling on the command line, such as in Azure CLI, run `az vmss scale` and specify the `--new-capacity` parameter, as shown here:

```
az vmss scale --name myScaleSet --new-capacity 3 --resource-group $resourceGroupName
```

Autoscaling is the real power in scale sets. Switch back to the Azure portal and click **Custom Autoscale** in the **Scaling** blade. The default scale condition is displayed; scroll to the bottom and click **Add A Scale Condition**. Multiple conditions can be added. Figure 1-31 shows examples of scale conditions for predictable and unpredictable loads.

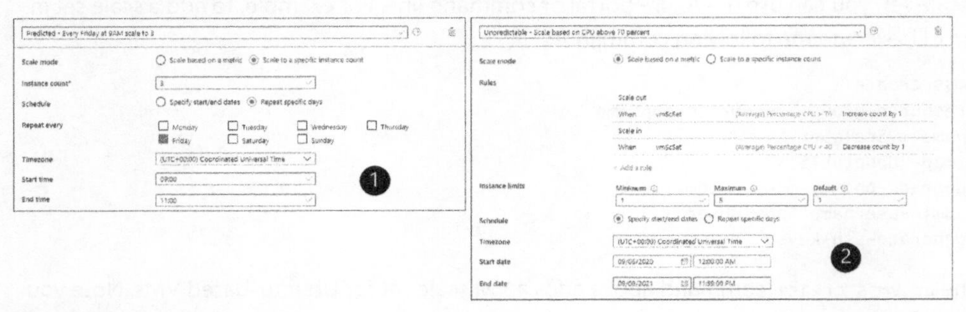

1. Predicted load
2. Unpredictable load

FIGURE 1-31 Predicted and Unpredictable load-scale conditions

The example predictable load scale condition in Figure 1-31 is shown on the left. The **Scale Mode** is set to **Scale To A Specific Instance Count** and the **Instance Count** can scale out to a specific instance count of **3**. The **Schedule** is set to **Repeat Specific Days** and **Repeat Every** is set to **Friday**. Lastly, the **Start Time** and **End Time** are **09:00** and **11:00**, respectively.

The unpredictable load scale condition in Figure 1-31 appears on the right. The **Scale Mode** is set to **Scale Based On A Metric**. The first metric rule is set to **Increase Count By 1** and **(Average) CPU Credits Consumed > 70** (the average CPU load across all instances is greater than 70 percent for at least 10 minutes). The second metric rule is set to **Decrease Count By 1** and **(Average) Percentage CPU < 40** (the average CPU load across all instances is less than 40 percent for 10 minutes). **Instance Limits** ensure the scale condition does not go beyond 5 instances.

Scaling in and scaling out is not limited to VM instance metrics; click **Add A Rule** in a scale set condition and see that **Storage** and **Service Bus** queues are available under **Metric Source**. Therefore, if the queues to your VMSS are large, you can scale out to reduce the queue.

While still in the **Scale Rule** panel, scroll down to **Actions**. This is where you can increase or decrease your instances.

> ***NEED MORE REVIEW?*** **VIRTUAL MACHINE SCALE SETS**
>
> **To learn about virtual machine scale sets, visit the Microsoft Docs article "Virtual Machine Scale Sets documentation" at *https://docs.microsoft.com/en-us/azure/virtual-machine-scale-sets/*.**

Implement Azure Dedicated Hosts

The VMs you have looked at so far in this skill have all been running on an underlying shared physical infrastructure. You have little control over where your VM has been placed, beyond specifying a region or availability zone. You have no control over whose workloads you are sharing the infrastructure with. In many use cases, this is not an issue, though some regulatory and compliance requirements must have isolated physical infrastructure. Azure Dedicated Hosts address these requirements by providing the following features:

- **Single tenant physical servers.** Only VMs you choose are placed on your host(s). This is achieved by hardware isolation at the physical server level.
- **Control over maintenance events.** This allows you to choose the maintenance windows for your host(s).
- **Azure hybrid benefit.** You can bring your own Windows Server and SQL licenses to reduce costs.

Azure Dedicated Hosts are grouped within a host group. When creating a host group, you can specify how many fault domains to use. If you specify more than one fault domain, you choose which fault domain a host is added into. The virtual machines automatically pick up this fault domain from the host. This feature is why availability sets are not supported in Azure Dedicated Hosts. In a host group, you have the option to specify an availability zone. You must create multiple host groups across availability zones if you require high availability across zones. A host requires the choice of a SKU-size family from the VM series and hardware generations supported in your host group's region.

When a VM is added to an Azure Dedicated Host, it must match the host region and size family. Existing VMs can be added, though they must meet the same requirements and be stopped/deallocated first.

> ***NEED MORE REVIEW?*** **AZURE DEDICATED HOSTS**
>
> **To learn about deploying Azure Dedicated Hosts in the portal, visit the Microsoft Docs article "Deploy VMs to dedicated hosts using the portal" at *https://docs.microsoft.com/en-us/azure/virtual-machines/windows/dedicated-hosts-portal.***

Skill 1.4: Automate deployment and configuration of resources

The speed of business has become much faster, and organizations are deploying changes and solutions to the cloud using agile methodologies. As an architect, you need to understand how to automate the deployment of your solutions, ensuring that the underlying infrastructure is reliable from the first to the nth time it is deployed. These deployments leverage Infrastructure as Code (IaC). In Azure, IaC is performed using an Azure Resource Manager (ARM) template, which is that a JSON (Javascript Object Notation)–based structure in which you declare what the end state of your resources will be in JSON.

Once a solution has been deployed, it might require some configuration. This can also be scripted and is known as "Configuration as Code." Configuration as Code aids configuration drift, where a server configuration alters over time because of manual interventions. In this section, you will explore using ARM templates for deployment and configuration and using an Azure automation runbook for state configuration.

This skill covers how to:

- Save a deployment as an Azure Resource Manager template
- Modify Azure Resource Manager template
- Evaluate location of new resources
- Deploy from a template
- Configure a virtual disk template
- Manage a template library
- Create and execute an automation runbook

NEED MORE REVIEW? **ARM TEMPLATES**

To learn about ARM templates, visit the Microsoft Docs article at *https://docs.microsoft.com/en-us/azure/azure-resource-manager/templates/*.

Save a deployment as an Azure Resource Manager template

The Azure portal provides the ability to export deployments to an ARM template. This can be especially useful when you are first starting out with ARM templates. You can export an environment you are used to working with and then explore the exported JSON. The Azure portal has two ways to export a template:

- **From a resource or resource group.** Generates an ARM template based on an existing resource or resource group.
- **Before a deployment or from a historical deployment.** Extracts the ARM template used for a deployment.

Exporting from a specific resource is, in the main, the same process regardless of the resource. In the Azure portal, click any resource, scroll down in the resource menu blade to **Settings**, and then choose **Export Template,** which brings up the **Export Template** blade, as shown in Figure 1-32.

FIGURE 1-32 Exporting a template from a resource in the Azure portal

Figure 1-32 shows an example of a single resource export. It is the public IP of a domain controller referred to in Skill 1.7 of this book. As shown in Figure 1-32, the **Export Template** blade shows the following options:

- **Download.** Downloads a zipped copy of the template.
- **Add To Library.** Saves the template to a library for later use. The template library is discussed in the section "Manage a template from a library" further on in this chapter.
- **Deploy.** Deploys the template as displayed in the editor.
- **Include Parameters.** Includes the parameters section of the template. If this option is not selected, the parameters section becomes an empty object—{}.
- **Template Structure.** The left side of the bottom pane defines the outline of the JSON structure of the template.
- **Template Editor.** The right side of the bottom pane enables live editing of the export.

Click **Download**. The resulting zip file contains two JSON files: The `template.json` file contains the definition of your resource(s), and the `parameters.json` file is used to pass in parameters to the `template.json` file for a deployment.

Exporting a resource group is similar, as the screenshot in Figure 1-33 shows.

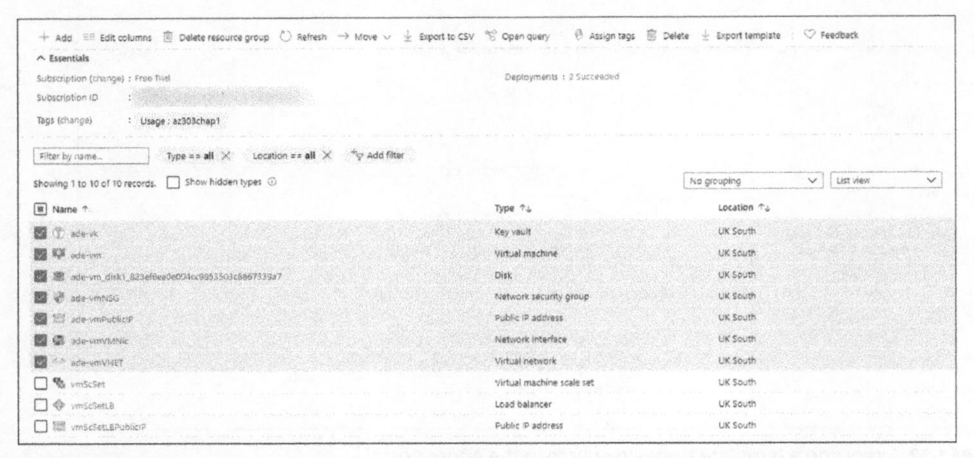

FIGURE 1-33 Selecting resources to export from a resource group in the Azure portal

Clicking the **Export Template** link at the top right will export all the resources from your resource group unless you specifically select the resources you want to export.

Modify Azure Resource Manager template

ARM templates are JSON files, and they can be modified with any text editor and stored alongside your company's code in source control. Microsoft's cross-platform source code editor, Visual Studio Code (VS Code), has some excellent extensions to assist with editing ARM templates. (See *https://docs.microsoft.com/en-us/azure/azure-resource-manager/templates/use-vs-code-to-create-template*.) Using the editor is not part of the exam, but the extensions will make it easier to see the key sections of an ARM template and to learn how to modify those sections.

To get started modifying a template, you can export a template from the portal as discussed in the previous section. Also, the Azure ARM Quickstart Template GitHub repository has hundreds of ready-built templates to help with learning ARM. The complexity of these templates ranges from smaller single resource templates to large templates containing best-practice, multi-tier architectures with built-in security, compliance, resiliency, and redundancy. The 100-level templates are the introductory templates. (See *https://github.com/Azure/azure-quickstart-templates/tree/master/100-blank-template*.) Copy the contents of the `azuredeploy.json` file into VS Code as shown in Figure 1-34.

```
{} azuredeploy.json ×
1.4 - Automation > 1.4.2 - Modifying a bank template > {} azuredeploy.json > ...
1   {
2       "$schema": "https://schema.management.azure.com/schemas/2019-04-01/deploymentTemplate.json#",
3       "contentVersion": "1.0.0.0",
4       "parameters": {
5       },
6       "variables": {
7       },
8       "resources": [
9       ],
10      "outputs": {
11      }
12  }
```

FIGURE 1-34 Blank ARM template structure

The blank ARM template shown in Figure 1-34 shows a clear view of the template structure:

- **$schema (required).** This is the location of the JSON schema definition for an ARM template. This does not change unless the schema is upgraded.
- **contentVersion (required).** This is used for source control and can be any format.
- **Parameters.** Parameters are passed into the template to customize deployment.
- **Variables.** Variables are values calculated from parameters, other variables or resources in the template and then used in the deployment.
- **Resources (required).** The resources for the deployment must be defined.
- **Outputs.** These are the outputs from resource deployments, such as an IP address or service endpoint.

The blank template can be deployed to Azure; it won't do anything, but it is a valid template.

Figure 1-35 displays an adapted version of the `101-storage-account-create quick start` template from the GitHub repository. The template has been separated out across the next four images so that you can clearly see the structure defined above.

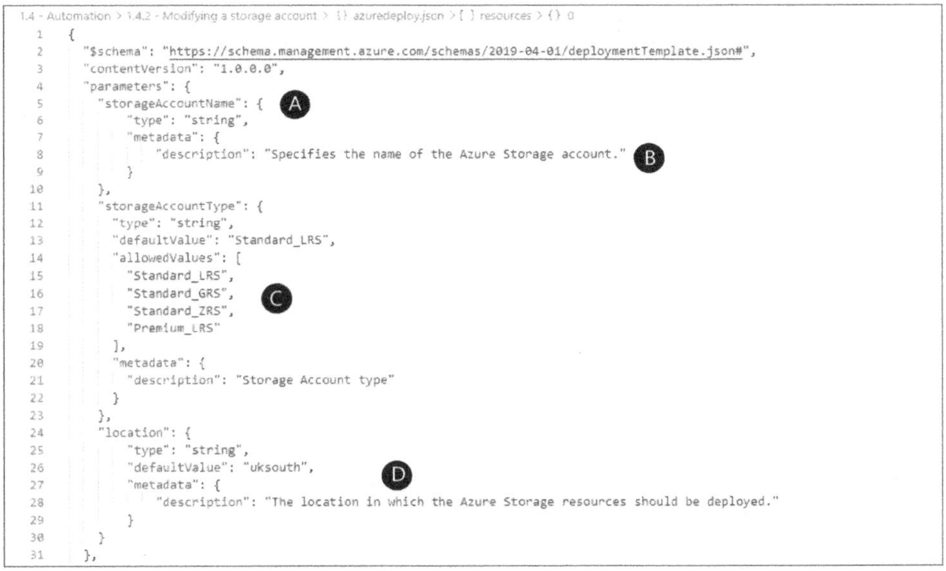

```
1.4 - Automation > 1.4.2 - Modifying a storage account > {} azuredeploy.json > [ ] resources > {} 0
1   {
2     "$schema": "https://schema.management.azure.com/schemas/2019-04-01/deploymentTemplate.json#",
3     "contentVersion": "1.0.0.0",
4     "parameters": {
5       "storageAccountName": {
6           "type": "string",
7           "metadata": {
8               "description": "Specifies the name of the Azure Storage account."
9           }
10      },
11      "storageAccountType": {
12        "type": "string",
13        "defaultValue": "Standard_LRS",
14        "allowedValues": [
15          "Standard_LRS",
16          "Standard_GRS",
17          "Standard_ZRS",
18          "Premium_LRS"
19        ],
20        "metadata": {
21          "description": "Storage Account type"
22        }
23      },
24      "location": {
25          "type": "string",
26          "defaultValue": "uksouth",
27          "metadata": {
28              "description": "The location in which the Azure Storage resources should be deployed."
29          }
30      }
31    },
```

FIGURE 1-35 ARM template parameters

Figure 1-35 shows the parameters section of the template; each parameter is defined in a slightly different way:

A. Each parameter has a name; the first one is `storageAccountName`. This name is how the parameter will be referenced in the template.

B. `metadata` can be set throughout the ARM template; in most cases, it is ignored. For a parameter, setting metadata with the name description can be seen during deployment and is mainly used as a help mechanism.

C. allowedValues uses a drop-down menu configuration. Only the values specified in allowedValues can be chosen.

D. defaultValue, if specified, means a value does not have to be passed to the parameter it is specified against when the template is deployed. For the parameters above, storageAccountName must always be supplied when the template is deployed as there is no defaultValue.

The next template section (see Figure 1-36) defines a variable.

```
32    "variables": {
33      "uniqueAccountName": "[concat(parameters('storageAccountName'), uniquestring(resourceGroup().id))]"
34    },
```

FIGURE 1-36 Defining a variable in an ARM template

In Figure 1-36, parameters('storageAccountName') is an example of how to use a parameter in an ARM template; it will return the value entered for the storageAccountName parameter. ARM templates have many built-in functions available. For example, concat is a string function that concatenates two strings. In the example above, it is concatenating the storageAccountName to another function that returns a unique string that is based on the resource group.

The resources section is normally the most involved; Figure 1-37 shows a single resource—a storage account.

```
35    "resources": [
36      {
37        "type": "Microsoft.Storage/storageAccounts",
38        "apiVersion": "2019-04-01",
39        "name": "[variables('uniqueAccountName')]",
40        "location": "[parameters('location')]",
41        "sku": {
42          "name": "[parameters('storageAccountType')]"
43        },
44        "kind": "StorageV2",
45        "properties": {}
46      }
47    ],
48    "outputs": {}
49  }
```

FIGURE 1-37 Storage account definition for a resource

Every resource deployed requires the following properties:

- **type.** This sets the type of resource. It is the namespace of the resource provider, which in this case, is something like Microsoft.Storage/storageAccounts, Microsoft.Compute/virtualMachines, or Microsoft.Network/virtualNetworks.
- **apiVersion.** This is the REST API version used to create the resource. Every provider has its own API version.
- **Name.** This is the resource name.

Most resources also require a location. In Figure 1-37, you can also see the storageAccountType parameter being used for the SKU. This is a good use case for allowedValues because SKUs are defined by Microsoft and therefore, have a fixed set of values. Another good use case for this is to limit the SKUs available for a virtual machine.

The outputs section of this template is empty.

EXAM TIP ARM TEMPLATES

You will be expected to be able to read and understand ARM templates and their JSON structures. Use the 101 quick-start templates for frequently used resources, such as virtual machines, networking, and storage, to build your knowledge.

Evaluate location of new resources

ARM template values can be extended using expressions. An ARM template expression is evaluated at runtime and often contains a function. In Figure 1-37, we used an expression to create the unique account name: `[reference(variables('uniqueAccountName')).primaryEndpoints]",` which can only be evaluated at runtime. Until runtime, the template does not know what the `resourceGroup()` function will return.

The output section of the ARM template described in the previous section could have contained an expression to be evaluated. For a storage account, you might want to return the created endpoints, as shown in Figure 1-38.

```
45     "outputs": {
46       "endPoints": {
47         "type": "object",
48         "value": "[reference(variables('uniqueAccountName')).primaryEndpoints]"
49       }
50     }
51   }
```

FIGURE 1-38 Outputting information for a newly created resource from an ARM template

The code shown in Figure 1-38 would have returned the following JSON output if it had been given a parameter of `az303arm` for `storageAccountName`:

```
"outputs": {
  "endPoints": {
    "type": "Object",
    "value": {
      "blob": "https://az303armfrslx5kksdvcu.blob.core.windows.net/",
      "dfs": "https://az303armfrslx5kksdvcu.dfs.core.windows.net/",
      "file": "https://az303armfrslx5kksdvcu.file.core.windows.net/",
      "queue": "https://az303armfrslx5kksdvcu.queue.core.windows.net/",
      "table": "https://az303armfrslx5kksdvcu.table.core.windows.net/",
      "web": "https://az303armfrslx5kksdvcu.z33.web.core.windows.net/"
    }
  }
},
```

Another common expression is to use the built-in function of `resourceGroup()` to return the location of the resource group to which the ARM template is being deployed. As previously shown in Figure 1-35, the definition for the `location` parameter would change to include the expression shown in Figure 1-39.

```
24       "location": {
25         "type": "string",
26         "defaultValue": "[resourceGroup().location]"
27       }
```

FIGURE 1-39 Evaluating the resource location within the template

The `.location` property returns the location of the supplied resource group. All resources within the template use this parameter, which ensures all resources are in the same location. Having all resources in the same location as the resource group they belong to enforces best practice.

Deploy from a template

Now that you have configured a template, it is time to deploy your resources into Azure. There are a few options for this, and in this section, we will explore the most widely used options: Azure portal, PowerShell, and Azure CLI.

An ARM template can be deployed to multiple scopes, tenants, management groups, subscriptions, and resource groups. The first three scopes are generally used for Azure policy and RBAC deployments. The resource group deployment is how most resources are deployed and is the focus of the exam. A resource group deployment requires an existing resource group to deploy to; you can explore deploying to a resource group by using the Azure portal:

> ***NOTE*** **ARM TEMPLATE FOR WALKTHROUGH**
>
> **Each of the deployments in this example utilizes the `101-simple-vm-windows` template from Azure Quickstart templates (*https://github.com/Azure/azure-quickstart-templates/tree/master/101-vm-simple-windows*). This template was, at the time of writing, built by a Microsoft employee. However, not all of them are, so verify what you are deploying.**

1. In the Azure portal enter **deploy** in the field at the top of the Azure portal. Choose **Deploy A Custom Template** from the top in the drop-down that is displayed as you type the resource name.
2. Custom template deployment allows you to paste your template into the **Build Your Own Template In The Editor**; create resources from **Common Templates**, or **Load A GitHub Quickstart Template**. Choose **Load A GitHub Quickstart Template**. Filter for the text "simple" and select **101-vm-simple-windows**. Click **Select Template**.
3. Note the **Custom Deployment** screen (Figure 1-40) looks very similar to the portal screens for adding any resource. If you open the `azuredeploy.json` file from the `101-vm-simple-windows quickstart` repository and compare the parameters, each parameter in `azuredeploy.json` has an input box on this page. The empty input boxes correspond to the parameters with no `defaultValue`. Select the **2016-Datacenter** drop-down menu; the options available to you are `the allowedValues` defined for the parameter.
4. Enter appropriate values for the virtual machine deployment and select **Review + Create**. Finally, click **Create**. Your virtual machine is deployed.

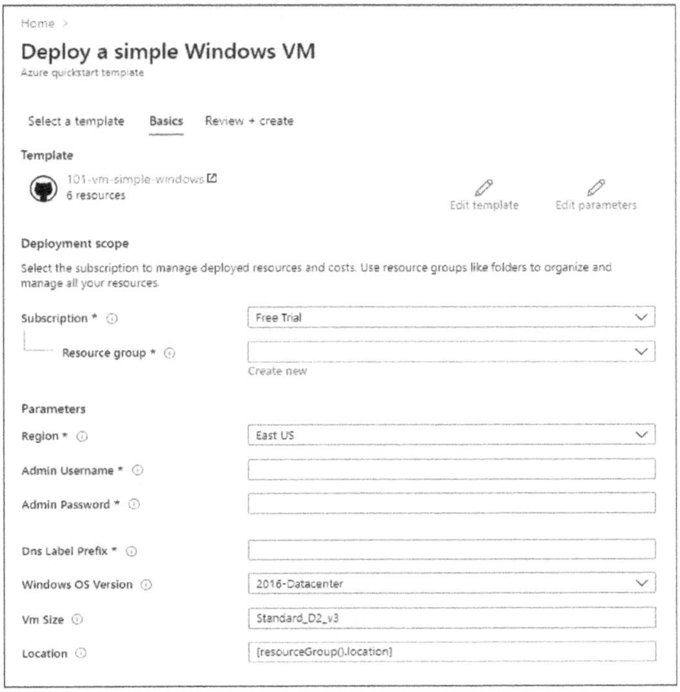

Home >

Deploy a simple Windows VM

Azure quickstart template

Select a template | Basics | Review + create

Template

101-vm-simple-windows
6 resources

Edit template | Edit parameters

Deployment scope

Select the subscription to manage deployed resources and costs. Use resource groups like folders to organize and manage all your resources.

Subscription * : Free Trial

Resource group * :
Create new

Parameters

Region * : East US

Admin Username * :

Admin Password * :

Dns Label Prefix * :

Windows OS Version : 2016-Datacenter

Vm Size : Standard_D2_v3

Location : [resourceGroup().location]

FIGURE 1-40 Deploying the 101-vm-simple-windows ARM template in the Azure portal

As an architect who wants to utilize IaC to speed up your deployments via automation, you are unlikely to be using the Azure portal to deploy your resources. This is where deployment scripted in PowerShell or the Azure CLI comes in. You will need a resource group and you will need to set your parameters. Parameters can be passed directly to the template on the command line with the Azure CLI, as shown in the following code:

```
#!/bin/bash

resourceGroupName="az303chap1_4-rg"
deploymentName="simpleWinVM"
templateUri="https://raw.githubusercontent.com/Azure/azure-quickstart-templates/
master/101-vm-simple-windows/azuredeploy.json"
adminUsername="adminuser"
adminPassword="secretP@ssw0rd"
dnsLabelPrefix="az303depvm"

az deployment group create --resource-group $resourceGroupName \
--name $deploymentName \
--template-uri $templateUri \
--parameters "adminUsername=$adminUsername" \
             "adminPassword=$adminPassword" \
             "dnsLabelPrefix=$dnsLabelPrefix"
```

Figure 1-41 shows the code block above being executed through VS Code:

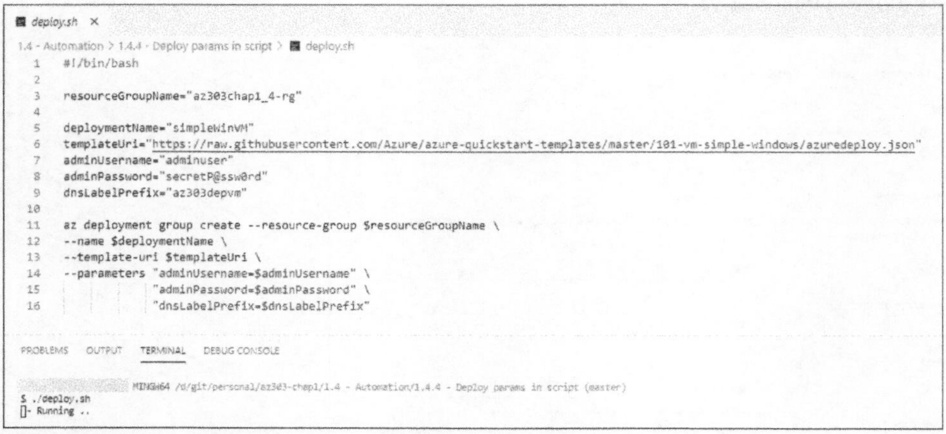

```
deploy.sh ×
1.4 - Automation > 1.4.4 - Deploy params in script > deploy.sh
1   #!/bin/bash
2
3   resourceGroupName="az303chap1_4-rg"
4
5   deploymentName="simpleWinVM"
6   templateUri="https://raw.githubusercontent.com/Azure/azure-quickstart-templates/master/101-vm-simple-windows/azuredeploy.json"
7   adminUsername="adminuser"
8   adminPassword="secretP@ssw0rd"
9   dnsLabelPrefix="az303depvm"
10
11  az deployment group create --resource-group $resourceGroupName \
12  --name $deploymentName \
13  --template-uri $templateUri \
14  --parameters "adminUsername=$adminUsername" \
15               "adminPassword=$adminPassword" \
16               "dnsLabelPrefix=$dnsLabelPrefix"

PROBLEMS   OUTPUT   TERMINAL   DEBUG CONSOLE

MINGW64 /d/git/personal/az303-chap1/1.4 - Automation/1.4.4 - Deploy params in script (master)
$ ./deploy.sh
- Running ..
```

FIGURE 1-41 Deploying 101-vm-simple-windows with the Azure CLI

The parameters in Figure 1-41 are set so that only those with no default value are passed to the template. Note the `templateUri` argument is taking the URL for the `azuredeploy.json` file straight from GitHub. The `templateUri` argument uses `raw.githubusercontent.com`, which passes the raw content of the file; without this change to the URL, the template will error.

If you recall exporting a resource from the previous section entitled "Save a deployment as an Azure Resource Manager template," the zip file contained a `parameters.json` file. This file is used to pass parameters to the template on deployment. It is referenced as part of the deployment command for Azure CLI and in the example shown in Figure 1-42, using PowerShell.

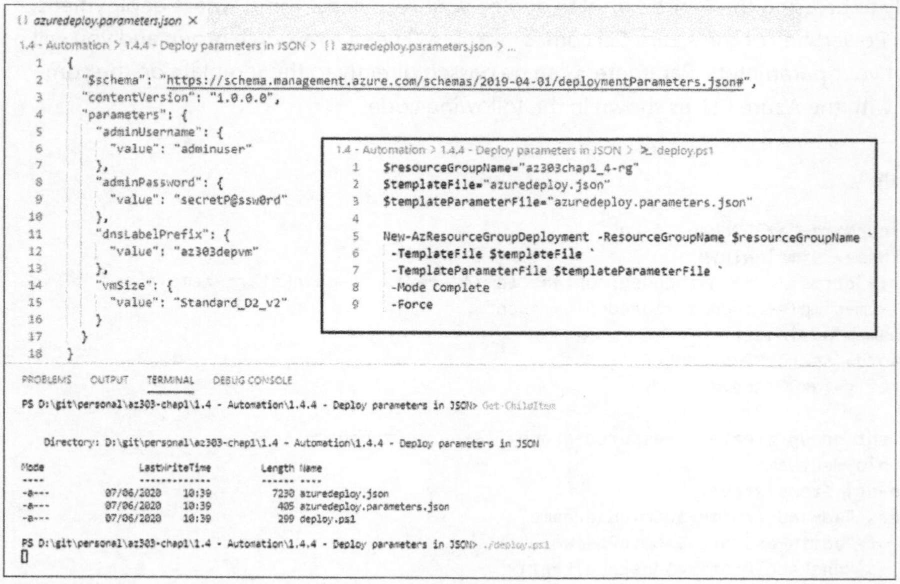

```
azuredeploy.parameters.json ×
1.4 - Automation > 1.4.4 - Deploy parameters in JSON > azuredeploy.parameters.json > ...
1   {
2     "$schema": "https://schema.management.azure.com/schemas/2019-04-01/deploymentParameters.json#",
3     "contentVersion": "1.0.0.0",
4     "parameters": {
5       "adminUsername": {
6         "value": "adminuser"
7       },
8       "adminPassword": {
9         "value": "secretP@ssw0rd"
10      },
11      "dnsLabelPrefix": {
12        "value": "az303depvm"
13      },
14      "vmSize": {
15        "value": "Standard_D2_v2"
16      }
17    }
18  }
```

```
1.4 - Automation > 1.4.4 - Deploy parameters in JSON > deploy.ps1
1   $resourceGroupName="az303chap1_4-rg"
2   $templateFile="azuredeploy.json"
3   $templateParameterFile="azuredeploy.parameters.json"
4
5   New-AzResourceGroupDeployment -ResourceGroupName $resourceGroupName `
6    -TemplateFile $templateFile `
7    -TemplateParameterFile $templateParameterFile `
8    -Mode Complete `
9    -Force
```

```
PROBLEMS   OUTPUT   TERMINAL   DEBUG CONSOLE

PS D:\git\personal\az303-chap1\1.4 - Automation\1.4.4 - Deploy parameters in JSON> Get-ChildItem

    Directory: D:\git\personal\az303-chap1\1.4 - Automation\1.4.4 - Deploy parameters in JSON

Mode          LastWriteTime       Length Name
----          -------------       ------ ----
-a---    07/06/2020   10:39         7230 azuredeploy.json
-a---    07/06/2020   10:39          405 azuredeploy.parameters.json
-a---    07/06/2020   10:39          299 deploy.ps1

PS D:\git\personal\az303-chap1\1.4 - Automation\1.4.4 - Deploy parameters in JSON> ./deploy.ps1
```

FIGURE 1-42 Deploying a local template with PowerShell

In Figure 1-42, the code on the right shows the PowerShell script, and the terminal winow below shows the command to call the script. The template and template parameters are stored locally, so the `TemplateFile` argument is used instead of the URI. For this example, the `101-vm-simple-windows azuredeploy.json` and `azuredeploy.parameters.json` have been copied to the directory from which the script is being run. Note the `-Mode` parameter; an ARM template that is run against a resource group that already has resources can run in two modes:

- **Incremental.** This is the default mode in which all resources that exist in the resource group but not in the template remain. Resources specified in the template are created or updated.
- **Complete.** All resources in the resource group are deleted and re-created.

The mode is defined as complete. When this PowerShell script is run, all resources in the defined resource group are deleted and re-created from scratch. This could be quite a destructive move, so PowerShell will ask if you are sure, though you can bypass this check with the `-Force` option.

On the left-hand side of Figure 1-42, you can see the parameters file that is being passed in by the PowerShell command. The top three parameters are the same as passed directly in the previous example from Figure 1-41 with Azure CLI. In the example in Figure 1-42, there is a fourth parameter, `vmSize`, which has a `defaultValue` within the ARM template. Specifying a parameter in the parameters file will override a `defaultValue` in the ARM template.

EXAM TIP ARM TEMPLATE DEPLOYMENT

You will be expected to understand how to execute deployments from the portal and command line. Having a good grasp of the options around these deployments could be beneficial.

Configure a virtual disk template

The Azure portal marketplace has many operating system images; however, these might not always be the best starting point for building your VMs in Azure. You might need to create your own base image or migrate a base image from on-premises. There are many ways to accomplish this, such as to `azcopy` a virtual disk (VHD) of the image to Azure Storage and reference it as part of an ARM template. To reference a VHD in an ARM template, the `storageProfile` must be set to point to the VHD. Look at the `storageProfile` for the Azure Quickstart template 101-vm-simple-linux as shown in Figure 1-43:

```
217                 "storageProfile": {
218                     "osDisk": {
219                         "createOption": "fromImage",
220                         "managedDisk": {
221                             "storageAccountType": "[variables('osDiskType')]"
222                         }
223                     },
224                     "imageReference": {
225                         "publisher": "Canonical",
226                         "offer": "UbuntuServer",
227                         "sku": "[parameters('ubuntuOSVersion')]",
228                         "version": "latest"
229                     }
230                 },
```

FIGURE 1-43 ARM template storageProfile for a managed operating system disk

Figure 1-43 shows the definition for a managed disk. The `osDisk` section means the disk will be created from an image and managed by Azure in `Standard_LRS` storage, which is set in the variable `osDiskType` at the top of the ARM template. The `imageReference` section determines which image will be used for the disk.

Configuring the ARM template to use a copy of a VHD from Azure Storage changes the `storageProfile` section to that shown in Figure 1-44.

```
203                 "storageProfile": {
204                     "osDisk": {
205                         "name": "[concat(parameters('vmName'),'-osDisk')]",
206                         "osType": "[parameters('osType')]",
207                         "caching": "ReadWrite",
208                         "image": {
209                             "uri": "[parameters('vhdUrl')]"
210                         },
211                         "vhd": {
212                             "uri": "[variables('osDiskVhdName')]"
213                         },
214                         "createOption": "FromImage"
215                     }
216                 },
```

FIGURE 1-44 ARM template storageProfile for an unmanaged VHD

The `osDisk` section (Figure 1-44) has expanded because this is an unmanaged disk. The template now sets the name of the managed disk as `osType` (Set to linux in the parameters) and the caching mechanism. The key part in this section is the image; this is where the VHD will be copied from. The `vhdUrl` is passed as a parameter, which is the full URL to the VHD in Azure Storage. There is no `imageReference` section; the operating system is already on the VHD, so it does not need to be selected. The `vhd` section defines where the new VHD will be stored. It is set in the variables section and is a storage account in the same region as the VM.

Manage a template library

The Azure portal has a template library where you can store and deploy templates. Open the Azure portal and search for **templates** in the resource name search box at the top of the Azure portal. Choose **Templates** from the drop-down menu that is displayed as you type the resource name and press Enter. The page that loads is the Template Library. Follow these steps to explore the library functionality:

1. Click **Add** at the top left. This process will add a template to the library. Enter a **Name** and **Description** (both of which are mandatory). Click **OK**. You can now build a template up from scratch in the editor on the right of the add page or paste in your own. Paste in a copy of `azuredeploy.json` from *https://github.com/Azure/azure-quickstart-templates/blob/master/101-vm-simple-linux/azuredeploy.json*. Click **OK**, then click **ADD**.
2. Your template is now stored in the portal. Click the name of the stored template in the portal. Note, you may need to click **Refresh** at the top of the **Templates** page to see the new template in the list.
3. As shown in Figure 1-45, the following options are available:
   - **Edit.** Edit the template in the online editor or paste another version over the top. The template description can also be edited, though the name is fixed.

- **Delete.** Delete the template.
- **Share.** RBAC for the selected template.
- **Deploy.** Opens the template in the **Custom Deployment** window. See "Deploy from a template," earlier in this chapter, for more information.
- **View Template.** Opens a read-only view of the template.

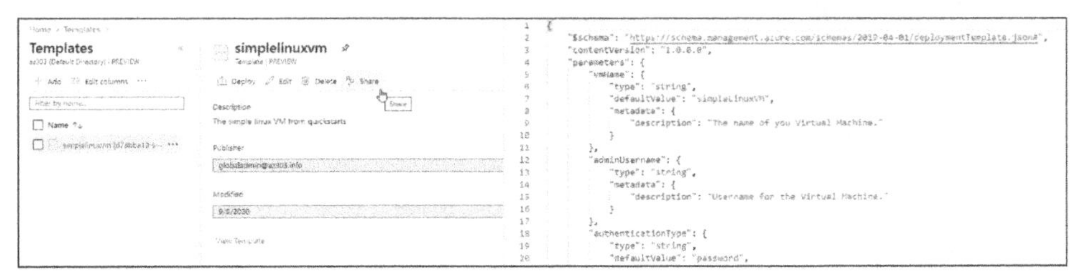

FIGURE 1-45 The Azure portal template library features

> ***NOTE*** **TEMPLATE LIBRARY**
>
> **Managing a template library is part of the exam specification. However, when saving a template to the library, the previous version is overwritten. Therefore, the library is not version controlled. As an architect, you should recommend the best practice, which is version control for storing Infrastructure as Code (IaC).**

Create and execute an automation runbook

Azure automation enables the automation and configuration of on-premises and cloud environments. Azure automation works across Windows and Linux, delivering a consistent way to deploy, configure, and manage resources. Azure automation has three main capabilities:

- **Configuration management.** You can manage configurations using PowerShell desired state configuration (DSC), update configuration, or stop configuration drift by applying configurations pulled from Azure.
- **Update management.** You can orchestrate update installation via maintenance windows.
- **Process automation.** You can automate time consuming, frequent, and sometimes error-prone tasks via runbooks.

An automation runbook is used for process automation. The runbook can be created with PowerShell or Python, or it can be created graphically through drag and drop in the Azure portal. A runbook can execute in Azure or on-premises on a hybrid runbook worker. On execution of the runbook, Azure automation creates a job that runs the logic as defined in the runbook.

Before an automation runbook can be created or executed, an automation account must be created. This can be performed on the command line, or as shown in this example, it can be created in the Azure portal:

1. In the Azure portal, search for **automation** in the resource name search bar at the top of the Azure portal and click **Automation Accounts**.
2. Click **Add** to add an Automation Account. Figure 1-46 shows the **Add Automation Account** screen where you can set the configuration options for the account:
   - **Name.** This is the name for the Automation Account.
   - **Resource Group.** This is the resource group where the Automation Account resides.
   - **Location.** This is the location of the automation account.
   - **Create An Azure Run As Account.** When set to **Yes**, this option creates a service principal, which has the Contributor role at the subscription level. This is used to access and manage resources. For this example, leave this set to **Yes**.

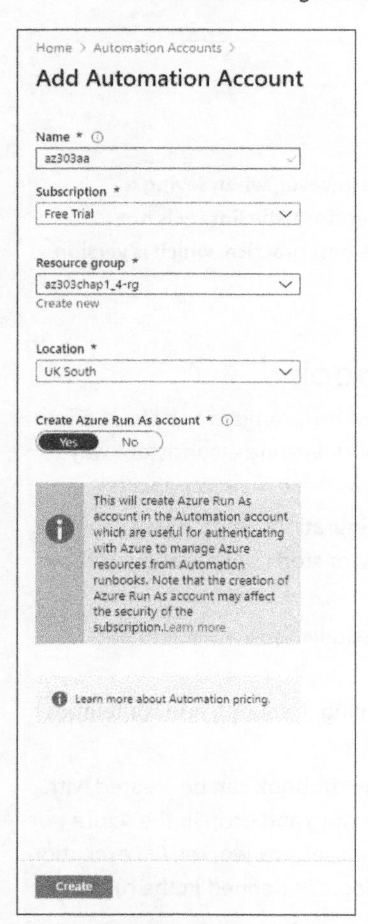

FIGURE 1-46 Add Automation Account

3. Once you have selected the appropriate values, clicking **Create** will create the automation account. You are returned to the Automation Accounts page.

4. Refresh the **Automation Accounts** page, and you will see the newly created account in the list. To add a runbook to the Automation Account, click the automation account name. The screen that loads is the Automation Account menu. Scroll down and click **Runbooks**. The runbooks listed were automatically created when you added the automation account. To add a runbook, click **Create A Runbook** and fill in the following parameters:
   - **Name.** This is the name of the runbook; for this example, enter **cleanDevResources**.
   - **Runbook Type.** From the drop-down menu, you can choose **PowerShell**, **Python 2**, **Graphical**, or **Workflow-Based** types. For this example, choose **PowerShell**.
   - **Description.** You have the option to enter a description for the nature of the runbook.
5. Click **OK**.

The runbook will open using the editor you chose under **Runbook Type**. In this case, we are using PowerShell. You can write your PowerShell script online or you can paste in the script from another editor. The use case for a runbook is process automation. The example PowerShell in the Runbook from Figure 1-47 deletes all resources in resource groups with a specific tag. This process could be used to clean up development resources at the end of a day.

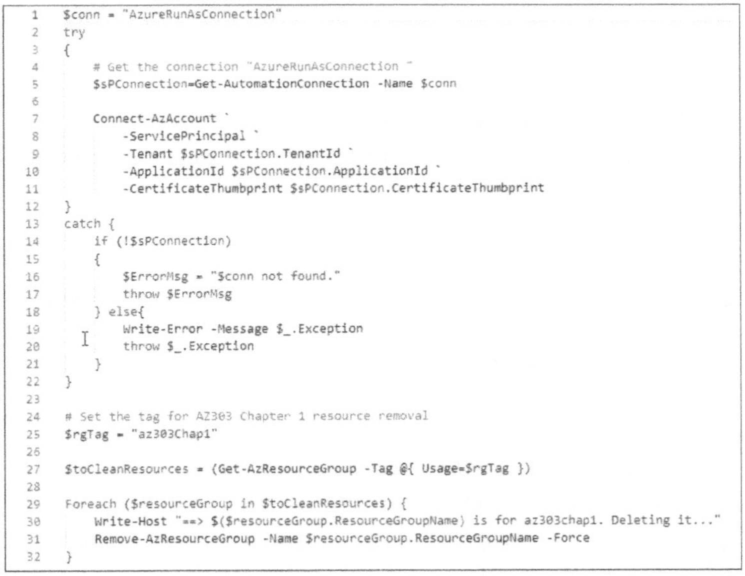

```
1   $conn = "AzureRunAsConnection"
2   try
3   {
4       # Get the connection "AzureRunAsConnection "
5       $sPConnection=Get-AutomationConnection -Name $conn
6
7       Connect-AzAccount `
8           -ServicePrincipal `
9           -Tenant $sPConnection.TenantId `
10          -ApplicationId $sPConnection.ApplicationId `
11          -CertificateThumbprint $sPConnection.CertificateThumbprint
12  }
13  catch {
14      if (!$sPConnection)
15      {
16          $ErrorMsg = "$conn not found."
17          throw $ErrorMsg
18      } else{
19          Write-Error -Message $_.Exception
20          throw $_.Exception
21      }
22  }
23
24  # Set the tag for AZ303 Chapter 1 resource removal
25  $rgTag = "az303Chap1"
26
27  $toCleanResources = (Get-AzResourceGroup -Tag @{ Usage=$rgTag })
28
29  Foreach ($resourceGroup in $toCleanResources) {
30      Write-Host "==> $($resourceGroup.ResourceGroupName) is for az303chap1. Deleting it..."
31      Remove-AzResourceGroup -Name $resourceGroup.ResourceGroupName -Force
32  }
```

FIGURE 1-47 PowerShell script to delete all resource groups with a given tag

The code listing for this example is below:

```
$conn = "AzureRunAsConnection"
try
```

```
{
    # Get the connection "AzureRunAsConnection "
    $sPConnection=Get-AutomationConnection -Name $conn

    Connect-AzAccount `
        -ServicePrincipal `
        -Tenant $sPConnection.TenantId `
        -ApplicationId $sPConnection.ApplicationId `
        -CertificateThumbprint $sPConnection.CertificateThumbprint
}
catch {
    if (!$sPConnection)
    {
        $ErrorMsg = "$conn not found."
        throw $ErrorMsg
    } else{
        Write-Error -Message $_.Exception
        throw $_.Exception
    }
}

# Set the tag for AZ303 Chapter 1 resource removal
$rgTag = "az303chap1"
$toCleanResources = (Get-AzResourceGroup -Tag @{ Usage=$rgTag })

Foreach ($resourceGroup in $toCleanResources) {
    Write-Host "==> $($resourceGroup.ResourceGroupName) is for az303chap1. Deleting
    it..."
    Remove-AzResourceGroup -Name $resourceGroup.ResourceGroupName -Force
}
```

Once the script has been added, click **Save**. Select **Test Pane** at the top of the screen, which runs the edited version of the runbook to test the results. This is useful if you are not ready to publish your runbook. Publishing a runbook overwrites the live copy. Click **Start** to start the test.

In this example, the runbook will error; PowerShell does not recognize `Connect-AzAccount`. This is because the automation account has the Legacy `AzureRM` PowerShell modules loaded by default, but not the `Az` modules. You must load the `Az` modules; to do this, return to the **Automation Account** menu blade and choose **Modules**. The modules that are loaded by default are displayed on the **Modules** blade. In this example, only the `AzureRM` modules are available. Click **Browse Gallery**, search for **Az**, choose **Az.Accounts**, and click **Import**. Next, choose **Browse Gallery**, search for **Az**, and choose **Az.Resources**. (You must do this because the PowerShell in the example runbook uses cmdlets from both modules.)

Once the modules show as imported in the **Module**s blade, go back to the **Runbook** blade and select `cleanDevResources`**,** the runbook name from step 4 above. Click **Edit** > **Test pane** > **Start** to test the runbook once more. The runbook should now run correctly.

The runbook has been verified as functioning, so now select **Publish** to make the runbook available to run. You are returned to the runbook blade for **cleanDevResources**. There are three ways to run a runbook:

- **Manually.** Choosing **Start** at the top of the runbook page will run the runbook.
- **Webhook.** Triggers the runbook by HTTP POST to a URL.
- **Schedule.** Schedules the runbook to execute.

The use case for this example is to delete developer resources at the end of the day. Therefore, click **Schedules** on the **Runbook** menu blade, and then choose **Add A Schedule** to add a schedule for the runbook, which opens the **Schedule Runbook** page, as shown in Figure 1-48.

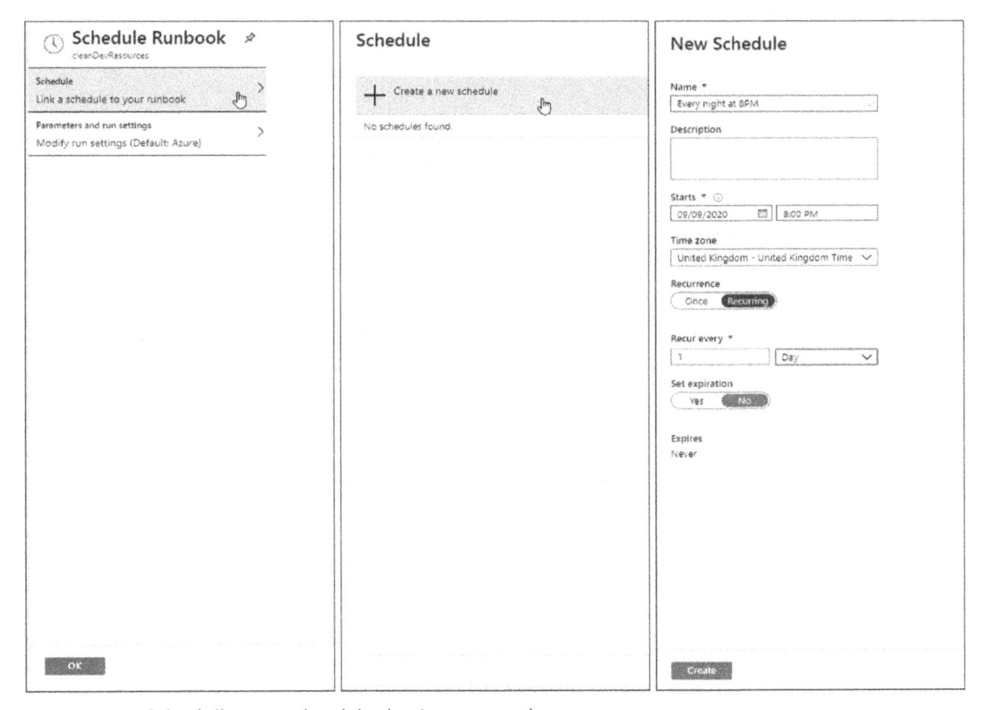

FIGURE 1-48 Scheduling a runbook in the Azure portal

You can set the following options: **Starts**, **Recurrence**, **Recur Every**, and **Set Expiration**. In the example shown in Figure 1-48, the runbook is set to run every night at 8 PM. The runbook will be created when you click **Create**.

NEED MORE REVIEW? **AZURE AUTOMATION**

To learn about Azure Automation in the portal, visit the Microsoft Docs article "An introduction to Azure Automation" at *https://docs.microsoft.com/en-us/azure/automation/automation-intro*. In particular, you should read the Desired State Configuration sections.

Skill 1.5: Implement virtual networking

Because AZ-303 is an expert certification, you are expected to already possess knowledge on how VNets are used to enable secure communication between resources in Azure. Also, you are expected to know how to create and maintain VNets and understand CIDR notation. This skill requires you to understand how to connect VNets to build out your private network within Azure, as well as the requirements that drive each method of connection.

> **This skill covers how to:**
> - Implement VNet-to-VNet connections
> - Implement VNet peering

Implement VNet-to-VNet connections

When encrypted traffic is listed as a security or compliance requirement for communication across a VNets in a virtual network, you will need to implement a VNet-to-VNet VPN gateway connection. When a VNet-to-VNet connection is created, it is like a site-to-site VPN connection; all traffic between the VNets flows over a secure IPsec/IKE tunnel. The tunnel is created between two public IP addresses that are dynamically assigned to the VPN gateways on creation. Figure 1-49 shows a diagram of an example implementation for VNet-to-VNet connections.

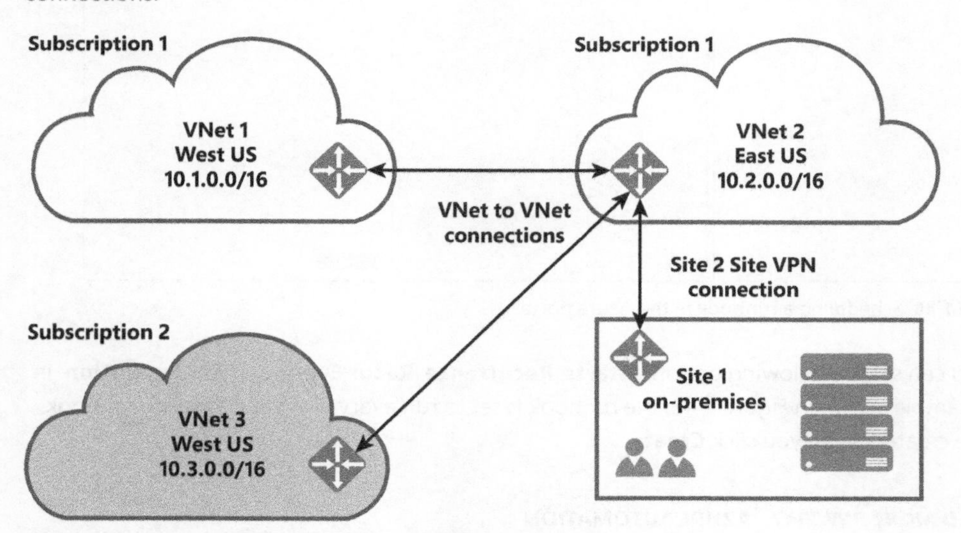

FIGURE 1-49 VNet-to-VNet connections across subscriptions and regions

Only one VPN gateway is permitted per VNet. However, a VPN Gateway may connect to multiple VNets and Site-to-Site VPNs. VNet-to-VNet connections can be across regions and subscriptions. In Figure 1-49, VNet 3 is in West US and is part of Subscription 2. VNet 3 is also connected to VNet 2 in East US, which is part of Subscription 1. In order to connect two VNets, there must be no crossover in the address ranges of the subnets.

Follow these steps to set up the connection for VNet 1 and VNet 2 within the same subscription but across regions.

1. Create two Linux Azure Virtual Machines (VMs)—one in VNet 1 and one in VNet 2 with address spaces, as shown in Figure 1-49. Ensure the VM in VNet 1 is in a subnet of 10.1.0.0/24, and VNet 2 is in a subnet of 10.2.0.0/24. This will ensure there is no overlap in existing subnets, which is a requirement of VPN gateway design. Ensure the VM in VNet 1 has a public IP address. To assist with creating this architecture, use the Azure QuickStart ARM template at *https://github.com/Azure/azure-quickstart-templates/tree/master/101-vm-sshkey*. You will need to edit the address and subnet prefixes accordingly.
2. Sign in to the Azure portal, and in the resource name search bar at the top, type **virtual network gateway**. Select **Virtual Network Gateway** from the drop-down menu that is displayed as you type the resource name. The Virtual Network Gateways page opens. Click **Add** to create a virtual network gateway.
3. As shown in Figure 1-49, create the VPN Gateway for VNet1 using the following values:
   - **Subscription.** Select the same subscription used to create the VNets and VMs in Step 1.
   - **Resource Group.** This is automatically filled when the VNet is selected.
   - **Name.** This is a unique name for the VPN gateway; for this example, enter **VNet1GW**.
   - **Region.** Select the region used for VNet 1; in Figure 1-49, this is West US.
   - **Gateway Type.** For a VPN gateway, this must be VPN.
   - **VPN Type.** Choose **Route-Based**. Route-based VPNs encrypt all traffic that passes through the VPN, whereas choosing **Policy-Based** encrypts some traffic as defined by the policy.
   - **SKU.** Choose **Basic**. SKUs for a VPN gateway differ by workloads, throughputs, features, and SLAs. (The higher the throughput, the higher the cost.)
     - **Basic.** Intended for proof of concept (POC) or development workloads.
     - **VpnGw1-3.** Supports BGP, up to 30 site-to-site VPN connections, and up to 10 gigabits per second (Gbps) throughput for the Gw3 SKU when combined with Generation 2.
     - **VpnGw1-3AZ.** These SKUs have the same feature set as VPNGw1-3, but they are availability-zone aware.
   - **Generation.** Choose **Generation 1**. The combination of Generation and SKU support various throughputs. A Basic SKU is only supported by Generation 1.
   - **Virtual Network.** Choose VNet 1. It should be listed as available if you selected the correct **Region** in Step 3d.

- **Gateway Subnet Address Range.** This will be automatically populated once the virtual network is selected. The subnet range is populated with /24; however, Microsoft recommends a /27 or /26 range, but no smaller than a /28 range. Enter **10.1.1.0/27**.
- **Public IP Address.** Choose this option to create a new Public IP address.
- **Public IP Address Name.** Enter a unique name; in this case, use **VNet1GW-ip**.
- **Enable Active-Active Mode.** Leave this option set to **Disabled**. Active-Active mode is used for highly available VNet-to-VNet connectivity.
- **Configure BGP ASN.** Leave this option set to **Disabled**. Border Gateway Protocol (BGP) is used to exchange routing information between two or more networks.
- **Click Review + Create.** Once the validation has passed, click **Create**. The validation process can take some time.

4. While VNet1GW is being created, follow the same steps to create a VNet named **VNet2GW**. Once more, select to add A VPN Gateway in the portal using the same directions from step 2. Using Figure 1-49 as a guide, enter the setup required for VNet2GW:
   - **Subscription.** Select the same subscription used to create the VNets and VMs in Step 1.
   - **Resource Group.** This is automatically filled when the VNet is selected.
   - **Name.** This is a unique name for the VPN gateway; for this example, enter **VNet2GW**.
   - **Region.** In Figure 1-49, this is East US.
   - **Gateway Type.** Choose **VPN**.
   - **VPN Type.** Choose **Route-Based**.
   - **SKU.** Choose **Basic**.
   - **Generation.** Choose **Generation 1**.
   - **Virtual Network.** Choose **VNet2**.
   - **Gateway Subnet Address Range.** Enter **10.2.1.0/27**.
   - **Public IP Address.** Choose to create a new public IP address.
   - **Public IP Address Name.** Enter a unique name for the Public IP address; for this example, enter **VNet2GW-ip**.
   - **Enable Active-Active Mode.** Leave this set to **Disabled**.
   - **Configure BGP ASN.** Leave this set to **Disabled**.
5. Click **Review + Create**. Once the validation has passed, click **Create**.
6. Once the two VPN gateways are created, they must be connected to each other before a tunnel can be created and traffic can flow. Navigate back to Virtual Network Gateways by entering **Virtual Network Gateway** in the resource name search box at the top of the Azure portal, then select **Virtual Network Gateways** in the drop-down menu that

opens as you start to type. The Virtual Network Gateways page opens, and the two new VPN gateways will be listed. Click the name given to the first VPN gateway you created; in this example, it is VNet1GW. On the VNet1GW menu blade, click **Connections** > **Add** to start creating the connection. Fill in these options:

- **Name.** Enter a unique name for the connection; for this example, enter **VNet1-VNet2**.
- **Connection Type.** Leave this set as **VNet-To-VNet**. The other two options cover on-premises to Azure solutions.
- **Second Virtual Network Gateway.** Select **VNet2GW**.
- **Shared Key (PSK).** This is a random string of letters and numbers used to encrypt the connection.
- **IKE Protocol.** Leave this set as IKEv2 for VNet-to-VNet. IKEv1 can be required for some on-premises site-to-site connections.

7. Click **OK** to add the connection.
8. You must now create a second connection from VNet2 to VNet1 using the process outlined in step 6, this time choosing **VNetGW2**.
9. Navigate to the **Connections** menu option on VNet1GW. Check that the **Status** of both connections is **Connected**. This can take a short while. Once both are connected, the connection is ready to test.
10. SSH to the VM in VNet 1 with the public IP address. You should now be able to ping the virtual machine in VNet 2. If you used the ARM template in Step 1 of this guide, port 22 will be open to VNet 2 to test SSH between the two VMs. This is a key point: Network Security Groups (NSGs) defined at the network interface (NIC) or subnet will still come into play across a VNet-to-VNet connection. Therefore, you might need to configure NSG rules to allow your traffic to flow.

> ***NOTE*** **VPN GATEWAY CONNECTIONS**
>
> **The Azure portal may only be used to create connections between VPN gateways in the same subscription. To connect two VPN gateways in different subscriptions, use PowerShell; see *https://docs.microsoft.com/en-us/azure/vpn-gateway/vpn-gateway-vnet-vnet-rm-ps*. Also, you can use Azure CLI; see *https://docs.microsoft.com/en-us/azure/vpn-gateway/vpn-gateway-howto-vnet-vnet-resource-manager-portal*.**

Implement VNet peering

Running two VPN gateways to connect VNets can be quite costly, as each VPN gateway is billed hourly along with egress traffic. The VPN gateway connections also limit the bandwidth available, as all traffic must flow through the gateway. VNet peering is equivalent to a VNet-to-VNet connection using VPN gateways because peering also enables resource communication between VNets. However, with a VNet peering, the traffic is routed through private IP addresses on the Azure backbone. This means VNet peering offers a lower latency, higher bandwidth option when compared to VNet-to-VNet using VPN gateways. When the peering is within the same region, the latency is the same as that within a single VNet. VNet peering is also a lower-cost option, as no VPN gateway costs are accrued; only ingress and egress fees are accrued. VNet peering can also connect VNets across Azure regions; this is known as Global VNet peering.

Figure 1-50 shows a common architecture pattern (a hub-and-spoke network topology) made available to an Azure architect by implementing VNet peering.

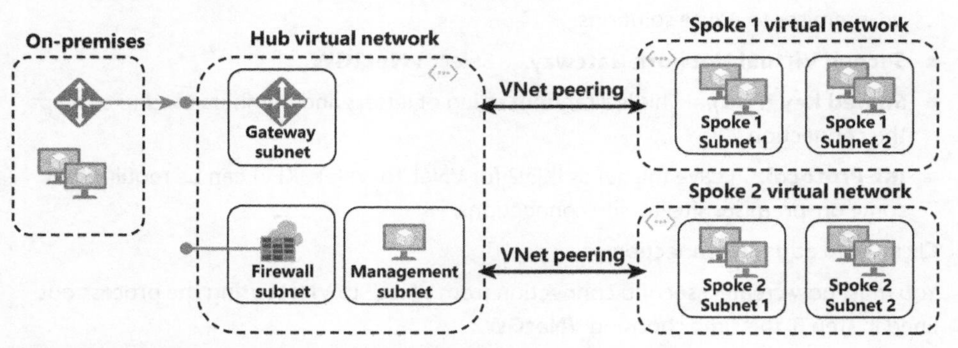

FIGURE 1-50 VNet peering to create a hub-and-spoke network topology

In a hub-and-spoke topology, the hub is a VNet, and it is the central point; the hub contains the connection to your on-premises network. The connection from on-premises to the hub can be via an ExpressRoute or VPN gateway. A hub is often used to group shared services that can be used by more than one workload, such as DNS or a security appliance (NVA).

Each spoke connects to the hub by VNet peering; a spoke can be in a different subscription from the hub. Peering across multiple subscriptions can be used to overcome subscription limits. Peering isolates workloads. As shown in Figure 1-50, if Spoke 1 was for your development department and Spoke 2 was for your production department, they would be isolated and could be managed separately. Configuring spokes in this way enables another architectural practice—the separation of concerns. Figure 1-50 shows how the spokes can communicate with the hub to use shared services but not with each other.

To see part of this topology in action, work through the following steps in the Azure portal to create a VNet peering between two VNets:

1. Create two Linux Azure Virtual Machines (VMs), one in each of the following VNet and subnet configurations:
   - VNet1: 10.3.0.0/24 – subnet 10.3.0.0/16
   - VNet2: 10.4.0.0/24 – subnet 10.4.0.0/16

   This setup ensures there is no overlap in existing VNet address spaces, which is a requirement of VNet peering. Make sure the VM in VNet1 has a public IP address. To assist with creating this architecture, use the Azure QuickStart ARM template at *https://github.com/Azure/azure-quickstart-templates/tree/master/101-vm-sshkey*. You will need to edit the address and subnet prefixes accordingly.

2. In the Azure portal, search for **vnet** in the search bar at the top and select **Virtual Networks** in the drop-down menu that is displayed when you start typing VNet. In the list of virtual networks displayed on the **Virtual Networks** page, select **VNet1**.
3. You can now configure VNet1; on the menu blade on the left of the **Overview** blade that is opened, scroll down, select **Peerings**, and click **Add**. You must now enter the following peering configuration settings:
   - **Name Of The Peering From VNet1 To Remote Virtual Network.** Enter a name for your peering; in this example, enter **Vnet1peerVNet2**.
   - **Virtual Network Deployment Model.** Choose **Resource Manager**. In step 1, you created a new VNet using ARM or the portal; in this step, you are creating the Resource Manager model.
   - **I Know My Resource ID.** Leave this unselected. If you know the resource ID of the VNet you are peering to, you can select this box and enter the ID instead of selecting the **Subscription** and **Virtual Network**.
   - **Subscription.** Select the subscription in which you created VNet2.
   - **Virtual Network.** Select **VNet2**.
   - **Name Of The Peering From VNet1 To VNet2.** Enter **Vnet2peerVNet1**.
   - **Configure Virtual Network Access Settings.** Leave both switches set to **Enabled**. This allows traffic to flow between the two VNets.
   - **Configure Forwarded Traffic Settings.** Leave both switches set to **Disabled**. This blocks traffic that does not originate from within the VNet being peered to from entering the VNet from which the peering originates. This is how traffic is isolated in the spokes.
   - **Allow Gateway Transit.** Select this option if the VNet being peered from contains a VPN gateway and you want to use it.
4. Click **OK** to create the peering.
5. When you click **OK**, you are returned to the **Peerings** blade in the portal. Once the **Peering Status** of the peering you just created shows **Connected**, you are ready to test the connection.
6. SSH to the VM in VNet 1 with the public IP address. You should now be able to ping the virtual machine in VNet 2. If you used the ARM template in step 1 of this guide, port 22 will be open to VNet 2 to test SSH between the two VMs. This is a key point: Network Security Groups (NSGs) defined at the network interface (NIC) or subnet will still come into play across a VNet-to-VNet connection. Therefore, you might need to configure the NSG rules to allow your traffic to flow.

Skill 1.6: Implement Azure Active Directory

Azure Active Directory (Azure AD) is Microsoft's cloud-based access management and identity platform. At a basic level, Azure AD signs users into Microsoft 365, Azure portal, and many other Microsoft SaaS applications. Azure AD can also sign in users to apps you have created on-premises and in the cloud.

This skill covers how to:

- Add custom domains
- Manage multiple directories
- Implement self-service password reset
- Configure user accounts for MFA
- Configure fraud alerts
- Configure bypass options
- Configure trusted IPs
- Configure verification methods
- Implement and manage guest accounts
- Configure Azure AD Identity Protection
- Implement Conditional Access including MFA

The first time a user from your organization signs up for a Microsoft SaaS service, an instance of Azure AD is created for your organization. An instance of Azure AD is called an Azure tenant. An Azure tenant has a one-to-many relationship with Azure subscriptions.

Azure AD comes in three tiers, and the features discussed in this skill might require the use of the two premium tiers, as shown in Table 1-3.

TABLE 1-3 Azure ad tier feature summary

	Free	Premium P1	Premium P2
Custom domains	Yes	Yes	Yes
Guest users	Yes	Yes	Yes
Multiple directories	Yes	Yes	Yes
Multifactor Authentication (MFA)	Yes (For admins)	Yes	Yes
Conditional Access (with MFA)		Yes	Yes
Self Service Password Reset—cloud and hybrid users		Yes	Yes

	Free	Premium P1	Premium P2
Guest access reviews			Yes
Azure Identity Protection			Yes
Privileged Identity Management			Yes

EXAM TIP HEADING HERE

Knowing which of the features described throughout this skill are free, P1, and P2 features will be beneficial.

As an architect, you need to have an excellent grasp of the features of Azure AD and how they can be configured. In this skill, you will explore these configurations.

Add custom domains

When an organization's Azure tenant is created, it is assigned a public DNS name in the format `tenantname.onmicrosoft.com`. The `tenantname` is generally the organization's domain name; for example, contoso.com would become `contoso.onmicrosoft.com`. Even though your organization's domain name is part of the public DNS name, it is not one that your employees or your customers will recognize as part of your brand. To associate your domain with your Azure tenant, you will need to add a custom domain name. You can add a custom domain name in the Azure portal. Follow these steps to try it out:

1. Log in to the Azure portal and search for **azure active directory** in the resources search bar at the top. Select **Azure Active Directory** in the search results that are displayed in the drop-down menu as you type the resource name. Now click **Custom Domain Names** in the menu on the left of the **Azure Active Directory** page. This lists the domain names associated with your Azure tenant. You will see the `tenantname.onmicrosoft.com` listed.
2. Select **Add Custom Domain** at the top of the **Custom Domain Names** page. You will be asked to enter a domain name. This domain name must be one you already own through a domain registrar; an example is shown in Figure 1-51. Click **Add domain**.
3. The settings required to verify your domain are now shown. You must add either the TXT or MX record to the DNS zone file. If you do not have access to your registrar, you can choose **Share These Settings Via Email**. You must use the exact values so that Microsoft can verify that you own the domain. An example is shown in Figure 1-51. Once the DNS record is added at the registrar, click **Verify.**
4. The **Verification Succeeded** page should appear as shown in Figure 1-51. If you receive an error you may need to wait for the DNS record changes to propagate before trying once more. If you want this newly added domain to be the default when new users are added, click **Make Primary** at the top of the verification successful page. Your domain is now listed in the **Custom Domain Names** page in the Azure portal.

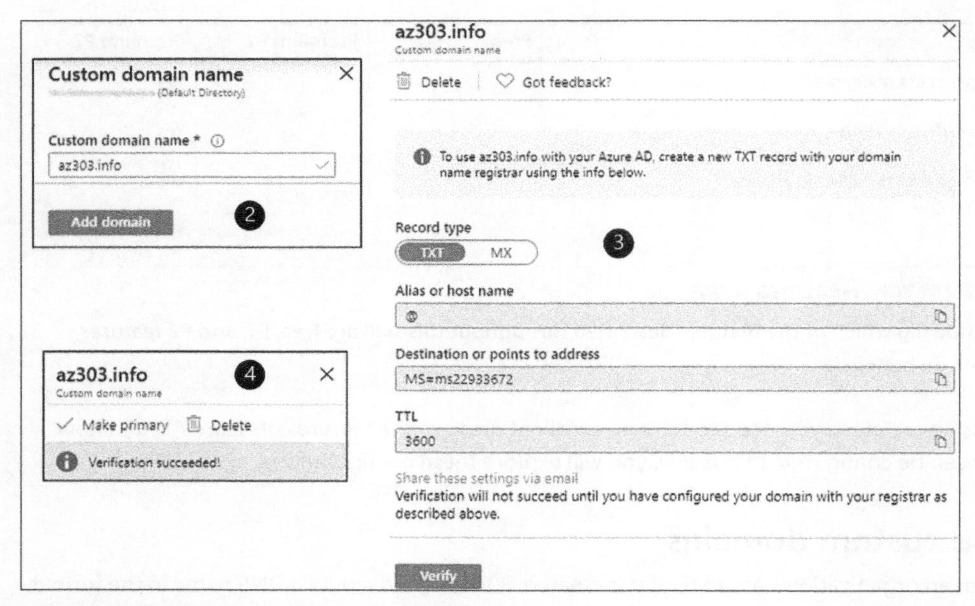

FIGURE 1-51 The steps to create a custom domain

Manage multiple directories

Azure AD is a multitenant environment. Each tenant can have multiple subscriptions and multiple domains, but tenants may have only one directory. A directory is the Azure AD service, which can have one or more domains. A directory may be assigned multiple subscriptions, but it can never be associated with more than one tenant. This one-to-one relationship between a tenant and a directory can lead to confusion with the words "tenant" and "directory" being used interchangeably without explanation in documentation and in the Azure portal.

You can have multiple directories and an identity can have permissions to access multiple directories. Each directory is independent of another, including administrative access to specific directories. If you are an administrator in one directory, you will not have administrator privileges in another directory unless is it granted. You might use multiple directories to separate your live directory from a test directory that is used to explore new features or configurations.

To create a new directory, you will need to create a new tenant and search for **azure active directory** in the resource name search bar at the top of the Azure portal. Select **Azure Active Directory** in the drop-down menu that is displayed as you type the resource name. After entering **Azure Active Directory**, **Overview** is displayed by default on the menu blade. At the top of Overview, click **Create A Tenant**. You are taken to the **Create A Tenant** page. Leave the **Directory Type** option at its default setting of **Azure Active Directory** and click the **Configuration** tab. The Configuration of the directory is displayed, as shown in Figure 1-52.

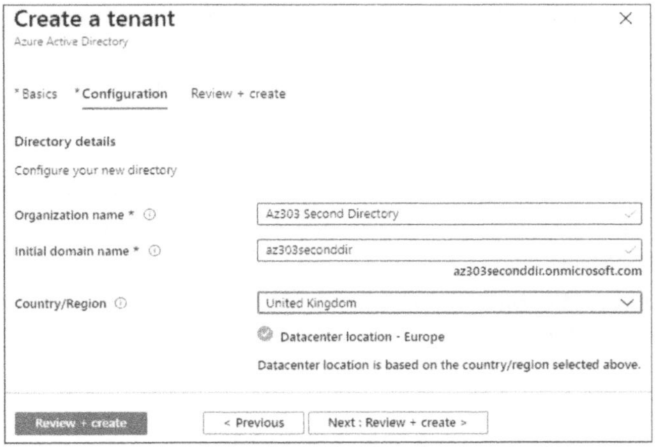

FIGURE 1-52 Configuring a new tenant

Enter your **Organization Name** and an **Initial Domain Name**. Note the domain name is tacked onto `.onmicrosoft.com`, as described in "Add custom domains" earlier in this chapter. The **Datacenter Location** setting has added importance if user information in this directory is subject to local legislation, so the **Country/Region** selection should reflect this. Click **Review + Create** to create the new tenant.

Your logged-in identity has created the new tenant and therefore a new directory. Azure has also automatically assigned your identity Global Administrator rights for the new directory as the identity that created the tenant. To access the new directory, you will need to switch to it. Navigate to Azure Active Directory **Overview** blade and click **Switch Tenant** at the top. This opens the **Switch Tenant** blade, which gives you the option to switch to a new tenant by clicking on it, or to set tenants as favorites.

You can also switch directories by clicking on your identity's avatar in the top right of the portal and choosing **Switch Directory**. This opens the **Directory + Subscription** blade, which has the following options:

- Select a directory to switch to
- Set a default Azure AD directory
- Set favorite directories, making them easier to find if you manage multiple Azure AD tenants

Implement self-service password reset

Any architect who has worked his or her way through a support desk will know that calls to reset user passwords on-premises can be quite time consuming. It is estimated that password reset accounts for 20 percent of an organization's IT spend. When architecting solutions for the number of users who could be given access to a cloud application, you will want users to reset their own passwords. Self-service password reset (SSPR) enables users to reset their own passwords without having to contact a support function. A user may change his or her password with any tier of Azure AD. However, using SSPR requires a premium tier or for a trial to be activated. Once a premium tier has been activated, follow these steps to enable SSPR within the Azure portal:

1. Search for **Azure Active Directory** in the resource name search bar at the top of the Azure portal. Note on the **Overview** page, the **Tenant** is now **Azure AD Premium P1 or P2**. Click **Password Reset** on the menu blade.
2. The **Self-Service Password Reset Enabled** option is to the default **None** setting. No users in the directory can utilize SSPR. If you switch this to **Selected**, administrators can specify which user group(s) can use SSPR. If you choose **All**, SSPR will be enabled for all users in the directory.
3. Click **Save**.

Once SSPR is now enabled, Azure will assign defaults to the SSPR configuration. As an architect you need to understand how the defaults affect your users' experiences. In the **Password Reset** menu blade, choose **Authentication Methods**.

Note that **Email** and **Mobile Phone** are selected because they are the authentication methods that will be available to your users. Also, you can choose **Mobile App** or **Office Phone**, and you can set up **Security Questions**. Now click **Registration**. The slider for **Require Users To Register Before Signing In** was set to **Yes** when SSPR was enabled. This setting forces users to set up SSPR for themselves on their first log-ins. The **Number Of Days Before Users Are Asked To Re-confirm Their Authentication Information** setting has defaulted to 180 days. This is the number of days before the user is asked to reconfirm his or her SSPR information. Click **Notifications**. The **Notify Users On Password Resets** has defaults to **Yes**. This setting will send an email to users when they reset their own passwords. If you choose to **Notify all admins when other admins reset their password?** an email will be sent to all admins when an admin resets his or her own password.

The final option on the **Password Reset** menu is **On-Premises Integration**. This is used in conjunction with hybrid identities. You will explore this in "Skill 1.7: Implement and manage hybrid identities."

> ***NOTE*** **SSPR AND AZURE AD PREMIUM**
>
> **Azure AD Premium is required for user SSPR. By default, administrators are enabled for SSPR on all Azure AD tiers.**

Your users may set up self-service password reset through the My Apps portal. To see the SSPR process, add a new user to the directory in which you just enabled SSPR. Ensure the user has a usage location set, which is a requirement for a Azure AD Premium license assignment.

Assign a Premium AD license to the user and use the new user to log in to the My Apps portal (https://myapps.microsoft.com). Now, follow these steps (which also are the steps you would communicate to your users):

1. In the top-right corner of the **My Apps** portal, click the avatar and then choose **Profile** > **Set Up Self-Service Password Reset**.
2. You have the option to set up a phone number or email address for password reset. Choose **Set It Up Now** next to **Authentication Phone Is Not Configured** to set up phone-based password reset.
3. Choose the country where your phone is registered and enter your telephone number.
4. Click **Text Me** or **Call Me** to choose a verification method.
5. Microsoft will text or call you with a verification code, depending on the method chosen in Step 4. Enter this verification code in the box next to **Verify**, and then click **Verify**.
6. Optionally, you can choose to verify an email address. Your users only need to use one of the verification methods that they choose.
7. Click **Finish**.

> ***NOTE*** **MY APPS PORTAL**
>
> **Microsoft have released new My Apps portal which can be accessed through (*https://myapplications.microsoft.com*). SSPR is accessed using View Account which can be accessed through the user's avatar in the myapplications portal. The password reset is as described above as the new portal redirects the user to the same pages.**

When your users log in to an application secured by Azure AD, they will now see a **Forgotten My Password** under the **Password** field. If the user has completed the set-up steps above and has been assigned a premium license, the user will be able to reset his or her own password. The steps for the resetting a password are shown in Figure 1-53.

> ***NEED MORE REVIEW?*** **SELF-SERVICE PASSWORD RESET (SSPR)**
>
> **To learn about enabling and deploying self-service password reset, visit the Microsoft Docs article "How it works: Azure AD self-service password reset" at *https://docs.microsoft.com/en-us/azure/active-directory/authentication/concept-sspr-howitworks*. For further reading, you should also review the Password Reset sections.**

> ***NOTE*** **SSPR AND BROWSER CACHING**
>
> **If the changes to the Azure AD tier and license assignments are not being picked up by your users, it is likely that your browser is caching old tokens. Clear your history and try again.**

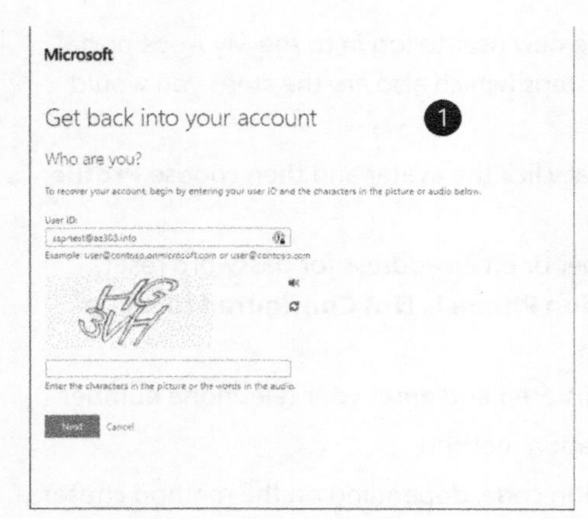

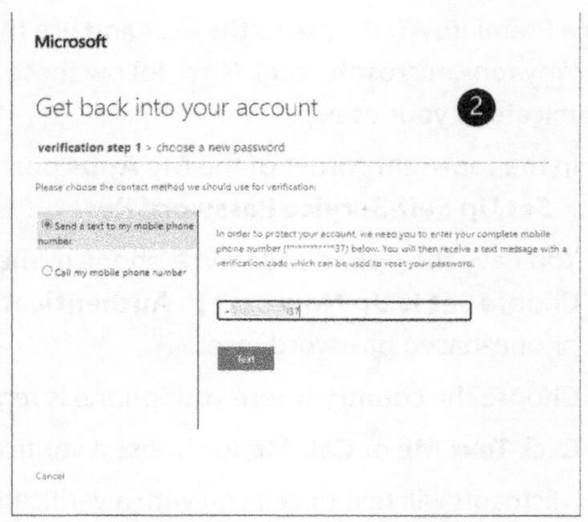

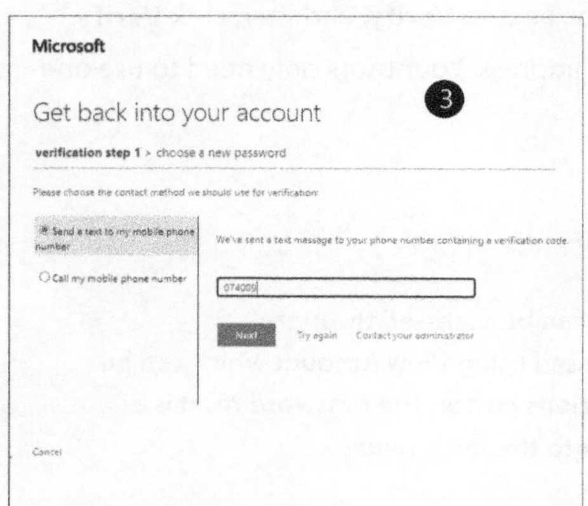

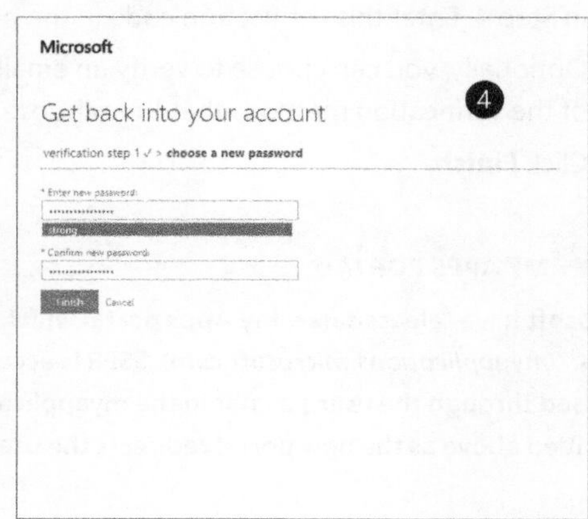

FIGURE 1-53 User self-service password reset steps

1. The user's log in is copied to the **User ID** field. The user must enter the CAPTCHA text. Click **Next**.
2. Password reset for a telephone number was enabled in the previous section. The user can choose to be called or to be sent a verification code via text. If email verification had also been enabled, you would see an option for that. Leave this set as **Send A Text** and enter the telephone number that was previously verified. Click **Text**.
3. Microsoft sends a verification code; enter it in the box and click **Next**.
4. The user is now able to choose a new password. The user will click **Finish** once the password reset is complete.

EXAM TIP SSPR

Be sure to have a good grasp of SSPR Authentication methods, registration, and notifications.

Configure user accounts for MFA

Your users live in a multi-platform, multi-device world. They can connect to applications on and off your organization's network with phones, tablets, and PCs—often from multiple platforms. This flexibility means that using passwords is no longer enough to secure your users' accounts. Azure multifactor authentication (MFA) provides an extra layer of security in the form of a secondary authentication method known as two-step verification. This secondary method requires the user to provide "something they have," which is often in the form of a token provided by SMS or an authenticator app.

As an architect, you need to know how to enable MFA in Azure AD and how to configure MFA settings for your use case. There are four main ways to enable MFA for a user in Azure AD:

- **Enable by changing state.** Users must perform MFA every time they log in.
- **Enable by security defaults.** Security settings preconfigured by Microsoft, including MFA.
- **Enable by conditional access policy.** This a more flexible, and two-step is required for certain conditions. This method requires premium Azure AD licenses.
- **Enable by Azure AD Identity Protection.** Two-step is required based on sign in risk. This method requires premium P2 Azure AD licenses.

In this section, you will look at the enable by changing state and enable by security defaults methods. The others are covered later in this skill. Note that the enable by changing state method is also known as "per-user MFA." To enable per-user MFA, navigate to the top of the Azure portal and search for **Azure Active Directory** in the resource name search bar at the top of the Azure portal. Select **Azure Active Directory** from the drop-down menu that is displayed as you type the name of the resource, and then follow these steps to configure per-user MFA by changing the state of a user:

1. Azure AD opens with **Overview** selected in the **Azure Active Directory** menu. Click **Users**.
2. Toward the top of the **All Users** blade is the **User Management** menu. Click the ellipses to the right of this menu and choose **Multi-Factor Authentication**.
3. Select the users for whom you want to enable MFA. If there are many users for whom you need enable or disable MFA at the same time, you can use the **Bulk Update** function to upload a CSV file of users to enable/disable, as shown in Figure 1-54.

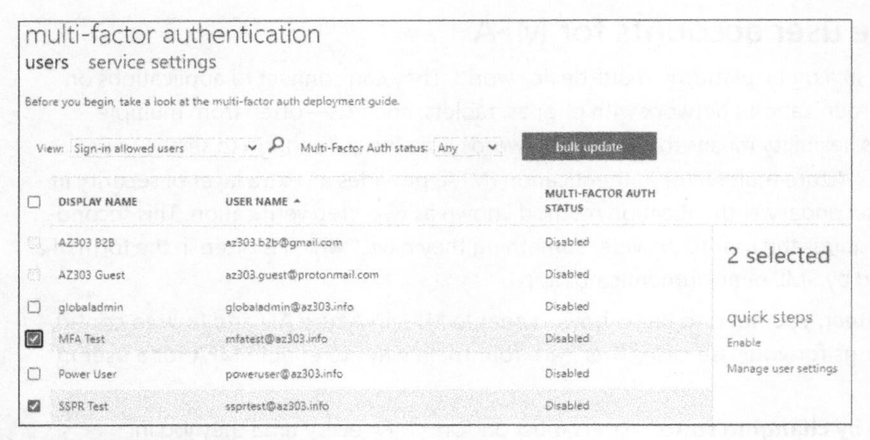

FIGURE 1-54 Enabling MFA for end users

4. In the **Quick Steps** section, click **Enable** and then click **Enable Multi-Factor Auth** in the popup.
5. You are taken back to the user list; the **Multi-Factor Auth Status** for the users you enabled is now set to **Enabled**. There are three user states for MFA:
   - **Disabled.** MFA has not been enabled.
   - **Enabled.** MFA is enabled, but the user has not registered.
   - **Enforced.** MFA is enabled, and the user has registered.

MFA is now configured, and at the enabled user's next log in, he or she will be required to register for MFA.

Using the method described above for changing a user's state to administer MFA has some drawbacks. If you study Figure 1-54, you can that this screen has not been integrated with the Azure portal. Therefore, the administrative experience is different, which can be confusing. The missing integration to the Azure portal also means that you cannot use role-based access control to grant access to administer per-user MFA. Only global administrators can access per-user MFA, and this is unlikely to adhere to the principle of least privilege in most organizations. Enabling per-user MFA also enables app passwords, which are a legacy form of authentication where the app password is securely stored on the device using the app. App passwords are used for legacy apps that cannot support MFA, where the app returns the app password to the Microsoft cloud service and MFA is bypassed. Microsoft does not recommend the use of app passwords to access cloud services because they can be difficult to track and ultimately revoke.

- If your organization does not have premium-tier Azure AD licenses and per-user MFA does not fit your organization's requirements, you also have the option to use the enable by security defaults method. Microsoft has created a set of preconfigured security settings to protect organizations against attacks such as phishing, password spray, and replay. These settings are grouped with the security defaults:

- All privileged access Azure AD administrators must perform MFA on every log in. This includes the following administrative roles: Global, SharePoint, Exchange, Conditional Access, Security, Helpdesk, Billing, User, and Authentication.
- All users must register for MFA. MFA for non-administrative users is performed when necessary, such as accessing a service through a new device, or when the user's refresh token expires.
- MFA is required for any user accessing the Azure Resource Manager API through the Azure portal, PowerShell, or CLI.
- Legacy authentication protocols such as app passwords are blocked.

Once enabled, all the security defaults listed above are applied automatically to the tenant, and you cannot choose a subset of them. The defaults are fully managed by Microsoft, which means they might also be subject to change.

To enable security defaults, navigate to the top of the Azure portal and search for **azure active directory** in the resource name search bar at the top of the page. Select **Azure Active Directory** from the drop-down menu that is displayed as you type the name of the resource and follow these steps to enable security defaults:

1. Azure AD opens with **Overview** selected in the **Azure Active Directory** menu. From the same menu, click **Properties**.
2. At the bottom of the **Properties** page, click **Manage Security Defaults**. The **Enable Security Defaults** blade appears.
3. On the **Enable Security Defaults** blade, enable **Enable Security Defaults** by moving the slider control to **Yes** and click **Save**.

NOTE **SECURITY DEFAULTS**

If your tenant was created after October 2019, security defaults might already be enabled for your tenant. Security defaults cannot be enabled if your tenant has at least one conditional access policy enabled. See "Implement Conditional Access including MFA," later in this chapter for information on conditional access policies.

NEED MORE REVIEW? **AZURE MULTI-FACTOR AUTHENTICATION**

To learn about enabling and deploying Azure Multi-Factor Authentication, visit the Microsoft Docs article "What are security defaults" at *https://docs.microsoft.com/en-us/azure/active-directory/fundamentals/concept-fundamentals-security-defaults* and "Configure Azure Multi-Factor Authentication settings" at *https://docs.microsoft.com/en-us/azure/active-directory/authentication/howto-mfa-mfasettings*. Note the second article is also recommended for the next four sections.

Configure fraud alerts

If a user account that is protected by MFA is accessed fraudulently, users will be contacted via their verification methods, even though they did not initiate the access. This allows users to know that the fraudulent log-in attempt is occurring. By configuring fraud alerts, you enable the users to report fraudulent attempts automatically and to lock their accounts to prevent further access attempts. To configure fraud alerts, open the Azure portal and follow these steps:

1. Search for **azure active directory** in the resource name search box at the top of the portal and press enter to select **Azure Active Directory** from the drop-down menu that is displayed when you type the resource name.
2. Click **Security** in the menu blade and then click **MFA** in the **Security** blade. Click **Fraud Alert** in the **MFA** blade.
3. The **Fraud Alert** blade opens, as shown in Figure 1-55. To enable fraud alerts, set **Allow Users To Submit Fraud Alerts** to **On**.

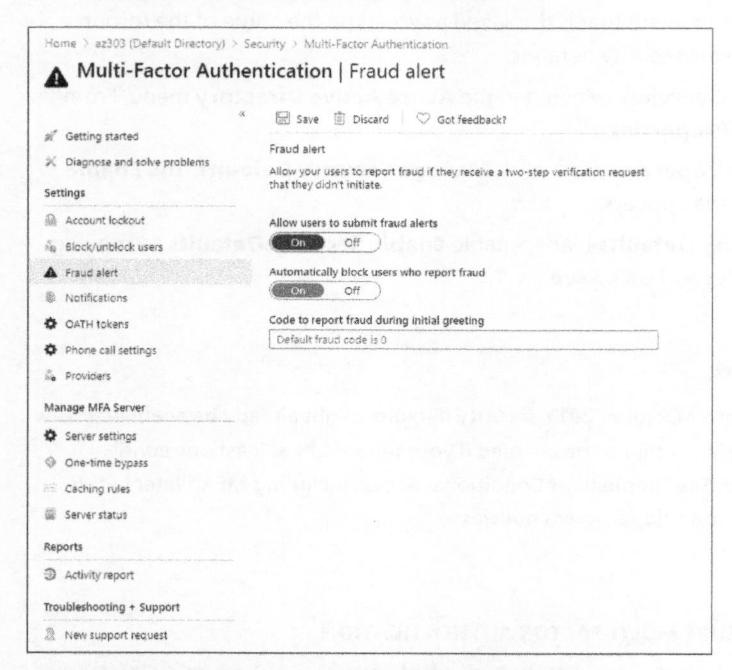

FIGURE 1-55 Enabling fraud alerts for MFA in the Azure portal

4. **Automatically Block Users Who Report Fraud** is set to **On** by default. This will block the user's account for 90 days or until an admin can unblock it.
5. **Code To Report Fraud During Initial Greeting** is set to 0 by default. This enables users who use call verification to report fraud.
6. Click **Save** at the top of the **Fraud Alert** page. Fraud alerts are now configured.

The fraud alert can be triggered by the user when using the Authenticator App (see "Configure verification methods," later in this chapter) or via call verification. If a user's account is blocked by triggering a fraud alert, an administrator needs to unblock the user before he or she can log in again. To unblock a user, follow these steps:

1. Search for **azure active directory** in the resource name search bar at the top of the portal and press Enter to select **Azure Active Directory**.
2. Click **Security** in the **Menu** blade, and then click **MFA** in the **Security** blade. In the **MFA** blade, click **Block/Unblock Users**. A list of blocked users is shown in Figure 1-56.

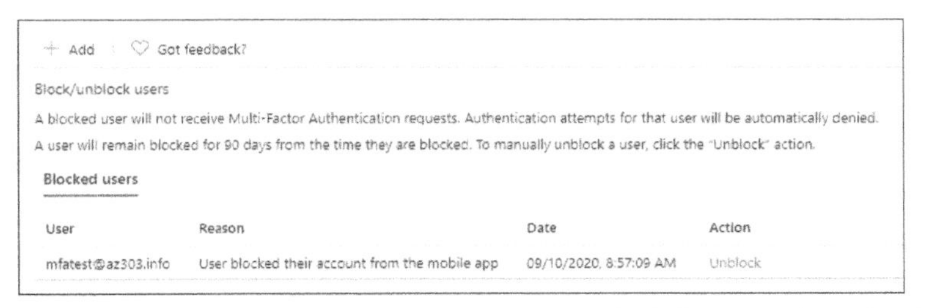

FIGURE 1-56 Unblocking a user whose log in was blocked after triggering a fraud alert

3. Click **Unblock,** enter a **Reason For Unblocking**, and click **OK**. The user is now unblocked.

If a user triggers a fraud alert, an email notification is sent to all email addresses that have been added to the **Notifications** configuration section of the **Multi-Factor Authentication** page. This section is located under the **Security** menu item for **Azure Active Directory**.

Configure bypass options

Two-step verification relies heavily on the user being able to receive the code notification via SMS messages or phone calls. These notifications might not be possible, for example, if one of your organization's facilities is underground or the user has lost his or her phone. In this instance, you need to recommend a secure way to bypass MFA. In Azure MFA, this is achieved with a one-time bypass that allows an administrator to set up a short window during which a user can log in with just his or her password. To see this feature in action, follow these steps in the Azure portal:

1. Search for **Azure Active Directory** in the resource name search box at the top of the portal and press Enter to select Azure Active Directory.
2. Click **Security** in the menu blade and then click **MFA** in the **Security** blade. Click **One-Time Bypass** in the **MFA** blade.
3. Note that **Default One-Time Bypass Seconds** is set to **300**, which means each user gets 5 minutes to complete his or her log in.
4. Click **Add**.

5. In the **User** field, add the user's email address that is being used for the log in. You can override the bypass time in the **Seconds** box (possibly to something shorter). Under **Reason**, provide a reason for the bypass, such as "Working underground."
6. Click **OK**. The user who was given a one-time bypass is added to the **Bypassed Users** list, as shown in Figure 1-57.

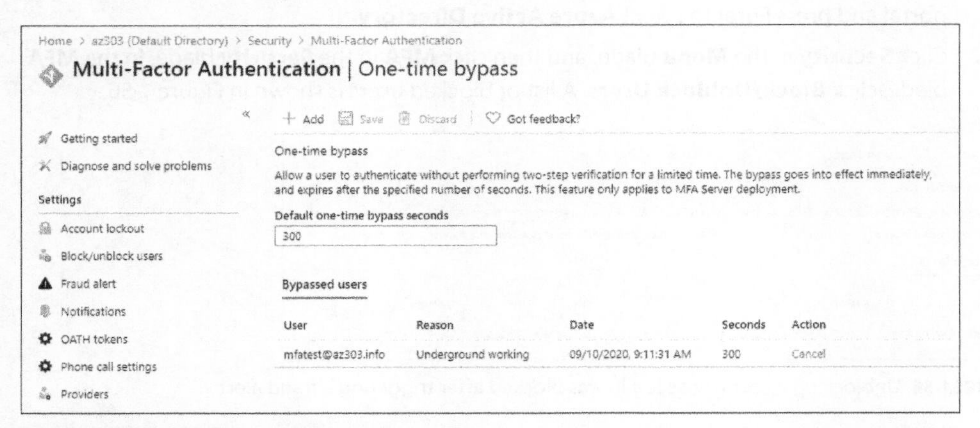

FIGURE 1-57 The One-Time Bypass blade

Note that an administrator can also cancel the request before the time expires, as shown in Figure 1-57.

Configure trusted IPs

Throughout the last three sections, you have been exploring the configuration of Azure MFA by using the enable by changing state method. This method requires a user to two-step verify for every log-in they perform. If a user is logging in from a workstation within your organization's intranet, it is highly likely that this is a valid access attempt. If you configure a trusted IP for this location, two-step verification will be bypassed for every log-in initiated from that IP. To enable trusted IPs using Azure MFA service settings, work through the following steps in the Azure portal:

1. Search for **azure active directory** in the resource name search box at the top of the portal and press Enter to select **Azure Active Directory**.
2. Click **Users** in the menu blade, and then click the ellipses in the top menu. Click **Multi-Factor Authentication** in the drop-down menu.
3. The **Multi-Factor Authentication** page opens on the **Users** tab. Click the **Service Settings** tab to open the **Service Settings** page, as shown in Figure 1-58.

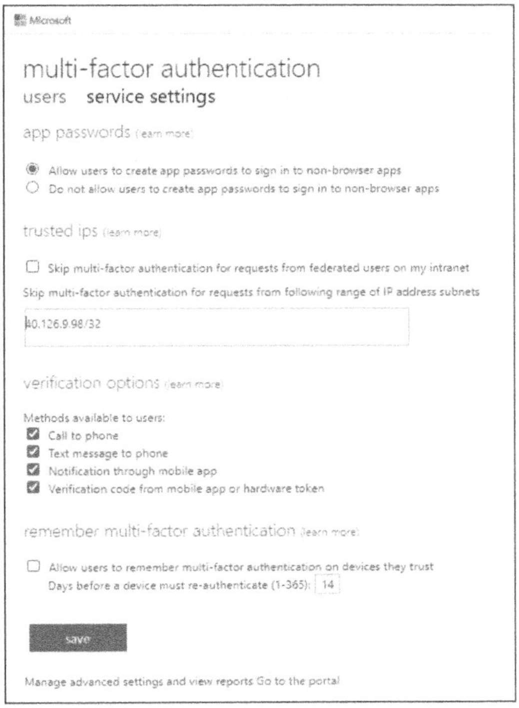

FIGURE 1-58 Configuring Trusted IPs for MFA on the Service Settings page

4. In the **Trusted IPs** box add the IP address or address range using CIDR notation. The example in Figure 1-58 sets just a single IP address. The **Skip Multi-Factor Authentication For Requests From Federated Users Originating From My Intranet** is for organizations utilizing single sign-on (SSO) through Active Directory Federation Services (ADFS).
5. Click **Save**, and then click **Close** on the **Updates Successful** screen. Trusted IP is now configured.

NOTE **TRUSTED IPS**

This method of trusted IPs only supports IPv4.

EXAM TIP MFA AND TRUSTED IPS

This method of configuring trusted IPs is not the method recommended by Microsoft. The recommended configuration is covered in the section, "Implement Conditional Access including MFA," later in this chapter. Therefore, if a question involves trusted IPs, it is likely regarding Conditional Access.

Configure verification methods

So far in this skill, you have seen SMS and phone calls as the main methods for the second part of two-step verification. These are the defaults given to users when they register for MFA. There are however, four methods of verification available to a user:

- **Call to phone.** An automated phone call. The user presses # on the keypad to verify the log in.
- **Text message to phone.** Sends a verification code in a text message. The user enters the code into the log-in screen when prompted to verify the log-in.
- **Notification through mobile app.** Sends a push notification to the Microsoft Authenticator app on the user's mobile. The user chooses **Verify** in the notification.
- **Verification code from mobile app or hardware token.** An OATH code is generated on the Microsoft Authenticator app every 30 seconds. The user enters this code into the log-in screen when prompted to verify the log in.

By default, all four verification methods are available to a user when MFA is enabled. However, a user must choose to specifically enable use of the Microsoft Authenticator app through the My Apps portal. To see how this process works, add a user to Azure AD and use this user's credentials to log in to the My Apps portal (*https://myapplication.microsoft.com*). Now follow these instructions within My Apps:

1. Click on the avatar at the top right and then select **View account**.
2. The **Profile** page is displayed for the logged in user. Click **Additional Security Verification** in the top-right **Security Info** widget.
3. The user will be asked to sign in again as an extra security measure.
4. The user can set up their preferred method of verification at the top of the page. In the **How Would You Like To Respond** section, the user can select from the verification methods that have been enabled for MFA.
5. Once the user has completed their choices, click **Save**, and they will be asked to log in and verify once more to save the changes.

To configure the verification methods available to a user, follow these steps in the Azure portal:

1. Search for **azure active directory** in the resource name search bar at the top of the portal and press Enter to select **Azure Active Directory**.
2. Click **Users** in the menu blade and then click the ellipses in the top menu. Click **Multi-Factor Authentication** in the drop-down menu.
3. The **Multi-Factor Authentication** page is opened to the **Users** tab. Click **Service Settings** to open the **Service Settings** page.

4. The **Verification Options** box on the **Service Settings** tab shows the available verification methods. Select or deselect the options as required.
5. Click Save and then click **Close** on the **Updates Successful** screen. The updated verification methods are now configured.

Implement and manage guest accounts

Azure AD brings guest access to your tenant with Azure AD business-to-business (B2B) collaboration. Through Azure AD B2B, access to services and applications can be securely shared. The external users do not have to be part of an Azure AD; they can use their own identity solutions, which means there is no overhead for your organization's IT teams. Adding guest users to your Azure AD is done by invitation through Azure portal. To explore how this works, follow these steps:

1. Search for **azure active directory** in the resource name search bar at the top of the portal and press Enter to select **Azure Active Directory**.
2. In the **Azure AD** menu blade, click **Users** > **New Guest User**.
3. You may now enter the guest user's information:
   - **Name.** The first and last name of the guest user.
   - **Email Address (Required).** The email address of the guest user. This is where the invite is sent to.
   - **Personal Message.** Include a personal welcome message to the guest user.
   - **Groups.** You can add the guest user to any existing Azure AD groups.
   - **Directory Role.** Direct assignment of administrative permissions if required.
4. Once you are happy that the guest credentials are correct, click **Invite**.
5. You are taken back to the list of all users in your tenant. Look at the row for the guest user you just added. The **User Type** is set to **Guest** and the **Source** is set to **Invited User**, as you can see in Figure 1-59. In this example, the invited guest user is *az303.guest@protonmail.com*. In the **Source** column shown in Figure 1-60, a value of **Invited User** is displayed, which shows that the user has not yet accepted the invitation and logged in.
6. The user receives an invite email with a **Get Started** link. The user logs in with the credentials for the Microsoft Account of the same username or is prompted to create a new account.
7. The user must grant the directory access to read a minimal amount of the user's data, as shown in Figure 1-59. Once the user clicks **Accept**, the account is added to the directory.

FIGURE 1-59 Review permissions for a user accepting an invitation to be a guest

- The user's **Source** will now be listed as **Microsoft Account**. An example of this is shown in Figure 1-60 for the *az303.b2b@gmail.com* user.

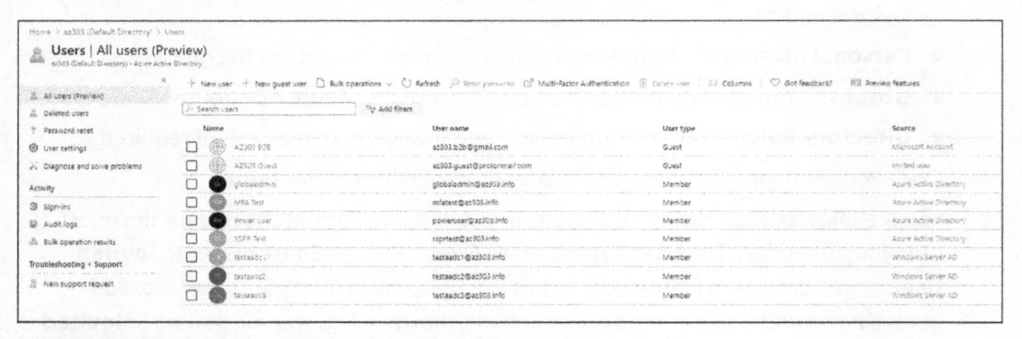

FIGURE 1-60 Guest user source types from Azure AD

> ***NOTE*** **B2B FEDERATION**
>
> **In the previous procedure, step 6 requires the guest user to have a Microsoft Account to log in. It is possible to federate your Azure AD to Google or other external providers through Direct federation(preview), which enables the user to have the same username and password. This set up is beyond the scope of the exam, though it is something to be aware of.**

Managing guests within Azure AD can be performed with Azure AD access reviews. Access reviews are a part of Identity Governance, which is a set of features that are part of the paid Azure AD Premium P2 SKU. Azure AD Access reviews cover group memberships and applications. Role and resource-based access reviews are part of Azure AD Privileged Identity Management (PIM).

Azure AD access reviews ensure that each user reviewed still requires their access. This is done by asking the user or a decision maker if the access is still appropriate. Because the review is performed over an Azure AD group or application, access reviews are not just for guest access. The user who creates the access review must be assigned a Premium P2 license and be a Global Administrator.

To explore Azure AD access reviews to manage guest users, walk through the following process in the Azure portal. Note for this walkthrough, an Azure AD group has already been created containing two guest users:

1. Search for **azure active directory** in the resource name search box at the top of the portal and press Enter to select **Azure Active Directory**. Click **Identity Governance** in the **Azure Active Directory** menu, which opens the **Identity Governance** menu.
2. In the **Identity Governance** menu, the **Access Reviews** section might be unavailable. To enable **Access Reviews**, you must click **Onboard** on the **Identity Governance** menu. If you have more than one directory with Premium P2 licenses, you can choose the directory to onboard. Click **Onboard Now** to allow the use of access reviews in the selected directory. Note if you do not onboard, you will receive a message stating that you do not have access to create an access review and to contact your global administrator.
3. Go back to the Azure portal and click **Identity Governance** in the menu blade.
4. The **Getting Started** blade opens. On the right of this blade, click **Create An Access Review**. The options for creating an access review are shown in Figure 1-61.
   - **Review name.** Mandatory name for the review.
   - **Description.** A brief description of the review.
   - **Start Date.** Mandatory start date of the review.
   - **Frequency.** You can choose between **One-Time**, **Weekly**, **Monthly**, **Quarterly**, or **Yearly** reviews. Choose **One-Time**.
   - **Duration And End.** If the frequency is not yearly, choose when to end a repeating review.
   - **Users To Review.** Assigned to an application or members of a group. For this explanation choose **Members Of A Group.**
   - **Scope.** This is key for managing guest users; you can choose from all users in the group or application, or you can just choose guest users. Choose **Guest Users Only**.
   - **Group.** Choose the group to review. If **Users To Review** had been set to **Assigned To Application**, an application name selector would appear instead. Select the Azure AD group you created for this walkthrough and choose some guest users. If you had created a review for this group previously, a banner stating this is displayed underneath the group, as shown in Figure 1-61.

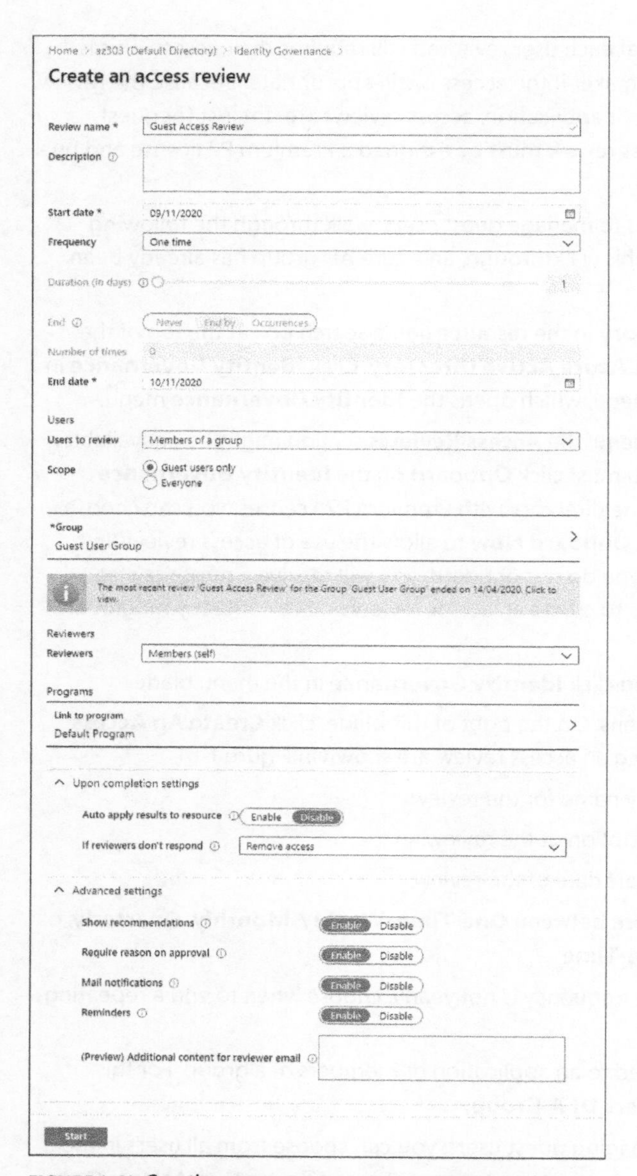

FIGURE 1-61 Creating a guest-management access review

- **Reviewers.** Drop-down menu of choices:
  - **Group Owners.** The owner of the group who reviews on behalf of the members.
  - **Selected Users.** Users selected from within the group.
  - **Members (Self).** The group members themselves.

5. Choose **Members(Self).** This will trigger an email to the users in the group to review their own access.
   - **Programs.** Allows you to create programs to collect data for specific compliance requirements. Leave this set to the default setting.
   - **Upon Completion Settings.** Options for automated actions on the completion of a review:
     - **Auto Apply Results To Resource.** If a review comes back that a user no longer requires access, it will be automatically removed.
     - **If Reviewers Don't Respond.** You can choose to remove or approve access, or you can leave your access settings as is. Choose **Remove Access**.
6. Once you have set up the access review options, click **Start**. You are returned to the **Access Reviews** blade, and your new review will be listed as **Not Started**. You can click the listed access review to edit the settings, to delete it, or to view the status of each user's review.

The access review will remain shown as **Not Started** until the start date is reached. The Review Status will change to **Initializing** as Azure sends out review notification emails to those selected as reviewers. Once the notifications are sent, the status shifts to **Active**.

When the notification email is received, you will see a **Review Access** link. When you click the link, the user or selected reviewer logs in and can review his or her access or the access of others in the group. If the review is a self-review, the user is asked whether he or she still requires access to the group or application. The user chooses **Yes** or **No** and fills in a reason for why the access is needed, which is reflected in the access review **Results**, as shown in Figure 1-62.

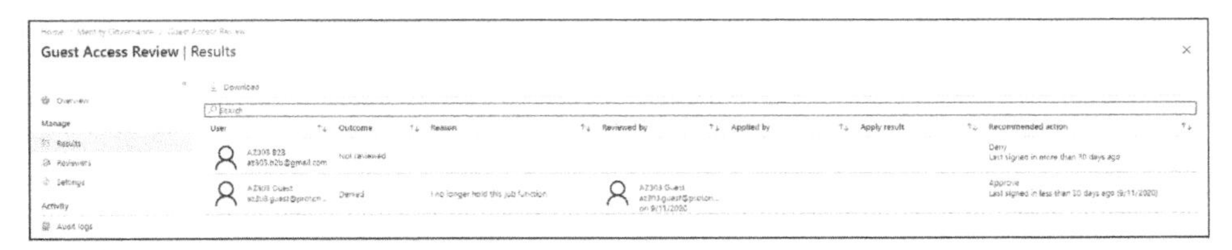

FIGURE 1-62 Reviewing the access review results in Azure portal

In this example, the `az303.guest user` has selected that he or she no longer requires access and has been automatically denied access based on the selection. The `az303.b2b user` has not logged in for 30 days, therefore, access would been automatically denied. If the `az303.b2b user` responds within the review period stating they still require access, access is restored.

> ***NOTE*** **CONDITIONAL ACCESS**
>
> **Microsoft recommends using conditional access with MFA for a B2B user log in. This can be performed by choosing All Guest Users in the Assignments section. For more details, see "Configure verification methods," earlier in this chapter.**

Configure Azure AD Identity Protection

Microsoft deals with millions of logins from Azure AD, Microsoft Accounts, and Xbox every day. Machine learning provides risk scores for each log in, and these risk signals are fed into Azure AD Identity Protection to provide three key reports:

- **Risky Users.** The probability that the account has been compromised.
- **Risky Sign-Ins.** The probability that the sign-in was not authorized by the account owner.
- **Risk Detections.** This is displayed when a P2 license is not available to show that either of the above two risks have been triggered.

Azure AD Identity Protection provides real-time data in the form of a security overview in the Azure portal. To access the Security Overview, navigate to **Azure AD** > **Security** > **Identity Protect** in the portal, as shown in Figure 1-63.

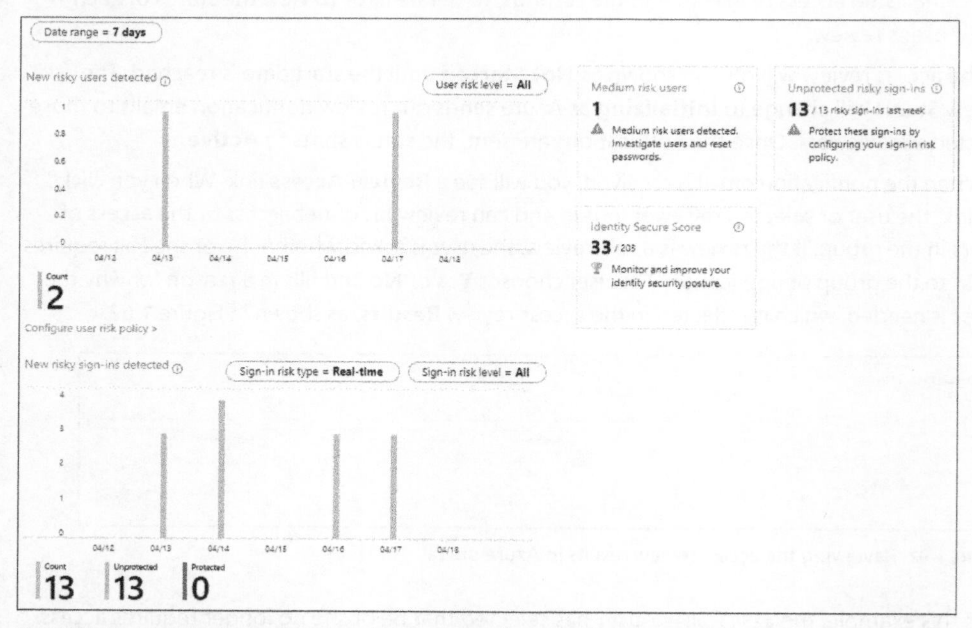

FIGURE 1-63 Identity Protection overview summary from the Azure portal

This is a new tenant with a scarce amount of data. The documentation states that Azure AD takes approximately 14 days of initial learning to build a model of your user's behavior. The top chart in Figure 1-63 displays the users who have been identified as risky. The bottom chart shows the number of risky sign-ins per day. This information can also be accessed via Microsoft Graph Azure AD Identity Protection APIs.

From the **Identity Protection** menu blade, scroll down to **Notify**. Here, you can configure two types of email notification:

- **Users At Risk Detected.** Set one or more admins (all global admins added by default), to receive an email alert based on Low, Medium, or High alert risk level.
- **Weekly Digest Email.** This is a summary of at-risk users, suspicious activities and detected vulnerabilities.

The users at-risk email contains a link to the risky users report; an administrator can access this report directly at **Azure AD** > **Security** > **Identity Protection** > **Risky Users**. As shown in Figure 1-64, the report shows a list of risky users, as well as their risk states and levels.

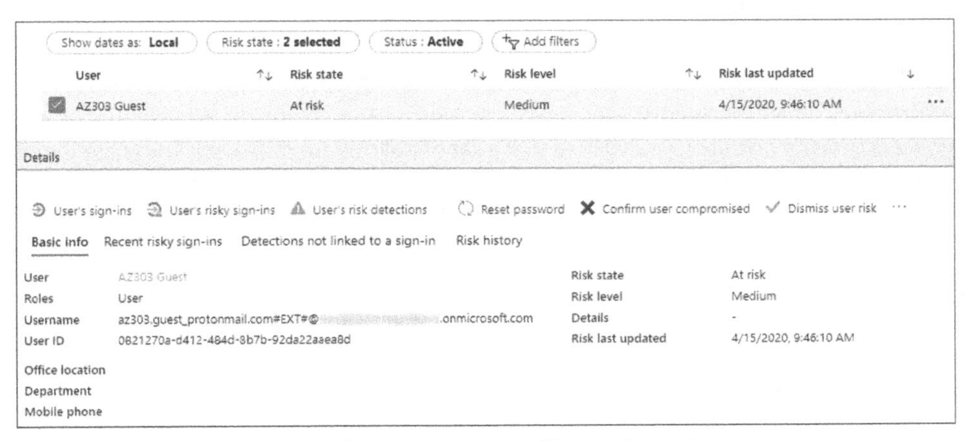

FIGURE 1-64 The risky users report from Azure AD Identification Protection

Note that in Figure 1-64, the actions that can be performed directly from the report: **Reset Password**, **Confirm User Compromised**, and **Dismiss User Risk**. These enable you to provide feedback on the risk assessments to Azure AD Identity Protection.

At the top of the Azure AD Identity Protection menu blade in Azure portal, there are three default policies that can be enabled to support Identity Protection:

- **User Risk Policy.** This is dependent on the user's risk level (**Low**, **Medium**, or **High**). The risk level for a User Risk Policy is the condition. You can choose to either block or allow access based on the condition. If you are allowing access, you have the option to enforce MFA.
- **Sign-In Risk Policy.** This is dependent on the user's sign-in risk level (**Low**, **Medium**, or **High**). The risk level for a Sign-in Risk Policy is the condition. You can choose to either block or allow access based on the condition. If you are allowing access, you have the option to enforce MFA.
- **MFA registration policy.** When enabled, this policy forces the selected users or groups to use Azure AD multifactor authentication.

Each of these policies can be set for a subset of users, for groups, or for all users. These policies have limited customization. If you need more control, you can use a conditional access policy. Conditional access policies are covered in the next section.

Implement Conditional Access including MFA

Until now, our discussion of MFA configuration has concentrated on MFA that is enabled per user by changing the user's state, or against a specific feature such as sign-in risk. This can be inflexible because it requires a second verification step being forced at every log in, regardless of the risk level of the information being accessed. Conditional Access gives you a framework to architect an access strategy for the apps and resources your organization uses, tailoring it to meet the resource access needs of your organization.

Conditional access is a P2 Premium Azure AD feature, which can be found in the **Azure Active Directory** under the **Security** section of the **Azure AD** menu blade. When you look at conditional access the first time, you will see that a set of policies are displayed. These are the baseline policies; they are legacy policies and should be ignored. You should create your policies from scratch.

Conditional access is highly configurable. To see how configurable, the following example looks at setting up conditional MFA. The use case for this example is: "If a log-in from a user in a specific group is outside the head office, an MFA, a domain joined machine, or a compliant device from Microsoft Intune is required." You will explore the other conditional access options available on each blade.

> ***NOTE*** **CONDITIONAL ACCESS**
>
> **If you still have per-user MFA configured from the previous section, you will need to disable it. Conditional Access is overridden by per user MFA.**

In this example, before creating a conditional access policy, you must first create a named location to simulate your head office. In the **Conditional Access** menu blade in the portal, click **Named Locations** and then follow these steps:

1. Click **Add Named Location**.
2. Enter a **Name** for the location; for this example, enter **Head Office**.
3. Select **Mark As A Trusted Location**, which will automatically lower sign-in risk for users who are logging in from this location. You will explore this later in this section.
4. In the **IP Ranges** field, enter the CIDR notation for the IP address you are currently using. Click **Create**.

The named location is created and is ready to be selected in the conditional access policy. To create the policy, stay in the Azure portal and select **Conditional Access** in the **Security** menu blade. Follow this walkthrough to create the use-case policy and explore the options on the blades, as shown as Figure 1-65.

FIGURE 1-65 The Conditional Access blades for assignments in the Azure portal

1. Click **New Policy**; the first blade in Figure 1-65 is displayed with each section set to 0 selections.
2. Click **Users And Groups**. In this blade (see Figure 1-65), the users to be included or excluded are displayed. For the example, the use case is: "Include users who are part of a specific group." Click **Select Users And Groups** to select the group. Click **Done**.
3. Click **Cloud Apps Or Actions**. Here, Microsoft apps, such as Microsoft 365, your own applications, or third-party applications that have been integrated with Azure AD can be selected. The use case states, "any log in" and does not refer to specific applications, so select all cloud apps and click **Done**.
4. Click **Conditions**. Information about the login conditions being used is passed in from Azure:
   - **Sign-in risk.** Filter to **Low**, **Medium**, or **High** (as described earlier in this chapter in "Configure Azure AD Identity Protection." For this example, leave **Configure** set to **No**.
   - **Device platforms.** Include or exclude based on the operating system type: Android, iOS, Windows, or macOS. For this example, leave **Configure** set to **No**.
   - **Location.** Include or exclude named and/or trusted locations. Part of the use case is to exclude the head office. Set the **Location** to exclude Head Office. (You created the head office location in the previous set of steps.)
   - **Client Apps (Preview).** Include or exclude based on the type of client application being used for the login. For this example, leave **Configure** set to **No**.
   - **Device State.** You can choose to exclude domain-joined or Microsoft Intune devices that are marked as compliant. For this example, leave **Configure** set to **No**.
5. Multiple conditions can be combined to filter to a specific set of circumstances. Click **Done**.
6. On the **New** blade, you now need to configure the access controls and click **Grant**. **Block Access** and **Grant Access** radio buttons appear at the top of the **Grant** blade, as

shown in Figure 1-66. The use case is to grant access to a user outside the head office if he or she passes MFA or has a compliant device. To configure the **Grant** policy settings to meet this use case, you will need to set the following:

- **Require Multi-Factor Authentication.** Requires a user to perform multifactor authentication. Select this checkbox to meet the use case requirement of "require MFA."
- **Require Device To Be Marked As Compliant.** Requires the user's device to meet Microsoft Intune–configured compliance requirements. Select this checkbox to meet the use case requirement of "a compliant device from Microsoft Intune."
- **Require Hybrid Azure AD Joined Device.** Select this checkbox to meet the use case requirement of "a domain joined device."
- **Require Approved Client App.** Requires the application the user is accessing to be one of the Microsoft approved client apps. Leave this checkbox unchecked, as it is not part of the use case requirement.
- **Require App Protection Policy.** Requires the application the user is accessing to have an enforced app protection policy. Leave this checkbox unselected, as it is not part of the use case requirement.

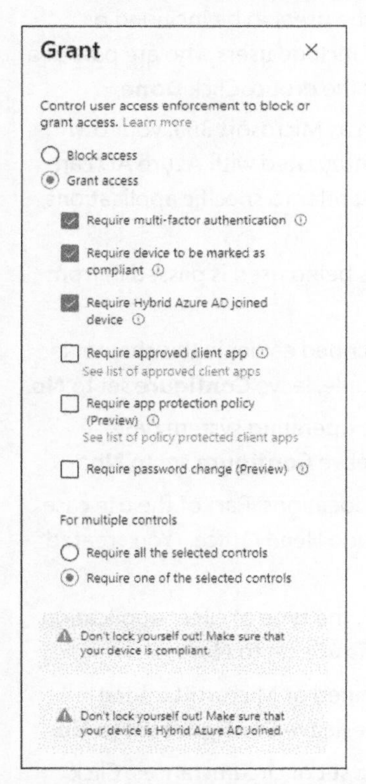

FIGURE 1-66 The Grant blade for creating a conditional access policy

7. The use case states that only one of the controls needs to be met; therefore, set **Multiple Controls** to **Require One Of The Selected Controls**. Click **Select**.

8. Click **Session**. This limits the access within specified Microsoft 365 applications. This is not required for the use case. Close the **Session** blade.
9. The use case requirement is now fulfilled; click **Create** to create the access policy.
10. The new policy is listed in the **Policies** blade. To test the policy, log in to My Applications (*https://myapplications.microsoft.com*) from the IP address set in the named location. You will need to perform this log in as one of the users who is part of the group selected in step 2 of this walkthrough. You are logged in correctly because this simulates logging in from the head office.
11. Now try logging in from your phone on mobile data; you will be asked to verify using MFA because conditional access flags the login as coming from outside the office.

To help troubleshoot conditional access policies, click the **What If** button on the **Conditional Access** blade. Here, you can see which conditional access policies will apply under various conditions.

> ***NEED MORE REVIEW?*** **CONDITIONAL ACCESS**
>
> **To learn about implementing conditional access, including MFA, visit the Microsoft Docs article "Conditional Access documentation" at *https://docs.microsoft.com/en-us/azure/active-directory/conditional-access/*.**

Skill 1.7: Implement and manage hybrid identities

Most organizations will have an on-premises identity solution in which applications span on-premises and in the cloud resources. Managing the users who access these apps can be challenging. As an architect you need to look to solutions that allow your users to have one set of credentials regardless of where their applications are housed. The identity solutions from Microsoft have cloud-based and on-premises capabilities. This creates a hybrid identity, which is a single common identity for authentication and authorization across locations. Active Directory on Windows Server is Microsoft's on-premises identity provider. The identities within Active Directory can be synchronized to Azure AD using Azure AD Connect, which creates a common identity for authentication and authorization to all resources, across all locations.

This skill covers how to:

- Install and configure Azure AD Connect
- Identity synchronization options
- Configure and manage password sync and password writeback
- Configure single sign-on
- Use Azure AD Connect Health

The walkthroughs in this skill require a domain controller so that a synchronization can be set up from Active Directory to Azure AD. If you have no prior experience working with Azure AD Connect, we recommend that you set up an environment to work through the process. This might seem daunting, but at a high level, it can be achieved in Azure with three steps:

1. Purchase a domain name and follow the instructions in Skill 1.6 to add a custom domain name and make it the primary domain in your Azure AD tenant.
2. Use the Azure Quick Start template to create a domain controller in Azure (*https://github.com/Azure/azure-quickstart-templates/tree/master/active-directory-new-domain)*. Click **Deploy To Azure** and then use the following parameters:
   - **Basics.** Enter a resource group name and choose a location.
   - **Settings.** Choose an admin username and password. For **Domain Name**, enter the domain name you purchased in step 1. For **DNS Prefix**, enter something that will be unique. Leave everything else set to the defaults.
3. Click **Purchase**.
4. Once deployed, RDP to the load balancer's public IP. Log in as the admin user you created in step 2. Server Manager will open automatically. Click **Tools** > **Active Directory Users And Computers** and create some users. You might want to create a new organizational unit (OU) in which you can place your test users when you explore Azure AD Connect filtering in the next section. Make sure one of the users is an Enterprise Admin.

Your domain controller in Azure will act as if it were on-premises.

Install and configure Azure AD Connect

Azure AD Connect is a tool that provides synchronization of identity data from on-premises domain controllers to Azure AD. It is a lightweight agent that can be installed on Windows Server 2012 or above. Azure AD Connect can even be installed on the domain controller itself, though this is not the best practice. Azure AD Connect works over a standard internet connection, and you do not need to set up a site-to-site VPN or Express Route. To explore the setup further, follow these steps:

1. Open the Azure portal, search for **azure active directory** in the resource name search bar at the top of the portal, and press Enter to select **Azure Active Directory**. Click **Azure AD Connect** in the menu blade. On the **Azure AD Connect** blade, click **Download Azure AD Connect**; this is the Azure AD Connect Agent. Copy the downloaded `AzureADConnect.msi` file to the server you will be installing from. For this walkthrough, you will be installing onto the domain controller.
2. Double click the `AzureADConnect.msi` file that you just copied to the server to start the installation. Agree to the license terms and click **Continue**.

3. The default installation of Express Settings is displayed in Figure 1-67. This process is automatic and will install **Azure AD Connect** using defaults. Click **Customize**, which will give you full control over the installation process, including the synchronization method.

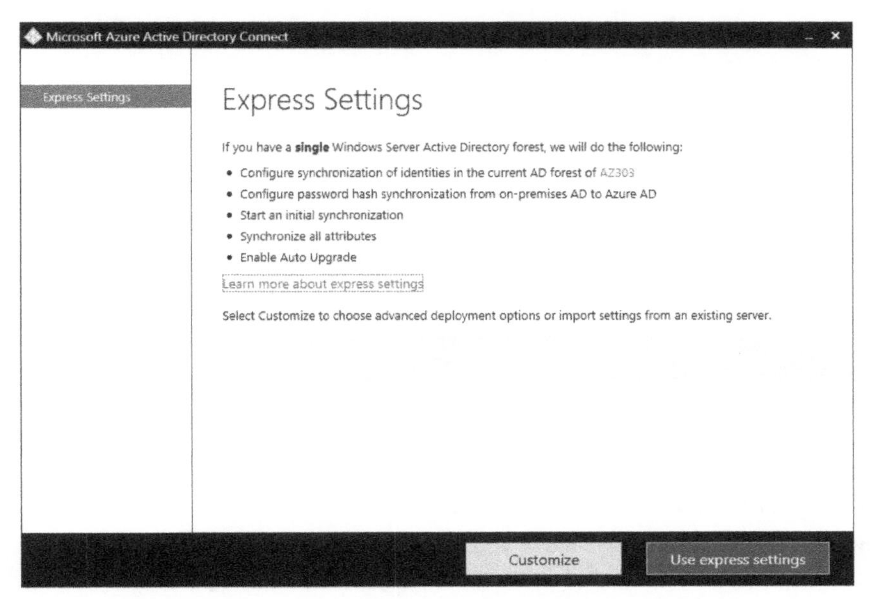

FIGURE 1-67 The automatic install process for Express Settings in Azure AD Connect

4. The **Required Components** screen provides you with a choice to use previously installed components. Leave these set to their default settings (not selected). Click **Install**. The required components will now install.
   - **Custom Install Location.** Choose where the Azure AD Connect agent files will be installed.
   - **Existing SQL Server.** You can specify a database server to house the Azure AD Connect database if you already have an SQL installation.
   - **Service Account.** You may already have a service account set up, though it will require the Log on as a service permission and that you are a system administrator on your chosen SQL server.
   - **Custom Sync Groups.** Local groups to the server.
5. The **User Sign-In** screen lists the synchronization options available, as shown in Figure 1-68. You will explore these in "Identity synchronization options," later in this chapter. Leave **Password Hash Synchronization** enabled. The **Enabling Single Sign-On** setting will also be explored in "Configure Single Sign-On," later in this chapter. For now, don't click this option. Click **Next**.

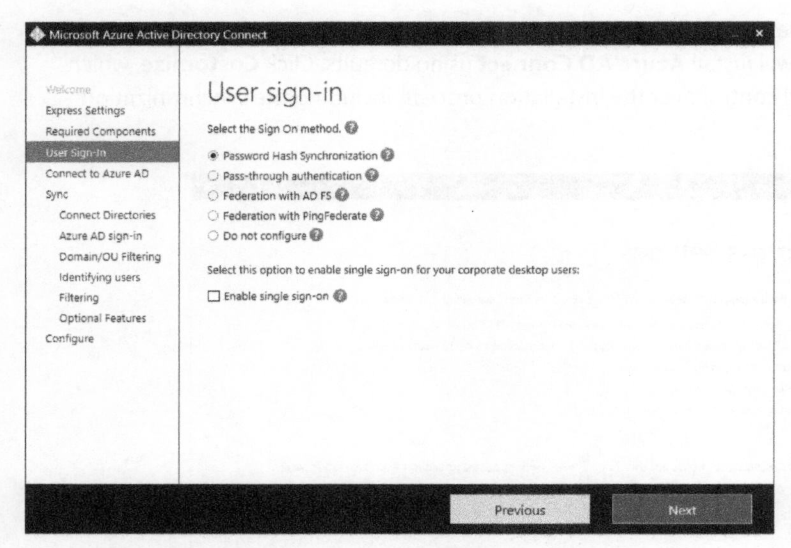

FIGURE 1-68 Choosing the sign-in method for users in Azure AD Connect

6. The connection to Azure AD requires global administrator credentials. Enter these credentials and click **Next**.
7. The **Connect To Azure AD** screen allows you to choose which directory type you want to connect. Choose the forest and click **Add Directory**, as shown in Figure 1-69. You now need to create an account with permissions to periodically synchronize your Active Directory. Under **Select Account Option**, leave **Create New AD Account** selected and enter enterprise admin credentials. This process is shown in Figure 1-69. Click **OK**.

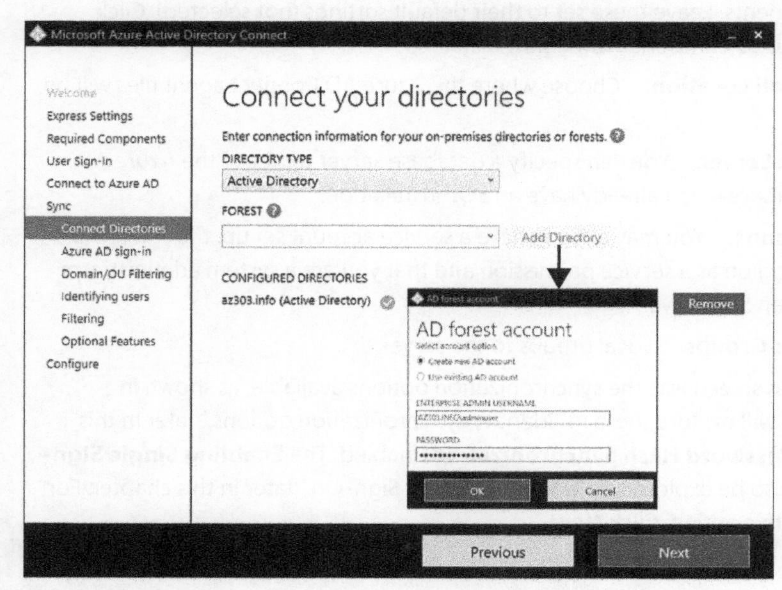

FIGURE 1-69 Azure AD Connect directory connect and enterprise admin log in

8. You are returned to the **Connect Your Directories** screen, as shown in Figure 1-70. The directory you just added is listed under **Configured Directories**. Click **Next**.

9. Azure AD Connect will now list the **UPN Suffixes** from your on-premises Active Directory, as displayed in Figure 1-70. For a user to log in without error, the custom domain in Azure AD must match a UPN suffix in the on-premises environment. You cannot use the tenant's default `*.onmicrosoft.com` domain name. When a UPN Suffix and Azure AD Domain match, it is marked as `Verified` in the **Azure AD Domain** column (see Figure 1-70).

In the past, many Active Directories were set up with `.local` as the domain. If your Active Directory is set up this way, you must add a UPN suffix to your forest, which must match the custom domain in Azure AD. This might also mean the selector for **User Principal Name (UPN)** is incorrect. The UPN will be taken as the username for the Azure log in. The UPN must have a suffix as verified in the list in Figure 1-70; otherwise, your users will not be able to log in. If the **Active Directory UPN Suffix** and **Azure AD Domain** do not match—for example, from a historical `.local` domain—you might need to use a different attribute, such as email address, for your user principal name. Click **Next**.

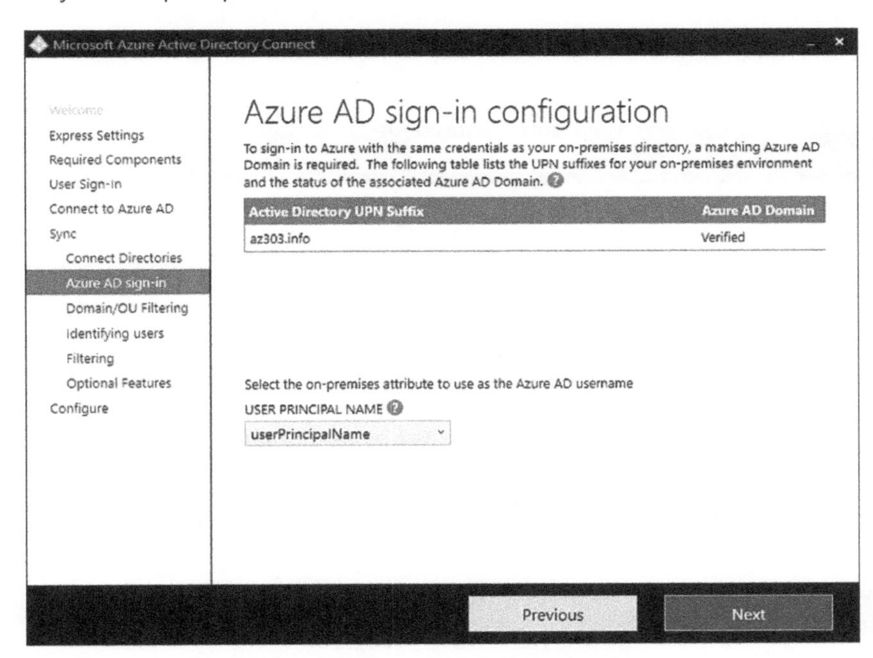

FIGURE 1-70 Azure AD Connect Sign-In Configuration verification

10. You may now choose which parts of your directory to synchronize. The default is to select all domains and OUs. However, you should filter for two reasons:
    - You do not want to waste expensive Azure AD licenses on non-user accounts.
    - You do not want to synchronize high-privilege accounts or service accounts to Azure AD unless necessary.

11. Choose **Sync Selected Domains And OUs**, and then select the OUs where your users reside, as shown in Figure 1-71. Click **Next**.

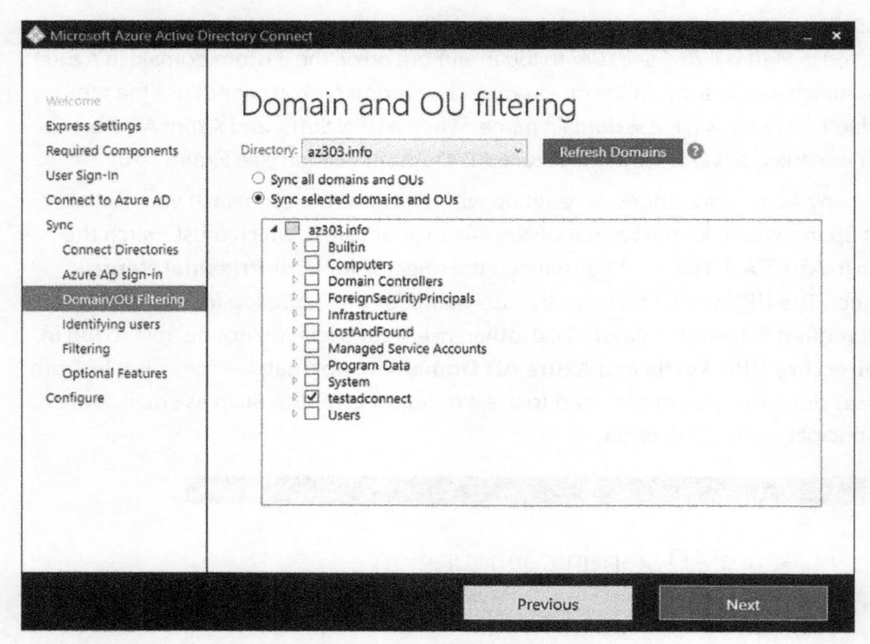

FIGURE 1-71 Azure AD Connect Domain And OU Filtering

12. On the **Uniquely Identifying Your Users** screen, click **Next** to continue. By default, Azure AD Connect uses the UPN attribute to identify your local AD accounts individually. In larger organizations that plan to synchronize users across AD domains and forests, you might need to choose another AD schema attribute to resolve account name conflicts.
13. **Filter Users And Devices** is used for a piloting phase of Azure AD Connect. If you want to pilot a subset of users, create a group in your on-premises AD and enter the group name at this point. Leave this selection set to **Synchronize All Users And Devices**. Click **Next**.
14. On the **Optional Features** screen, click **Next**. You will explore these features in the next four sections of this skill.
15. The **Ready To Configure** screen shown in Figure 1-72 displays the synchronization that has been set up on your server. Choosing **Start The Synchronization Process When Configuration Completes** will start synchronization as soon as the configuration is complete.
16. If you select **Enable Staging Mode: When Selected, Synchronization Will Not Export Any Data To AD or Azure AD**, changes to Azure AD Connect will be imported and synchronized, but they will not be exported to Azure AD. This means you can preview your changes before making your synchronization live. Once installed, to leave

staging mode, you will need to edit your Azure AD Connect configuration and turn off staging mode, which will start synchronization. Click **Install**. Azure AD Connect will now install and start to synchronize your users to Azure AD.

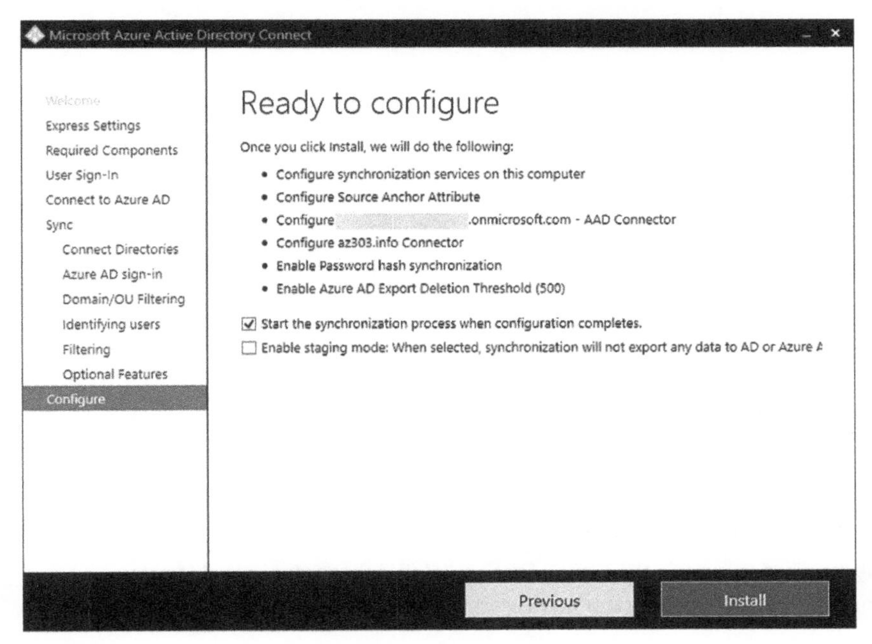

FIGURE 1-72 Azure AD Connect Ready To Configure

You can now verify your users have synchronized to Azure AD by switching to the Azure portal. Search for **azure active directory** in the resource name search bar at the top of the portal. After clicking **Users** in the menu blade, you should now see your users listed, as shown in Figure 1-73. In the **Source** column, synchronized users are shown with **Windows Server AD**.

New user | New guest user | Bulk activities | Refresh | Reset password | Multi-Factor Authentication | Delete user | Columns | Preview features

Search users | Add filters

Name	User name	User type	Source
SSPR Test	ssprtest@az303.info	Member	Azure Active Directory
MFA Test	mfatest@az303.info	Member	Azure Active Directory
globaladmin	globaladmin@az303.info	Member	Azure Active Directory
testaadc1	testaadc1@az303.info	Member	Windows Server AD
testaadc2	testaadc2@az303.info	Member	Windows Server AD
testaadc3	testaadc3@az303.info	Member	Windows Server AD

FIGURE 1-73 Synchronized users are identified with Windows Server AD.

Click any of the users who have synchronized from an on-premises Active Directory. You can see from Figure 1-74 that most of the detail cannot be edited because it is unavailable. Only items that are used in the cloud are available, such as **Usage Location**. The Windows Server Active Directory is the master directory. If edits are to be made, they must be made on-premises.

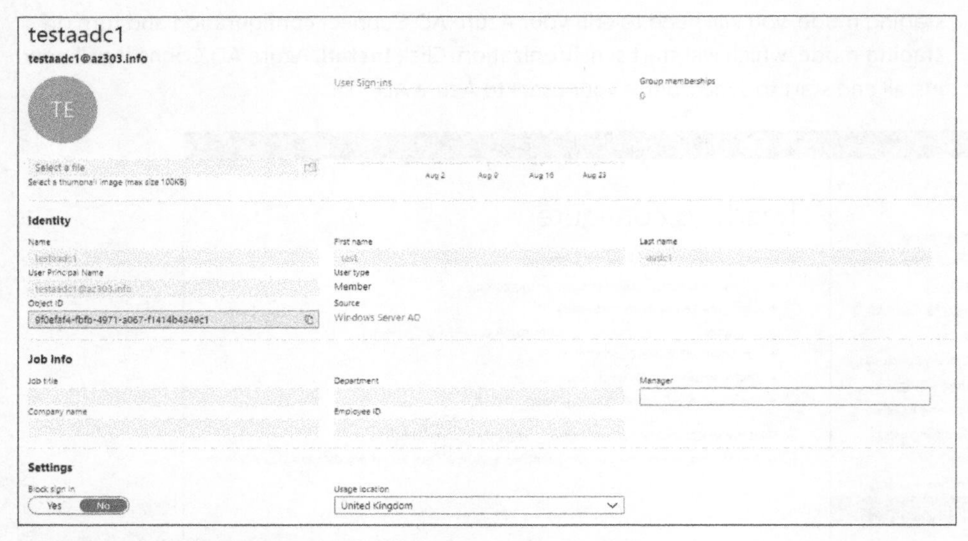

FIGURE 1-74 Only cloud items are editable.

EXAM TIP* *USER PRIVILEGES FOR AZURE AD CONNECT

You might be required to explain the types of user privileges that are required to set up Azure AD Connect (global administrator and enterprise administrator).

NEED MORE REVIEW? **INSTALL AD CONNECT**

To learn about installing Azure AD Connect, visit the Microsoft Docs article "Custom installation of Azure AD Connect" at *https://docs.microsoft.com/en-us/azure/active-directory/hybrid/how-to-connect-install-custom*.

Identity synchronization options

In the previous section, you learned how to install and configure Azure AD Connect. You set **Password Hash Synchronization** as the synchronization option. However, there were five other options available. Each of these options has different advantages and therefore, different use cases. As an architect, you need to understand when each option should be used.

- **Do Not Configure.** Users can sign in using a federated sign-in that is not managed by Azure AD connect. These sign-ins do not use the same password, just the same user-name. This should be chosen when a third-party federation server is already in place.
- **Password Hash Synchronization.** Users can sign into Office 365 and other Micro-soft cloud services using the same password they use on-premises. Azure AD Connect synchronizes a hash of the password to Azure AD, and authentication occurs within the cloud. This method should only be used when storing a user's password hash in the

cloud complies with your organization's compliance requirements. It is also important to remember that because Azure AD performs the authentication, not all Active Directory policies will be followed. For example, if an account has been expired but the account is still active, Azure AD will still authenticate. Password hash synchronization supports seamless single sign-on.

- **Pass-Through Authentication.** Users can sign in to Microsoft cloud services with their own passwords. However, with pass-through authentication, the authentication happens in the on-premises Active Directory. The key benefit of pass-through authentication is that no passwords are stored in the cloud, which can be a compliance requirement for many organizations. Because the authentication happens at the on-premises Active Directory, the AD security and password policies can also be enforced.
- **Federation With AD FS.** Federation is a collection of domains that have established trust between them. Trust can contain authentication and authorization. Historically, federation was used to establish trust between organizations for shared resources. Azure AD can federate with on-premises AD FS, allowing users to use their own passwords and use single sign-on (SSO). Federation with AD FS authenticates against the on-premises AD FS server, so no passwords or password hashes are stored in the cloud. AD FS with Azure AD Connect should be used when third-party applications require it and when AD FS is already in use.
- **Federation With PingFederate.** This is a third-party alternative to AD FS. This option should be selected for businesses that already use PingFederate for token-based SSO.

EXAM TIP AD FS

Microsoft recommends that customers move from Federation with AD FS to Pass-through Authentication with seamless SSO where possible. Keep this in mind if you are asked about password methods in the cloud and single sign-on.

Configure and manage password sync and password writeback

With Azure AD self-service password reset enabled, users can unlock their accounts and update their passwords from cloud-based applications. If these users are members of your on-premises Active Directory that is being synchronized using Azure AD Connect to Azure AD, your users might find that their passwords are out of sync.

Password writeback is a feature of Azure AD Connect that writes back password changes in real-time to an on-premises directory. Password writeback is supported by password hash synchronization, pass-through authentication, and ADFS. Password writeback does not require any firewall changes; it uses an Azure service bus relay through the Azure AD Connect communication channel.

Password writeback is a paid feature requiring at least a premium P1 license to be assigned to your users in Azure AD. Password write back must be configured in the on-premises Active Directory and within Azure AD. To configure the on-premises Active Directory, follow these steps through an RDP session to the server to which you will need to sign in as a domain administrator:

1. Open Azure AD Connect, which has already been installed and click **Configure** > **View Current Configuration**. The current Azure AD Connect settings are shown in Figure 1-75.

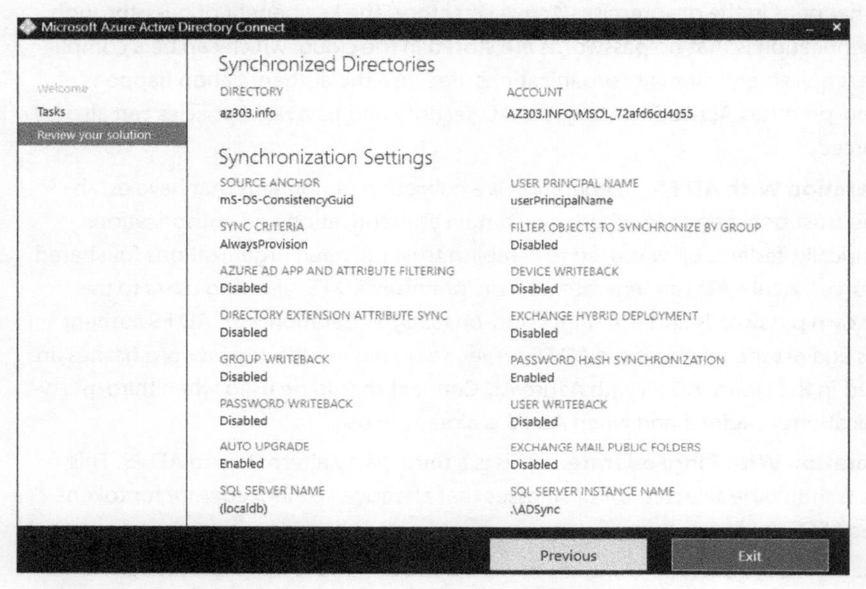

FIGURE 1-75 Current Azure AD Connect synchronization set up

2. Note the **Account** shown at the top right. This is the service account created by Azure AD Connect for the synchronization process. This account needs to have the following permissions added to it for password writeback:
   - Reset password
   - Write permissions on `lockoutTime`
   - Write permissions on `pwdLastSet`
   - Extended rights for `Unexpire Password` on either
     - The root object of each domain in that forest
     - The user organizational units (OUs) you want to be in scope for SSPR
3. Open **Active Directory Users And Computers**. Under **View** at the top, choose **Advanced Features**. Right-click the root of the domain and choose **Properties**.
4. Click the **Security** tab at the top and then click **Advanced**. Click **Add**. The first three permissions should be listed in the **Access** column of the **Permissions Entry** pane for the account noted in step 2. The account name from Figure 1-75 should be selected in the **Principal**. If any are missing, add them.

5. The last permission listed in Step 2 is achieved by setting **Minimum Password Age** to **0** in Group Policy. Open **Server Manager**, click **Tools** in the top right, and then click **Group Policy Management**.
6. Edit the relevant policy for the OU scope of your users. **Minimum Password Age** is found by selecting **ComputerConfiguration** > **Policies** > **WindowsSettings** > **Security Settings** > **Account Policies**. Click **OK**, close **Group Policy Management**, and execute `gpupdate /force` on the command line to force the policy update.
7. Switch back to Azure AD Connect and click **Previous** > **Customize Synchronization Options**. Enter the credentials for a global administrator and click **Next**.
8. Click **Next** twice to get to the **Optional Features** page. Select **Password Writeback**, as shown in Figure 1-76, click **Next**, and then click **Configure**.

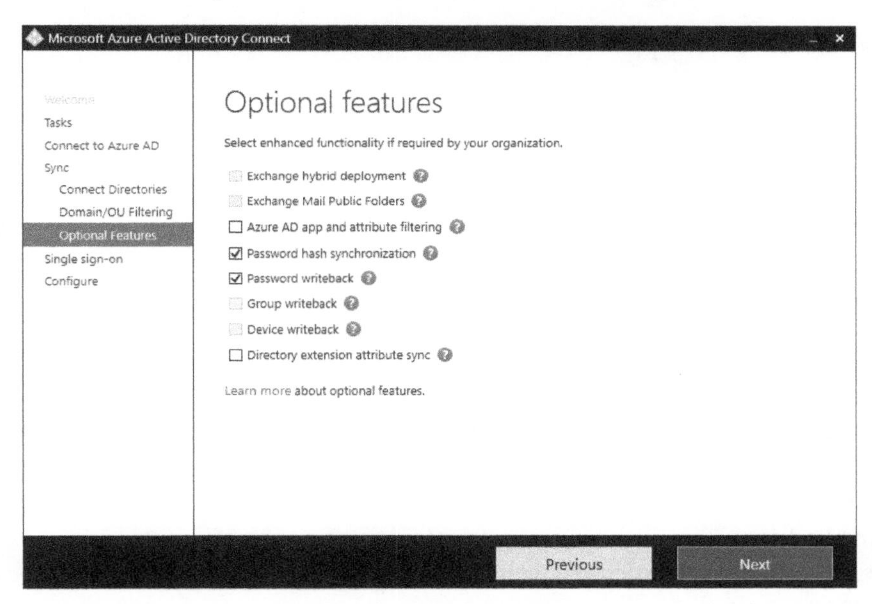

FIGURE 1-76 Selecting Password Writeback on the Azure AD Connect Optional Features

Azure AD Connect will now enable password writeback and configure the appropriate services on the on-premises server.

The final part is to configure self-service password reset (SSPR) to write password changes back to the domain controller. It is assumed that SSPR has already been configured, but if you haven't enabled it, see "Implement self-service password reset" earlier in this chapter. To configure password writeback with SSPR, sign in to the Azure portal as a global administrator:

1. Open the Azure portal and search for **azure active directory** in the search resources box at the top of the portal. Press Enter to select **Azure Active Directory** and then select **Password Reset** in the menu blade.
2. Select **On-premises Integration** on the **Password Reset** menu blade. The previous steps 1 to 8 of the last section of enabling password writeback has set **Write Back**

Passwords To Your On-Premises Directory? to **Yes**. The **Your On-Premises Client Is Up And Running** message is shown in Figure 1-77.

3. Optionally, you can change the **Allow Users To Unlock Accounts Without Resetting Their Password?** setting to **No**.

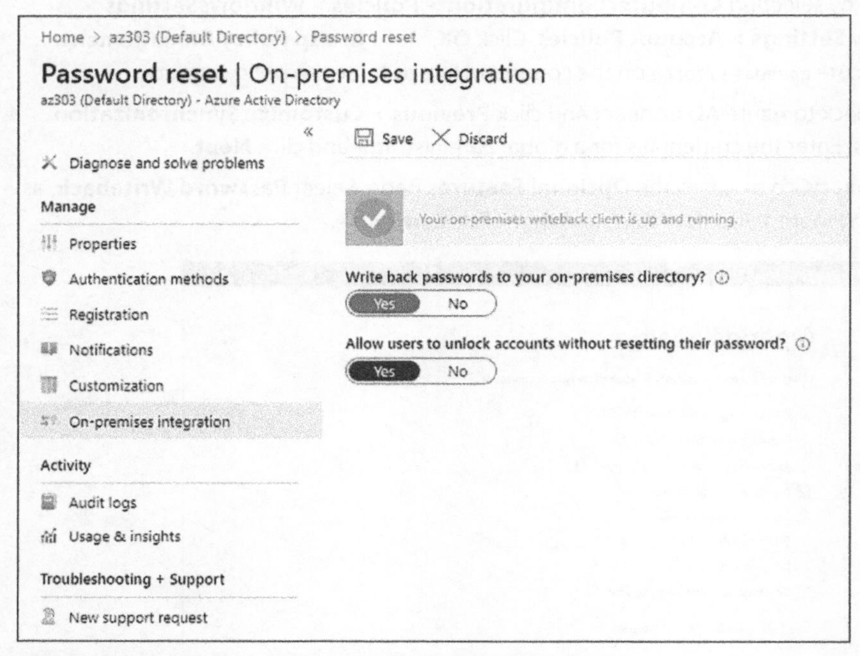

FIGURE 1-77 Enabling password writeback for Azure AD SSPR

4. Click **Save**.

Password writeback is now enabled. You can test this by resetting a user's password using My Apps (*https://myapps.microsoft.com*) and then logging the user in to a server or workstation on your domain.

> ***NEED MORE REVIEW?*** **CONFIGURE PASSWORD WRITEBACK**
>
> **To learn about configuring password sync and writeback, visit the Microsoft Docs article "Tutorial: Enable Azure Active Directory self-service password reset writeback to an on-premises environment" at *https://docs.microsoft.com/en-us/azure/active-directory/authentication/concept-sspr-writeback*.**

Configure Single Sign-On

Your users may now use the same credentials across on-premises and cloud applications; however, they must enter their credentials on every log-in. Azure AD seamless single sign-on (Azure AD seamless SSO) is a feature of Azure AD that automatically signs a user in to their cloud applications without the user having to type the password.

Azure AD Seamless SSO is enabled through a setting in Azure AD Connect. When enabled, a computer account named AZUREADSSOACC is created on the on-premises Active Directory. This computer account represents Azure AD, and the accounts password is securely stored with Azure AD. When users enter their usernames at an Azure AD sign-in page, a JavaScript script runs in the background for the user to access AZUREADSSOACC. The on-premises Active Directory returns a Kerberos ticket to the browser, which is encrypted with the accounts secret. The Kerberos ticket is securely passed to Azure AD, which decrypts the ticket. The Kerberos ticket includes the identity of the user signed in to the device. Azure AD evaluates the ticket and returns an authentication token back to the application or prompts for MFA. On success, the user is signed in to the application.

Azure AD seamless SSO requires the device the user is logged in to to be domain-joined. It also required the sign-in method to be password hash synchronization or pass-through authentication. Azure AD seamless SSO does not support ADFS.

To enable Azure AD seamless SSO on an already installed and configured Azure AD Connect, follow these steps:

1. RDP to the server where Azure AD Connect is installed. Open Azure AD Connect and click **Configure**.
2. Click **Change User Sign-In** on the **Additional Tasks** page. Enter the credentials for an Azure AD global administrator account. Click **Next**.
3. The **User Sign-In** page is displayed, which is identical to that shown in Figure 1-68 in "Configure and manage password sync and password writeback." Select **Enable Single Sign-On**. Note **Enable Single Sign-On** is only available if **Password Hash Synchronization** or **Pass-Through Authentication** are selected, as these are the supported options. Click **Next**.
4. The **Enable Single Sign-On** page appears, as shown in Figure 1-78. Click **Enter Credentials** and enter the credentials for a user with domain admin privileges. Click **OK**. These credentials will be used to configure Active Directory for single sign-on.
5. You are returned to the **Enable Single Sign-On** page. **Enter Credentials** should now be selected. Click **Next**, and then click **Configure**.

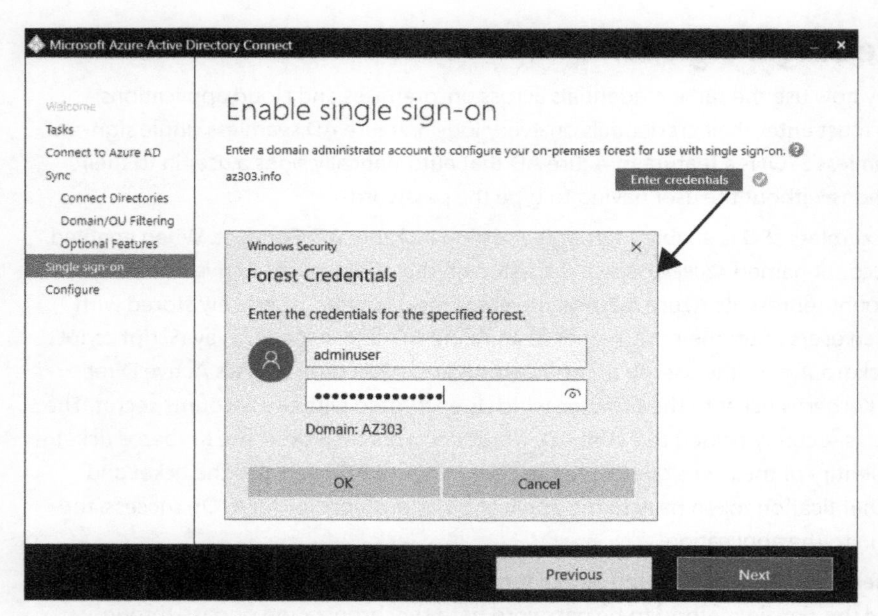

FIGURE 1-78 Entering domain administrator credentials to Enable Single Sign-On in Active Directory for Azure AD Connect.

Azure AD Seamless SSO is now enabled. To verify this switch to the Azure portal, search for **azure active directory** in the search resources bar at the top of the portal. In the menu blade select **Azure AD Connect**. The **Azure AD Connect page** should now display that Seamless single sign-on is Enabled as shown in Figure 1-79.

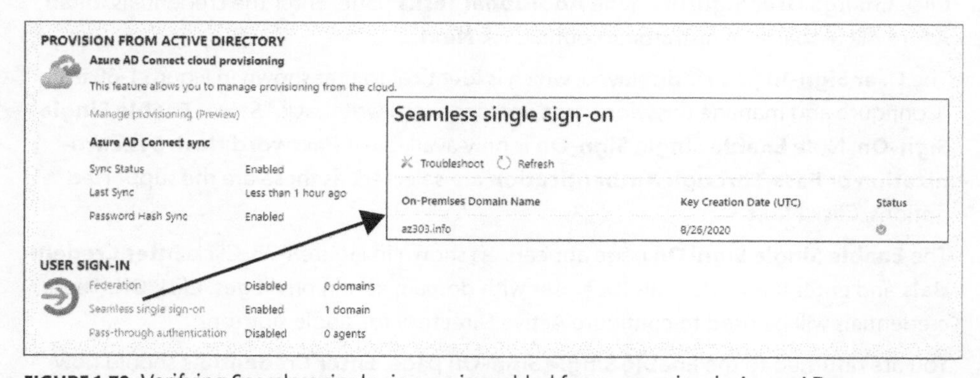

FIGURE 1-79 Verifying Seamless single sign-on is enabled for on-premises in Azure AD.

Although Azure Seamless SSO is now enabled, if you logged in as one of your users on a domain-joined device, you will still be asked for the password. This is because of the Kerberos ticket; a browser will not send the ticket to a cloud endpoint unless it is part of the user's intranet zone. This means that the ticket is being generated correctly, but it is not getting to Azure AD to be evaluated. To allow the ticket to be passed to Azure AD, you need to add the endpoint to each user's intranet zone. Also, you to need to allow the JavaScript that returns the

Kerberos token permission to send it to the Azure AD endpoint. To achieve this, you need to edit the group policy on the on-premises domain controller, which also means you can gradually roll out this feature. To edit the group policy, do the following on your domain controller:

1. Open **Server Manager**, click **Tools** at the top right and click **Group Policy Management**.
2. Edit the appropriate policy for your users. Browse to **User Configuration** > **Policy** > **Administrative Templates** > **Windows Components** > **Internet Explorer** > **Internet Control Panel** > **Security Page**. Then select **Site To Zone Assignment List**.
3. Enable the policy, and then click **Show** in the **Zone Assignments**. Set the following:
   - **Value name** – https://autologon.microsoftazuread-sso.com
   - **Value** – 1
4. Click **OK**, then **OK** once more.
5. Staying in the policy editor, browse to **User Configuration** > **Policy** > **Administrative Templates** > **Windows Components** > **Internet Explorer** > **Internet Control Panel** > **Security Page** > **Intranet Zone**, and then select **Allow Updates To Status Bar Via Script.**
6. Enable the policy and then click **OK**.

To determine that Azure AD Seamless SSO is functioning correctly, you can log in to *(http://myapps.microsoft.com)*. Make sure you have cleared your browser cache and that you run `gpupdate` in a command prompt first. If the steps in this section have been followed correctly, you will only need to enter your username but not your password. Instead, you will see the **Trying To Sign You In** page before you are signed in to MyApps.

If you have set up a test domain controller in Azure for this Skill, you could add a Windows 10 VM to your virtual network and domain join it to your domain controller. You will then be able to complete this test.

Use Azure AD Connect Health

Now that you have configured Azure AD Connect, you need to ensure that the service is reliable. Azure AD Connect Health monitors your Azure AD Connect identity synchronization and uses agents to record the metrics. If you are using password hash synchronization or pass-through authentication, the agent is installed as part of Azure AD Connect. If you are using ADFS, you will need to download an agent from Azure AD. The metrics returned to Azure AD Connect Health are displayed as dashboard components in the Azure AD Connect Health portal. These dashboard components cover usage, performance, and alerts. Azure AD Connect Health is a Premium Azure AD feature, so it requires a purchased SKU.

You can explore the features of Azure AD Connect Health in the Azure portal. Search for **azure active directory** in the resource name search bar at the top of the portal and press Enter. You will enter **Azure Active Directory** on the **Overview** blade. At the top of the overview blade is the **Azure AD Connect Health** dashboard widget, which provides a quick summary of whether your Azure AD Connect synchronization is healthy. Click the widget, and the **Azure AD Connect** blade opens. At the bottom, click **Azure AD Connect Health** in the **Health And Analytics** section.

Click **Sync Errors** in the **Azure AD Connect Health** menu blade. Doing so displays dashboard widget summaries of sync errors from Azure AD Connect, such as attribute duplicates and data mismatches. If errors are listed here, you can click the widget and drill in to investigate further.

Now click **Sync Services** in the **Azure AD Connect Health** menu blade. Sync services lists services that are synchronizing on this Azure AD tenant. The **Status** column displays whether the service is healthy or unhealthy, as shown in Figure 1-80. Clicking the service line will drill into the servers that make up the service, as displayed in Figure 1-80.

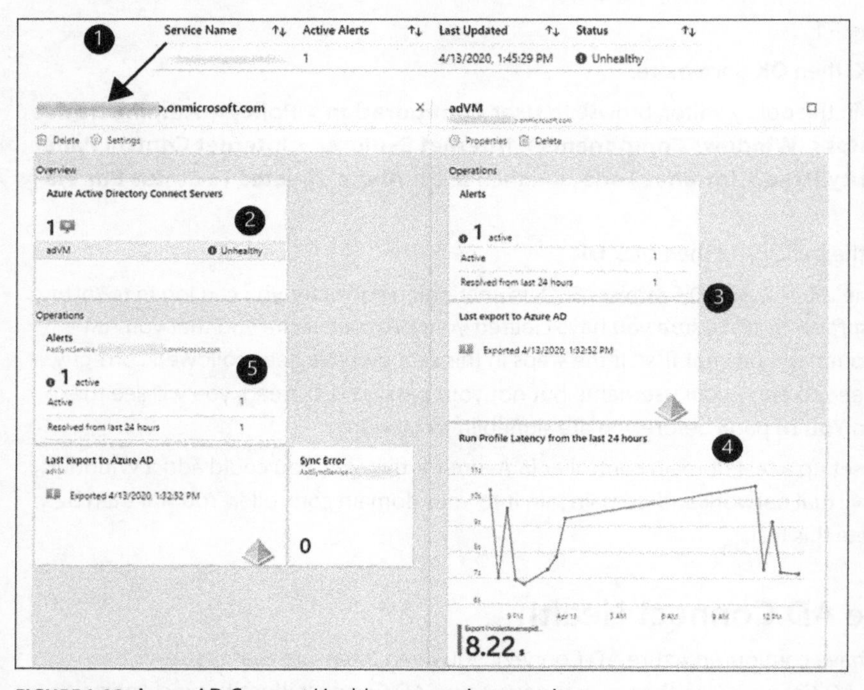

FIGURE 1-80 Azure AD Connect Health sync services metrics

Following is a brief overview of the numbered dashboard widget from Figure 1-80:

1. Sync services from Azure AD Health Connect.
2. This is a list of servers connected to the service via Azure AD Connect. The list shows whether the synchronization from the servers is healthy. Selecting a listed VM will display a drilled-in view, which is shown on the right in Figure 1-80.
3. This is shown when drilled through from selecting tile 2. This is a list of all alerts and the export status of the last export from an on-premises Active Directory to Azure AD.
4. Drilled in from selecting the second tile. By default, this is the latency of the export from an on-premises Active Directory to Azure AD. You can click this chart and edit it to show

other connectors. Note the lack of metric points during the night hours on April 13. This shows an unhealthy synchronization during this time period. This was simulated by deallocating the domain controller.

5. Current alerts from the connected servers. Click the **Alerts** widget to drill for more information, as shown in Figure 1-81.

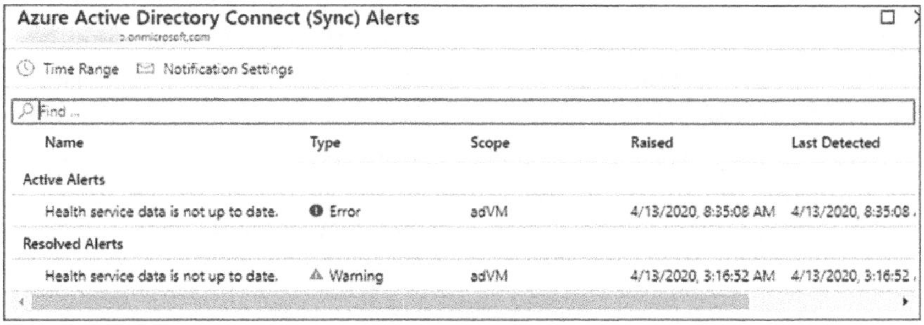

Azure Active Directory Connect (Sync) Alerts

.onmicrosoft.com

Time Range Notification Settings

Find ...

Name	Type	Scope	Raised	Last Detected
Active Alerts				
Health service data is not up to date.	Error	adVM	4/13/2020, 8:35:08 AM	4/13/2020, 8:35:08
Resolved Alerts				
Health service data is not up to date.	Warning	adVM	4/13/2020, 3:16:52 AM	4/13/2020, 3:16:52

FIGURE 1-81 Azure AD Connect Health Sync Alerts

Click an alert to see the full details of the alert and suggested links to help fix the issue. At the top of the **Azure Active Directory Connect (Syncs) Alerts** page is a **Notification Settings** link (see Figure 1-81). By default, alerts are emailed to all global admins. Click this link to configure the notification settings.

Chapter summary

- Azure Security Center and Azure Sentinel give you the ability to monitor the security of your infrastructure.
- You can implement Log Analytics as a centralized store for your services logging and metrics. You can report from Log Analytics using Workbooks, KQL, and Metrics Explorer through Azure Monitor.
- Azure Monitor for insights should be used when you require deep insights into the performance of VMs, applications, networks, and containers.
- Azure Storage can be configured to provide multiple levels of data backup and high availability of data. Azure Storage should be secured using Azure AD authentication where possible.
- Azure Storage has limits to the amount of IOPS each account can provide. Therefore, when configuring storage for VMs you should check the required IOPS and spread disks across storage accounts where required.
- Virtual network peering allows communication between networks in Azure without need for a VPN with global VNet peering connecting VNets across regions. When encrypted communications are required between networks in Azure you should consider a VNet-to-VNet VPN.

- Hybrid identities give your users a common user identity for authentication and authorization both in the cloud and on-premises. If you are looking to use single sign on with hybrid identities but cannot store passwords in the cloud, look to use pass-through authentication.
- Azure AD Identity Protection is an Azure AD Premium P2 feature that uses Microsoft's Intelligent Security Graph to detect potential vulnerabilities with your user identities.
- Use multifactor authentication to prevent malicious actors from accessing accounts by using a second factor of authentication. When implementing multifactor authentication, use conditional access to meet best practice requirements.
- Infrastructure as Code using Azure ARM templates gives you the ability to automate your infrastructure deployments, thus making them repeatable. When deploying resources using infrastructure as code to store your secrets in Azure Key Vault.

Thought experiment

In this thought experiment, demonstrate your skills and knowledge of the topics covered in this chapter. You can find the answers to thought experiment questions in the next section, "Thought experiment answers."

You are an Azure solutions architect hired by Wide World Importers to help with a "lift-and-shift" migration of their on-premises VMs into Azure. Wide World Importers currently has no infrastructure in any private cloud; however, it does have enterprise-wide Microsoft 365 usage. During discussions with Wide World Importers, the following items are identified as requirements:

Workloads running in the cloud must be isolated so that communication is private to each workload. The workloads will be managed from a central point. Five of the workloads have identical infrastructure which backs the development process of Wide World Importers' smart inventory tracking application. These workloads must be removed and re-created with minimum effort.

Wide World Importers has been receiving reports that the users of their .Net-based smart inventory tracking application have been experiencing frequent downtime and exceptions. The developers of the smart inventory tracking application are struggling to find a resolution.

Single sign-on is used for internal application authentication. This requirement must be carried forward, but credential security is a concern.

Admin-level users in Azure need to use strong passwords and another level of authentication. All the admins are smartphone users. All internal application users that are not based in the office must use more than one method of authentication on login.

Considering the discovered requirements, answer the following questions:

1. What would you recommend for deployment of the infrastructure and isolation of communication?

2. Which monitoring tool would be best suited for assisting the developers in troubleshooting their application exceptions and tracking availability?
3. What solution will address Wide World Importers' credential concerns while continuing to provide single sign-on capabilities?
4. How can the administrative and user account security requirements be met?

Thought experiment answers

This section contains the solution to the thought experiment for this chapter. Please keep in mind there might be other ways to achieve the desired result. Each answer explains why the answer is correct.

1. It is best practice to deploy infrastructure to Azure using infrastructure as code (IaC). Azure resource manager (ARM) templates are the recommended method of deploying to Azure using IaC. An ARM template can be reused for multiple environments using parameters, which meets the criteria for being reusable with minimal effort. VNets isolate network traffic within Azure. By implementing VNet peering using a hub-and-spoke topology, Wide World Importers can isolate workload traffic while maintaining a central hub for maintenance.
2. The key points here are the singular use of the word tool and the types of issues the developers need assistance to rectify. Application Insights is an application performance management (APM) service which analyzes an application in real time. Application Insights supports dotnet, which means the developers can use it for application instrumentation to view the exceptions. Application insights also includes application availability tracking and alerting, enabling development and operations teams to respond to events faster.
3. There was a small clue here in the summary at the top of the previous page. If Wide World Importers already use Microsoft 365, it is possible Azure AD Connect is already being used to synchronize user identities to Azure AD. Azure AD Connect with pass-through authentication provides seamless single sign-on capability. With pass-through authentication, no passwords are stored in the cloud, which addresses Wide World Importers credential security concerns.
4. Azure AD comes with multifactor authentication (MFA) capability for Azure admins. However, conditional access policies are the Microsoft-recommended way of implementing MFA. Conditional access policies can be used to fulfill both the admin and out-of-office user requirements for Wide World Importers. Conditional access requires a Premium P1 Azure AD tier; therefore, Wide World Importers' AD licenses might need to be upgraded.

CHAPTER 2

Implement management and security solutions

Organizations are still working out the details of getting to the cloud. With all the hardware and servers running in datacenters and co-location spaces, moving to the cloud still takes a bit of effort.

Architecting solutions in Azure is not just development or infrastructure management in the cloud. It's much more than that, and you need to understand how the Azure resources an organization needs to operate will sometimes be centered in development and sometimes in infrastructure. It's up to you to know enough about these topics.

This chapter helps you understand how you can bring your existing workloads to Azure by allowing the use of some familiar resources (IaaS Virtual Machines) and others that may be new (such as serverless computing) to your environment. In addition, the use of multifactor authentication (MFA) is covered here to ensure your cloud environment is as secure as possible. An Azure Solutions Architect might face all these situations in day-to-day work life and needs to be ready for each of them.

Skills covered in this chapter:

- Skill 2.1: Manage workloads in Azure
- Skill 2.2: Implement disaster recovery using Azure Site Recovery
- Skill 2.3: Implement application infrastructure
- Skill 2.4: Manage security for applications
- Skill 2.5: Implement application load balancing and network security
- Skill 2.6: Integrate an Azure virtual network and an on-premises network
- Skill 2.7: Implement and manage Azure governance solutions
- Skill 2.8: Implement multifactor authentication (MFA)

Skill 2.1: Manage workloads in Azure

Because most organizations have been operating on infrastructure running in house, there is a significant opportunity to help them migrate these workloads to Azure, which might save some costs and provide efficiencies for these servers that their datacenters might not. Also, some organizations might want to explore getting out of the datacenter business. How can you help your organization or customer move out of a datacenter into the Azure cloud?

The recommended tool for this is Azure Migrate, which offers different options depending on the type of workload you're migrating (physical or virtual). Azure Site Recovery has not gone away, though it is used primarily for disaster-recovery scenarios where Azure is the target for disaster recovery. See Skill 2-2, "Implement disaster recovery using Azure Site Recovery," for more info.

This skill covers:

- Configure the components of Azure Migrate
- Migrate Virtual Machines to Azure
- Migrate data to Azure
- Migrate web applications
- Configure the components needed to migrate databases to Azure SQL or an Azure SQL–managed instance

Configure the components of Azure Migrate

Azure Migrate uses migration projects to assess and manage any inbound migration of workloads to Azure. To create a migration project and get started, follow these steps:

1. Determine the workload type to migrate:
   - **Servers.** Virtual or physical servers
   - **Databases.** On-premises databases
   - **VDI.** Virtual Desktop Infrastructure
   - **Web Apps.** Web-based applications
   - **Data Box.** Offline data migration to Azure
2. Add the tools for the selected migration to create a Migrate Project
3. Perform a migration of the selected workloads to Azure

Azure Migrate Assessment Tools

Before executing the migration of any workload to Azure, with the exception of a Data Box migration, the assessment of the current status of on-premises resources will help determine the type of Azure resources needed, as well as the cost to migrate them to Azure.

There are two assessment tools for migrating servers to Azure:

- **Azure Migrate Server Assessment.** This service has been the built-in assessment tool for some time and has roots in Site Recovery. It will discover and review VMware, Hyper-V, and physical servers to determine if they are ready and able to make the transition to Azure.

- **Movere.** This assessment tool was a third-party company until late 2019, which was acquired by Microsoft to broaden the tools available for getting resources into Azure. With the assessments performed by Movere, an agent is loaded within the on-premises environment and scans are performed to determine the volume of servers in the environment. Additional information, including SQL Server instances, SharePoint instances, and other applications, are also reported by Movere.

In addition to server assessments, Azure Migrate has tools to review existing web applications with the Web App Migration Assistant and on-premises SQL Server databases with the Database Migration Service. The assessment for SQL Server will also review the fit of the databases discovered within the three Azure offerings for SQL Server: Azure SQL Database, Managed Instance SQL, and SQL Server running on VMs in Azure.

> ***NOTE*** **AZURE SQL ADDITIONAL FIXES MAY BE REQUIRED**
>
> **When migrating SQL databases, there might be additional steps identified by the assessment that need to be remedied based on the destination implementation of the chosen SQL. In our experience, Azure SQL Database will have the most items for review because it is the most different (and potentially feature-restricted) option.**

Azure Migrate Server Assessment Tool

The Server Assessment Tool provides the following information to help your organization make the best decisions when preparing to move resources to Azure:

- **Azure Readiness.** This tool determines if the servers discovered on-premises are good candidates for moving to Azure.
- **Azure Sizing.** This tool estimates the size of a virtual machine once it has migrated to Azure, based on the existing specifications of the on-premises server.
- **Azure Cost Estimation.** This server assessment tool will help to estimate the run rate for machines that are migrated to Azure.

No agents are required by the Server Assessment tool. Server assessment is configured as an appliance and runs on a dedicated VM or physical server in the environment being evaluated.

Once an environment has been scanned for assessment, administrators can review the findings of the tool and group servers for specific projects or lifecycles. (The grouping of servers is done after assessment.) Then, groups of servers can be evaluated for migration to Azure.

When reviewing server groups for migration, be sure to consider things like connectivity to Azure and any dependencies that applications or servers being moved may have.

To complete a server environment assessment, perform the following steps:

1. Locate Azure Migrate within the Azure Portal.
2. Create an Azure Migrate resource from the Azure portal by selecting **Assess and Migrate Servers** on the **Overview** blade, as shown in Figure 2-1.

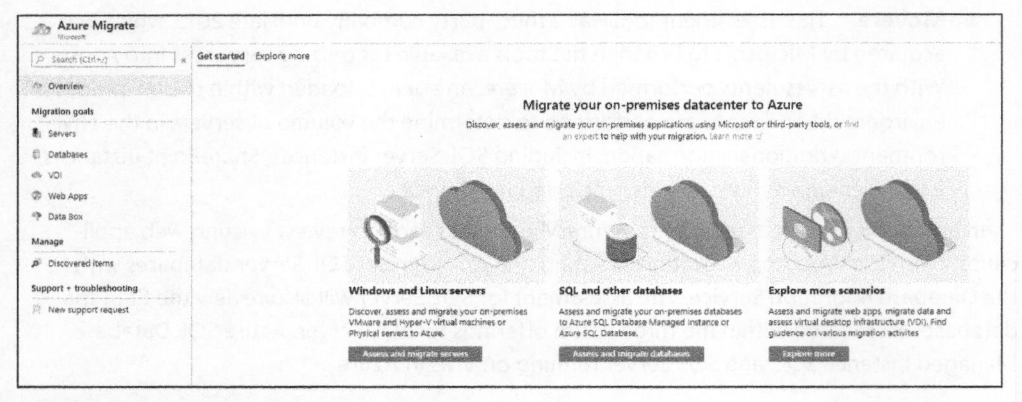

FIGURE 2-1 Choosing Assess And Migrate Servers

3. Select **Add Tool(s)** to create a project and select assessment and migration tools, as shown in Figure 2-2.

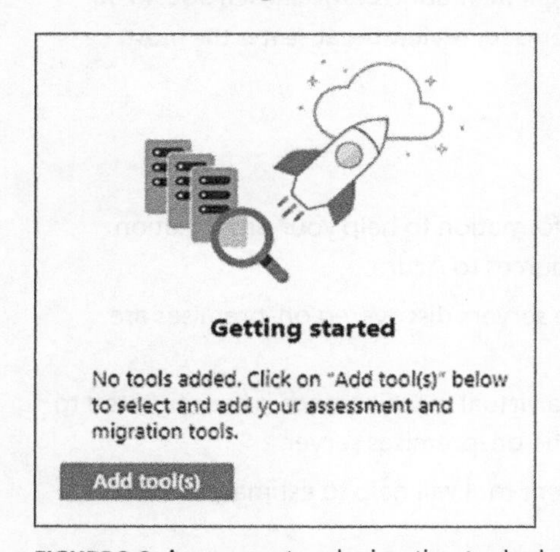

FIGURE 2-2 Assessment and migration tool selection

4. Enter the details required for the migration project for servers, as shown in Figure 2-3.
5. Select a **Subscription**.
6. Select a **Resource Group**.
7. Enter a name for the Azure Migrate project.

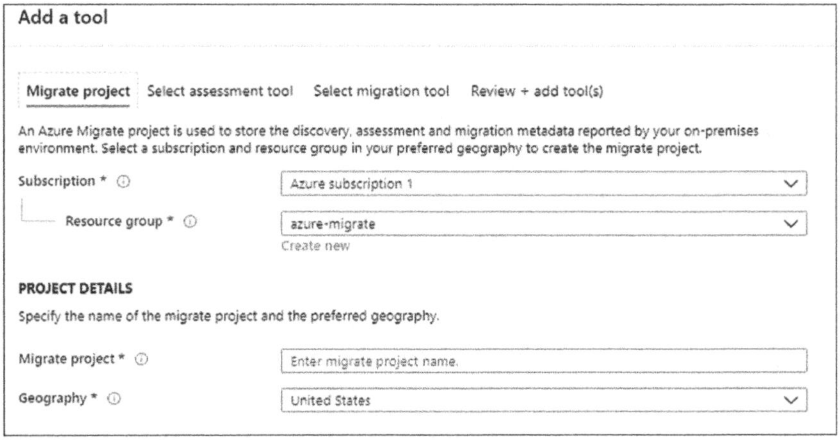

Add a tool

Migrate project Select assessment tool Select migration tool Review + add tool(s)

An Azure Migrate project is used to store the discovery, assessment and migration metadata reported by your on-premises environment. Select a subscription and resource group in your preferred geography to create the migrate project.

Subscription * Azure subscription 1

Resource group * azure-migrate

Create new

PROJECT DETAILS

Specify the name of the migrate project and the preferred geography.

Migrate project * Enter migrate project name.

Geography * United States

FIGURE 2-3 Details for configuration of server migration project

8. Select the **Azure Migrate: Server Assessment** tool and click **Next**, as shown in Figure 2-4.

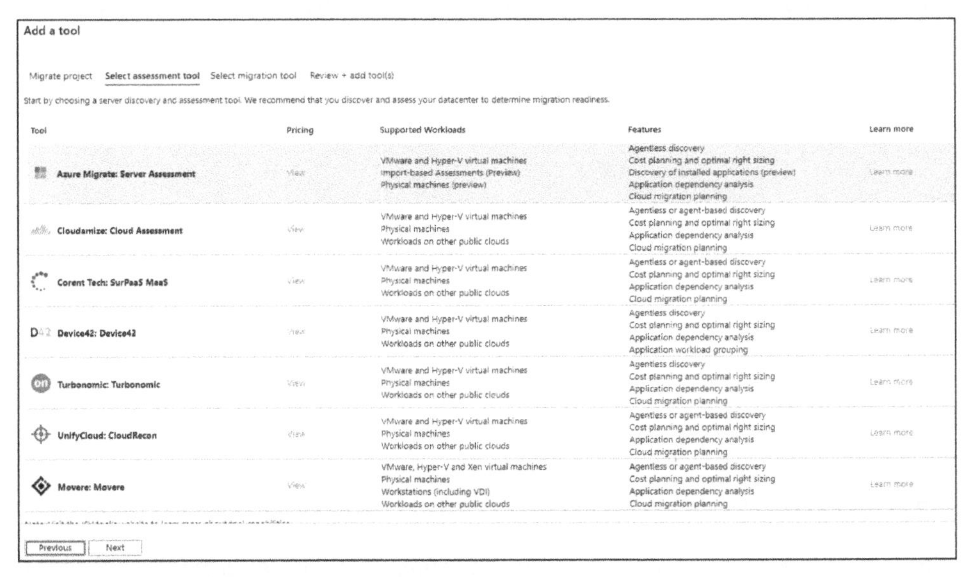

FIGURE 2-4 Tools for server assessment to Azure

9. Select the **Skip Adding A Migration Tool For Now** check box and click **Next**, as shown in Figure 2-5.

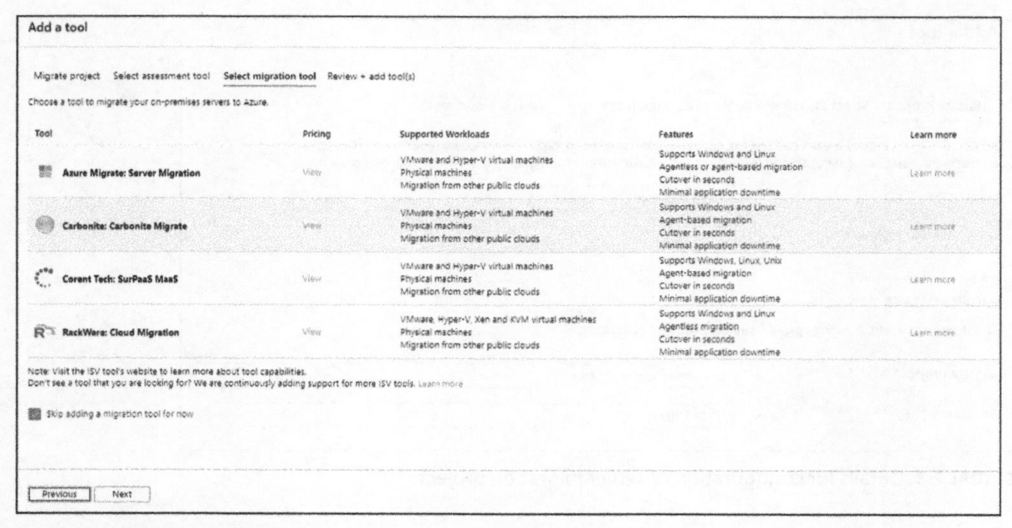

FIGURE 2-5 Server migration tools

10. Review the assessment selections made and click **Add Tool(s)**, as shown in Figure 2-6.

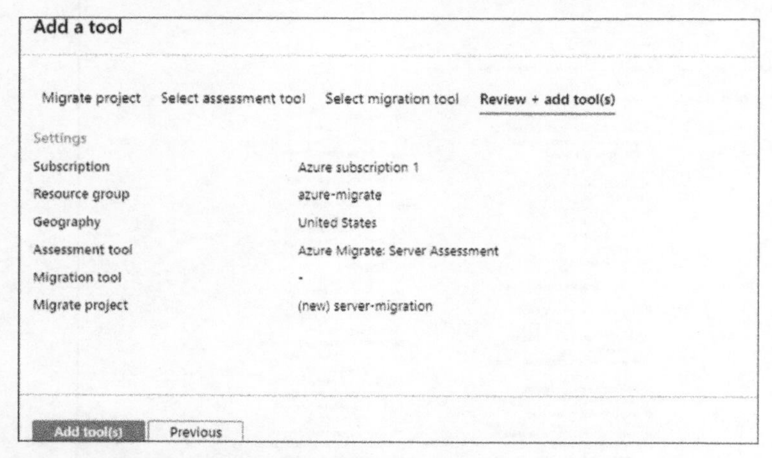

FIGURE 2-6 Review choices and continue

11. Once the assessment tool has been chosen in Azure, additional setup of the appliance is necessary.
12. Click **Discover** under **Assessment Tools**. The **Azure Migrate: Server Assessment** dialog box shown in Figure 2-7 below.

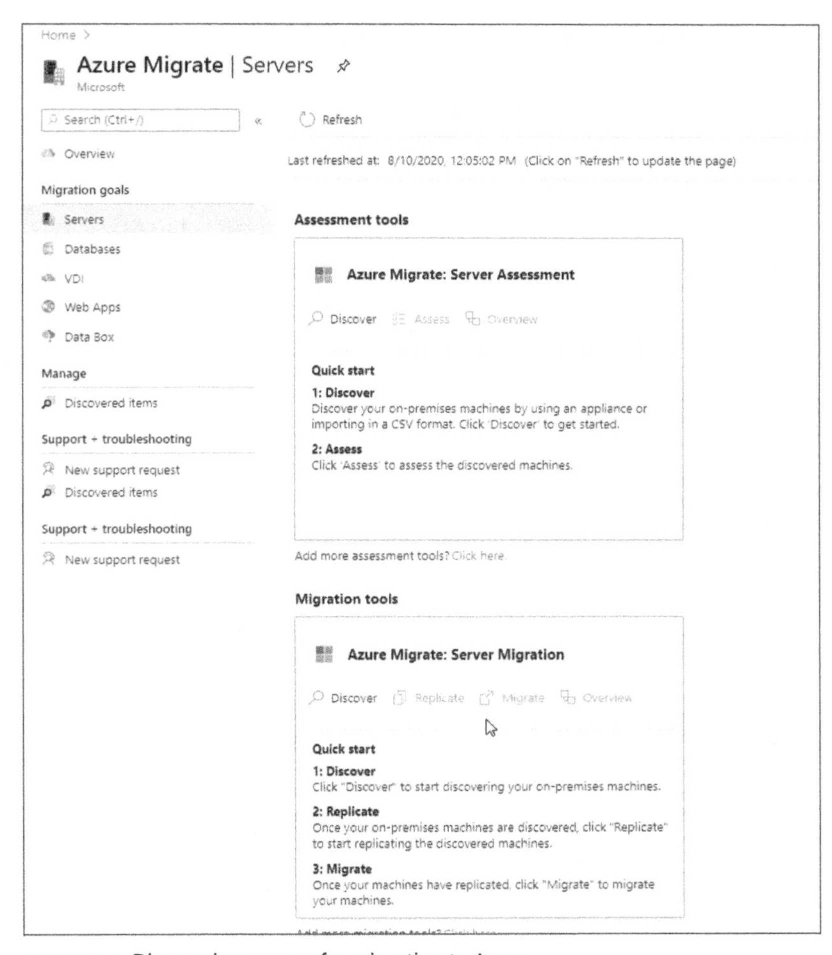

FIGURE 2-7 Discovering servers for migration to Azure

13. To use an appliance, select **Discover Using Appliance**, as shown in Figure 2-8.

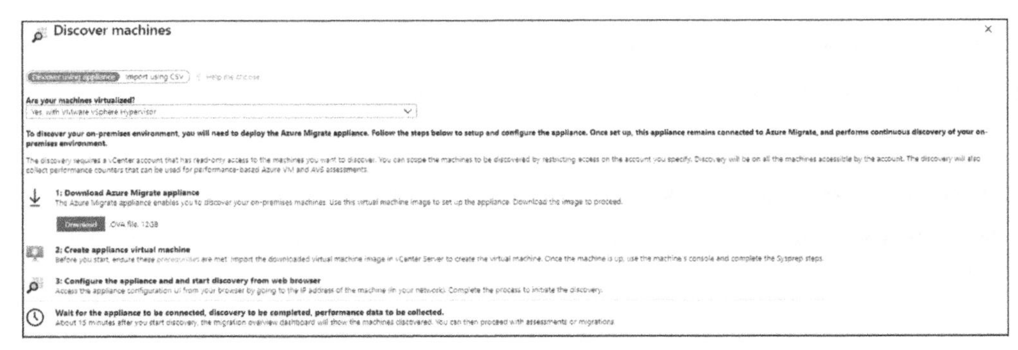

FIGURE 2-8 Discovering servers using a self-hosted appliance

14. Choose the hypervisor type used in the environment: **Hyper-V**, **VMware**, or **Physical Servers**.
15. Download the appliance and install it in the environment.
16. Using a browser, visit the IP address of the appliance, configure it to reach the Azure Migrate project, and then start discovery.

After about 15 minutes, machines that are discovered will begin to appear in the Azure Migrate Discovery Dashboard.

You can also complete a CSV template, which supplies the details of your environment, and then upload it to the Azure Migrate project if you would rather not use the discovery appliance. This is shown in Figure 2-9.

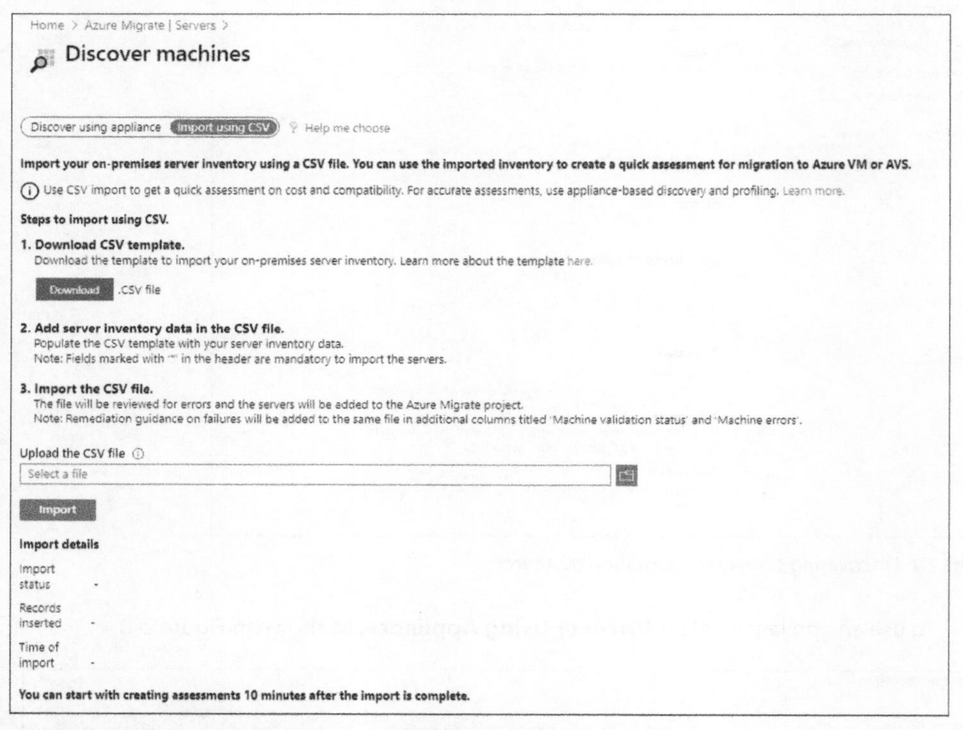

FIGURE 2-9 CSV template download to provide information about environment

> ***NOTE*** **ASSESSMENT AND MIGRATION – BETTER TOGETHER**
>
> **Assessment and migration are discussed together here because the same tool is used for both operations.**

To complete a web app assessment and migration, complete the following steps:

1. Inside the existing Azure Migrate project, select **Web Apps** from the **Migration Goals** section of the navigation bar.
2. Select **Add Tool(s)** and choose the **Azure Migrate: Web App Assessment** tool, as shown in Figure 2-10.

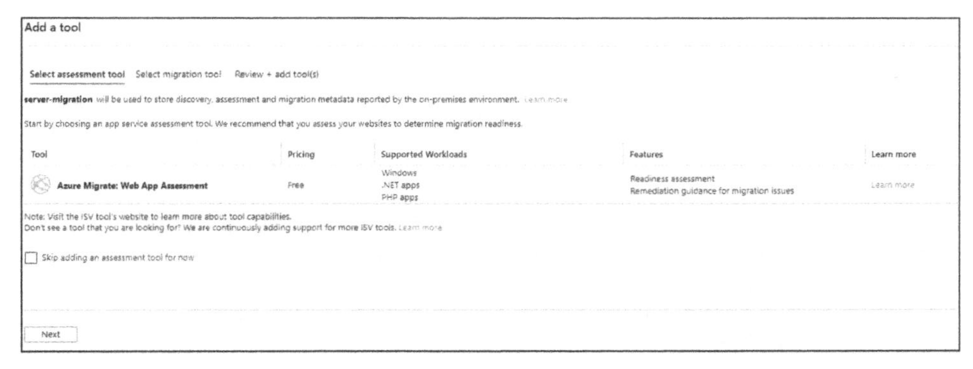

FIGURE 2-10 Adding Azure Migrate: Web App Assessment tool

3. Click **Next**.
4. Select the **Skip Adding A Migration Tool** check box and click **Next**.
5. After reviewing the configuration, click **Add Tool(s)**.
6. Once the web app assessment tool has been added, download the Azure App Service Migration Assistant to assess internal web applications. If the application has a public URL, it can be scanned via the public Internet.
7. Install the assessment tool on any web servers containing applications for migration. IIS 7.5 and administrator access on the server(s) are the minimum requirements to complete an assessment. Currently, PHP and .NET apps are supported for migration, with more application types coming soon.
8. The migration tool will determine whether the selected websites are ready to migrate to Azure, as shown in Figure 2-11.

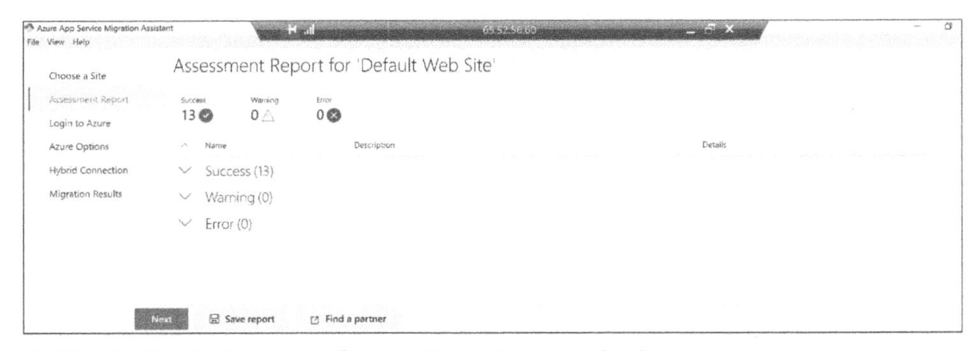

FIGURE 2-11 Website Assessment for migration to Azure App Services

9. Once the assessment tool has reviewed the chosen web applications, click **Next** to log in to Azure using the provided device code and link provided in the wizard, show in Figure 2-12.

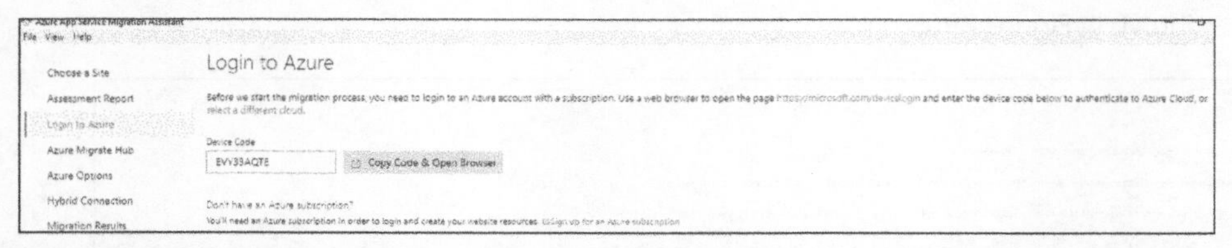

FIGURE 2-12 Use the link provided to open a browser and log in to your Azure Migrate project

10. Click Azure Options in the left-side navigation pane and set the **Subscription**, **Resource Group**, **Destination Site Name**, **App Service Plan**, **Region**, **Azure Migrate Project**, and **Databases** options, as shown in Figure 2-13.

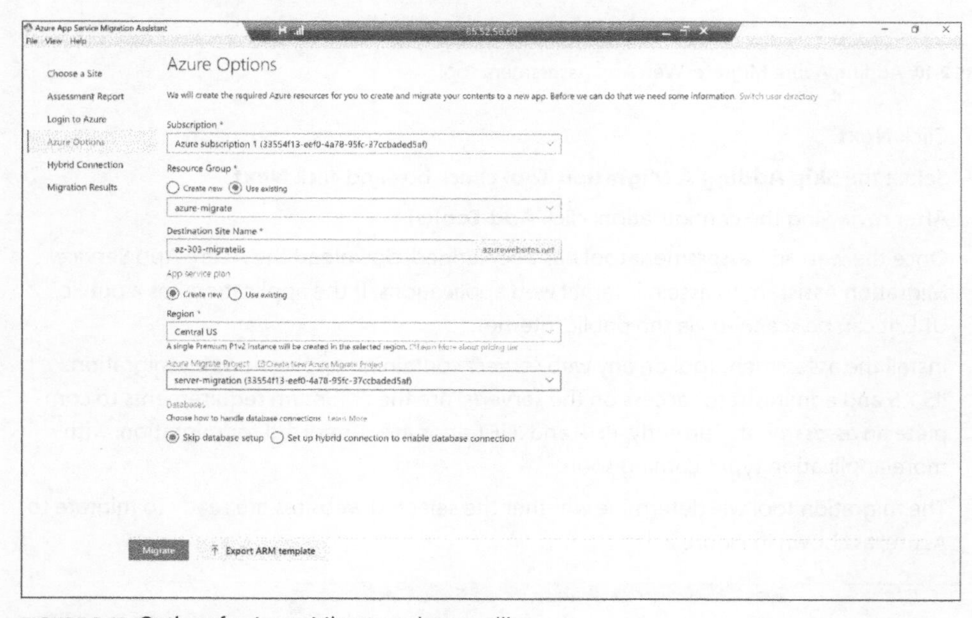

FIGURE 2-13 Options for Azure Migrate web app utility

11. If your application has a database back end, select the **Set Up Hybrid Connection To Enable Database Connection** option and enter the name of the on-premises database server and the port on which to connect in the On-Premises Database Server field shown when the option is selected.
12. Click **Migrate** to migrate the application as is or click the **Export ARM Template** button on the **Azure Options** screen to produce the JSON-based ARM template for the application for later deployment to Azure.
13. The migration progress is shown in Figure 2-14. You will also be able to see the resources once they are migrated in the Azure portal.

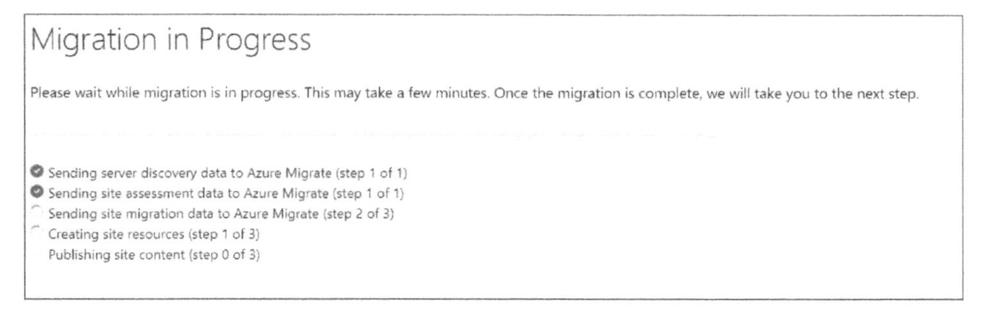

FIGURE 2-14 Migration in process

Complete a SQL database assessment and migration using the following steps:

1. Within the Azure Migrate project, select **Databases** > **Add Tool(s)**.
2. Select the **Azure Migrate: Database Assessment** tool and click **Next**, as shown in Figure 2-15.

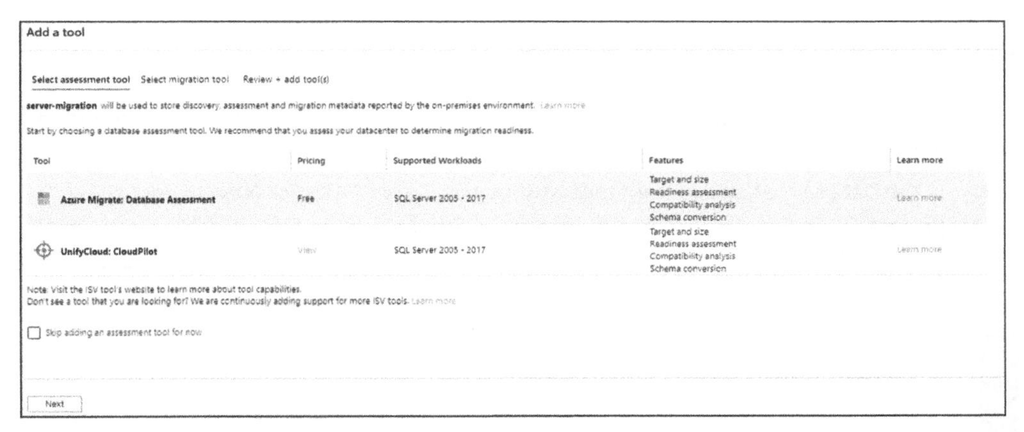

FIGURE 2-15 Database Assessment tool selection in Azure Migrate

3. To proceed with a migration if the assessment produces the expected outcome, select the **Azure Migrate: Database Migration** tool.
4. If you are assessing production workloads and/or extremely large databases, select the **Skip Adding A Migration Tool For Now** check box to allow further review of the assessment to correct any issues found.
5. Once the tools have been added to the migration project, as shown in Figure 2-16, click the **Download** link to download the Database Migration Assessment tool to start the assessment.

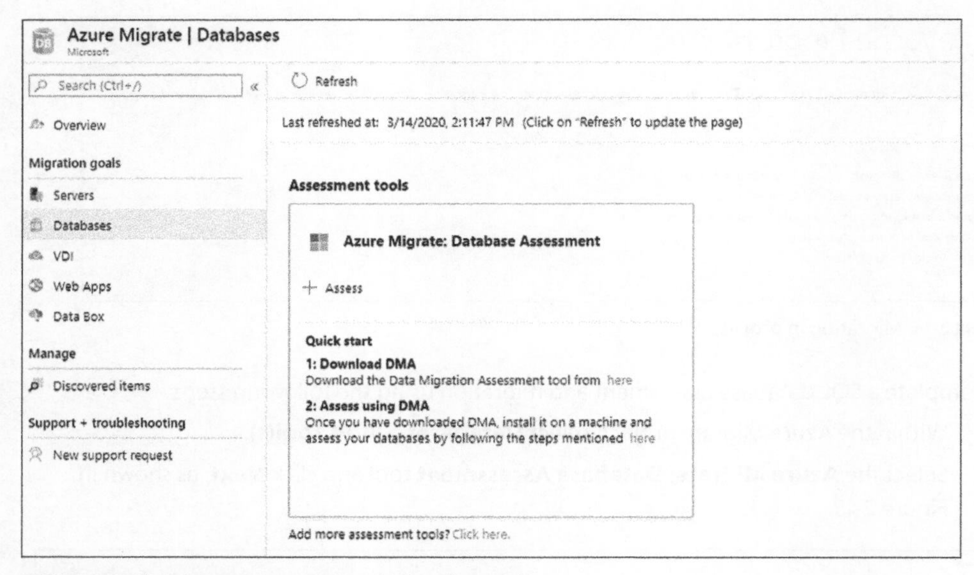

FIGURE 2-16 Database Assessment and Migration tools

6. Install and run the Data Migration Assistant Tool on the SQL server(s) to be migrated to Azure.
7. In the Data Migration Assistant tool, as shown in Figure 2-17, click **New** to add a new project.

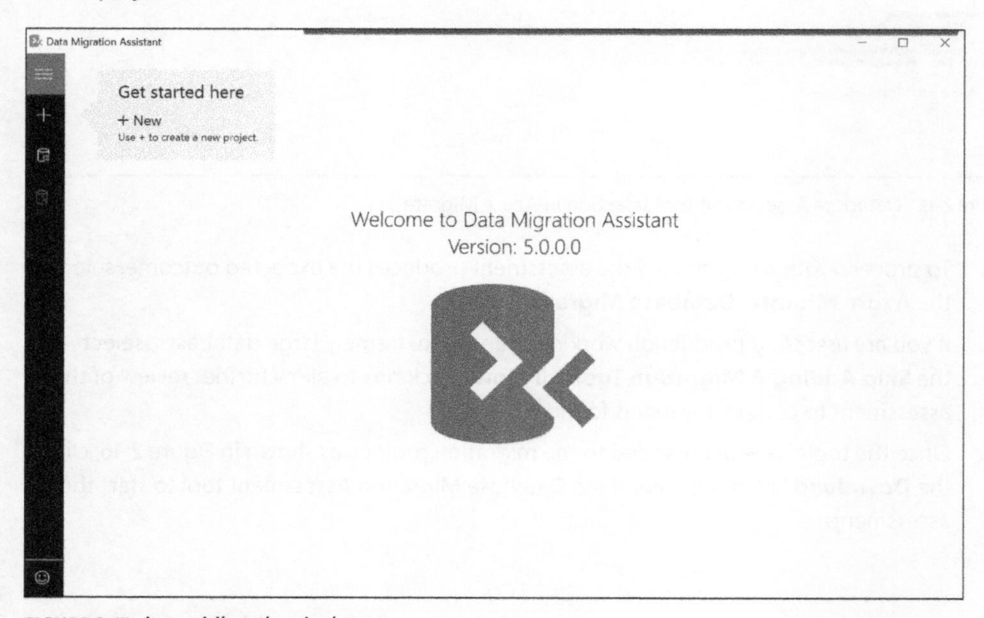

FIGURE 2-17 Azure Migration Assistant

8. Enter a name for the project and select the following for the SQL server data being migrated:
   - **Assessment Type.** Choose either database engine or integration services.
   - **Source Server Type.** Choose either SQL Server or AWS RDS For SQL Server.
   - **Target Server Type.** Choose from Azure SQL Database, Azure SQL Database Managed Instance, SQL Server On Azure Virtual Machines, or SQL Server.
9. On the **Options** screen within the created project, following are the selected (and default) options:
   - **Check Database Compatibility.** This will check an existing database for any issues that would prevent it from running in Azure SQL.
   - **Check Feature Parity.** This option looks for unsupported features in the source database.
10. Select the SQL server(s) and choose the appropriate authentication method(s) for the SQL server:
    - **Windows Authentication.** Use the currently logged-in Windows credentials to connect.
    - **SQL Server Authentication.** Use specific credentials stored in the SQL server to connect.
    - **Active Directory Integrated Authentication.** Use the logged-in Active Directory user for authentication.
    - **Active Directory Password Authentication.** Use a specific Active Directory user or service account to authenticate.
11. Select the properties for the connection:
    - **Encrypt connection.** Check this box if the SQL Server (and/or your organization's information security team) requires connections to be encrypted.
    - **Trust Server Certificate.** If the SQL Server is using certificates, the Data Migration Assistant can trust these certificates to simplify future connections.
12. Click **Connect**.
13. From the list of databases found, select any that should be included in the assessment, as shown in Figure 2-18.
14. Click **Add**.

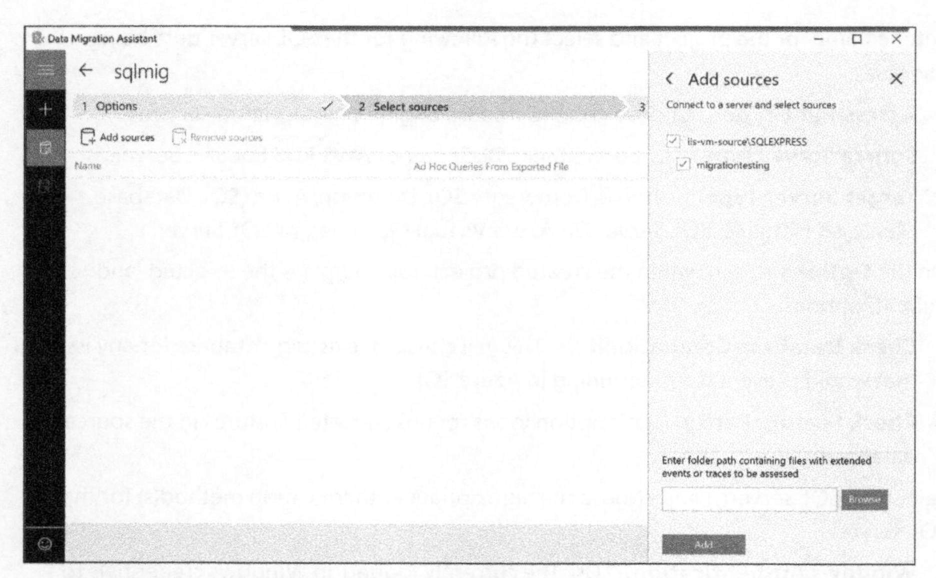

FIGURE 2-18 Include selected databases in Assessment

15. Once the databases are added to the assessment, if there are log files or extended events to include, click **Browse** to locate and include them, as shown in Figure 2-19.

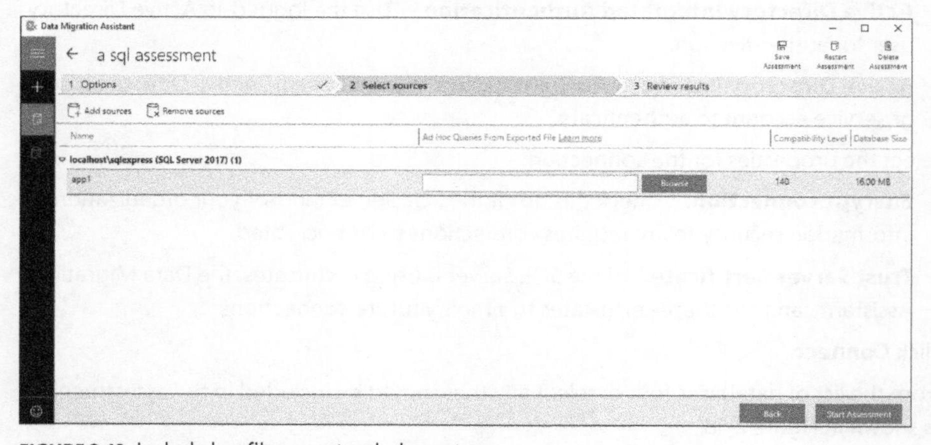

FIGURE 2-19 Include log files or extended events

16. Review the assessment for both feature parity and compatibility and fix any issues found. If there are discrepancies, they will need to be resolved before the migration can proceed.

> ***NOTE*** **SOME ITEMS MAY REQUIRE ADDITIONAL WORK**
>
> **The assessment will return items that are unsupported by Azure SQL but are in use within the source database(s). It will also find any compatibility issues within the data in the source database. These items will need to be remedied before migrating the data to Azure SQL.**

17. Click **Upload To Azure**.
18. You will be prompted to sign in if you are not already signed in on the computer where the assessment is running.
19. Select the **Subscription** and **Resource Group** and then click **Upload**.

Migrating information is straightforward as well, though there must be an existing Azure SQL database in which to migrate the SQL data. You should create this Azure SQL database beforehand because the tools will not build Azure SQL or other types of SQL in Azure as part of the process.

To complete a migration after the assessment of SQL databases, complete the following steps:

1. In the Data Migration Assessment tool, select the **Migrations** option.
2. Specify the source SQL instance and log-in method.
3. Specify the target Azure SQL Server name and credentials, and then click **Connect**.

> ***NOTE*** **ACCESS REQUIRED TO PROCEED**
>
> **You will need to ensure the system where the migration is running has access to the Azure SQL DB by allowing access from the IP address of the client within the Azure SQL Server networking details.**

4. Select the database to migrate and click **Next**, as shown in Figure 2-20.

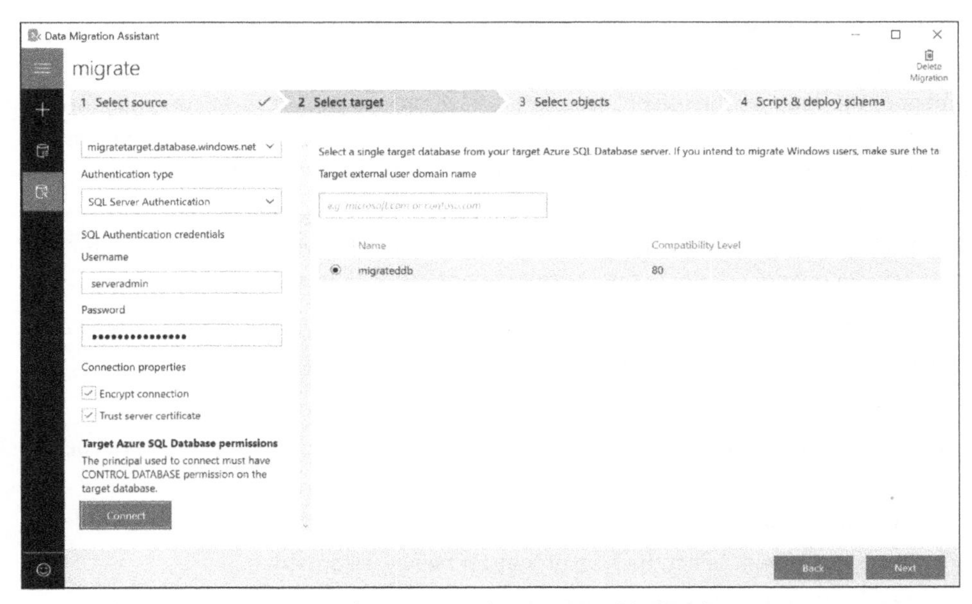

FIGURE 2-20 Connect to Azure to migrate source data to Azure SQL Database

5. Once the preparation completes and has been reviewed, click **Generate SQL Script** to create a script. A generated script is shown in Figure 2-21.

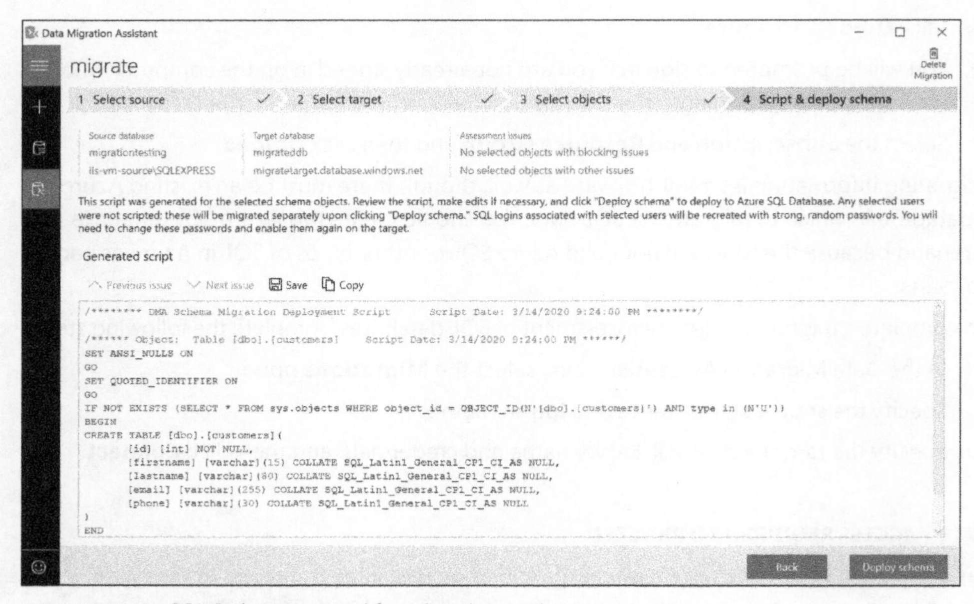

FIGURE 2-21 An SQL Script generated for migration work

6. To push this data to a specified instance of Azure SQL Database using the Data Migration Assistant, click **Deploy Schema**.

Migrate virtual desktop infrastructure to Azure

Azure Migrate also allows you to bring virtual desktop infrastructure (VDI) into Azure. The assessment of VDI requires the use of Lakeside: Systrack, a third-party tool, to complete the assessment of VDI environments. The migration process, however, follows the same path as a server migration, allowing workloads from VMware or Hyper-V to be migrated.

Azure Data Box allows offline migration of existing data to Azure. The Data Box itself is a ruggedized NAS that is capable of storing up to 100 TB of data with AES 256 encryption for transporting your data physically to the Azure datacenter(s) for ingestion.

To complete a Data Box offline migration of workloads to Azure, complete the following steps:

1. From within an Azure Migrate project, select **Data Box** as the **Migration Goal**.
2. Provide the following details about the data being ingested:
   - **Subscription.** Select the name of the Azure Subscription where the data will be transferred.
   - **Resource Group.** Select the resource group where the data will be transferred.
   - **Transfer Type.** Select the type of transfer being performed.
   - **Source Country/Region.** Select the country or region where the data lives today.
   - **Destination Azure Region.** Select the region in Azure where the data should reside after transfer.

3. Click **Apply**.
4. Select the appropriate Data Box option for your migration, as shown in Figure 2-22.

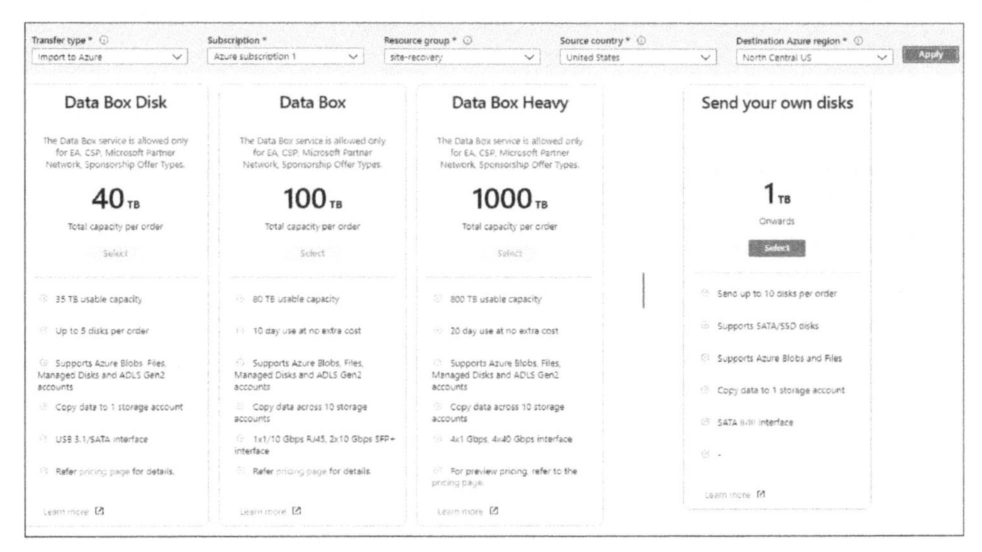

FIGURE 2-22 Select the appropriate Data Box size for your migration

Note that Data Box disks provided by Microsoft are only allowed with the following subscription offers:

- **EA.** Enterprise Agreement
- **CSP.** Cloud solution provider partnership
- **Microsoft Partner Network.** Partner organizations
- **Sponsorship.** A limited, invite-only Azure subscription offer provided by Microsoft

If you do not have an offer tied to your Azure subscription that meets the above requirements to use a provided Data Box, you can send in data on your own disks. If you provide your own disk, the following requirements apply:

- Up to 10 disks per order
- 1 TB per disk
- Copying data to one storage account
- $80 per disk import fee

These Data Box options are for offline transfers to Azure. Using the Data Box Gateway, a virtual appliance within your environment, will perform an online data migration to Azure.

5. Once you have selected a disk option, you will be able to configure the options for your environment (see Figure 2-22). You will choose the following options shown in figure 2-23:
   - **Type.** Import to or export from Azure.
   - **Name.** The name of the job to identify it to Azure.

- **Subscription.** Select the subscription for the job.
- **Resource Group.** Select an existing resource group or create a new one for the job.

6. After clicking **Next: Job Details**, you will supply the following information, shown in Figure 2-24:
    - **Upload Journal Files.** Specify the path to the journal file for each drive being used for import.
    - **Import Destination.** Specify a storage account to consume ingested data and the region the data will be stored in.
    - **Provide Return Shipping Information.** Specify the name and address details to allow your disk to be returned along with carrier information as shown in Figure 2-24.

Review and confirm your choices.

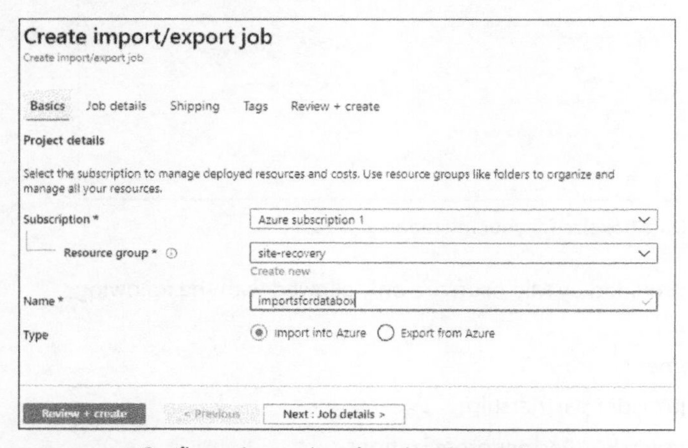

FIGURE 2-23 Configuration options for migration environment

FIGURE 2-24 Provide job details

If you have shipped your own drives for this process, you will need to supply return information.

NOTE **ONLY OPTION**

Supplying your own drives is the only option available for some Azure subscription types.

As discussed above, if you are not using a EA,CSP, Partner, Sponsorship subscription in Azure, or one with a special offer designation, you might be required to use your own drive(s) with Data Box. If that is the case, return shipping information is required, as shown in Figure 2-25.

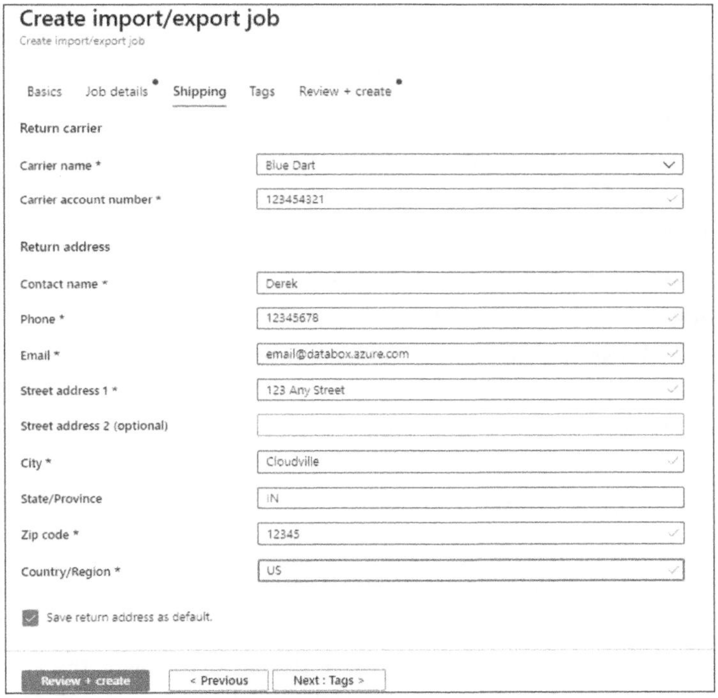

Create import/export job
Create import/export job
Basics Job details Shipping Tags Review + create
Return carrier
Carrier name * Blue Dart
Carrier account number * 123454321
Return address
Contact name * Derek
Phone * 12345678
Email * email@databox.azure.com
Street address 1 * 123 Any Street
Street address 2 (optional)
City * Cloudville
State/Province IN
Zip code * 12345
Country/Region * US
Save return address as default.
Review + create < Previous Next : Tags >

FIGURE 2-25 Return shipping information

There are other assessment and migration tools such as Movere or other third-party tools. These tools might require additional spend to assess your environment. Movere is free and can be used as part of this process because it was acquired by Microsoft, but this book focuses on the Azure tools for assessment and migration.

Implementing Azure Update Management

An organization that is seeking to move workloads to the cloud is probably (hopefully) already ensuring these servers are patched regularly and kept as close to truly up to date as their governance and infosec organizations will allow. Migrating a server to Azure does not necessarily remove this burden from server administration teams. The last thing to cover in this section on workload management and migration is managing updates in the cloud. As you might expect, Azure has a method for that, and here, we will look at the implementation of this feature set.

> ***NOTE*** **IF IT IS WORKING, MAYBE IT SHOULD STAY WORKING**
>
> **Just because Azure brings an update management tool to the party does not mean it will be the best patch management strategy for your organization. In the event your organization has mostly Windows domain-joined systems or a well-oiled strategy for patching Linux, there might be no reason for you to change the way things are. Sure, you should evaluate the situation, but make sure the new tools fit the needs of your organization.**

To configure Azure Update Management, complete the following steps:

1. Log in to the Azure portal and navigate to a running virtual machine.
2. In the **Operations** section of the left navigation menu for the VM, select **Update Management**.
3. Supply the following information:
   - **Log Analytics Workspace Location.** Select the region for the account.
   - **Log Analytics Workspace.** Choose (or create) a log analytics workspace.
   - **Automation Account Subscription.** Select the Azure subscription to house this resource.
   - **Automation Account.** Choose or create an automation account for Update Management.
4. Click **Enable** and wait for the deployment to complete (between 5 and 15 minutes).

> ***NOTE*** **BE PATIENT WITH DATA COLLECTION**
>
> **Once the solution is enabled, the solution will need to collect data about your system(s) to help ensure the best update management plan. This can take several hours to complete. The Azure portal dialog box recommends allowing this to run overnight.**

5. Once the solution has finished onboarding virtual machines, revisiting the **Update Management** blade for one or more VMs will display information as it becomes available.
6. Selecting the **Update Agent** readiness troubleshooter will help determine which items might interfere with the use of the Update Management solution (see Figure 2-26).

Troubleshoot Update Agent

server-to-dr

Click the button below to run a troubleshooting utility in the Azure VM. This uses the RunCommand API. The results will be available in about a minute.

Run checks

Troubleshooting documentation

Prerequisite Checks

Check	Result	Details
Operating system	Passed	Operating system version is supported.
.Net Framework 4.5+	Passed	.NET Framework version 4.5+ is found.
WMF 5.1	Passed	Detected Windows Management Framework version: 5.1.14393.3471.
TLS 1.2	Passed	TLS 1.2 is enabled by default on the operating system.

Connectivity Checks

Check	Result	Details
Registration endpoint	Passed	TCP test for 5ac509ad-1b73-4c40-8ebf-184009c6ba2a.agentsvc.azure-automation.net (port 443) succeeded.
Operations endpoint	Passed	TCP test for eus2-jobruntimedata-prod-su1.azure-automation.net (port 443) succeeded.

Monitoring Agent Service Health Checks

Check	Result	Details
Monitoring Agent service status	Passed	Microsoft Monitoring Agent service (HealthService) is running.
Monitoring Agent service events	Passed	Microsoft Monitoring Agent service Event Log (Operations Manager) does not have Error event 4502 logged in the last 24 hours.

Access Permission Checks

Check	Result	Details
MachineKeys folder access	Passed	Permissions exist to access C:\ProgramData\Microsoft\Crypto\RSA\MachineKeys.

Machine Update Settings

Check	Result	Details
Automatically reboot after install	Passed	Windows Update reboot registry keys are not set to automatically reboot
WSUS Server Configuration	Passed	Windows Updates are downloading from the default Windows Update location. Ensure the server has access to the Windows Update service
Automatically download and install	Passed with warning	Auto Update is enabled on the machine and will interfere with Update management Solution

FIGURE 2-26 Update Agent Readiness configuration

7. If your VM is running Windows Auto Update, you will want to disable it before proceeding with Update Management in Azure.

Once the onboarding process has completed and after waiting for configuration to complete, visit the **Update Management** blade for a VM to see the **Missing Updates** for the system, which are broken out by **Critical**, **Security**, and **Others**, as shown in Figure 2-27.

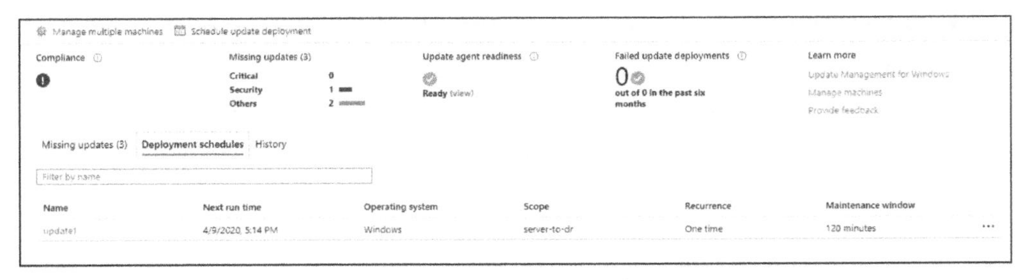

FIGURE 2-27 Security fixes needed before migration can proceed

Selecting an update from the **Missing Updates** list will open Log Analytics and insert a query looking for that update; running the query will display the update as a result.

When a server has onboarded into Update Management, it can be patched by configuring a schedule for update deployment. To do that, complete the following steps:

1. From the **Update Management** blade, click **Schedule Update Deployment**.
2. Enter the following information about the schedule:
   - **Name.** A name for the deployment.
   - **Update Classification.** The update types to be included.
   - **Include/Exclude Updates.** Optionally, select the updates to include or exclude.
   - **Schedule Settings.** When the deployment should happen.
   - **Pre/Post Scripts.** Any scripts that should run before or after deployment.
   - **Maintenance Window.** Specify the length of the maintenance window for deploying updates.
   - **Reboot Options.** Choose the reboot options for the update(s).
3. Click **Create** on the update deployment schedule.

The deployment that has been scheduled will be listed on the **Deployment Schedule** tab. Also, any deployments will be defaulted to 30 minutes after the current time to allow the schedule to push to Azure.

After these items are configured, the updates will be applied as per the schedule that has been set up.

This section took a high-level overview covering the various types of migrations to Azure using built-in Azure tools. As this technology changes and Azure evolves, this will surely expand.

NEED MORE REVIEW? **AZURE MIGRATE**

Check out these resources:

- **Azure Migrate Guidelinesfor Hyper-V.** *https://docs.microsoft.com/en-us/azure/migrate/migrate-support-matrix-Hyper-V#assessment-appliance-requirements*
- **Azure Migrate Overview.** *https://docs.microsoft.com/en-us/azure/migrate/*
- **Update Management Solution in Azure.** *https://docs.microsoft.com/en-us/azure/automation/update-management/overview*
- **An Overview of Azure VM Backup.** *https://docs.microsoft.com/en-us/azure/backup/backup-azure-vms-introduction*

Skill 2.2: Implement disaster recovery using Azure Site Recovery

With the growing number of organizations moving to Azure, one of the first things that comes to mind is leveraging the cloud as a target for disaster recovery. If an organization has an existing co-location for DR data, Azure can provide some or all the services needed to replace this secondary (or multiple secondary) datacenter(s). In this section, the use and configuration of Azure Site Recovery are covered.

NOTE **BEFORE THERE WAS MIGRATE, THERE WAS SITE RECOVERY**

Before Azure Migrate, Azure Site Recovery was the Microsoft solution for both disaster recovery and migration of servers to Azure.

This skill covers:

- Configure Azure components of Site Recovery
- Configure on-premises components of Site Recovery
- Replicate data to Azure
- Migrate by using Azure Site Recovery

Configure Azure components of Site Recovery

Azure Site Recovery provides a way to leverage the scale of Azure while allowing Resources to be failed back to your on-premises datacenter should the need arise as part of a business continuity and disaster recovery (BCDR) scenario. Since the introduction of Azure Migrate and the additional workloads covered previously in this chapter, Site Recovery has become the primary disaster recovery tool for use with Azure.

Follow these steps to configure the Azure resources to use Site Recovery for DR to Azure:

NOTE **CONSIDER CREATING THE AZURE RESOURCES FIRST**

Creating the Azure resources first prepares the destination and ensures that nothing is missed. Because the process moves files into Azure, this can minimize issues when the transfer begins because the target resources will be identified up front.

1. Log in to your Azure subscription.
2. Create a resource group to hold your Azure Backup Vault.

3. Create a new resource and select **Backup And Site Recovery** from the **Storage** grouping in the **Azure Marketplace**, as shown in Figure 2-28.

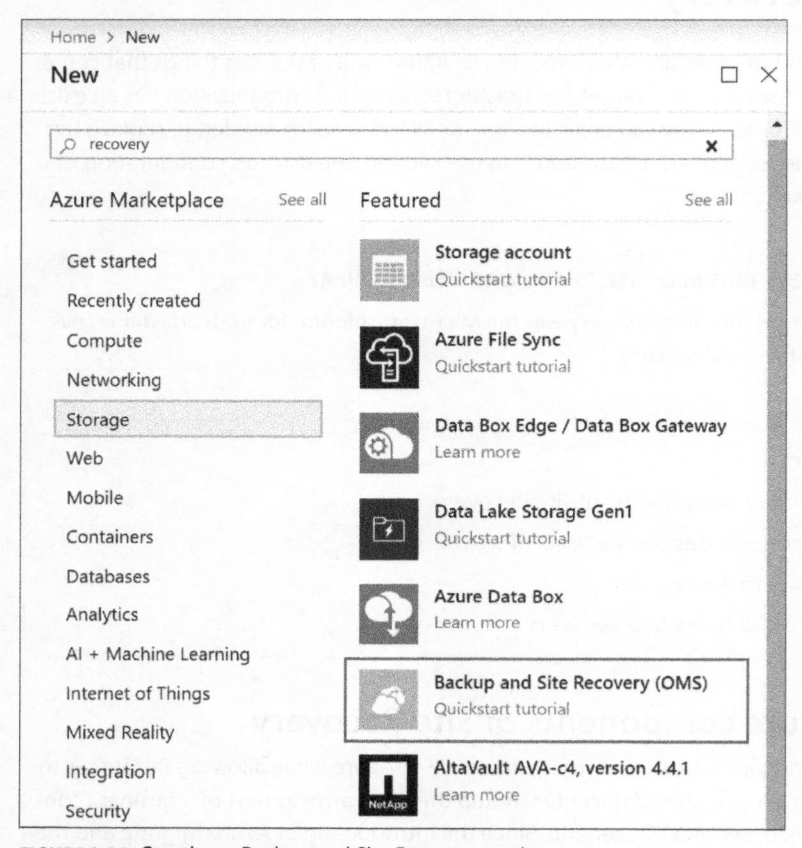

FIGURE 2-28 Creating a Backup and Site Recovery vault

4. In the Recovery Services **Vault Creation** blade shown in Figure 2-29 complete the form:
   - **Subscription.** Specify an active Azure subscription.
   - **Resource Group.** Create a new resource group or select an existing resource group for the Recovery Services vault.
   - **Name.** Choose a unique name for your Recovery Services vault.
   - **Location.** Select the region to use for the Recovery Services vault.
5. Click the **Create** button to build the resource, which may take a few moments to complete.

> ***NOTE*** **FEATURE NAME CHANGES HAPPEN AT CLOUD SPEED, TOO**
>
> **Backup and Site Recovery is the new name for the Recovery Services vault resource. As of this writing, the names have not been updated throughout the portal.**

FIGURE 2-29 Creating a Recovery Services vault

Once the Recovery Services vault is ready, open the **Overview** page by clicking the resource within the resource group. This page provides some high-level information, including any new things related to Recovery Services vault.

Configure on-premises components of Site Recovery

Use the following steps to get started with a site recovery (migration in this case):

1. Click the **Site Recovery** link under **Getting Started** in the **Settings** pane, as shown in Figure 2-30.

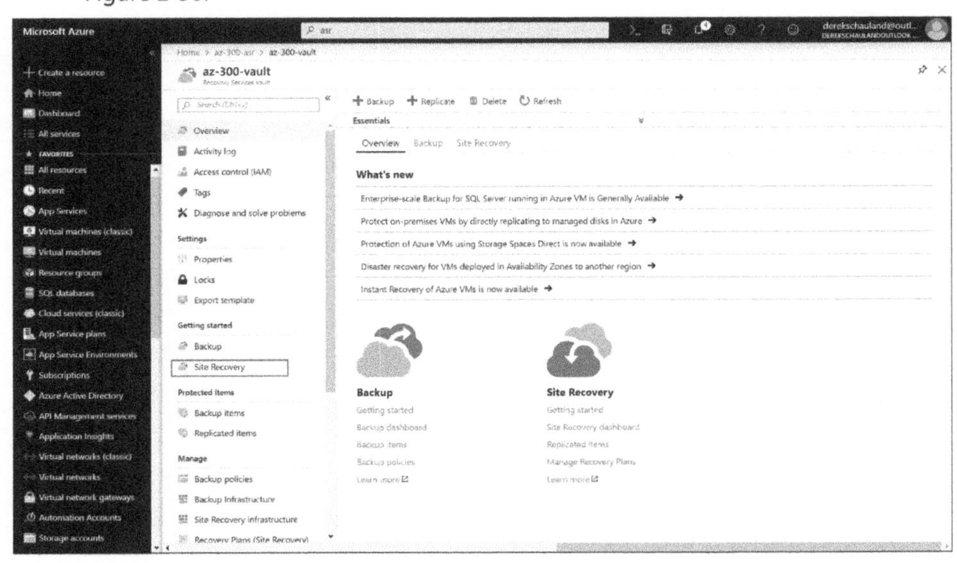

FIGURE 2-30 Getting Started with Site Recovery

2. Select the **Prepare Infrastructure** link to begin readying on-premises machines.
3. Complete the **Prepare Infrastructure** steps (shown in Figure 2-31):
   - **Where Are Your Machines Located?** Choose **On-Premises**.
   - **Where Do You Want To Replicate Your Machines To?** Choose **To Azure**.
   - **Are You Performing A Migration?** Select **Yes** or **No**.
   - **Are Your Machines Virtualized?** Select the appropriate response:
     - **Yes, With VMware**.
     - **Yes, With Hyper-V**.
     - **Other/Not virtualized**.

NOTE **ABOUT PHYSICAL SERVERS**

Migrating Physical Servers using P2V, which is covered later in this chapter, uses the Physical/ Other option of the Azure Site Recovery configuration mentioned here. Aside from this step, the Azure configuration is the same as discussed here.

NOTE **ABOUT HYPER-V**

If you select Hyper-V as the virtualization platform, you will also need to indicate if you are using System Center VMM to manage the virtual machines.

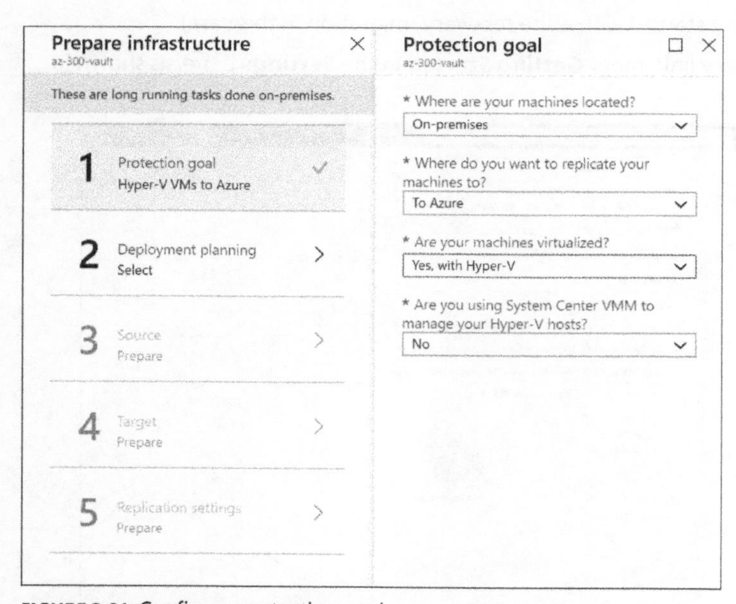

FIGURE 2-31 Configure protection goals

4. Click **OK** to complete the **Protection Goal** form.

Step 2 of infrastructure preparation is deployment planning, which helps to ensure that you have enough bandwidth to complete the transfer of virtualized workloads to Azure. The wizard will estimate the time needed to completely transfer the workloads to Azure based on the machines found in your environment.

Click the **Download** link for the deployment planner, located in the middle pane of the deployment planning step, to download a zip file to get started.

This zip file includes a template that will help in collecting information about the virtualized environment as well as a command-line tool to scan the virtualized environment to determine a baseline for the migration. The tool requires network access to the Hyper-V or VMware environment (or direct access to the VM hosts where the VMs are running). The command-line tool provides a report about throughput available to help determine the time it would take to move the scanned resources to Azure.

> ***NOTE*** **ENSURE RDP IS ENABLED BEFORE MIGRATION**
>
> **Ensuring the local system is configured to allow remote desktop connections before migrating it to Azure is worth the prerequisite checks. There will be considerable work to do—including the configuration of a jumpbox that is local to the migrated VM's virtual network—if these steps are not done before migration. It's likely that this will be configured already, but it's never a bad idea to double-check.**

After the tool has been run, in the Azure portal, specify that the deployment planner has been completed and click **OK**.

Next, the virtualization environment will be provided to Azure by adding the Hyper-V site and server(s).

> ***NOTE*** **ALL HYPERVISORS WELCOME**
>
> **At the time of this writing, the lab used for the examples consists of Hyper-V infrastructure. The examples provided will use Hyper-V as the on-premises source, but ASR is compatible with VMware as well.**

To add a Hyper-V server, download the Azure Site Recovery Provider and the vault registration key (see Figure 2-32), and install them on the Hyper-V server. The vault registration info is necessary because ASR needs to know which recovery vault the VMs belong to once they are ready to migrate to Azure.

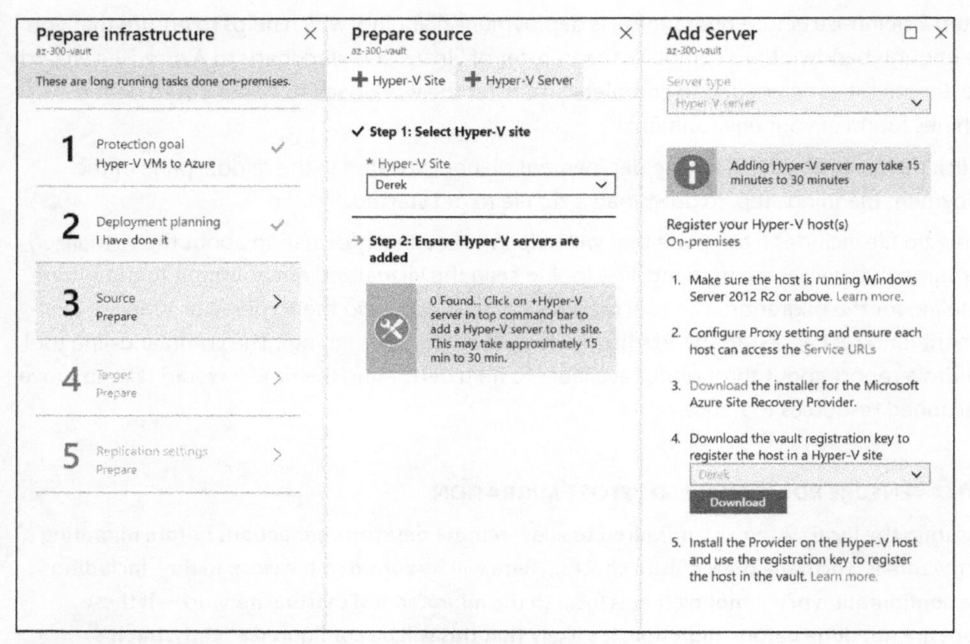

FIGURE 2-32 Preparing the source virtualization environment

If you're using Hyper-V, install the Site Recovery Provider on the virtualization host, as shown in Figure 2-33.

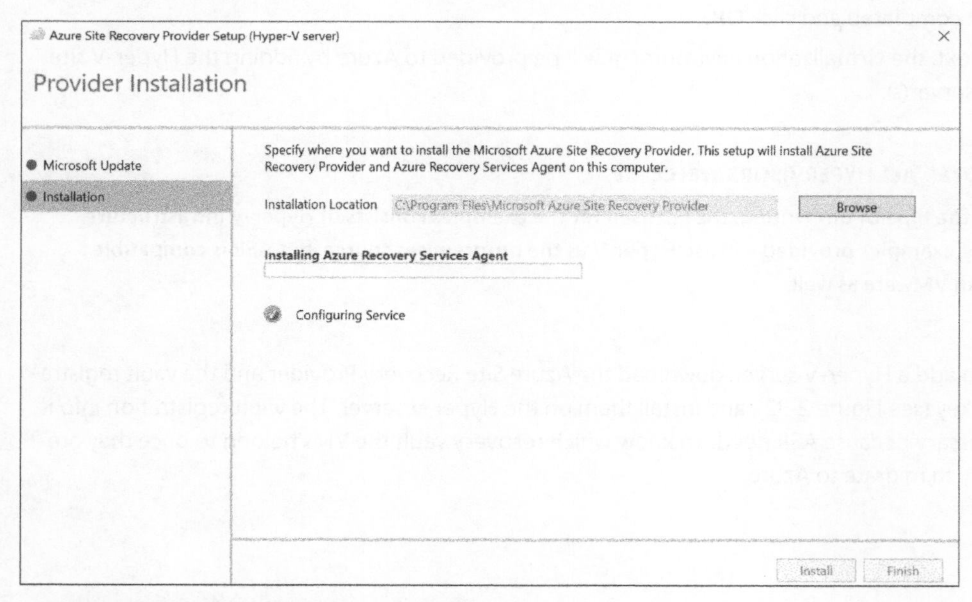

FIGURE 2-33 Installation of Site Recovery Provider

After installation and registration, it might take some time for Azure to find the server that has been registered with Site Recovery vault.

Proceed with infrastructure prep by completing the **Target** section of the wizard, as shown in Figure 2-34.

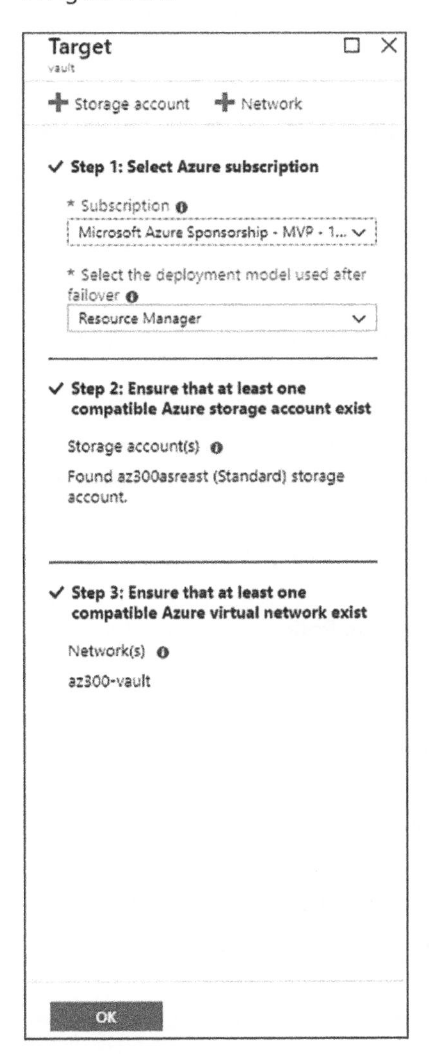

FIGURE 2-34 Preparing the Azure Target

Select the **Subscription** and the **Deployment Model** used. (Generally, the **Deployment Model** will be **Resource Manager**.)

> ***NOTE*** **ENSURE THAT STORAGE AND NETWORKING ARE AVAILABLE**
>
> **A storage account and network are necessary within the specified subscription in the same Azure region as the Recovery Services vault. If this exists when you reach this step, you can select the resources. If the storage account and network don't exist, you can create them at this step.**

Click the **Storage Account** button at the top of the **Target** blade to add a storage account. Provide the following storage account details:

- Storage account name
- Replication settings
- Storage account type

When this storage account is created, it will be placed in the same region as the replication services vault.

If a network in the same region as the vault isn't found, you can click the **Add Network** button at the top of the **Target** blade to create one. Much like storage, the network region will match the vault. Other settings, including **Address Range** and **Name**, will be available for configuration.

The last requirement for preparing infrastructure is to configure a replication policy. Complete the following steps to create a replication policy:

1. Click **Create And Associate** at the top of the **Replication Policy** blade. Enter the following information:
   - **Name** The name of the replication policy.
   - **Source Type** This should be prepopulated based on previous settings.
   - **Target Type** This should be prepopulated based on previous settings.
   - **Copy Frequency** Enter the replication frequency for subsequent copies to be captured.
   - **Recovery Point Retention In Hours** How much retention is needed for this server.
   - **App Consistent Snapshot Frequency In Hours** How often an app-consistent snapshot will be captured.
   - **Initial Replication Start Time** Enter a time for the initial replication to begin.
   - **Associated Hyper-V Site** Filled in based on previous settings.
2. Click **OK** to create the policy, and Azure builds and associates these settings with the specified on-premises environment.

Replicate data to Azure

After the completion of the on-premises settings, you return to the **Site Recovery** blade to continue configuration.

To enable replication, complete the following steps:

1. Select the source of the replication—**On-Premises**, in this case.
2. Select the **Source** location—the Hyper-V server configured within your environment.
3. Click **OK** to proceed to the target settings.
4. Select the **Subscription** to use with this replication.
5. Provide a post failover resource group, which is a resource group for the failed-over VM.
6. Choose the deployment model for the failed-over virtual machine.
7. Select or create the storage account to use for storing disks for the VMs being failed-over.
8. Select the option for when the Azure network should be configured: **Now** or **Later**.
9. If you selected **Now**, select or create the network for use post-failover.
10. Select the subnet for use by these VMs from the list of subnets available for the chosen network.
11. Click **OK**.
12. Select the virtual machines to failover as part of Azure Site Recovery.
13. Specify the following default properties and the properties for the selected virtual machines:
    - **OS Type** Whether the OS is Linux or Windows (available as default and per VM).
    - **OS Disk** Select the name of the OS Disk for the VM (available per VM).
    - **Disks To Replicate** Select the disks attached to the VM to replicate (available per VM).
14. Click **OK**.
15. Review the replication policy settings for this replication. They will match the replication policy settings configured in step 5 of the **Prepare Infrastructure** wizard, but you can select other policies if they exist.
16. Click OK.
17. Click Enable Replication.

With replication options configured, the last part of the configuration to complete is the recovery plan. To configure the recovery plan, use the following steps:

1. On the **Site Recovery** blade, select **Step 2: Manage Recovery Plans** and click the **Add Recovery Plan** button at the top of the screen.
2. Provide a name for the recovery plan and select the deployment model for the items to be recovered.
3. Select the items for a recovery plan. Here you will choose the VMs that will be included in recovery.
4. Click **OK** to finalize the recovery plan.

5. Once the items are protected and ready to failover to Azure, you can test the failover by selecting the **Site Recovery** vault resource and choosing **Recovery Plans (Site Recovery)** from the **Manage** section of the navigation pane.
6. Select the appropriate recovery plan for this failover. This overview screen shows the number of items in the recovery plan in both the source and target, as shown in Figure 2-35.

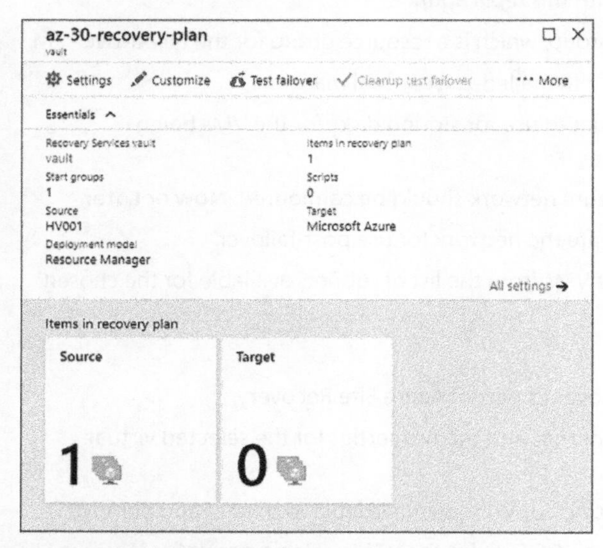

FIGURE 2-35 Site Recovery plan overview

To test the configuration, click the **Test Failover** button at the top of the **Site Recovery Plan** blade and complete the following steps:

1. Select the recovery point to use for the test.
2. Select the **Azure Virtual Network** for the replicated VM.
3. Click **OK** to start the test failover.

Once the failover completes, the VM should appear in the resource group that was specified for post-failover use, as shown in Figure 2-36.

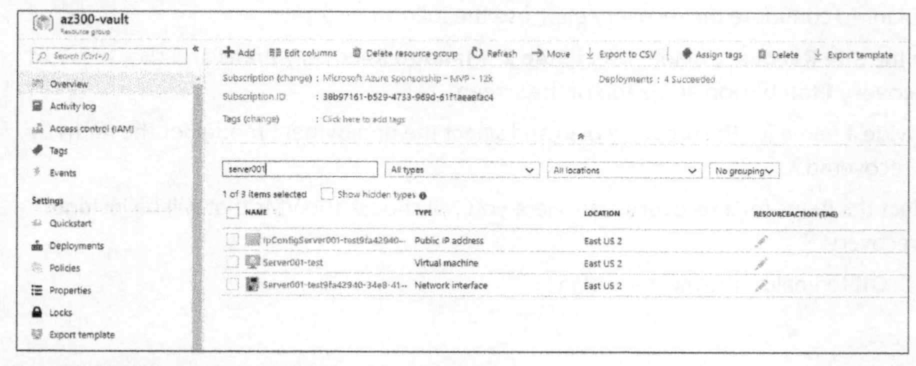

FIGURE 2-36 Resources after failover running in Azure

Migrate by using Azure Site Recovery

Once the test failover has completed, your VM is running in Azure, and you can see that things are as expected. When you're happy with the result of the running VM, you can complete a cleanup of the test, which will delete any resources created as a part of the test failover. Select the item(s) in the **Replicated Items** list and choose the **Cleanup Test Failover** button shown previously at the top of the recovery plan blade (see Figure 2-35). When you are ready to migrate, use an actual failover by completing the following steps:

1. Select **Replicated Items** in the **ASR Vault Protected Items** section.
2. Choose the item to be replicated from the list.
3. Once the item has synchronized, click the **Failover** button to send the VM to Azure.

Following the failover of the VM to Azure, the on-premises environment is cleaned up as part of the completion of the migration to Azure. This ensures that the restore points for the migrated VM are cleaned up and that the source machine can be removed because it will be unprotected after these tasks have been completed.

You might need to tweak settings to optimize performance and ensure that remote management is configured once the system has landed (meaning it has been migrated to Azure), such as switching to managed disks—the disks used in a failover are standard disks.

There may might be some networking considerations after migrating the VM. External connectivity might require network security groups to ensure that RDP or SSH is active to allow connections. Remember that any firewall rules that were configured on-premises will not necessarily be completely configured post migration in Azure.

After verification that the migrated resource is operating as needed, the last step of the migration is to remove the on-premises resources. In terms of Azure, the resources are still in a failover state because the process was to fail them over with the intention of bringing them back to an on-premises location.

Although migrating to Azure using Site Recovery still works by using the cutover and cleanup process, Azure Migrate is a newer version of this tool that is used specifically for moving workloads (VMs, Databases, and so on) to Azure. Azure Migrate was covered earlier in this chapter.

> ***NEED MORE REVIEW?*** **AZURE DISASTER RECOVERY RESOURCES**
>
> **For additional material, see "Prepare Azure resources for disaster recovery of on-premises machines" at *https://docs.microsoft.com/en-us/azure/site-recovery/tutorial-prepare-azure*.**

Skill 2.3: Implement application infrastructure

In the age of the cloud, even using servers is considered legacy technology in some instances because there are platform-based services that will run the provided code rather than deploying applications, functions, or other units of work to a server. The cloud provider—Azure, in this case—takes care of the workings under the hood, and the customer only needs to worry about the code to be executed.

There are more than a few resources in Azure that run without infrastructure—or serverless:

- Azure Storage
- Azure Functions
- Azure Cosmos DB
- Azure Active Directory
- Azure Key Vault

These are just a few of the services that are available for serverless compute. Serverless resources are the managed services of Azure. They're not quite Platform as a Service (PaaS), but they're not all Software as a Service (SaaS), either. They're somewhere in between.

Serverless objects are the serverless resources to be used in an architecture. These are the building blocks used in a solution, and there will be several types created, depending on the solution being presented.

Two of the most popular serverless technologies supported by Azure are logic apps and function apps. The details of configuring these are discussed in the text that follows.

A logic app is a serverless component that handles business logic and integrations between components—much like Microsoft Flow but with full customization and development available.

This skill covers:

- Create a simple logic app
- Manage Azure functions
- Manage Azure Event Grid

Create a simple logic app

To build a simple logic app that watches for files in a OneDrive folder and sends an email when they're found, complete the following steps:

1. Select **Create A Resource** from the Azure Navigation menu.
2. Type **Logic Apps** in the marketplace search and select the Logic App resource.
3. Click **Create** in the Logic App description.
4. Complete the **Logic App Create** form and click **Create**.
   - **Name.** Provide a name for the logic app.
   - **Subscription.** Choose the subscription where the resource should be created.
   - **Resource Group.** Select **Create** or **Use Existing** to choose the resource group where the logic app should be created. If you select **Use Existing**, choose the appropriate resource group from the drop-down menu.
   - **Location.** Select the region where the logic app should be created.
   - **Log Analytics.** Set **Log Analytics** to either **On** or **Off** for this resource.

NOTE LOG ANALYTICS WORKSPACE IS REQUIRED

To enable the log analytics feature for a logic app, ensure that the log analytics workspace that will collect the information exists beforehand.

Once a logic app resource exists, you can apply the code to get it to act on resources through predefined templates, custom templates, or using a blank app and adding code to perform actions for the application.

To add code to copy Azure storage blobs from one account to another, complete the following steps:

1. Open the resource group specified when you created the logic app resource.
2. Select the name of the logic app. The **Logic App** page opens so you can add templates, actions, and custom code to the logic app (see Figure 2-37).

FIGURE 2-37 Creating a logic app resource

3. From the initial designer page, select the **When A New File Is Created On OneDrive** common trigger, as shown in Figure 2-38.

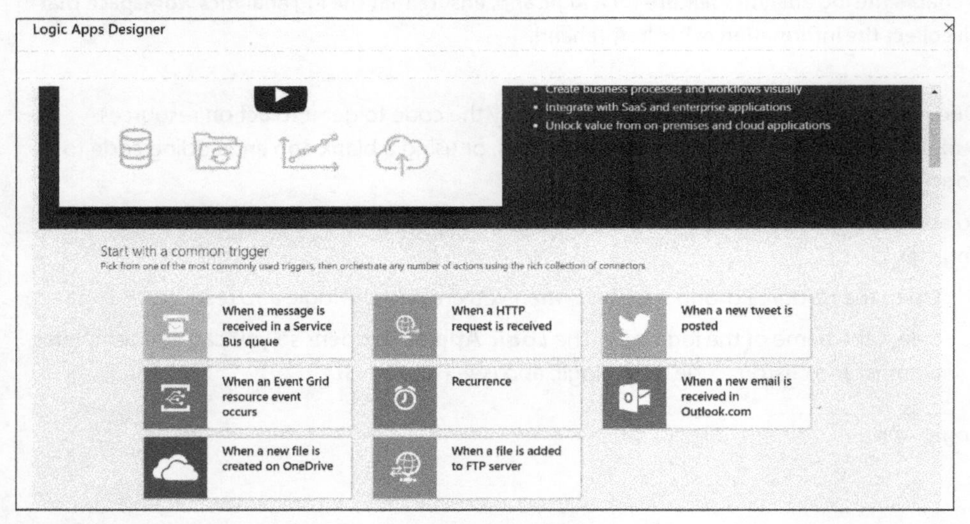

FIGURE 2-38 Logic Apps Designer with common templates

In this example, the logic app watches for new files in OneDrive and sends an email when a new file is landed. It is very simple, but it is designed to showcase the tools available to work with logic apps.

NOTE **CONNECT TO ONEDRIVE**

A connection to OneDrive will be needed to use this template; choosing to connect a One-Drive account will prompt you to log in to the account.

4. Specify the account credentials for OneDrive to be watched for files and click **Continue**.
5. Specify the folder to be watched and the interval for how often the folder should be checked by the logic app, as shown in Figure 2-39.
6. Choose a folder to monitor by clicking the folder icon at the end of the folder text box and choosing the root folder.
7. Set an **Interval**. The default is 3 minutes.
8. Click **New Step** to add an action to the logic app.
9. Select **Office 365 Outlook Template**.
10. Choose the **Send An Email** option.
11. Sign in to Office 365.
12. Specify the **To**, **Subject**, and **Body** of the email, as shown in Figure 2-40.

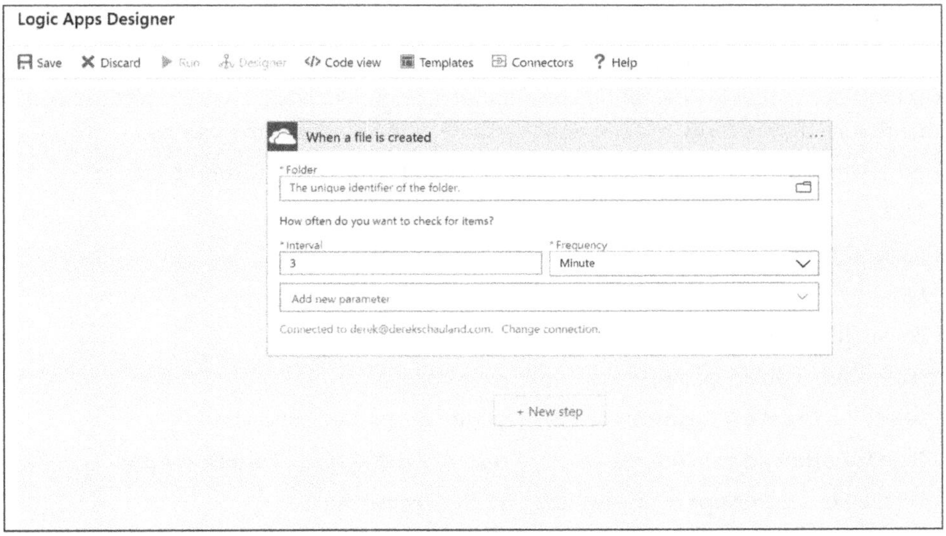

Logic Apps Designer

Save Discard Run Designer Code view Templates Connectors Help

When a file is created

* Folder

The unique identifier of the folder.

How often do you want to check for items?

* Interval * Frequency

3 Minute

Add new parameter

Connected to derek@derekschauland.com. Change connection.

+ New step

FIGURE 2-39 Specifying the OneDrive folder to be watched for new files

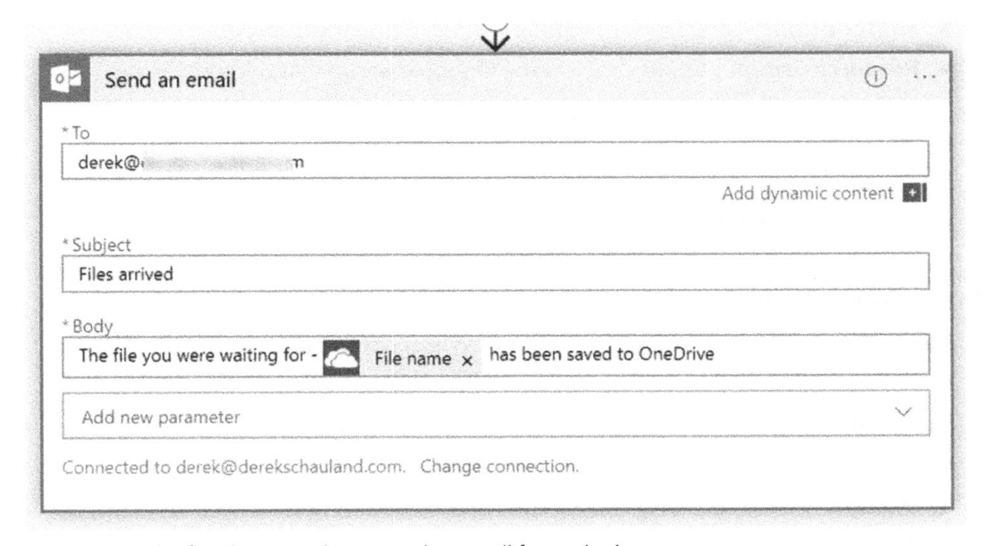

FIGURE 2-40 Configuring an action to send an email from a logic app

13. Click **Save** at the top of the **Logic Apps Designer** window to ensure the changes made to the logic app are not lost.
14. Click the **Run** button in Logic Apps Designer to make the app start watching for files.
15. Place a new file in the folder being watched by the logic app.
16. The Logic Apps Designer should show the progress of the app and that all steps for finding the file and sending the mail message have completed successfully.

Manage Azure Functions

Azure Functions allows the execution of code on demand, with no infrastructure to provision. Whereas logic apps provide integration between services, function apps run any piece of code on demand. How they're triggered can be as versatile as the functions themselves.

As of this writing, Azure Functions support the following runtime environments:

- .NET
- JavaScript
- Java
- PowerShell (which is currently in preview)

To create a function app, complete the following steps:

1. Select the **Create A Resource** link in the Azure portal Navigation bar.
2. Type **function apps** in the marketplace search box and select **Function Apps**.
3. On the **Function Apps** overview hub, click the **Create** button.
4. Complete the **Function App Create** form shown in Figure 2-41:
   - **App Name.** Enter the name of the function app.
   - **Subscription.** Enter the subscription that will house the resource.
   - **Resource Group.** Create or select the Resource Group that will contain this resource.
   - **OS.** Select the operating system that the function will use (Windows or Linux).
   - **Hosting Plan.** Select the pricing model used for the app: **Consumption** (pay as you go) or **App Service** (specifically sized app service).

> ***NOTE*** **NEW APP SERVICE PLAN IF NEEDED**
>
> **If you select the App Service hosting plan, a prompt to select/create it will be added.**

   - **Location.** Select the Azure region where the resource will be located.
   - **Runtime Stack.** Select the runtime environment for the function app.
   - **Storage.** Create or select the storage account that the function app will use.
   - **Application Insights.** Create or select an Application Insights resource for tracking usage and other statistics about this function app.
5. Click **Create** to build the function app.

In the Resource Group where you created the function app, select the function to view the settings and management options for it.

FIGURE 2-41 Creating a function

The **Overview** blade for the function app provides the URL, app service, and subscription information along with the status of the function (see Figure 2-42).

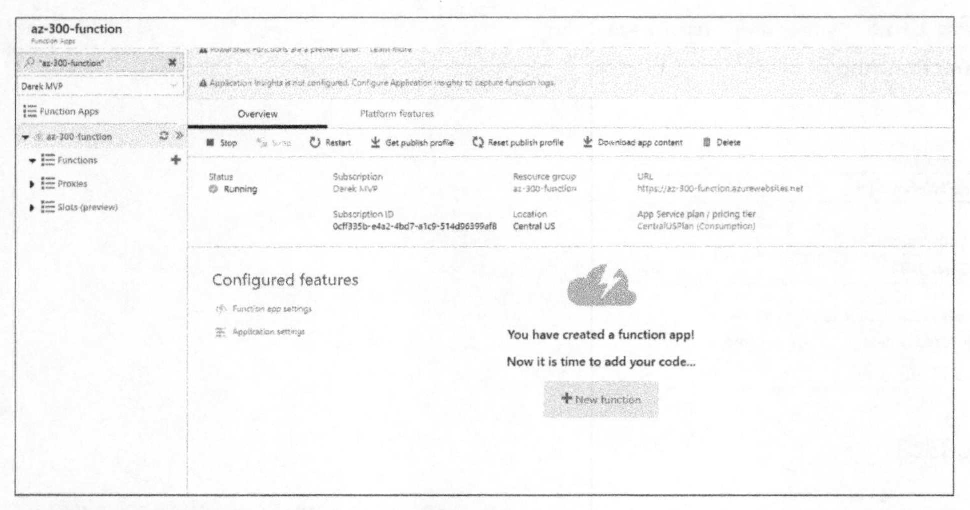

FIGURE 2-42 The Overview blade for an Azure function

Function apps are built to listen for events that kick off code execution. Some of the events that functions listen for are

- HTTP Trigger
- Timer Trigger
- Azure Queue Storage
- Azure Service Bus Queue trigger
- Azure Service Bus Topic trigger

IMPORTANT **MULTIPLE TYPES OF AUTHENTICATION POSSIBLE**

When configuring a function for the HTTP Trigger, you need to choose the Authorization level to determine whether an API key will be needed to allow execution. If another Azure service trigger is used, you might need an extension to allow the function to communicate with other Azure resources.

In addition to the **Overview** blade, there is a **Platform Features** blade, which shows the configuration items for the App Service plan and other parts of Azure's serverless configuration for this function. Here, you configure things like networking, SSL, scaling, and custom domains, as shown in Figure 2-43.

Within the **App Settings** blade for function apps is the Kudu console, which is shown as **Advanced Tools (Kudu)**. This console operates much like being logged into the system or app back end. Because this is a serverless application, there is no back end to be managed; this tool is used for troubleshooting a function app that isn't performing as needed. Figure 2-44 shows the Kudu back end.

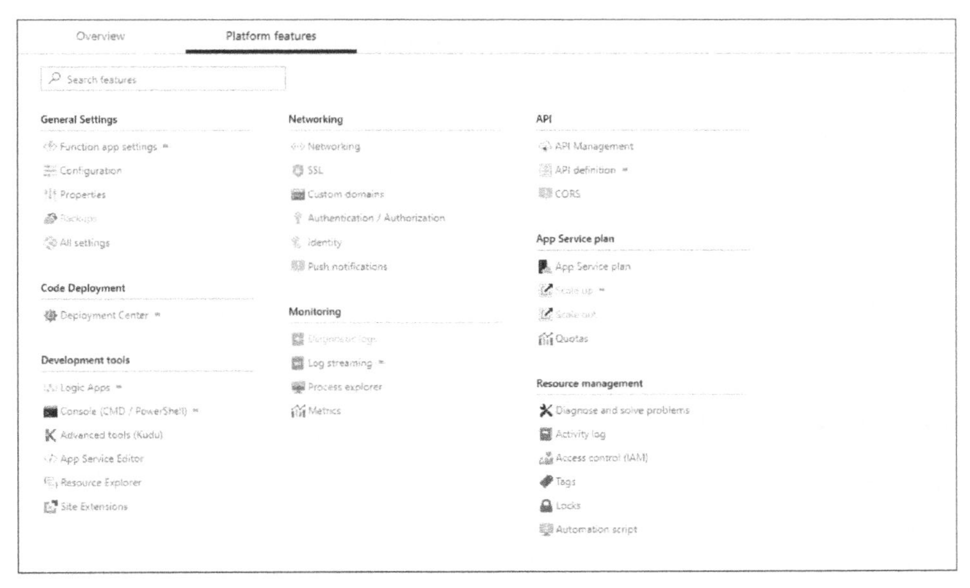

FIGURE 2-43 The Platform Features blade for an Azure function app

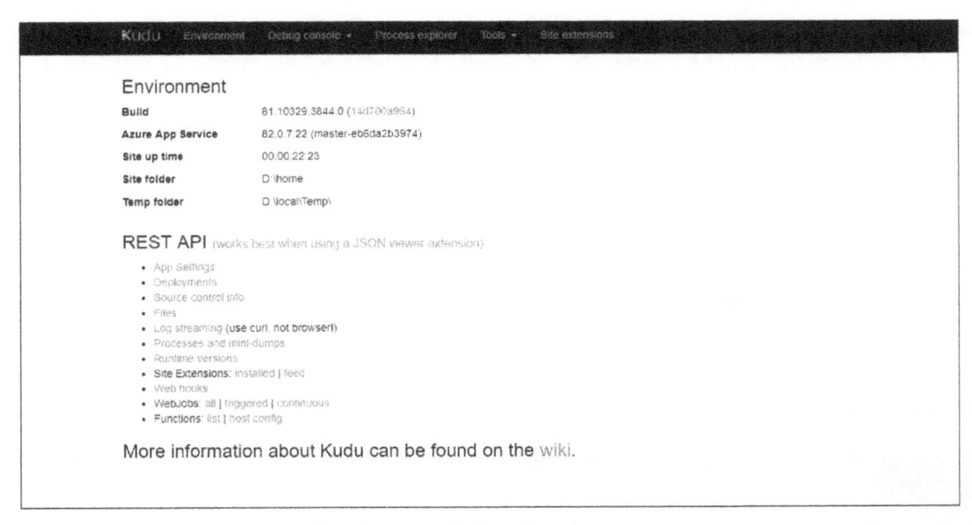

FIGURE 2-44 The Kudu troubleshooting console for a function app

> ***NOTE*** **AZURE HAS A CUSTOM CONSOLE FOR TROUBLESHOOTING**
>
> You can access the Kudu console by inserting `.scm.` into the URL of the Azure function. *https://myfunction.azurewebsites.net* would be *https://myfunction.scm.azurewebsites.net.*

NEED MORE REVIEW? **AZURE FUNCTIONS CREATION AND TROUBLESHOOTING**

For additional information, see

- "Using Kudu and deploying apps into Azure" at *https://blogs.msdn.microsoft.com/uk_faculty_connection/2017/05/15/using-kudu-and-deploying-apps-into-azure/*
- "Azure Functions Documentation" at *https://docs.microsoft.com/en-us/azure/azure-functions/*
- "Execute an Azure Function with triggers" at *https://docs.microsoft.com/en-us/learn/modules/execute-azure-function-with-triggers*

Manage Azure Event Grid

Event Grid is an event-consumption service that relies on publish/subscription (pub/sub) to pass information between services. Suppose I have an on-premises application that outputs log data and an Azure function that's waiting to know what log data has been created by the on-premises application. The on-premises application would publish the log data to a topic in Azure Event Grid. The Azure function app would subscribe to the topic to be notified as the information lands in Event Grid.

The goal of Event Grid is to loosely couple services, allowing them to communicate, using an intermediate queue that can be checked for new data as necessary. The consumer app listens for the queue and is not connected to the publishing app directly.

To get started with Event Grid, complete the following steps:

1. Open the **Subscriptions** blade in the Azure portal.
2. Select **Resource Providers** under Settings.
3. Filter the list of providers by entering **Event Grid** in the **Filter By Name** box.
4. Click the **Microsoft.EventGrid** resource provider and then click **Register** at the top of the page.

Once the registration completes, you can begin using Event Grid by navigating to the **Event Grid Topics** services in the portal, as shown in Figure 2-45.

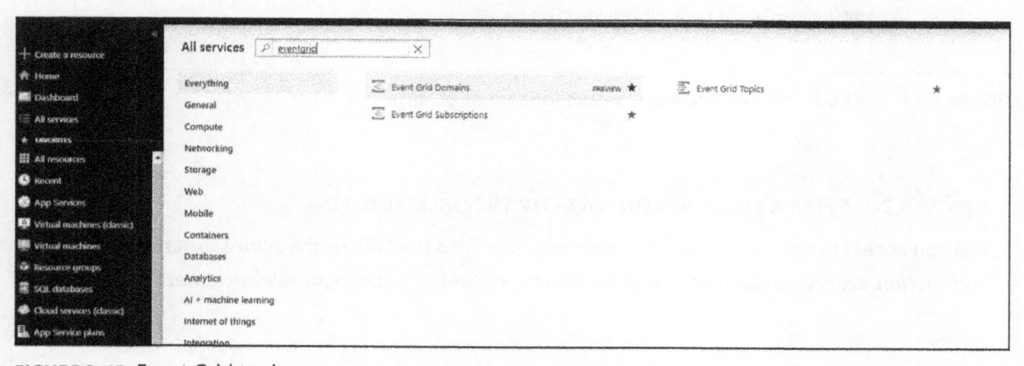

FIGURE 2-45 Event Grid topics

Once a subscription has topics created, each topic will have specific properties related to the subscription. Click the event grid subscription from the list. From the **Topic Overview** blade, the URL for the topic endpoint, the status, and the general subscription information are available. You can manage the following items from this point:

- **Access Control.** The Azure IAM/Role-Based configuration for which Azure users can read, edit, and update the topic. Access Control is discussed later in this chapter.
- **Access Keys.** Security keys used to authenticate applications publishing events to this topic.

Ensuring that the applications pushing information to this topic have a key to do so will ensure that the amount of noise sent to the topic is controlled. If the application sends an overly chatty amount of information, the noise might not be reduced.

IMPORTANT **SECURITY ITEM**

To ensure the access keys for a topic are secured and kept safe, consider placing them in a Key Vault as secrets. This way, the application that needs them can refer to the secret endpoint and avoid storing the application keys for the topic in any code. This prevents the keys from being visible in plain text and only makes them available to the application at runtime.

Once a topic has been created and is collecting information, consuming services that require this information need to subscribe to these events and an endpoint for the subscription. In this case, an endpoint is an app service with a URL that the subscriber services will access to interact with the topic.

Event subscriptions can collect any and all information sent to a topic, or they can be filtered in the following ways:

- **By Subject.** Allows filtering by the subject of messages sent to the topic—for example, only messages with `.jpg` images in them
- **Advanced Filter.** A key-value pair one level deep

NOTE **ADVANCED FILTER LIMITATIONS**

These are limited to five advanced filters per subscription.

In addition to filtering information to collect for a subscription, when you select the **Additional Features** tab when you're creating an event subscription, additional configurable features are shown, including the following:

- **Max Event Delivery Attempts** How many retries there will be.
- **Event Time To Live.** The number of days, hours, minutes, and seconds the event will be retried.
- **Dead-Lettering.** Select whether the messages that cannot be delivered should be placed in storage.

- **Event Subscription Expiration Time.** When the subscription will automatically expire.
- **Labels.** Any labels that might help identify the subscription.

> ***NEED MORE REVIEW?*** **WORKING WITH EVENT GRID**
>
> **Check out the articles at the following URLs for additional information:**
>
> - **"Concepts in Azure Event Grid" at *https://docs.microsoft.com/en-us/azure/event-grid/concepts***
> - **"Understand event filtering for Event Grid subscriptions" at *https://docs.microsoft.com/en-us/azure/event-grid/event-filtering***
> - **"Event sources in Azure Event Grid" at *https://docs.microsoft.com/en-us/azure/event-grid/event-sources***

Manage Azure Service Bus

Azure Service Bus is a multi-tenant asynchronous messaging service that can operate with first-in first-out (FIFO) queuing or publish/subscribe information exchange. Using queues, the message bus service will exchange messages with one partner service. If you are using the publish/subscribe (pub/sub) model, the sender can push information to any number of subscribed services.

A service bus namespace has several properties and options that can be managed for each instance:

- **Shared Access Policies.** The keys and connection strings available for accessing the resource. The level of permissions, manage, send, and listen are configured here because they're part of the connection string.
- **Scale.** The service tier used by the messaging service: Basic or Standard.

> ***NOTE*** **A NOTE ABOUT SKU**
>
> **A namespace can be configured with a premium SKU, which allows geo recovery in the event of a disaster in the region where the service bus exists. Selection of a premium SKU is available only at creation time.**

- **Geo-Recovery.** Disaster recovery settings that are available with a Premium namespace.
- **Export Template.** An ARM automation template for the service bus resource.
- **Queues.** The messaging queues used by the service bus.

Each configured queue displays the queue URL, max size, and current counts about the following message types:

- **Active Messages.** Messages currently in the queue.
- **Scheduled Messages.** These messages are sent to the queue by scheduled jobs or on a general schedule.
- **Dead-Letter Messages.** Dead-letter messages are undeliverable to any receiver.
- **Transfer Messages.** Messages that are pending transfer to another queue.
- **Transfer Dead-Letter Messages.** Messages that failed to transfer to another queue.

In addition to viewing the number of messages in the queue, you can create shared access permissions for the queue. This will allow manage, send, and listen permissions to be assigned. Also, this provides a connection string leveraging the assigned permissions that the listener application will use as the endpoint when collecting information from the queue.

In the **Overview** blade of the selected message queue, the following settings can be updated:

- **Message Time to Live**
- **Message Lock Duration**
- **Duplicate Detection History**
- **Max Delivery Count**
- **Max Size**
- **Dead Lettering**
- **Forward Messages To**

The settings for a message queue are similar to those discussed earlier in the "Manage Azure Event Grid" section because they serve a similar purpose for the configured queues.

NEED MORE REVIEW? **SERVICE BUS MESSAGING**

Check out the articles at the following URLs for additional information:

- "What is Azure Service Bus?" at *https://docs.microsoft.com/en-us/azure/service-bus-messaging/service-bus-messaging-overview*
- "Choose between Azure messaging services—Event Grid, Event Hubs, and Service Bus" at *https://docs.microsoft.com/en-us/azure/event-grid/compare-messaging-services?toc=https%3A%2F%2Fdocs.microsoft.com%2Fen-us%2Fazure%2Fservice-bus-messaging%2FTOC.json&bc=https%3A%2F%2Fdocs.microsoft.com%2Fen-us%2Fazure%2Fbread%2Ftoc.json*
- "Choose a messaging model in Azure to loosely connect your services" at *https://docs.microsoft.com/en-us/learn/modules/choose-a-messaging-model-in-azure-to-connect-your-services*

Skill 2.4: Manage security for applications

Azure Active Directory is available for registering applications and users for access to services and applications. This section discusses how applications and other Azure resources are registered with Azure Active Directory and how confidential values are managed using a service called Azure Key Vault.

This skill covers:

- Using Azure Key Vault to store and manage application secrets
- Using Azure Active Directory Managed Identity
- Azure Active Directory application registration

Using Azure Key Vault to store and manage application secrets

Applications need access to resources outside of what is being developed. Placing credentials, API keys, or other potentially sensitive information in code is something that might get developers hauled into meetings with InfoSec—which could spell trouble. Azure has a service that can solve this issue—Key Vault.

Azure Key Vault is an encrypted storage service specifically created for storing the following items:

- Keys
- Secrets
- Certificates

All these items are encrypted at rest and are only visible to the user accounts, service principals (registered applications), or managed identities that are granted access to use them.

Key Vault, like all other resources, can have access controlled by IAM, which in this case, means the user or group's ability to see or access the Key Vault resource. This does not apply to the items contained within the Key Vault. For access to secrets, keys, and certificates, the user or application will need to be identified in an access policy specific to the particular Key Vault containing these items.

To create the Key Vault resource, follow these steps:

1. Log in to the Azure portal *https://portal.azure.com.*
2. Select the **Create A Resource** button from the home screen.
3. Search for **Key Vault** in the **New Resources** blade.

4. On the **Key Vault** marketplace blade, click **Create**.
5. Select the **Subscription** that will house the Key Vault resource.
6. Select a **Resource Group** (or create one) that will be used to manage the Key Vault resource.
7. Enter a **Name** for the Key Vault resource.
8. Select a **Region** for the Key Vault resource.
9. Choose a **Pricing Tier**:
   - **Standard.** Software-based only key-management solution
   - **Premium.** Software and Hardware Security Module (HSM)–backed key management solution

> ***NOTE*** **WHEN TO CHOOSE PREMIUM**
>
> **Only choose premium Key Vault pricing if you require HSM-backed data. This is the only difference in the two tiers; all other pricing is the same. If you need the HSM features, the price does increase a bit.**

10. Enable **Soft Delete**.
11. Determine the retention period if **Soft Delete** is enabled.
12. Enable **Purge Protection**.
13. Click **Next** to create an access policy.

Soft Delete marks a value or key vault for deletion after a configured number of days before removing the stored items permanently. The number of days is determined by the retention period chosen when the Key Vault is created.

> ***NOTE*** **ONE TIME ONLY**
>
> **When a retention value is set, it cannot be changed or removed from the Key Vault. The same goes for Purge Protection; once set to true, items kept in the Key Vault are held for 90 days before being permanently deleted.**

An access policy manages the security for the items contained within a Key Vault. One Key Vault can have multiple access policies.

Create an access policy by completing the following steps while referring to Figures 2-46 and 2-47.

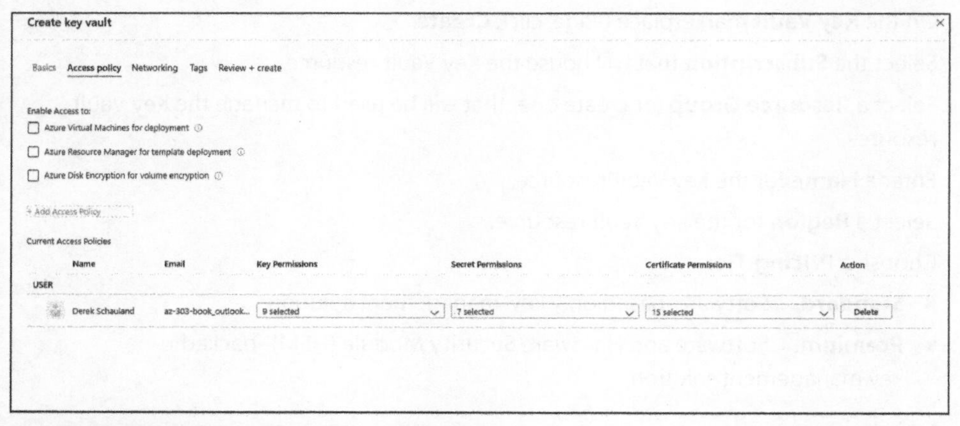

FIGURE 2-46 Create an Azure Key Vault access policy

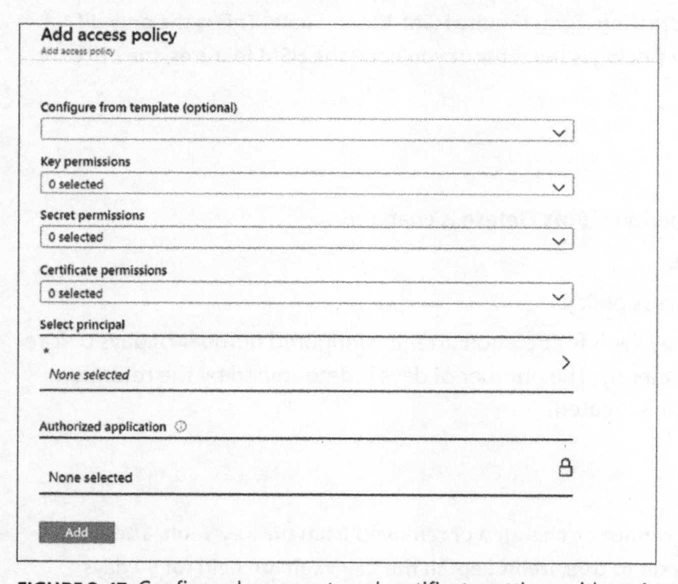

FIGURE 2-47 Configure key, secret, and certificate settings with an Azure Key Vault access policy

1. From the **Key Vault** resource blade in the Azure portal, select **Access Policy** from the navigation list.
2. Specify whether this Key Vault can be used for VM deployment.
3. Specify whether this Key Vault can be used by deployment templates during deployment—think administrative credential storage.
4. Specify whether this Key Vault should be used for Azure Disk Encryption information.
5. Click the **Add Access Policy** link.
6. If desired, select a template for configuration of an access policy.
7. Select permissions for the key values stored in this key vault:

Key Management Operations

- **Get.** Retrieve key values
- **List.** List keys contained in Key Vault
- **Update.** Modify existing key values
- **Create.** Create new keys
- **Import.** Import key values
- **Delete.** Remove keys
- **Recover.** Recover deleted keys
- **Backup.** Backup keys
- **Restore.** Restore key backups

Cryptographic Operations

- **Decrypt.** Decrypt cryptographically stored data
- **Encrypt.** Encrypt data to store
- **Unwrap Key.** Decrypt symmetric key data
- **Wrap Key.** Encrypt symmetric key data
- **Verify.** Provides verification of key data stored in Key Vault
- **Sign.** Uses key data stored to sign applications and resources

Privileged Key Operations

- **Purge.** Permanently remove key data from Key Vault

8. Select permissions to secrets stored in this Key Vault:
    - **Get.** Allows access to secret values
    - **List.** Allows access to see what secrets are stored in Key Vault
    - **Set.** Write a secret and its value to Key Vault
    - **Delete.** Remove a secret from Key Vault
    - **Recover.** Bring a removed secret back to Key Vault
    - **Backup.** Capture an external copy of a secret stored in Key Vault
    - **Restore.** Import an external copy of a secret to Key Vault
    - **Purge.** Permanently remove a secret from Key Vault after the configured retention period
9. Select permissions for certificates stored in Key Vault:
    - **Get.** Allow access to certificate values
    - **List.** Allow access to see which certificates are stored in Key Vault
    - **Update.** Allow existing certificate values stored to be updated
    - **Create.** Add new certificates to Key Vault from the portal
    - **Import.** Import existing certificates to Key Vault

- **Delete.** Remove a certificate from Key Vault
- **Recover.** Bring a deleted certificate back into Key Vault
- **Backup.** Create an external file backup of a certificate
- **Restore.** Create a certificate value in Key Vault from an external backup
- **Manage Contacts.** Add or edit contacts associated with a stored certificate
- **Manage Certificate Authorities.** Add, edit, or remove certificate authorities for certificates stored in the Key Vault
- **Get Certificate Authorities.** Review existing certificate authority information in Key Vault
- **List Certificate Authorities.** List certificate authorities stored in Key Vault
- **Set Certificate Authorities.** Update/create certificate authority data stored in Key Vault
- **Delete Certificate Authorities.** Remove certificate authority data stored in Key Vault
- **Purge.** Permanently remove certificate data stored in Key Vault per the retention days set for they Key Vault resource

10. Select the principal for the access policy—the user, group, or application to which this policy applies.
    - Search for the user or group needed and click **Select**.
11. Specify any authorized applications that can access this Key Vault via this access policy. (This option is usually locked and unavailable for selection.)
12. Click **Add** to create the policy.

NOTE **SOME THINGS ARE BETTER TOGETHER**

When you are looking to assign read permissions, consider keeping get and list access together within an access policy. It is easier to select the correct secret endpoint when all secrets can be listed.

NOTE **ABOUT KEY VAULTS**

A Key Vault is a great way to store sensitive information, but it has a downside as well. When you configure an access policy, that access is assigned to the key vault. It is not specific to an individual record within the Key Vault. If you can see one secret, you can see them all—something to keep in mind when using a Key Vault.

Once the permissions are assigned via an access policy, do not forget to click the **Save** button inside the resource to write the policies to the Key Vault.

Accessing an endpoint

Once a value is stored within a Key Vault, it gets assigned an HTTPS endpoint to allow access. If the entity accessing the endpoint is listed on an access policy with permission to use the value, the value is used in place of the endpoint. A Key Vault is a great way to keep sensitive information only accessible to the applications or users that need it. It lives within Azure and does not require third-party services or subscriptions to manage this information for an organization.

Using Azure Active Directory Managed Identity

Azure Active Directory is a great way to authenticate user accounts and provide services like single sign-on for applications. Managed Identity extends these features to other Azure resources, including but not limited to

- App services
- Function apps
- Virtual machines

The above examples are services that can have a managed identity assigned to them that allows interaction with other Azure services. Azure allows two types of managed identities: system-assigned and user-assigned:

- **System-assigned managed identity.** This type of managed identity is enabled on a service instance in Azure, and the identity for the service is created in Azure Active Directory and is trusted by the subscription containing the instance of the service. The service instance credential lifecycle is directly tied to the lifecycle of the service instance with no additional management of the assigned credentials required.
- **User-assigned managed identity.** This type of managed identity is created as an independent resource within Azure and assigned a service principal within Azure Active Directory. Once the service principal is created, it can be assigned to one or more applications or Azure instances. The lifecycle of a user-assigned identity is managed independently of the resource(s) to which it is assigned.

Unless your organization has specific requirements for managing these identities, system-assigned managed identities reduce the management overhead and provide the same level of security and access as user-assigned managed identities.

For example, a key vault can hold sensitive information and allow other resources to access that information. If, for example, my application needs to connect to a database, it will require a connection string to do so. The connection string likely contains a user ID and Password or key that provides the database a way to verify that the application requesting access should be allowed to connect. Because the connection string is a sensitive piece of information, storing it in Key Vault makes sense because it will be encrypted and will only be accessible to those who have access policies assigned.

As an administrator of the Key Vault, the user Derek would be able to add the connection string as a secret and view it once added. However, Derek is not the application, so if the application called an endpoint for the connection string, the connection would fail or return an error about an invalid identity.

Assigning a managed identity to the application provides a registration within Azure Active Directory and returns the following credentials for the application:

- **Client ID.** This is an identifier within Azure Active Directory for the application and its service principal (managed identity).
- **Principal ID.** This is the `objectID` of the application within Azure Active Directory for the application.
- **Azure Instance Metadata Service.** This is a rest endpoint accessible only from within Azure Resource Manager VM resources on a well-known and non-routable IP address (169.254.169.254).

Once a managed identity is assigned, the application can be assigned role-based access to resources in Azure, and just like the user account, Derek can be assigned these permissions. In addition, in the case of a Key Vault, the application can have an access policy assigned to it. This will grant permissions set in the access policy to all the items within the Key Vault.

With Managed Identity enabled for the application and with an access policy configured, the application code can reference the connection string for the needed database(s) simply by calling the secret endpoint.

To enable managed identity for an Azure App Service, follow these steps:

1. Log in to the Azure portal.
2. Browse to the app service resource to which the managed identity will be assigned.
3. In the navigation pane shown in Figure 2-48, select **Identity** from the **Settings** section.

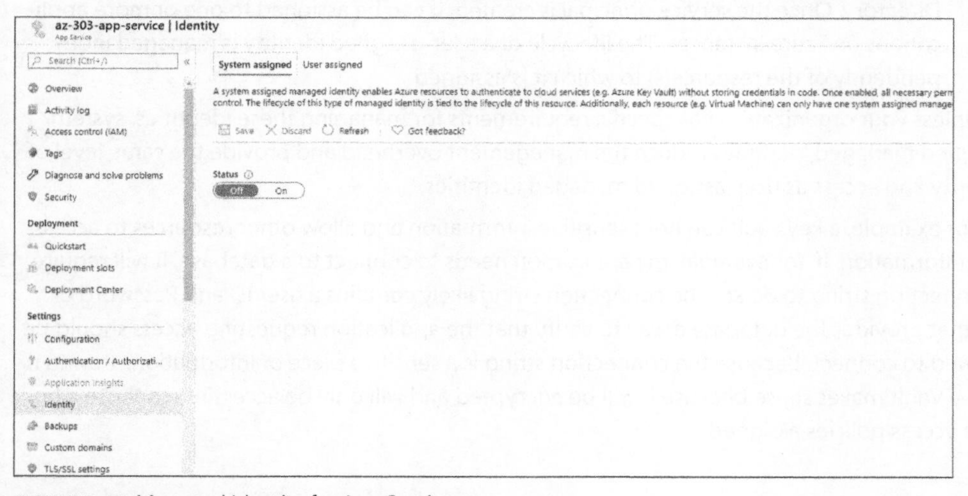

FIGURE 2-48 Managed Identity for App Service

4. On the **System Assigned** tab, toggle the **Status** to **On** and click **Save** to use a system-assigned identity.
5. To use a user-assigned identity, select the **User Assigned** tab and click **Add**.
6. Select the user-assigned managed identity you want to assign to this application.

APPLICATIONS AND AZURE MANAGE CREDENTIALS

Once the managed identity is assigned, you do not need to know or manage the client secret (password). This password is completely managed by Azure and the application.

For services that support enabling the managed identity option, managed identity creates an application registration for the resource where the feature is enabled; at least in part, it does this by creating a service principal within Azure Active Directory. Application registrations are covered in detail in the next section, "Azure Active Directory application registration."

Azure Active Directory application registration

Like Managed Identities, application registrations in Azure Active Directory are a method used to identify applications to allow access and roles to be assigned to them. An application or app registration can be created for applications that are created by your organization or for third-party applications that might be leveraging single sign-on capabilities provided by Azure Active Directory.

To create an application registration in Azure Active Directory using the Azure portal, complete the following steps and refer to Figure 2-49:

1. From the Azure portal navigation menu, select **Azure Active Directory**.
2. Ensure the appropriate tenant of Azure Active Directory is selected. Many organizations only have one tenant, but more than one Azure Active Directory tenant is allowed.
3. Select **Enterprise Applications**.
4. Select **New Application**.
5. Choose the application type to register:
   - An application you are developing.
   - An on-premises application via application proxy.
   - A non-gallery application, which is any other application not in the gallery.
   - A gallery (marketplace) application. As of this writing, there are 3,388 applications in the gallery.

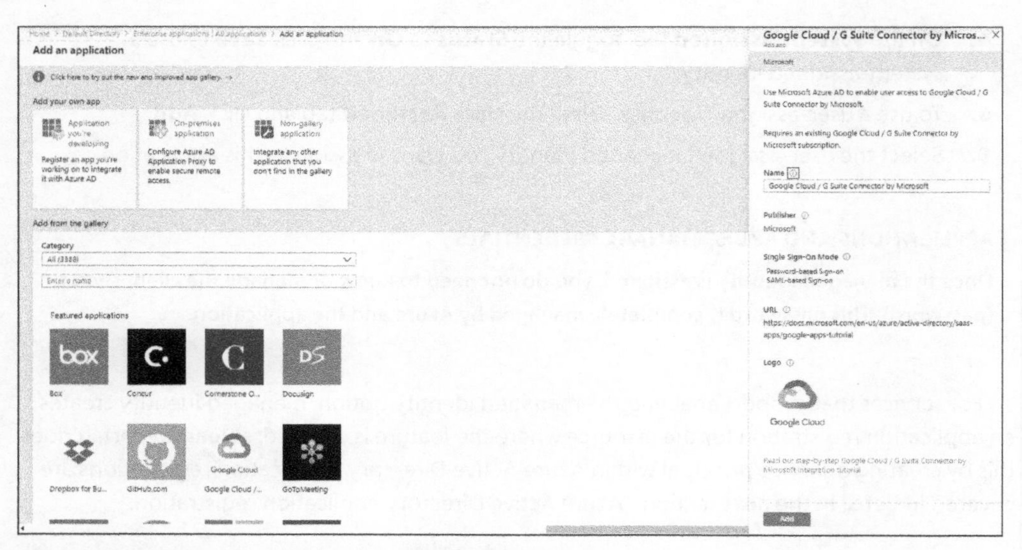

FIGURE 2-49 Registering an enterprise/gallery application

6. For a gallery application, select or search for the application and click the gallery to be registered.
7. Enter a name and other details for the registration, if required, and click **Add**.

For an application, your organization is working on, complete the following steps and refer to Figure 2-50:

1. From the Azure Active Directory navigation menu, select **App Registrations**.
2. Click **Register An Application**.
3. Supply a **Name** for the application.
4. Select the context in which the application will be available:
   - **Accounts In This Organizational Directory Only (Default Directory Only - Single Tenant)**
   - **Accounts In Any Organizational Directory (Any Azure AD Directory - Multitenant)**
   - **Accounts In Any Organizational Directory (Any Azure AD Directory - Multitenant And Personal Microsoft Accounts, such as Skype or Xbox)**
5. Enter an optional **Redirect URI**.
6. Click **Register**.

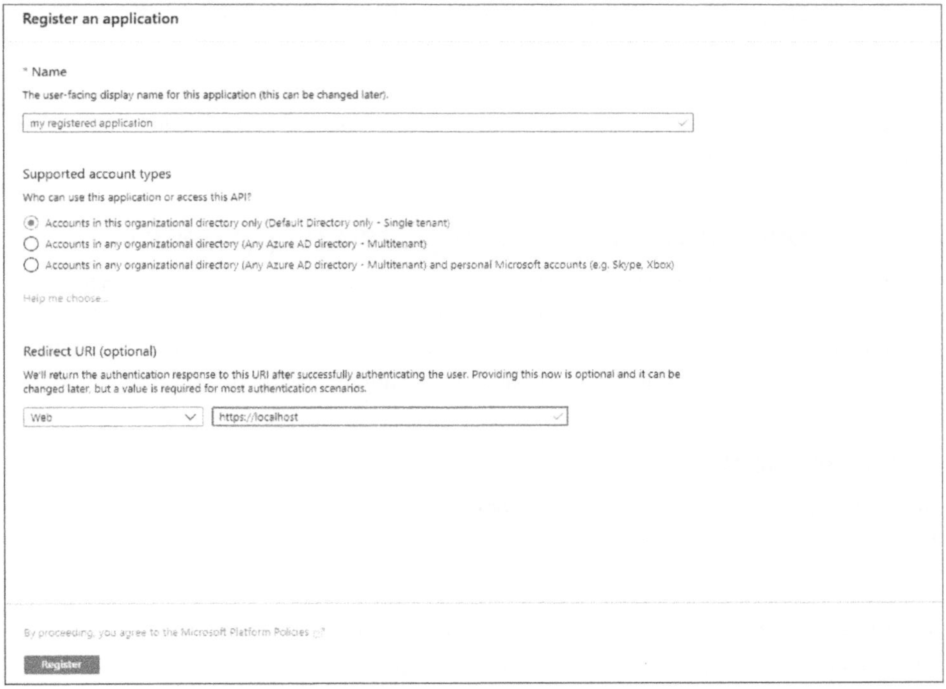

Register an application

* Name

The user-facing display name for this application (this can be changed later).

my registered application

Supported account types

Who can use this application or access this API?

Accounts in this organizational directory only (Default Directory only - Single tenant)

Accounts in any organizational directory (Any Azure AD directory - Multitenant)

Accounts in any organizational directory (Any Azure AD directory - Multitenant) and personal Microsoft accounts (e.g. Skype, Xbox)

Help me choose...

Redirect URI (optional)

We'll return the authentication response to this URI after successfully authenticating the user. Providing this now is optional and it can be changed later, but a value is required for most authentication scenarios.

Web | https://localhost

By proceeding, you agree to the Microsoft Platform Policies

Register

FIGURE 2-50 Registering an internally developed application

The tenancy of the application determines

- If only your organization can use the application registration.
- If any other Azure Active Directory tenant can use the application registration.
- If in addition to any Azure Active Directory tenant, any personal Microsoft account services (Xbox or Skype) can access the application.

The type of application being registered and/or company policy might dictate this selection.

The redirect URI is optional, and can be filled in as *https://localhost* if there is not a redirect URI required by the application. This URI determines where the authentication response will be sent.

To create an application registration in Azure Active Directory using PowerShell, execute the following code:

```
Connect-AzureAD -tenantid <your azure ad tenant id>
$applicationName = "my latest application"
$AppURI  = "https://myapp.azurewebsites.net"

If(!($myapp = get-azureadapplication -filter "DisplayName -eq '$($applicationName)'"))
{
        $myapp = new-azureadapplication -displayname $applicationName -identifierUris
$appURI
}
```

You will need to have the Azure AD module installed to register an application via PowerShell.

This code specifies the name and application URL for the app and then checks Azure AD to ensure that the application being registered is not already registered in the tenant. If the application is not found, it is registered in Azure AD.

Creating application secrets for registered applications

Now that the next big application has been registered in Azure Active Directory, it has an Application (client) ID just like the previously mentioned Application ID for managed identities and can be found in Azure AD. It does not have a client secret configured yet because the manual process of application registration requires the admin to create the secret as well.

> ***NOTE*** **TWO IDS ONE USE**
>
> **The Application ID and Client ID for registered applications are the same; however, Microsoft has as generally had two nomenclatures for this value.**

To add a client secret for your app registration, complete the following steps:

1. Within Azure Active Directory, select **App Registrations**.
2. Search for and select your registered application.
3. In the navigation menu, select **Certificates And Secrets**.
4. Click **New Client Secret** to create a secret value for this application and set the expiration info.
5. Enter a description for the secret and select an expiration.
6. Click **Add**.

> ***NOTE*** **SECRETS ARE SECRET**
>
> **When adding a new secret, the value is shown in the portal only while you are on the screen where the secret first displays. It should disappear if you navigate away from this screen and cannot be retrieved once dismissed. Make sure you copy the value somewhere for safe keeping before leaving the screen. A Key Vault is a great place to store these values.**

If you are adding a client secret via PowerShell, you can choose any expiration date you like; for example, you could set this to 5 years. You can also collect the client secret from PowerShell for an existing application registration after the fact. To add a client secret in PowerShell, execute the following code:

```
$application = get-azureadapplication
$secretStartDate = get-date
$secretExpireDate = (get-date).addyears(5)
$aadClientSecret = new-azureadapplicationpasswordcredential -objectid $application.
objectid -customkeyidentifier "App Secret" -startdate $secretStartDate -enddate
$secretEndDate
```

> ***NOTE*** **REVIEW POWERSHELL BEFORE COPYING IT FROM THE INTERNET**
>
> Make sure that you understand how this PowerShell works and have examined it. Also, the variable values listed here will not generally work unless you edit them to be used within your environment.

> ***NEED MORE REVIEW?*** **MORE INFORMATION ABOUT AZURE APPLICATION SECURITY**
>
> Check out the articles at the following URLs for additional information:
>
> - "Azure Key Vault basic concepts" at *https://docs.microsoft.com/en-us/azure/key-vault/basic-concepts*
> - "What are managed identities for Azure resources?" at *https://docs.microsoft.com/en-us/azure/active-directory/managed-identities-azure-resources/overview*
> - "Registering your application in Azure AD" at *https://docs.microsoft.com/en-us/skype-sdk/trusted-application-api/docs/registrationinazureactivedirectory*

Skill 2.5: Implement load balancing and network security

Azure has a couple of different options for load balancing: the Azure load balancer that operates at the transport layer of the networking stack and the Application gateway that adds to the load balancer at layer 4 and adds layer 7 (HTTP) load balancing on top of this configuration using additional rules. With some recent additions to the security space, there are additional resources being added constantly to improve the security posture of customers using Azure services. The new services include

- Azure Firewall
- Azure Front Door
- Azure Traffic Manager
- Network and Application Security Groups
- Azure Bastion

This skill covers how to:

- Configure Application Gateway and load balancing rules
- Implement front-end IP configurations
- Manage application load balancing
- Configure and manage Azure Firewall
- Configure and manage Azure Front Door
- Implement Azure Traffic Manager
- Implement Application and Network Security Groups

Configure Application Gateway and load balancing rules

An Application Gateway has the following settings that you can configure to tune the resource to meet the needs of an organization:

- **Configuration.** Settings for updating the tier, SKU, and instance count; indicate whether HTTP/2 is enabled.
- **Web Application Firewall.** Allows adjustment of the firewall tier for the device (Standard or WAF) and whether the firewall settings for the gateway are enabled or disabled.
  - Enabling the WAF on a gateway defaults the resource itself to a **Medium** tier by default.
  - If **Firewall Status** is enabled, the gateway evaluates all traffic except the items excluded in a defined list (see Figure 2-51). The firewall/WAF settings allow the gateway to be configured for detection only (logging) or prevention.

NOTE AUDITING AT THE FIREWALL REQUIRES DIAGNOSTICS

When using the Firewall Settings in WAF mode, enabling detection mode requires diagnostics to be enabled to review the logged settings.

- **Back-end Pools** The nodes or applications to which the application gateway will send traffic.

NOTE ANYTHING CAN BE A BACK-END POOL

The pools can be added by FQDN or IP address, Virtual Machine, VMSS, and App Services. For target nodes not hosted in Azure, the FQDN/IP Address method allows external back-end services.

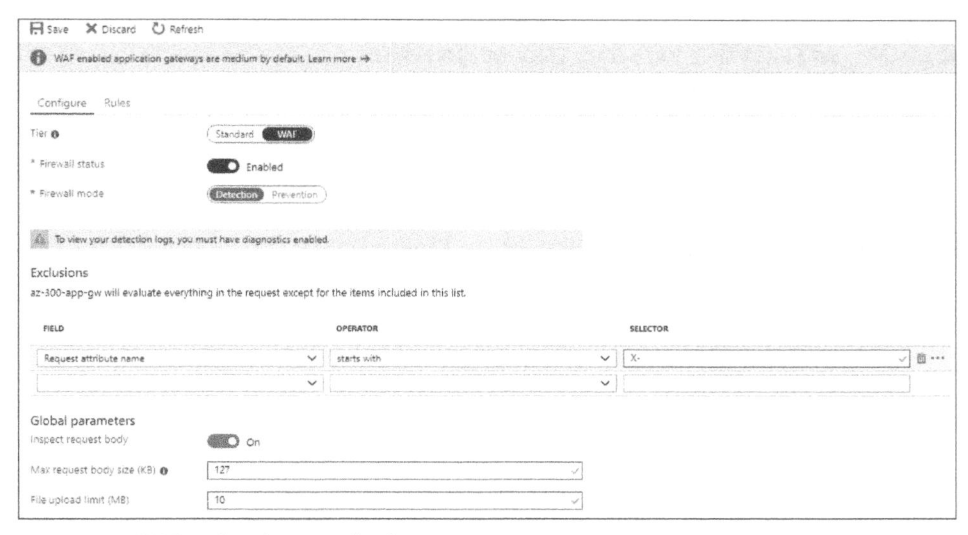

FIGURE 2-51 WAF settings in an application gateway

- **HTTP Settings.** These are the port settings for the back-end pools. If you configured the gateway with HTTPS and certificates during set up, this defaults to 443; otherwise, it starts with port 80. Other HTTP-related settings managed here are as follows:
  - Cookie-Based Affinity (sticky sessions)
  - Connection draining, which ensures sessions in flight at the time a back-end service is removed will be allowed to complete
  - Override paths for back-end services, which allow specified directories or services to be rerouted as they pass through the gateway
- **Listeners.** These determine which IP addresses are used for the front-end services managed by this gateway. Traffic hits the front end of the gateway and is processed by configured rules as it moves through the application gateway. Listeners are configured for IP address and port parings.
- **Rules.** The rules for the gateway connect listeners to back-end pools, allowing the gateway to route traffic landing on a specific listener to a back-end pool using the specified HTTP settings.

Even though each of these items is configured separately in the application gateway, rules bring these items together to ensure traffic is routed as expected for an app service.

Health Probes are used to ensure the services managed by the gateway are online. If there are issues with one of the configured back-end services, the application gateway removes the resource from the back end of the gateway. This ensures that the back-end service being used by the gateway will be less likely to display errored pages for resources that may be down.

IMPORTANT AT LEAST ONE BACK-END SERVICE IS NEEDED

If all back-end services are unhealthy, the application gateway is unable to route around the issue.

The interval at which health probes are evaluated, the timeout period, and retry threshold can all be configured to suit the needs of the back-end applications, as shown in Figure 2-52.

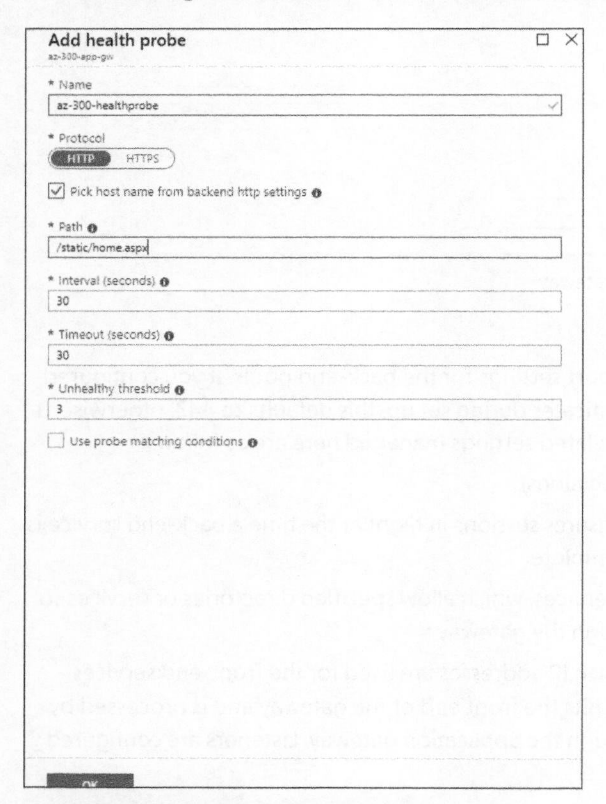

FIGURE 2-52 Configuring a new health probe

EXAM TIP MULTIPLE OPTIONS AVAILABLE FOR LOAD BALANCING

Azure supports different types of load balancing services that can be used in concert with one another. Be sure to understand when to use an application gateway and when to use a network load balancer.

Implement front-end IP configurations

An application gateway defaults to a front-end configuration using a public IP address, but you can configure it to use a private IP address for the front end. This might be useful in a multitiered application configuration. Using one application gateway to direct traffic from the Internet to an "internal" gateway that has a private front-end configuration might be a useful configuration in some scenarios.

Configuring virtual IP addresses (VIPs) happens in the settings for the application gateway in the **Front-End IP Configuration** section, which is shown in Figure 2-53.

FIGURE 2-53 The front-end configuration for an application gateway

When you set the front-end configuration, the default public settings include a configured listener. Each configuration needs a listener to allow it to properly distribute traffic to back-end resources.

Setting up private front-end configurations requires a name and private IP address to be specified if the original header will be modified to a known IP value.

NOTE **UPDATE TIME MAY BE REQUIRED**

When saving settings to some areas of the application gateway resource, the time to update may take longer than expected.

Manage application load balancing

The application gateway handles load balancing at layer 7 (the application layer) of the OSI model. This means it handles load balancing techniques using the following methods:

- **Cookie-Based Affinity.** This will always route traffic during a session to the same back-end application where the session began. The cookie-based method works well if there is state-based information that needs to be maintained throughout a session. For client computers to leverage this load balancing type, the browser used needs to allow cookies.

Cookie-Based Affinity management happens in the **HTTP Settings/Backend HTTP Settings** blade of the resource (see Figure 2-54).

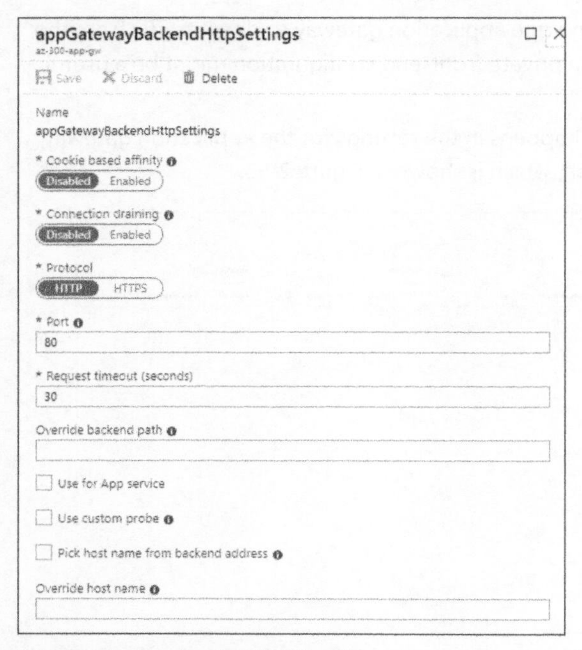

FIGURE 2-54 Configuring HTTP settings

- **Connection Draining.** Enable this setting to ensure that any connections that are being routed to a resource will be completed before the resource is removed from a back-end pool. In addition, enter the number of seconds to wait for the connection to timeout.
- **Protocol.** Set HTTP or HTTPS here. If you choose HTTPS, you need to upload a certificate to the application gateway.

URL Path-Based Routing

URL Path-Based Routing uses a configuration called a URL Path Map to control which inbound requests reaching the gateway are sent to which back-end resources. There are a few components within the Application Gateway needed to take advantage of URL Path-Based Routing:

- **URL Path Map.** The mapping of requests to back-end resources
- **Backend Listener.** Specifies the front-end IP configuration and port that the routing rules will be watching
- **Routing Rules.** The rules associate the URL Path Map and the listener to ensure that specific requests are routed to the correct back-end pool.

PowerShell is necessary to add the configurations to an application gateway for the settings needed for URL Path-Based Routing.

EXAM TIP

Leveraging the examples to help create a PowerShell script that works in your environment is advisable. When reviewing code supplied by others, be sure to look over it in an editor that supports the language—like Visual Studio Code—to help you understand what the code does before you run it in your environment.

A useable example of the following code is at *https://docs.microsoft.com/en-us/azure/application-gateway/tutorial-url-route-powershell*:

```
#Configure Images and Video backend pools
$gateway = Get-AzApplicationGateway '
  -ResourceGroupName Az-300-RG-Gateway'
  -Name AppGateway
Add-AzApplicationGatewayBackendAddressPool '
  -ApplicationGateway $gateway '
  -Name imagesPool
Add-AzApplicationGatewayBackendAddressPool '
  -ApplicationGateway $gateway '
  -Name videoPool

Add-AzApplicationGatewayFrontendPort '
  -ApplicationGateway $gateway '
  -Name InboundBEPort '
  -Port 8080
$backendPort = Get-AzApplicationGatewayFrontendPort '
  -ApplicationGateway $gateway '
  -Name bport
#configure a backend Listener
$fipconfig = Get-AzApplicationGatewayFrontendIPConfig '
  -ApplicationGateway $gateway

Add-AzApplicationGatewayHttpListener '
  -ApplicationGateway $gateway '
  -Name backendListener '
  -Protocol Http '
  -FrontendIPConfiguration $fipconfig '
  -FrontendPort $backendPort
#Configure the URL Mapping
$poolSettings = Get-AzApplicationGatewayBackendHttpSettings '
    -ApplicationGateway $gateway '
    -Name myPoolSettings

$imagePool = Get-AzApplicationGatewayBackendAddressPool '
    -ApplicationGateway $gateway '
    -Name imagesBackendPool

$videoPool = Get-AzApplicationGatewayBackendAddressPool '
    -ApplicationGateway $gateway '
    -Name videoBackendPool

$defaultPool = Get-AzApplicationGatewayBackendAddressPool '
    -ApplicationGateway $gateway
    -Name appGatewayBackendPool
```

```
$imagePathRule = New-AzApplicationGatewayPathRuleConfig '
    -Name imagePathRule '
    -Paths "/images/*" '
    -BackendAddressPool $imagePool '
    -BackendHttpSettings $poolSettings

$videoPathRule = New-AzApplicationGatewayPathRuleConfig '
    -Name videoPathRule '
    -Paths "/video/*" '
    -BackendAddressPool $videoPool '
    -BackendHttpSettings $poolSettings

Add-AzApplicationGatewayUrlPathMapConfig '
    -ApplicationGateway $gateway '
    -Name urlpathmap '
    -PathRules $imagePathRule, $videoPathRule '
    -DefaultBackendAddressPool $defaultPool '
    -DefaultBackendHttpSettings $poolSettings

#Add the Routing Rule(s)
$backendlistener = Get-AzApplicationGatewayHttpListener '
    -ApplicationGateway $gateway '
    -Name backendListener

$urlPathMap = Get-AzApplicationGatewayUrlPathMapConfig '
    -ApplicationGateway $gateway '
    -Name urlpathmap

Add-AzApplicationGatewayRequestRoutingRule '
    -ApplicationGateway $gateway '
    -Name rule2 '
    -RuleType PathBasedRouting '
    -HttpListener $backendlistener '
    -UrlPathMap $urlPathMap

#Update the Application gateway
Set-AzApplicationGateway -ApplicationGateway $gateway
```

IMPORTANT **BE PATIENT WHEN UPDATING APPLICATION GATEWAY**

An update to the application gateway can take up to 20 minutes.

EXAM TIP SPEND SOME TIME WITH THE CLI

Remember to work with the Azure Command-Line Interface (CLI) to understand how the commands work and that they differ from PowerShell. Although PowerShell can handle the command-line work in Azure, there may be some significant Azure CLI items on the exam, and it's good to know your way around.

Once the URL map is configured and applied to the gateway, traffic is routed to the example pools (images and videos) as it arrives. This is not traditional load balancing where traffic would be routed based on load of the device; a certain percentage of traffic goes to pool one and the rest to pool two. In this case, the content type is helping to drive the incoming traffic.

Implement Azure Load Balancer

Application Gateway includes layer 7 (HTTP or HTTPS) load-balancing capabilities to ensure increased performance of websites or web apps throughout an organization's Azure environment(s). There will be times when requirements come up for a more traditional, layer 4 load balancing solution and Azure Load Balancer has this covered.

> ***NOTE*** **LAYER 4 AND LAYER 7**
>
> **The layers mentioned above call out positioning in the OSI networking model. Layer 7 is the top layer and works at the application and browser level. Layer 4 is a middle layer that deals with communication transport—the TCP area. A discussion of what these layers bring is beyond the scope of this text. More info can be found at *https://osi-model.com*.**

The Azure Load Balancer works to handle TCP and other protocol-based communication and ensure requests are handled appropriately.

To configure Azure Load Balancer, complete the following steps (shown in Figure 2-55):

1. Log in to the Azure portal.
2. Click **Create A Resource** and search for **Load Balancer** to begin creating the load balancer.
3. Click **Create**.
4. Supply the following items to create a load balancer:
   - **Subscription.** Select the Azure subscription to use with this resource.
   - **Resource Group.** Select or create the resource group for the load balancer.
   - **Name.** Enter a name for the resource that meets organizational naming standards.
   - **Region.** Select the region for the load balancer.
   - **Type.** Select the type:
     - **Internal.** Used to provide connectivity for VMs within your virtual network to the front-end VMS as needed.
     - **Public.** Provides outbound connections for the virtual machines on a virtual network via address translation.
   - **SKU.** Select the pricing SKU for the load balancer:
   - **Basic.** Offered at no charge, but it is limited and has no SLA.
   - **Standard.** Used for large pools of targets or for additional functionality.
   - **Public IP Address.** Select an existing or create a new public IP.
   - **Public IP Address Name.** Name the public IP address resource.

- **Assignment.** Select the assignment type for the public IP.
  - **Dynamic.** Assigned when the load balancer is online and released if the load balancer goes away.
  - **Static.** Assigned permanently for use within Azure.
- Add a **Public Address**. Choose to enable IPv6 if needed.

5. Click **Next** to add tags.
6. Click **Review + Create** to review settings and build the load balancer.

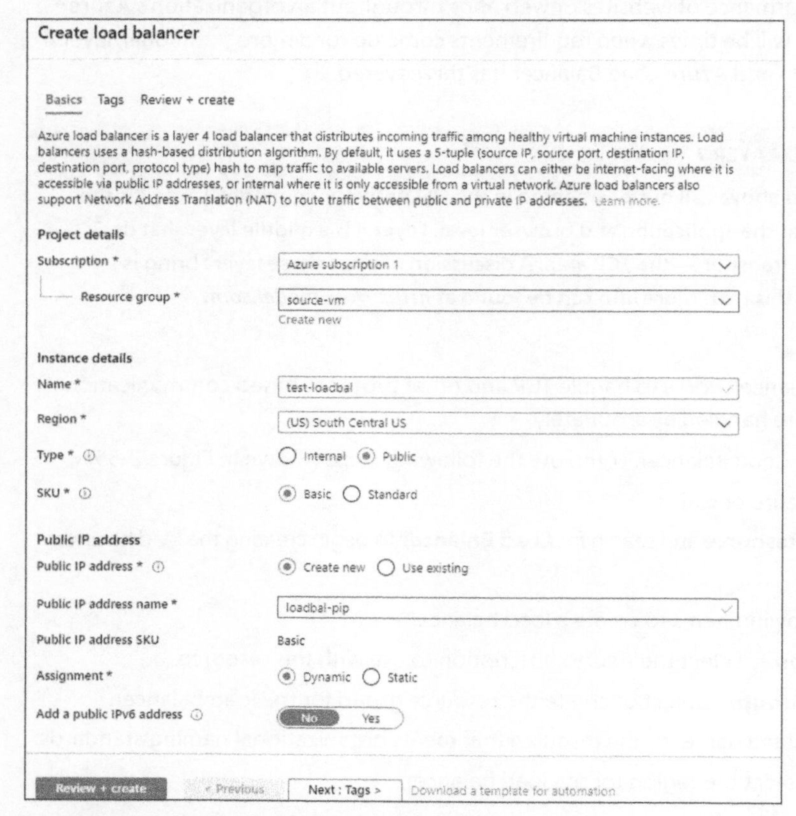

FIGURE 2-55 Creating an Azure Load Balancer

EXAM TIP TAGS AND ORGANIZATION

Using tags is a good way to ensure certain information is captured for resources being created. Azure keeps some information in the Activity Log, but this data gets purged regularly. If the information has been removed and you need to see who created a resource or the date the resource was added, you might be out of luck. This is where tags come in handy and can save much frustration with resources in Azure. There are other uses for them as well, but this one is a primary use we have found for tags.

Once the load balancer exists in Azure, it needs some configuration to get it working properly in your environment. Specifically, the following items need to be configured:

- **Frontend IP Configuration.** The public IP address and external endpoint for the resource.
- **Health Probes.** Method(s) to ensure the back end is healthy and online so the load balancer knows when to shift traffic.
- **Backend Pools.** The resources being load balanced.
- **Rules.** This expresses how traffic should be routed through the load balancer.

The front-end IP configuration is the easiest part of a simple load balancer. The IP was assigned during resource creation and requires no further changes to operate successfully. Additional IP addresses can be added to the load balancer if required by an organization.

Back-end pools are the resources targeted by users and the load balancer. This is where those needing access to things are headed. One note about back-end pools is that they are designed to be extremely similar. For example, placing three servers running your application behind a load balancer would be one backend pool. Requests coming in would then receive the same result no matter which resource they were directed toward.

To configure a back-end pool, complete the following steps:

1. From the **Load Balancer Resource** in Azure, select **Backend Pools** in the **Settings** section of the navigation pane.
2. Click **Add**.
3. Supply the **Name** of the pool.
4. Supply the **Virtual Network** that should be used for resources.
5. Select the **IP Version**. (Generally, IPv4 will be used.)
6. Select the association for the back-end pool:
   - **Single Virtual Machine**
   - **Virtual Machine Scale Set**
7. Select the virtual machine (or scale set) to associate with.
8. Select the IP address of the back-end resource to use.
9. Click **Add** to create the pool.

> ***NOTE*** **BE MINDFUL OF REGIONS**
>
> **When setting up a load balancer, it should exist in the same region as the virtual network that will be used for its backend pool. Accessing virtual networks across regions will not work natively.**

With the front end configured and the back-end pool online, the next item in the order of operations is health probes. Before we start flooding the back-end pool with traffic, the resources should be healthy. To configure a health probe, complete the following steps:

1. Select health probes from the settings list in the navigation menu for the load balancer.
2. Click **Add** to create a health probe and supply the following:
   - **Name.** The name of the health probe.
   - **Protocol.** Select the protocol the probe should use.
   - **Port.** Specify the port to watch; make sure the port is open or listening on the VM.
   - **Interval.** The number of seconds between checks.
   - **Unhealthy Threshold.** The number of consecutive failures before the pool is deemed unhealthy.
3. Click **OK**.

With a healthy back-end pool ready to go, the last step is to set up the rule(s) needed to move traffic between the front end and the back end. Depending on the type of load balancing you will be doing, there are two rule types to be aware of:

- **Load balancing rules.** These ensure traffic is being routed to healthy resources or pools.
- **Inbound NAT rules.** Forwards traffic from a source port on the front end to a destination port on the back-end pool.

Complete the following steps to configure a load balancing rule:

1. Select the **Load Balancing Rules** blade from **Settings** and click **Add**.
2. Provide the following information for the rule:
   - **Name.** A name for the rule.
   - **IP Version.** Whether the rule should be used with IPv4 or IPv6.
   - **Protocol.** Select either TCP or UDP.
   - **Port.** Specify the port the rule should be leveraging.
   - **Backend Pool.** Choose a back-end pool.
   - **Health Probe.** Choose a health probe.
   - **Session Persistence.** This helps ensure that the server you connected to will maintain your session for its duration.
   - **Idle Timeout.** Specify the number of minutes to wait before timing out.
   - **Floating IP (Direct Server Return).** Select whether a floating IP should be used. Unless you are configuring SQL AlwaysOn or other sensitive resources, a floating IP is not necessary.
3. Click **OK**.

Complete the following steps to configure an inbound NAT rule:

1. From the **Settings** section of the navigation pane, select **Inbound NAT Rules**.
2. Click **Add**.
3. Supply the following information:
   - **Name.** A name for the NAT rule.
   - **Frontend IP Address.** Select the load balancer front end to use.
   - **Service.** The service that will be used with NAT.
   - **Protocol.** The protocol for the service (**TCP** or **UDP**).
   - **Idle Timeout.** The number of minutes the session should be allowed idle.
   - **Network IP Configuration.** Select the resource that will be used with NAT.
   - **Port Mapping.** Choose to use the default port or a custom port with NAT.
4. Click **OK**.

With the load balancer configured, accessing allowed resources using the IP address of the load balancer works the same way as using the IP address of the resource itself. This allows any directly attached public IP addresses to be removed from resources in a back-end pool. Before taking this step, be sure anything using those IP addresses has shifted to the load balancer IP.

> ***NOTE*** **USING SPECIFIC PORTS**
>
> **Using Inbound NAT rules can help ensure that well-known ports for certain workloads are not exposed to the Internet. For example, you could configure a front-end port of 2020 to send traffic to 3389 on your internal network to obfuscate where RDP is happening. Note that 2020 was just a random port number selected as an example.**

The load balancer configured for this text was a basic load balancer. Visit the Azure pricing documentation for the Load Balancer resource to learn more about the SLAs and additional features provided by other load balancer SKUs. See *https://azure.microsoft.com/en-us/pricing/details/load-balancer/*.

Configure and manage Azure Firewall

Azure Firewall is a stateful next generation firewall service that can be configured on a virtual network. When Azure Firewall is enabled, the default mode is to deny traffic to resources on the same VNet. Only after rules are configured will access to resources be allowed. Keep this in mind if adding Azure Firewall to an existing VNet.

To get Azure Firewall running on a virtual network, complete the following steps:

1. Log in to the Azure portal and locate the VNet resource to which Azure Firewall will be added.
2. With the VNet selected, choose **Firewall** under **Settings**.

3. Click the **Click Here To Add a New Firewall** link to add a new firewall and supply the following information:
   - **Subscription.** This should be the same subscription that holds the previously selected VNet.
   - **Resource Group.** The resource group should default to the resource group for the VNet.
   - **Name.** The name of the Azure Firewall instance.
   - **Region.** The region for the Azure Firewall instance, which should match the region of the VNet as well.
   - **Choose A Virtual Network.** Create or select an existing Virtual Network.
   - **Virtual Network Name.** The name of a new VNet if you chose to create one.
   - **Address Space.** The address space of the new VNet.
   - **Subnet.** This will be filled in as `AzureFirewallSubnet` and cannot be changed. If you choose an existing VNet, this subnet will need to exist before creating the instance of Azure firewall.
   - **Subnet Address Space.** The IP address range for the `AzureFirewallSubnet`.
   - **Firewall Public IP Address.** The public IP address (required) for use with Azure Firewall.
   - **Forced Tunneling (Preview).** This feature will force all traffic to flow through the firewall; it is in preview at the time of this writing.
4. Click **Review + create** to review the selected settings.
5. Click **Create** to deploy Azure Firewall.

NOTE **FORCED TUNNELING ADDITIONAL CONFIG**

If you choose to enable forced tunneling, a management IP address (public) will be required to ensure the firewall can always be reached for configuration and to ensure that management traffic is handled separately from traffic passing through and affected by the firewall.

EXAM TIP ***BUILT-IN TEMPLATES***

As you work through building these resources, there will be templates built in the background for ARM-based deployment. Downloading the templates for review will help improve your understanding of the templates and prepare you for automation of resource deployment in Azure. In addition, you will not be building or attempting to build ARM templates from scratch.

Once the deployment has completed, additional configuration will be needed to ensure that resources behind the firewall are available. By default, anything behind the firewall will not be accessible until there are rules in place to allow it.

Configuring rules for Azure Firewall

To configure rules for Azure Firewall, complete the following steps:

1. On the **Azure Firewall** resource blade, select **Rules** under the **Settings** section of the navigation pane shown in Figure 2-56.
2. Select one of the following rule types to configure:
   - **NAT Rule Collection.** This is a collection of rules used to share a single inbound IP address with many internal resources, depending on the chosen port. Microsoft might refer to this as Destination Network Azure Translation (DNAT).
   - **Network Rule Collection.** This is a collection of outbound rules to allow connection to external resources based on IP address and/or port.
   - **Application Rule Collection.** This is a collection of outbound rules meant to target external FQDN resources, such as *google.com*, and allow or deny traffic out to the specified target(s) based on the port and FQDN.

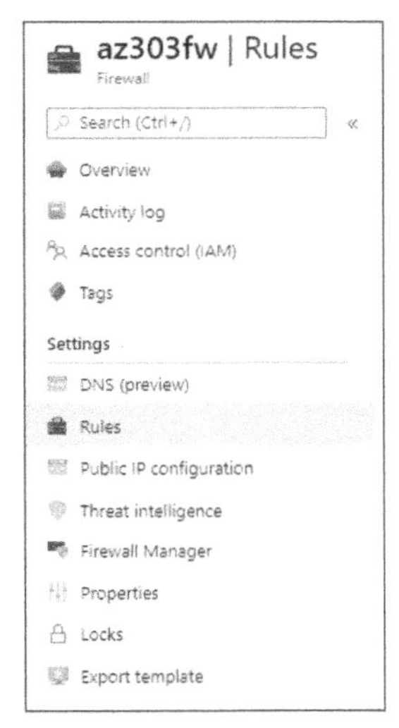

FIGURE 2-56 Configuring or adding rules to Azure Firewall

EXAM TIP* *RULES HAVE PROCESSING ORDER

When used, network rules are processed in order of assigned priority. If no matches are found for the outbound request, application rules are checked for matches. Once a match is found, no further rule processing is attempted.

3. Click **Add NAT Rule** and provide the following information:
   - **Name.** The first name is for the rule collection; similar types of rules can be added to the same collection.
   - **Priority.** This is the priority of the collection; keep these adequately spaced if you are using more than one type of rule collection to allow room for rule expansion.

- **Name.** This is the name of the individual rule being configured (for example, RDP).
- **Protocol.** Select **TCP** or **UDP** (or both) for the rule.
- **Source Type.** Select **IP Address** for a single source address or **IP Address Group** for a load-balanced group of source addresses.
- **Source.** Enter the IP address (or * for any) if the source type is an IP address, or select the named IP address group if source type is an IP address group.
- **Destination Address.** For a NAT rule, this should be the public IP address of the Azure Firewall Resource.
- **Destination Ports.** The network ports expected on the outside of the firewall, if using obfuscation; this is where the custom port number should be used.
- **Translated Address.** This is the internal IP address of the resource targeted by the rule; this address should be inside the VNet where the firewall is configured.
- **Translated port.** This is the target port for the service used by the rule; for example, RDP uses port 3389.

4. Repeat this information to add additional rules to the collection.
5. Click **Add**.
6. Click the **Network Rule Collection** tab to create network rules.
7. Supply the following information for a network rule collection:
   - **Name.** The name of the rule collection.
   - **Priority.** The priority for evaluation.
   - **Action.** Choose **Allow** or **Deny**.
   - **Name.** The name of the rule.
   - **Protocol.** Select **TCP**, **UDP**, or both.
   - **Source Type.** An IP address or IP address group.
   - **Source.** Enter an IP address (* for any) or select an IP address group.
   - **Destination Type.** An IP address or IP address group.
   - **Destination Address.** Enter an IP address (* for any) or select an IP address group.
   - **Destination Ports.** Specify the port that should be matched for the rule to be applied.

Service tags can also be configured in network rule sets—these are used to denote designated Azure services as the destination for the network rule—they are configured as individual rules within a rule set.

1. Click **Add** to create the rules and rule set.
2. To create an application rule collection, provide the following information:
   - **Name.** The name for the application rule collection.
   - **Priority.** The priority for the rule collection.
   - **Action.** Choose **Allow** or **Deny**.

- **FQDN Tags.** These allow outbound access to Azure-based services, such as Windows Update:
  - **Name.** The name of the FQDN tag rule.
  - **Source Type.** IP address or an IP address group.
  - **Source.** Enter the IP address (enter * for any) or select IP address groups.
  - **FQDN Tags.** Select the services that this rule should apply to.
- Target FQDNs. External domain names that should be allowed (or denied) from this rule collection.
  - **Name.** The name of the rule.
  - **Source Type.** IP address or a IP address group.
  - **Source.** Enter the IP address (enter * for any) or select IP address groups.
  - **Protocol:Port.** Specify a well-known protocol or protocol and port number to allow outbound access on.
  - **Target FQDNs.** specify a comma-separated list of FQDNs to which to allow outbound access.

3. Click **Add** to create the firewall rules and collections.

With rules configured, traffic will begin flowing through the Azure Firewall (if allowed). Without any rules, the default action of Azure Firewall is to deny any requests.

Once a firewall has been configured, it might make sense to lock the resource so it cannot be deleted by accident. On the **Overview** blade for the firewall resource, click the **Lock** option to lock the resource. Once enabled, clicking the **Unlock** option will remove the lock from an Azure Firewall Instance.

Configuring threat intelligence

Microsoft is constantly fielding networking attacks and other threats across Azure and other properties it manages. This data is aggregated to allow customers to work with data collected and managed by Microsoft. Note that this does not mean your environment is exposed to any of these attacks or threats; instead, it means when configured, threat intelligence can prevent them.

Telemetry data from all this aggregation is made available inside Azure Firewall to allow items to be alerted on or for items to be alerted on and denied by an instance of Azure Firewall.

To configure threat intelligence, choose one of the following options from the **Threat Intelligence Settings** blade:

- **Off.** Disable threat intelligence.
- **Alert Only (Default).** Receive high-confidence alerts for traffic routed through an instance of Azure Firewall in your environment that is going to or from known malicious IP addresses or domains.
- **Alert And Deny.** In addition to alerting on these events, traffic of this nature will be blocked.

Azure Firewall Manager (Preview)

Microsoft has introduced a policy-based firewall management service for Azure Firewall, which is in preview at the time of this writing. This service will allow rules and configurations to be shared across multiple instances of Azure Firewall. This feature is not covered in detail because it is in preview.

Configure and Manage Azure Front Door

Azure Front Door brings together monitoring, management, and routing of inbound HTTP and HTTPS traffic to an environment by allowing users to connect to points of presence (POPs) nearest their location to leverage Azure's backplane and network configurations to provide the best experience and access to your organization's applications.

Think of Front Door as the service that combines load balancing, Traffic Manager, and app gateway into a single offering for customers that wish to leverage it.

To get started with Azure Front Door, complete the following steps:

1. Log in to the Azure portal (*https://portal.azure.com*).
2. Select **Create A Resource** from the Azure navigation menu.
3. In the **Search The Marketplace** text box, enter **Front Door** to locate Azure Front Door.
4. Click **Create**.
5. Provide the following information for configuration:
   - **Subscription.** Select the subscription that will house your Azure Front Door implementation.
   - **Resource Group.** Create or select an existing resource group to house your Azure Front Door implementation.
6. Click **Next: Configuration**.
7. Complete the configuration wizard, as shown in Figure 2-57.

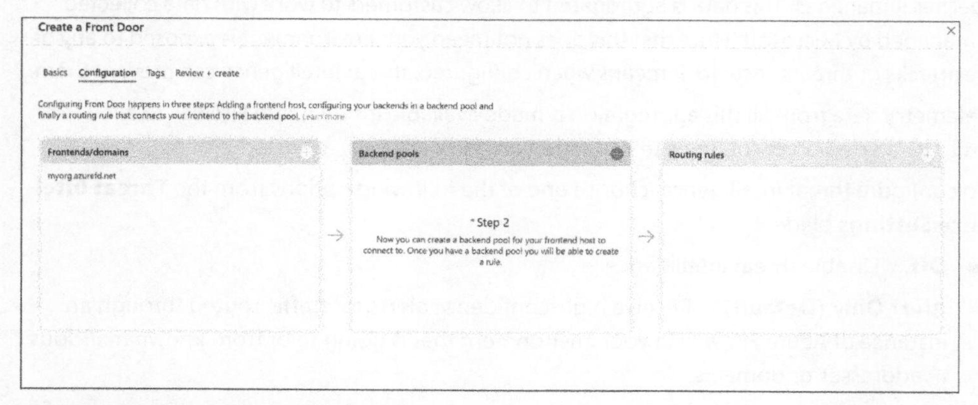

FIGURE 2-57 Azure Front Door configuration

- Configure Frontends/Domains.
  - Enter the host name.
  - Select to enable or disable session affinity.
  - Select to enable or disable the web application firewall.
  - Click **Add**.
- Configure Back-End Pools.
  - Enter a name for the back-end pool.
  - Click **Add A Backend** to configure a host within the backend pool.
  - Specify a path for the health probe for this back-end pool. Consider a static application or page to ensure the path does not change.
  - Specify the protocol: **HTTP** or **HTTPS**.
  - Specify the probe method for the health probe (**Head** or **Get**).
  - Define the interval in seconds for the frequency of polling.
  - Specify a load balancing sample size.
  - Specify successful samples required.
  - Specify latency sensitivity.

8. Click **Add**.

- Define the Routing Rules to determine which traffic is distributed to which back-end pool.
  - Specify a name for the rule.
  - Select the protocol to be accepted.
  - Specify the front domains (configured previously).
  - Specify patterns to match. This will determine which traffic is routed by this rule.
  - Select a route type for the rule (**Forward** or **Redirect**).
  - Select the back-end pool to pass traffic to.
  - Select the forwarding protocol (**HTTPS**, **HTTP**, or **Match Request**).
  - Select to enable or disable URL Rewrite.
  - Select to enable or disable Caching.

9. Click **Add.**
   - Click **Review + Create**.
   - Click **Create** to deploy Azure Front Door**.**

Once Front Door is online and running, you can view the Front Door designer to add additional front ends, back ends, and routing rules. This will follow the same process outlined above.

In addition to these configuration options, you can enable and configure the Web Application Firewall options for Front Door separately.

Within the Azure Front Door resource, select **Web Application Firewall** and then select the configured front end you wish to assign a policy to. Policies are specific to front end configurations so that they can be different for each configured front end.

Web application firewall policies are separate entities from Front Door and must exist within the subscription where front door is deployed. In the search bar at the top of the Azure portal, search for **Web Application Firewall** to see Web Application Firewall policies (WAF), shown in Figure 2-58.

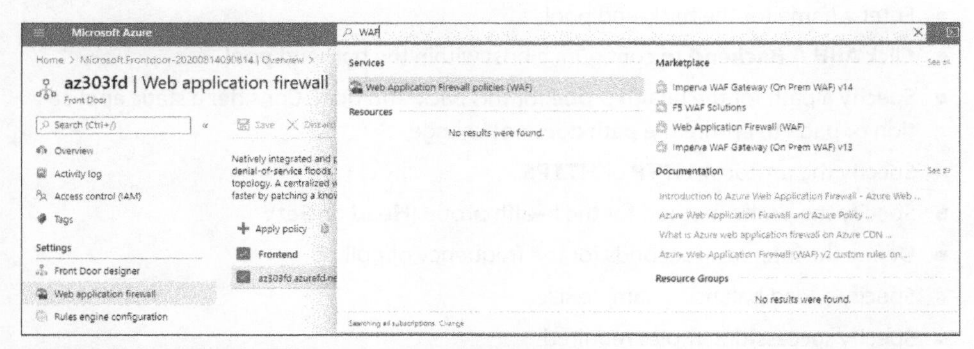

FIGURE 2-58 Adding Web Application Firewall Policy items

> ***NOTE*** **WHY CREATE WAF POLICIES?**
>
> **Front Door supports policies to allow the centralized management of configuration settings for an environment. These can be custom and created to follow an organization's security policy (which should be created) and/or they can use pre-created Azure policies, which take into account things that have been detected and have occurred across the Azure cloud. Using items from both will allow you to fine-tune policies and reduce the amount of things that must be considered/included within custom policy.**

To create a custom WAF policy, complete the following steps:

1. Provide project details about what this policy will cover.
2. Select where the policy will apply:
   - Global WAF (Azure Front Door)
   - Regional WAF (Application Gateway)
   - Azure CDN (preview at the time of this writing)
3. Select a subscription and resource group for the policy.
4. Supply an instance name for the policy and choose whether the policy is enabled or disabled.

> ***NOTE*** **CONFIGURATION CONSIDERATION**
>
> **We would recommend starting out with policies disabled to ensure all the necessary options are configured and documented as your organization requires before enabling them. Enabling these settings could cause traffic to your environment to be denied.**

5. Click **Next: Policy Settings** to define the following about the policy.
   - **Mode.** Select whether the policy will prevent (block) traffic or only detect (audit).
   - **Redirect URL.** This is the URL used to redirect requests if configured.
   - **Block Response Status Code.** This is the error code to return when a request is blocked.
   - **Block Response Status Body.** The message to return to the browser when a request is blocked.
6. Click **Next: Managed Rules** to configure the items managed by Azure.
   - Select the managed rule set to apply or choose **None** to skip managed rules.
7. Click **Next: Custom Rules** to add rules specific to an organization.
   - Click **Add Custom Rule**.
   - Supply the following information to configure a custom rule:
     - **Rule Name.** The name of the rule.
     - **Status.** Enabled or disabled.
     - **Rule Type.** Select Match to match specific patterns or Rate Limit to trigger the rule based on incoming requests.
     - **Priority.** Specify the priority of the rule, lower numbers process first.
8. Configure conditions for the rule:
   - Specify a match type and values to match against.
   - Specify the then condition. This specifies what to do when a match for conditions is found: **Allow**, **Deny**, **Log**, or **Redirect**.
   - When all the conditions needed for a rule have been added, click **Add**.
9. Click **Next: Association** to associate this policy with an environment.
   - Click **Add A Front-End Host**.
   - Select the Front Door instance, and then choose from the list of front-end hosts configured to associate the policy.
   - Click **Review + Create** to continue.
   - Click **Create** to build the configured policy and assign it.

NOTE SIMPLE, CUSTOM, AND AZURE PRECONFIGURED

When defining policy, it is a good idea to set up a policy that contains only Azure pre-configured rules and another that contains only custom rules. This way, when you are managing them later, only one set of items must be managed at a time. This also means you won't be wading through a mixture of custom rules and Azure provided rules.

- Like any other firewall or rule configuration, keeping rules within a policy containing related items is a good idea for WAF policy. More policies can be created to bring out more rules, but keeping your rules for certain types of traffic together can make for easier troubleshooting.
- Remember: Azure Front Door is a one-stop shop for applications and resources within an environment, and applying individual policies to the front-end configurations within Front Door removes the need to configure multiple instances of the Front Door service.

TIP ***PERIODICAL POLICY REVIEWS***

When leveraging services like Azure Front Door, it is a good idea to periodically review the configuration of the service, specifically any policies and associated rules, to ensure they still apply to your organization and that they are still providing the intended result. If not, you should adjust them accordingly.

Implement Azure Traffic Manager

Azure Traffic Manager is a DNS load balancer that allows DNS-based traffic to be sent to configured hosts to ensure specific hosts are not overloaded. In a similar fashion to the way a traditional load balancer ensures traffic going to IP address 1.2.3.4 is evenly spread across a pool of resources, Traffic Manager does the same for DNS-based traffic. Balancing traffic across Azure regions is possible using Traffic Manager profiles as well, which can make it a key component of a service failover solution, which removes the need to update DNS records during a failover scenario.

To configure Azure Traffic Manager, complete the following steps:

1. Log in to the Azure portal (*https://portal.azure.com*).
2. From the navigation pane select **Create A Resource**.
3. Search for **Traffic Manager Profile** and click **Create**.
4. Provide the following information to configure a Traffic Manager profile:
    - **Name.** This is the resource name, which will get an Azure DNS name of `<name>.trafficmanager.net`.
    - **Routing Method.** Choose the method for routing traffic:

    - **Performance.** Use this routing when resources are geographically dispersed, and you want to send the user to the closest endpoint to their location.
    - **Weighted.** Use this to distribute traffic across nodes evenly or by a weight you specify.
    - **Priority.** Use this to select one endpoint as the primary and specify additional resources as backups.
    - **Geographic.** Use this routing to send specific users to a defined geographic location based on where the DNS query originates.
    - **MultiValue.** Use this for profiles where only IPv4 or IPv6 addresses can be endpoints. When queried, all values will be returned.
    - **Subnet.** Use this to map sets of user IP address ranges to a specific Traffic Manager endpoint.
- **Subscription.** Select the subscription that will house the Traffic Manager profile.
- **Resource Group.** Select or create the resource group that will house the Traffic Manager profile.
- **Resource Group Location.** Select the region where the resource group will be located.
- Click **Create**.

The configuration of Traffic Manager does place the resource in an Azure region initially. However, the Traffic Manager is a global resource that exists across all regions and does not only operate in specific datacenters.

After the initial configuration and deployment, Traffic Manager will be enabled and ready for use, but it does not contain any endpoints out of the box. This means anything sent to the Traffic Manager has nowhere to go. This will need to be configured by providing endpoints to the service. To do this, complete the following:

1. From the Traffic Manager resource, select **Endpoints** under the **Settings** area of the navigation pane.
2. Click **Add** to add an endpoint and provide the following information:
    - **Type.** The type of resource this endpoint is:
        - **Azure Endpoint.** A resource running in Azure.
        - **External Endpoint.** A resource running in another cloud or a corporate datacenter.
        - **Nested Endpoint.** Leverages another instance of Traffic Manager as an endpoint.
    - **Name.** The name of the endpoint.
    - **Target Resource Type.** The type of service this endpoint points to:
        - **Cloud Service.** PaaS cloud services running in Azure.
        - **App Service.** Web apps running in Azure.
        - **App Service Slot.** Specific slots of web applications running in Azure.
        - **Public IP Address.** Specify a load balancer or the DNS name of an IP address tied to a virtual machine running in Azure.

- **Target Resource.** If the endpoint is an Azure endpoint, the target can be selected from a list of available resources.
- **Custom Header Settings.** Header information the target might be expecting.
- **Add As Disabled.** If this is checked, the endpoint will not be available to receive traffic as soon as it is deployed.

3. Click **OK** to add the endpoint.

> ***NOTE*** **LAYERS AND LAYERS OF TRAFFIC**
>
> **A new addition to Traffic Manager endpoints is the nested endpoint. This allows one Traffic Manager to reference another instance as an endpoint to which it can route traffic. For example, an application sitting behind DNS at *www.contoso.com* might need to send traffic to *apac.contoso.com*, and this site might need to be load balanced between two endpoints specific to Asia Pacific. With a nested endpoint, this is easy to setup.**

Configuring additional settings

In addition to endpoints, Traffic Manager must be configured to ensure the endpoints are being monitored properly. Without configuring monitoring for Traffic Manager, or at least reviewing it to ensure correct settings are implemented, this might affect endpoint usage. If an endpoint cannot be monitored or reached by Traffic Manager, it will be marked as down and unavailable for use.

The following items are available within the configuration settings for Traffic Manager:

- **Routing Method.** Select the routing method used by the Traffic Manager overall.
- **DNS Time To live (TTL).** The number of seconds the client should cache a record before re-querying Traffic Manager for updated information.
- **Endpoint Monitor Settings:**
  - **Protocol.** Should endpoints be monitored over HTTP, HTTPS, or TCP.
  - **Port.** The port used for monitoring.
  - **Path.** The path on the endpoint used for monitoring. If there is a status page that should be used instead of the root path, enter the relative path here.
- **Custom Header Settings.** Any custom header info that should be applied for all endpoints.
- **Expected Status Code.** Configure any status code ranges that should be considered during evaluation of an endpoint. For example, a status code range might be configured if an endpoint does not return 200 as a success message or if you are expecting the endpoint to be down rather than up.
- **Probing Interval.** How often should an endpoint be checked.
- **Tolerated Number Of Failures.** How many consecutive failures are okay before an endpoint is considered down.
- **Probe Timeout.** Number of seconds before a probe times out when checking an endpoint.

Traffic Manager has two traffic monitoring options outside of the endpoint monitoring options used to route traffic that may be useful for seeing how traffic movement is going: real user measurements and traffic view.

Real user measurements

To enable real user measurements, select the **Real user measurements** item from the settings section of the navigation pane within the traffic manager resource then click the **Generate Key** button and include the key in your application, much like an instrumentation key in Application Insights. Once configured, any latency measurements between a client browser and Azure Traffic Manager help keep an eye on latency experienced by the user.

Traffic view

When traffic view is configured, it can collect data about latency from user connections to endpoints behind Traffic Manager. Select the **Traffic View** item from the settings section of the navigation pane within the traffic manager resource, then click the **Enable Traffic View** to turn this on. Initial enablement might take up to 24 hours to populate the heat map and display data regarding user connections.

> ***NOTE*** **APPLIES TO ALL INSTANCES**
>
> **When the real user measurements key is created, it applies to all instances of Traffic Manager within a subscription, not just the instance where the Generate Key button was clicked.**

Manage and configure Network and Application Security Groups

Security in the cloud is something that should be considered at every step in the process. Microsoft leverages Network Security Groups (NSGs) to provide a method for allowing and denying traffic destined for Azure Resources. Application Security Groups take this a step further by allowing a grouping of similar resources to be targeted by NSG rules. Using these resources can keep security simplified and leverages cloud-native technology that will grow as Azure continues to evolve.

Network Security Groups

Network Security Groups are much like Access Control Lists (ACLs) used in early firewall devices. They allow traffic through to a specified resource or network segment over a specified port or set of ports. At a high level, Network Security Groups provide an allowed/denied method of control for traffic coming into or going out from the resources to which they are applied.

To add a Network Security Group for a virtual machine, complete the following steps:

1. Log in to the Azure portal (*https://portal.azure.com*).
2. Navigate to the resource group containing the virtual machine that will be covered by the NSG.

3. Select the **Add** button at the top of the **Resource Group** page and search for and select **Network Security Group**. Click **Create** to start creating the resource.
4. Specify the **Subscription** and **Resource Group** that will house the NSG.
5. Provide the **Name** of the NSG.
6. Choose the **Region** for the resource.
7. Click **Next: Tags**.
8. Specify any tags used by your organization by adding the name for the tag and its value in the corresponding fields. If you have used a tag previously, its name and value will be selectable once you enter each field. This limits the need to keep a list of used tags outside of Azure.

> ***NOTE*** **TEXT ONLY**
>
> **Tags are text only. If the plan is to create a tag for username, the value can be anything—tags do not support any logic.**

9. Click **Review + Create** to review the resource options that will be submitted for deployment.
10. Click **Create** to build the resource.

> ***NOTE*** **NSG RESOURCE PLACEMENT**
>
> **Deciding whether to place NSG resources near the network or near the resource depends on whether the NSG will be associated to the network or one or more subnets. If the NSG will be associated to the network interface card of a virtual machine, place it with the machine. If it will be associated with one or more subnets, place it with the virtual network resource. Remember, this is arbitrary and may not work for everyone, but is a good place to start.**

EXAM TIP

When assigning a Network Security Group, even if there is only one virtual machine on a network segment, using a subnet association for the NSG will significantly reduce the number of places where the group is not configured when there is a need for troubleshooting.

Once the network security group is created, it will need some configuration to be useful. With the new resource selected, the initial rules available are:

- **Allow VnetInBound.** All traffic from resources on the same VNet is allowed in.
- **AllowAzureLoadBalancerInBound.** Any traffic from the Azure Load Balancer is allowed in.
- **DenyAllInBound.** Any inbound traffic that does not meet another rule is denied in.
- **Allow VnetOutBound.** All traffic to other resources on the same VNet is allowed out.

- **AllowInternetOutBound.** All traffic destined for the Internet is allowed out.
- **DenyAllOutBound.** Any outbound traffic that does not meet another rule is denied.

You might notice the priority on these rules is 65,000 or higher, placing them at the bottom of the list. The priority number is how rules within an NSG are evaluated, lower numbers first. The default rules created within an environment are evaluated last and any rules added would be hit before them. These are catch-all rules to ensure most traffic is not blocked as soon as the resource is configured. The initial configuration of an NSG is shown in Figure 2-59.

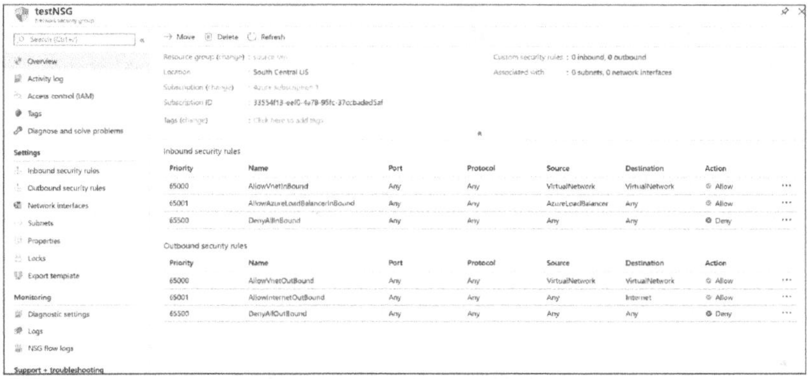

FIGURE 2-59 Network Security Group configuration

To add rules to the NSG, complete the following steps:

1. Select **Inbound Security Rules** from the NSG navigation menu.
2. Click **Add** and supply the following information:
   - **Source.** Select **IP Address**, **Azure Service Tag**, **Application Security Group**, or **Any**.
     - **IP Address.** A specific resource IP address.
     - **Virtual Network.** The name of an existing virtual network.
     - **Application Security Group.** The name of an existing application security group.
     - **Any.** Any resource that exists on the network where this NSG is configured.
   - **Source Port Ranges.** The port numbers this rule will apply to.
   - **Destination.** The resource(s) that will be targeted by this rule:
     - **IP Address.** A specific resource IP address.
     - **Virtual Network.** The name of an existing virtual network.
     - **Application Security Group.** The name of an existing application security group.
     - **Any.** Any resource that exists on the network where this NSG is configured.
   - **Destination Port Ranges.** The ports on the inside of this NSG that will be affected by this rule; these do not necessarily need to match the source ports, unless there is a reason to do so.
   - **Protocol.** Specify the protocol this rule will affect.
   - **Action.** Specify if the rule will allow or deny access when this rule is triggered.
   - **Priority.** Specify where in the rules list a rule should be processed. Lower numbers will evaluate at the top.

- **Name.** Specify a name for the NSG rule.
- **Description.** Specify an optional description.

3. Click **Add** to create the rule.

Remember, rules in an NSG are one way—either inbound or outbound. To add an outbound security rule, select the **Outbound Security Rules** option from the NSG navigation menu and repeat the above process.

With some rules in place to control traffic, the NSG needs to be associated with resources to control traffic. To assign it to a subnet, click the **Subnets** option in the navigation menu, click **Associate**, and choose the virtual network (and subnet) where this group should be used.

EXAM TIP SAME REGION REQUIRED

Network security groups being associated with subnets must be in the same region as the virtual network where the subnet exists. If they are not, no networks will be available to associate with.

Association with a network interface is like subnet association: select the **Network Interfaces** option from the navigation menu, click **Associate**, and select the network interface resources that this rule should be used with.

That is all there is to configuring NSGs, though this does not mean that there will not be troubleshooting needed or review of rules as things grow, but the process of configuration is straightforward.

One more thing about NSGs

To review the effective security rules applied by a group, complete the following steps:

1. Select the **Effective Security Rules** option from the navigation menu for the NSG.
2. Select the virtual machine (if associated with a VM) or the virtual network (if associated with a VNet).
3. Rules that are currently in effect on the selected resource(s) will be displayed.

Application Security Groups

Application Security Groups (ASGs) are used as targets within NSGs to ensure the correct traffic is allowed to reach resources within an ASG. They do not specifically allow or deny traffic, but they do provide a way to keep resources of a certain type—web servers, for example—grouped so that all of the traffic coming in on ports 80 or 443 can be routed to one destination and reach any and all configured web servers.

To create an ASG, complete the following steps:

1. Log in to the Azure portal (*https://portal.azure.com*).
2. From the navigation menu, click the **Create A Resource** button, search for **Application Security Group**, select **Application Security Group** from the results, and click **Create**.
3. Specify the subscription and resource group that will house the ASG.

4. Supply a name for the ASG and select the appropriate region.
5. If your organization uses tags, click **Next: Tags** to add them; if not, skip this step.
6. Click **Review + Create** to review the resource options that will be submitted for deployment.
7. Click **Create** to build the resource.

Like Network Security Groups, Application Security Groups will need some additional configuration once created. Because these groups help to bring servers performing similar tasks together, the addition of members to an Application Security Group happens from within the VMs being configured.

To add a virtual server as a member of an ASG, complete the following steps and refer to Figure 2-60:

1. Navigate to the virtual machine resource being added.
2. Select the **Networking** option in the navigation menu.
3. Select the **Application Security Groups** tab.
4. Click **Configure The Application Security Groups**.
5. Select the ASG to which this VM will become a member.
6. Click **Save**.

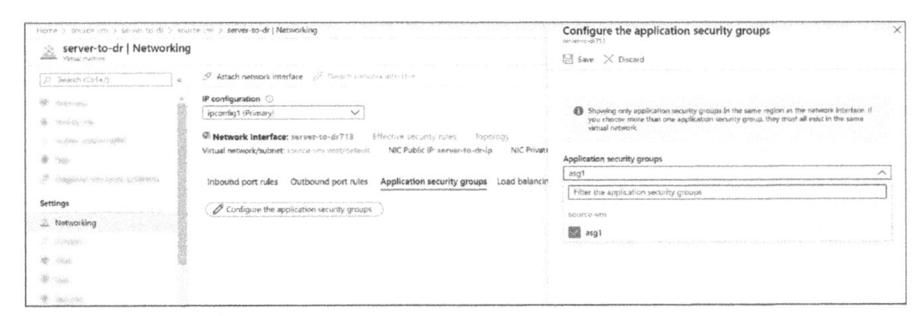

FIGURE 2-60 Application Security Group configuration

Once the ASG has members assigned, it can be used to help simplify NSGs and the rules used to define traffic flow within an environment.

Because it is likely that ASGs are fairly ambiguous at first—largely because they don't have individual configuration options—it is ideal practice to ensure that the names of the groups are very specific to the action(s) for which they will be used.

For example, if there is a requirement to configure a rule to allow access to a database but only from specific servers, it might make sense to specify an ASG as the source of the rule. This means only servers in that group would be allowed to access the database resource.

Implement Azure Bastion

Azure Bastion is the Azure service equivalent to a jump or bastion host. Using these machines to access resources on specific networks allows more security to be applied to the targeted environment. For example, my organization might need a specific network to be completely walled off from the Internet, which would remove any public IP addresses or access from other Internet-connected networks. When configured in the same environment, Azure Bastion will allow management access without requiring a multihomed virtual machine or public access to the target servers.

To get Azure Bastion up and running, complete the following steps:

1. Log in to the Azure portal (*https://portal.azure.com*).
2. From the navigation menu, select **Create A Resource**.
3. In the search box for new resources, type **Bastion**, select the **Bastion** option, and click **Create**.
4. Provide the following information to configure Azure Bastion in your environment:
   - **Subscription.** Select the subscription that will house the Bastion resource.
   - **Resource Group.** Select or create a resource group for the Bastion resource.

TIP LOCATION, LOCATION, LOCATION

Keep the Bastion service close to the network it will service. Placing it in the same resource group as the virtual network will ensure it is in the required region.

   - **Name.** The name of the instance of Azure Bastion being configured.
   - **Region.** Specify the region for the Bastion resource.
   - **Virtual Network.** Select or create a virtual network for use with Azure Bastion.
   - **Subnet.** Azure Bastion requires a subnet named `AzureBastionSubnet` to exist or be created on the VNet used. If this subnet exists, it is automatically selected.
   - **Public IP Address.** Select an existing or create a new public IP address for Azure Bastion.
5. Click **Next: Tags** to continue and add tags to the Azure Bastion instance.
6. Once tags have been added, click **Next: Review + Create** to review your selections.
7. Click **Create** to provision Azure Bastion.

An instance of Azure Bastion deployed provides browser-based connectivity to both Windows (over RDP) and Linux (over SSH) for management and general use. Using Azure Bastion does not require these systems to have a publicly accessible IP address or a private IP address reachable from a management station. The Bastion service handles the connection to the target system.

Two things to note:

- Azure Bastion, when used for Administrative actions only, does not require a Client Access License for the target system.
- Also, there is currently a limit on the number of hosts that Bastion can connect to concurrently. For RDP sessions, this is 25 and for SSH 50, both depending on the number of other sessions hitting the target system(s).

To connect to a server using Azure Bastion, complete the following steps:

1. Log in to the Azure portal.
2. Locate the virtual machine to which you wish to connect and select it to view its options.
3. Click the **Connect** option under the **Settings** section of the navigation menu.
4. Select **Bastion** as the connection type.
5. Enter the username and password and click **Connect**, as shown in Figure 2-61.

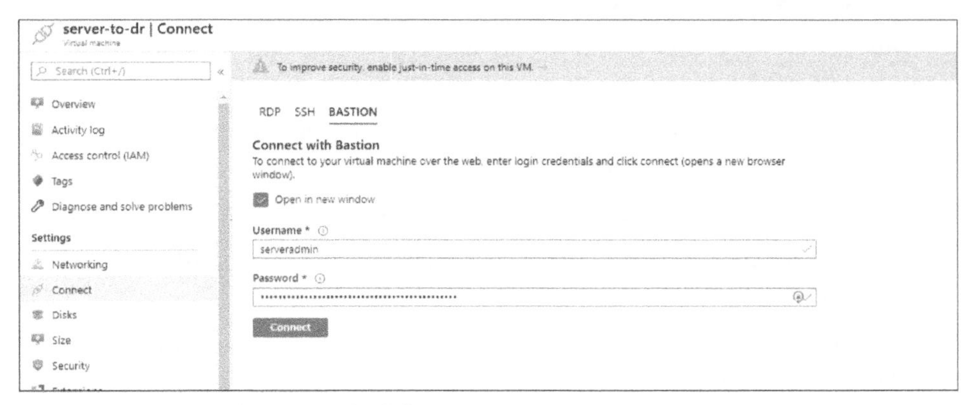

FIGURE 2-61 Azure Bastion connection info

By default, the Bastion connection opens in a new tab, which is sometimes blocked by pop-up blockers.

Once connected, the view though Bastion is the same as with the standard connection tools. It just occurs in a browser tab rather than external applications (see Figure 2-62).

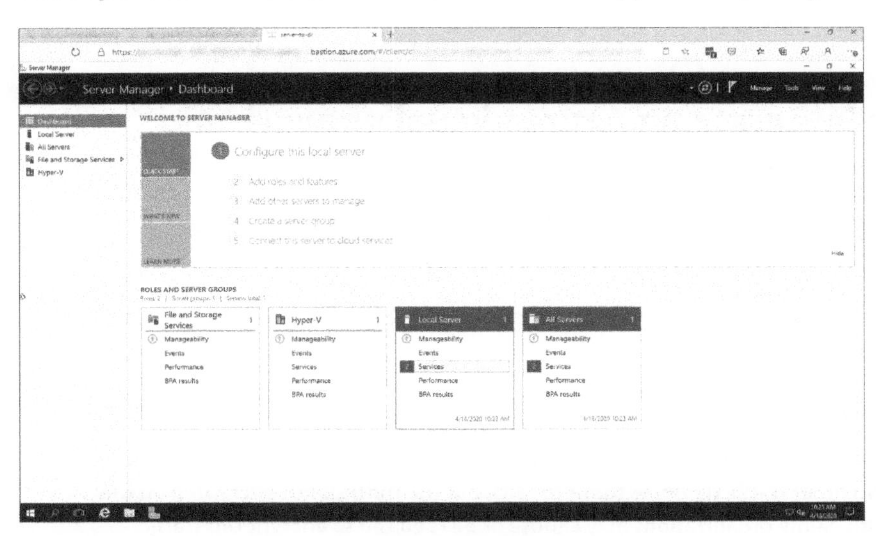

FIGURE 2-62 Connected to an Azure VM using Azure Bastion

Using this connection method removes the need to manage access via NSGs and prevents the addition of another host to patch and manage. In a traditional Bastion host scenario, the Bastion host itself would require maintenance and patching, but because Azure Bastion is a PaaS service, it does not require any additional maintenance.

NEED MORE REVIEW? **ADDITIONAL RESOURCES FOR LOAD-BALANCING OPTIONS**

Check out the articles at the following URLs for additional information:

- "What is Azure Application Gateway?" *https://docs.microsoft.com/en-us/azure/application-gateway/overview*
- "What is Azure Load Balancer?" *https://docs.microsoft.com/en-us/azure/load-balancer/load-balancer-overview*
- *"What is Azure Firewall?"* *https://docs.microsoft.com/en-us/azure/firewall/overview*
- *"What is Traffic Manager?"* *https://docs.microsoft.com/en-us/azure/traffic-manager/traffic-manager-overview*
- *"Network Security Groups Overview"* *https://docs.microsoft.com/en-us/azure/virtual-network/security-overview*
- *"Application Security Groups Examples"* *https://docs.microsoft.com/en-us/azure/virtual-network/application-security-groups*
- *"What is Azure Bastion?"* *https://docs.microsoft.com/en-us/azure/bastion/bastion-overview*

You also can review the Azure CLI documentation at *https://docs.microsoft.com/en-us/cli/azure/get-started-with-azure-cli?view=azure-cli-latest.*

Skill 2.6: Integrate an Azure virtual network and an on-premises network

Azure supports connectivity to external or on-premises networks via two methods:

- **VPN** An encrypted connection between two networks via the public Internet
- **ExpressRoute** A private circuit-based connection between an organization's network and Azure

NOTE **SECURITY DETAILS**

The connection made by ExpressRoute runs over private circuits between an organization and Azure. No other traffic traverses these circuits, but the traffic is not encrypted on the wire by default. Some organizations may choose or be required to encrypt this traffic with a VPN.

This skill covers how to:

- Create and configure Azure VPN Gateway
- Create and configure site-to-site VPN
- Verify on-premises connectivity
- Manage on-premises connectivity with Azure
- Configure ExpressRoute

Create and configure Azure VPN Gateway

The virtual network gateway is a router endpoint specifically designed to manage inbound private connections. The resource requires the existence of a dedicated subnet, called the gateway subnet, for use by the VPN.

To add a gateway subnet to a virtual network, complete the following steps:

1. Select the virtual network that will be used with the virtual network gateway.
2. Open the **Subnets** blade of the network resource.
3. Click **Gateway Subnet** at the top of the **Subnets** blade.
4. Specify the address range of the subnet. Because this is dedicated for connecting VPNs, the subnet can be small depending on the number of devices that will be connecting.
5. Edit the route table as necessary (not needed by default).
6. Choose any services that will use this subnet.
7. Select any services this network will be dedicated to supporting.
8. Click **OK**.

IMPORTANT **ABOUT NETWORKING**

Be mindful of the address space used for virtual networks created as any subnets, including the gateway subnet; they must fit within the address space and have no overlap.

To create a virtual network gateway, complete the following steps:

1. From the Azure portal, select or create the resource group that will contain the virtual network gateway.
2. Click **Add Link** at the top of the **Resource Group** blade.
3. Enter **virtual network gateway** in the resource search box. Select **Virtual Network Gateway** in the search results.
4. Click the **Create** button to begin creating the resource.

5. Complete the **Create Virtual Network Gateway** form shown in Figure 2-63:

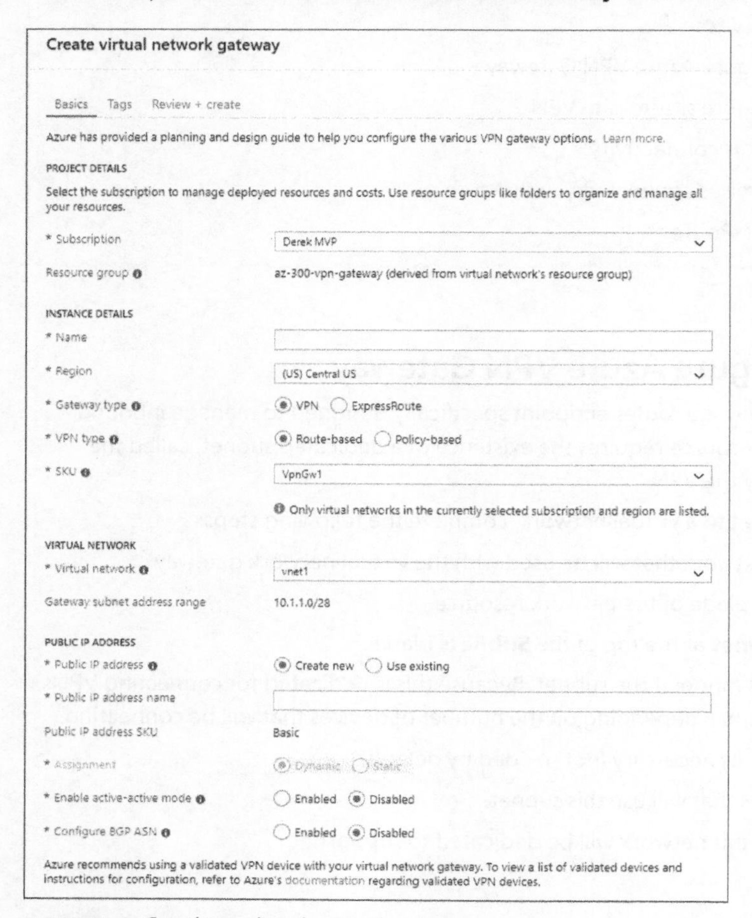

FIGURE 2-63 Creating a virtual network gateway

- **Subscription.** The Azure subscription that will contain the virtual network gateway resource.
- **Name.** The name of the virtual network gateway.
- **Region.** The region for the virtual network gateway. There must be a virtual network in the region where the virtual network gateway is created.
- **Gateway Type.** Choose **ExpressRoute** or **VPN**.
- **VPN Type.** Choose **Route-Based** or **Policy-Based**.
- **SKU.** The resource size and price point for the gateway.
- **Virtual Network.** The network to which the gateway will be attached.

- **Public IP Address.** The external IP address for the gateway (new or existing).
- **Enable Active-Active Mode.** Allow active/active connection management.
- **Enable BGP/ASN.** Allow BGP route broadcasting for this gateway.

6. Click **Review + Create** to review the configuration.
7. Click **Create** to begin provisioning the gateway.

NOTE **PROVISIONING TIME**

Virtual network gateways can take anywhere from 15 to 45 minutes to be created. In addition, any updates to the gateway also can take between 15 and 45 minutes to complete.

IMPORTANT **ABOUT NETWORKING RESOURCES**

When you configure networking resources, there's no way to deprovision them. Virtual machines can be turned off, but networking resources are always on and billing if they exist.

Create and configure site-to-site VPN

Once the virtual network gateway(s) are configured, you can begin configuring the connection between them or between one gateway and a local device.

There are three types of connections available using the connection resource in Azure:

- **VNet to VNet.** Connecting two virtual networks in Azure—across regions perhaps
- **Site to Site.** An IPSec tunnel between two sites: an on-premises datacenter and Azure
- **ExpressRoute.** A dedicated circuit-based connection to Azure, which we discuss later in this chapter

For a site-to-site configuration, complete the following steps:

1. In the Azure portal, open the resource group containing the virtual network gateway and VNet to be used in this configuration.
2. Collect the public IP address and internal address space for the on-premises networks being connected to Azure and the virtual network gateway public IP address and address space.
3. Create a pre-shared key to use in establishing the connection.
4. Add a connection resource in the same resource group as the virtual network gateway.
5. Choose the connection type for the VPN, site-to-site, the subscription, resource group, and location for the resource.

IMPORTANT **KEEP IT TOGETHER**

The resource group and subscription for connections and other related resources should be the same as the configuration for the virtual network gateway.

6. Configure the settings for the VPN as shown in Figure 2-64:
   - **Virtual Network Gateway.** Choose the available virtual network gateway based on subscription and resource group settings already selected.
   - **Local Network Gateway.** Select or create a local network gateway. This will be the endpoint for any on-premises devices being connected to this VPN.
7. Name the local network gateway.
8. Enter the public (external) IP address of the on-premises device used.
9. Enter the address space for the internal network on-premises. More than one address range is permitted.
10. The **Connection Name** is populated based on the resources involved, but you can change it if you need to make it fit a naming convention.
11. Enter the **Shared Key (PSK)** for the connection.
12. Enable BGP if needed for the connection. This will require at least a standard SKU for the virtual network gateway.
13. Review the summary information for the resources being created and click **OK**.

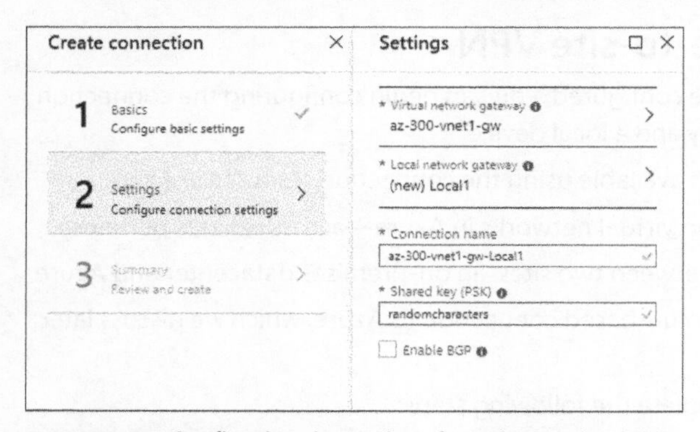

FIGURE 2-64 Configuring the settings for a site-to-site VPN

Verify on-premises connectivity

Once the site-to site-VPN configuration has been completed, verification of the connection will work, or it won't. If you have everything configured correctly, accessing resources in Azure should work like accessing other local resources.

Connecting to the machines connected to the Azure virtual network using local IP addresses should confirm that the VPN is connected, as the ping test shows in Figure 2-65.

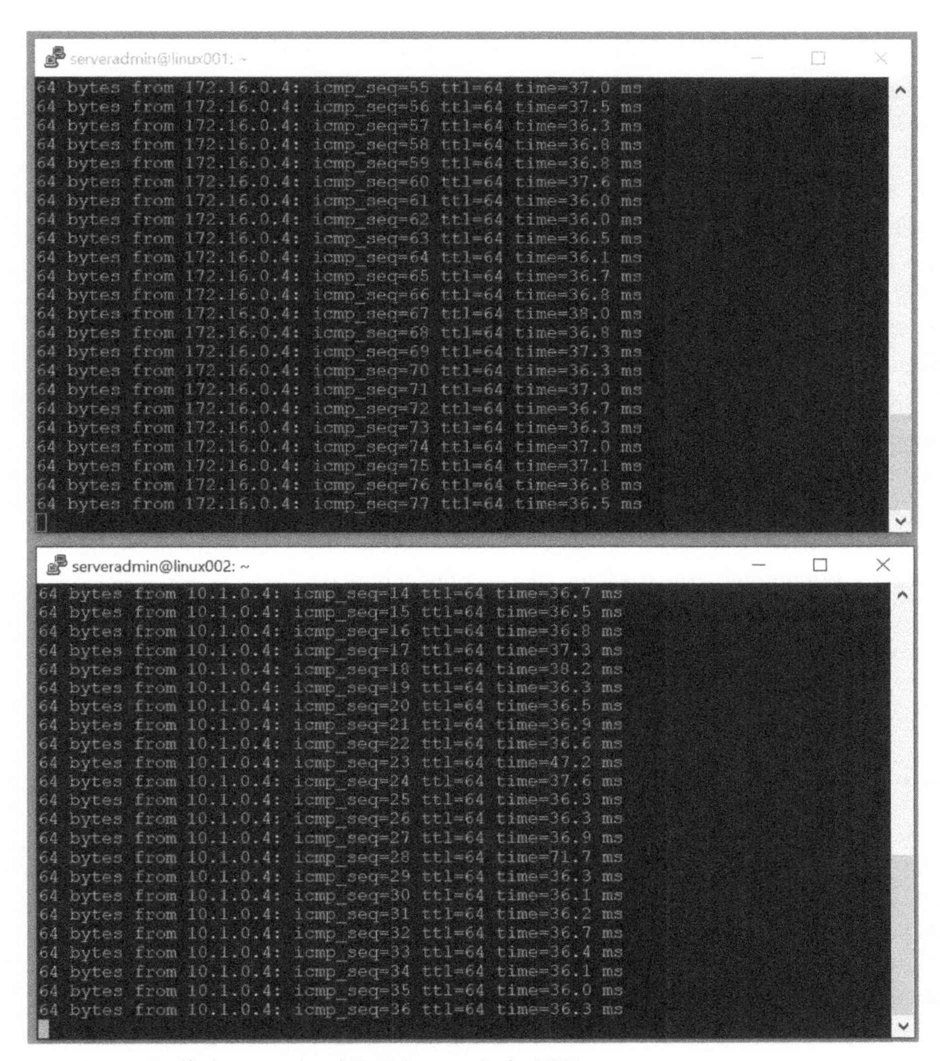

FIGURE 2-65 Traffic between local IP addresses via the VPN

In addition to the ping testing and connections between systems on these networks, the **Summary** blade for the local connection in Azure shows traffic across the VPN. This is shown in Figure 2-66.

FIGURE 2-66 An active VPN connection in the Azure portal

Manage on-premises connectivity with Azure

In many cases, VPN connections to Azure will be low maintenance once they are connected and in use. There may be times, though, that certain connectivity might need restrictions placed on it—for example, if a server in Azure should be accessed through a load balancer or be accessible only from the local network.

Azure allows these resources to be created without public IP addresses, making them accessible only across the VPN. This is part of the management of these resources; simply removing the public IP takes the machine off of the Internet, but an organization may have additional requirements in that systems in a production environment cannot talk directly to systems in a nonproduction environment. The segregation can be handled via network security groups and routing table entries.

A network security group serves as an ACL list for access (or denial) to resources, so it would help to open or block ports to and from certain machines.

Figure 2-67 shows a simple network security group where port 22 is allowed but only from a source tagged as a virtual network. This allows other resources on Azure virtual networks to reach the device, but nothing from the Internet can connect directly.

Inbound security rules

PRIORITY	NAME	PORT	PROTOCOL	SOURCE	DESTINATION	ACTION	
100	Port_22	22	Any	VirtualNetwork	10.1.0.4	Allow	...
65000	AllowVnetInBound	Any	Any	VirtualNetwork	VirtualNetwork	Allow	...
65001	AllowAzureLoadBalancerInBound	Any	Any	AzureLoadBalancer	Any	Allow	...
65500	DenyAllInBound	Any	Any	Any	Any	Deny	...

Outbound security rules

PRIORITY	NAME	PORT	PROTOCOL	SOURCE	DESTINATION	ACTION	
65000	AllowVnetOutBound	Any	Any	VirtualNetwork	VirtualNetwork	Allow	...
65001	AllowInternetOutBound	Any	Any	Any	Internet	Allow	...
65500	DenyAllOutBound	Any	Any	Any	Any	Deny	...

FIGURE 2-67 Network security groups

You can use network security groups at the network interface level for a virtual machine or at the subnet level.

EXAM TIP* *SIMPLIFY CONFIGURATION AT THE SUBNET LEVEL

Configuring network security groups at the subnet level ensures uniform rule behavior across any devices in the planned subnet and makes management of connectivity much less complicated.

NOTE **SECURITY**

If your organization has requirements for one-to-one access and connectivity, a network security group configured at the interface level for the VM might be necessary to ensure restricted access from one host to another.

Network security groups also allow the collection of flow logs that capture information about the traffic entering and leaving the network via configured network security groups. To enable this, you need two additional resources for all features, as shown in Figure 2-68:

- A storage account to collect the flow log data
- A Log Analytics workspace for traffic analysis

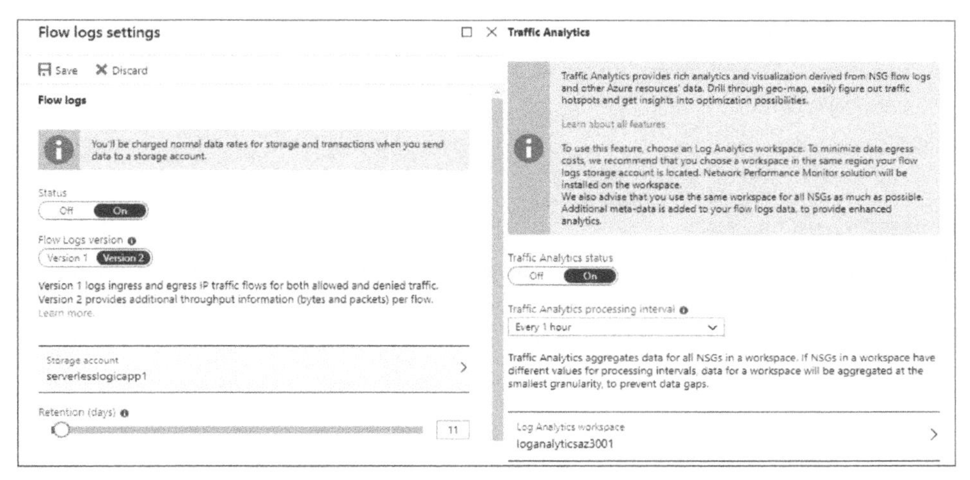

FIGURE 2-68 Flow Log and Traffic Analytics configuration

In addition to network security groups, route table entries can be used to control traffic flow between network resources. With a route table entry, you can force all the traffic between subnets to pass through a specific network or virtual network appliance that handles all the rules and access controls. There are reference architectures for this type of configuration in the Azure documentation that walk through configuring this type of network topology.

Configure ExpressRoute

Before you can use ExpressRoute as a VPN connection type, you need to configure it and prepare it as an Azure resource. Complete the following steps to configure the ExpressRoute Circuit resource in Azure:

1. In the Azure portal, click **Create A Resource**.
2. Select **ExpressRoute** from the **Networking** category.
3. On the **Create ExpressRoute Circuit** page, select to create a new circuit rather than importing from a classic configuration. To complete ExpressRoute setup, provide the following information:
   - **Circuit Name.** The name of the circuit resource.
   - **Provider.** Select the name of the provider delivering the circuit.
   - **Peering Location.** The location where your circuit is terminated; if you're using a partner like Equinix in their Chicago location, you would use Chicago for the Peering Location.

- **Bandwidth.** The bandwidth provided by the provider for this connection.
- **SKU.** This determines the level of ExpressRoute you are provisioning.
- **Data Metering.** This is for the level of billing and can be updated from metered to unlimited but not from unlimited to metered.
- **Subscription.** The Azure subscription associated with this resource.
- **Resource Group.** The Azure resource group associated with this resource.
- **Location.** The Azure region associated with this resource; this is different from the peering location.

4. Click **Create** the resource.

> ***NOTE*** **COSTS AND BILLING**
>
> **When you configure ExpressRoute in Azure, you receive a service key. When Azure issues the service key, billing for the circuit begins. Wait to configure this until your service provider is prepared with the circuit that will be paired with ExpressRoute to avoid charges while you're waiting for other components.**

Once the service key is issued and your circuit has been provisioned by a provider, you provide the key to the carrier to complete the process. Private peering needs to be configured and BGP allowed for ExpressRoute to work.

ExpressRoute also requires the virtual network gateway to be configured for it. To do this, when creating a virtual network gateway, select **ExpressRoute** as the **Gateway Type** (as shown in Figure 2-69).

Configuring the peering settings for ExpressRoute happens from within the ExpressRoute configuration settings once the circuit has been set up in Azure. From there, you see three types of peerings:

- **Azure Public.** This has been deprecated; use Microsoft peering instead.
- **Azure Private.** Peering with virtual networks inside subscriptions managed by your organization.
- **Microsoft.** Peering directly with Microsoft for the use of public services like Dynamics and Office 365.

You need to meet the following requirements for peering:

- A /30 subnet for the primary link.
- A /30 subnet for the secondary link.
- A valid VLAN ID to build peering on; no other circuit-based connections can use this VLAN ID. The primary and secondary links for ExpressRoute must use this VLAN ID.
- An AS number for peering (2-byte and 4-byte are permitted).
- Advertised prefixes, which is a list of all prefixes to be advertised over BGP.

- Optionally, you can provide a customer ASN if prefixes that do not belong to you are used, a routing registry name if the AS number is not registered as owned by you, and an MD5 hash.

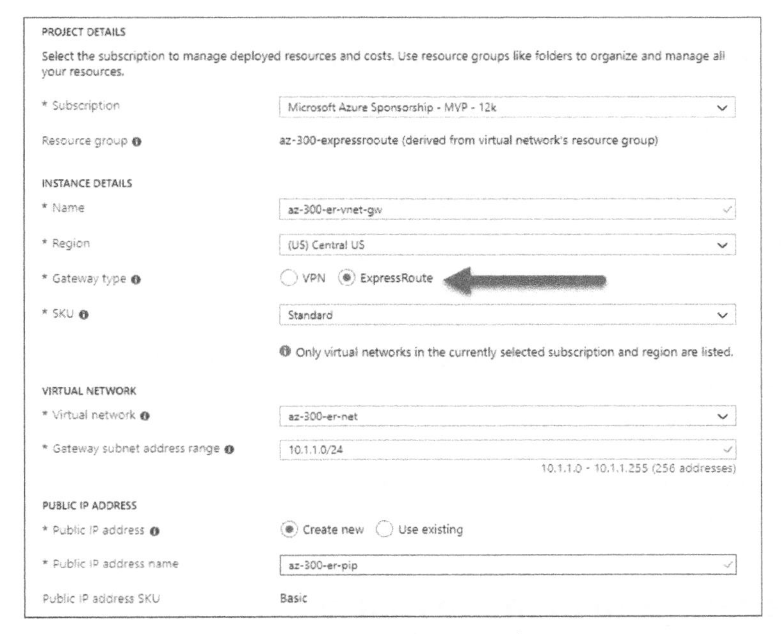

FIGURE 2-69 Configuring a virtual network gateway for ExpressRoute

Review the peering information and complete the following steps to finish configuring ExpressRoute:

1. Select the type of peering needed and provide the previously mentioned information.
2. Save the connection.

> ***IMPORTANT*** **VALIDATION**
>
> **Microsoft might require you to specify proof of ownership. If you see validation needed on the connection, you need to open a ticket with support to provide the needed information before the peer can be established. You can do this from the portal.**

3. Once you have successfully configured the connection, the details screen shows a status of `configured`.
4. Linking (or creating a connection to) ExpressRoute also happens from within the ExpressRoute resource. Choose the **Connections** option within the settings for ExpressRoute and provide the following:
   - **Name.** The name of the connection.
   - **Connection Type.** ExpressRoute.

- **Virtual Network Gateway.** Select the gateway with which to link ExpressRoute.
- **ExpressRoute Circuit.** Select the configured circuit with which to connect.
- **Subscription.** Select the subscription containing the resources used in this connection.
- **Resource Group.** Select the resource group containing the resources used in this connection.
- **Location.** Select the Azure region where the resources used in this connection are located.

This is like creating a site-to-site connection, as described earlier, but it uses different resources as part of the connection.

EXAM TIP

ExpressRoute is a private connection to Azure from a given location, and it requires high-end connectivity. Much of the discussion of ExpressRoute presented here relies on Microsoft Documentation because we don't currently have access to an ExpressRoute circuit.

The settings and configurations discussed are high level, but we've provided an overview of the concepts for ExpressRoute for the exam.

Skill 2.7: Implement and manage Azure governance solutions

Governance within a cloud environment plays an ever-growing part in the ability of organizations to move to the cloud and keep up with ever-changing technologies. Azure brings solutions centered around governance to the forefront to help organizations of all sizes manage access to resources and ensure that workloads are being deployed and maintained appropriately.

This skill covers how to:

- Implement Azure Policy
- Configure Azure Blueprint
- Implement and leverage Management Groups

Implement Azure Policy

Azure Policy provides a way to enforce and audit standards and governance throughout an Azure environment. Using this configuration involves two top-level steps:

1. Creating or selecting an existing policy definition
2. Assigning this policy definition to a scope of resources

Using Policy can streamline auditing and compliance within an Azure environment. However, it can also prevent certain resources from being created depending on the policy definition settings.

> ***IMPORTANT*** **REMEMBER TO COMMUNICATE**
>
> **Although the intent might be to ensure, for example, that all resources are created in a specified region within Azure, remember to overcommunicate any enforcement changes to those using Azure. The enforcement of policy generally happens when the Create button is clicked, not when the resource is discovered to be in an unsupported region.**

Collections of policy definitions, called *initiatives*, are used to group like policy definitions to help achieve a larger goal of governance rather than assigning 10 policy definitions separately. To hit this goal, they can be grouped into one initiative.

To assign a policy, complete the following steps:

1. From the **Navigation** pane in the Azure portal, select **All Services**.
2. Search for **Policy**.
3. Click the star next to the name of the service. (This will be helpful in the future.)
4. Click the name of the policy service to go to the resource.
5. On the **Policy Overview** blade, compliance information will be displayed (100 percent compliant if this is not in use yet).
6. Select the **Assignments** item.
7. On the **Policy Assignments** blade, shown in Figure 2-70, click **Assign Policy**.

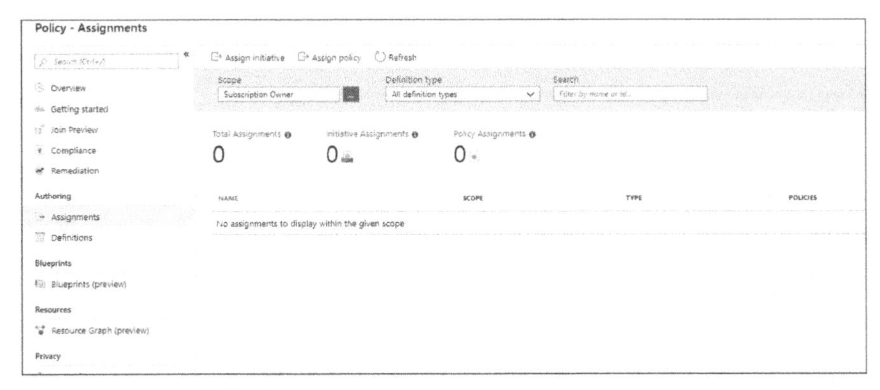

FIGURE 2-70 Azure Policy Assignments

8. Complete the following information on the Assign Policy screen:
   - **Scope.** Select the scope at which the chosen policy will be configured.
   - **Exclusions.** Select any resources that will be exempt from the policy assignment.
   - **Policy Definition.** Select the policy definition to be assigned.

- **Assignment Name.** Enter the name for this policy assignment.
- **Description.** Enter a description for the expected outcome of the policy assignment.
- **Assigned By.** The name of the Azure logged-in user who is assigning the policy will be listed.

9. Click **Assign** to save these settings.

When selecting from the list of available definitions, shown in Figure 2-71, pay attention to the name of the policy. Audit policies are used to capture information about what would happen if the policy were enforced. These will not introduce any breaking changes. Policies that aren't labeled audit may introduce breaking changes.

FIGURE 2-71 Policy definitions

Once a policy has been assigned, its compliance state may show as **Not Started** because the policy is new and has not yet been evaluated against resources. Click **Refresh** to monitor the state of compliance. It might take some time to reflect the state change.

If a policy runs against a scope and finds items in noncompliance, it may require remediation tasks to be performed. These tasks are listed under the **Remediation** section in the **Policy** blade, and they're only applicable to policies that will deploy resources if they are not found.

Kubernetes gets policy, too

In recent updates to the Azure Policy framework, Azure Kubernetes Service (AKS) has been integrated with the policy services. This allows policy to be applied during the scale out/up process of a container environment to ensure that containerized workloads are following the same rules as other services used within an organization's Azure environment.

Being able to audit the creation of things like virtual machines and other frontline Azure resources and ensure they are only allowed within certain regions was a great beginning, but if resources deployed inside a container on AKS could be moved to any regions in Azure, this could pose a compliance problem for Azure administrators. By using existing open-source tools to include AKS in Azure Policy, even containerized workloads are subject to organizational governance policy.

> ***NOTE*** **LIMITED PREVIEW ALERT**
>
> **Policy for AKS is in limited preview at the time of this writing. It supports only the built-in policy definitions, but as this continues to roll toward general availability, more options are likely to come along for the ride.**

To enable the Azure Kubernetes Service Policy, complete the following steps:

1. Opt in to the preview by registering the `Microsoft.ContainerService` and `Microsoft.PolicyInsights` resource providers in the Azure portal.
2. Browse to **Azure Policy**.
3. Select the option to join the preview.
4. Choose the subscription(s) to be included in the preview by checking the boxes for each.
5. Click the **Opt-In** button.

Once the opt-in has been completed for the preview, there is some work to complete to get the agent for policy installed. Install the Azure Policy Add-on by completing the following steps:

1. From the Azure CLI, install the preview extension using this code:

```
Az aks list
Az extension add --name aks-preview
#verify the version of the extension
Az extension show --name aks-preview --query [version]
```

2. Once the preview extension is configured, install the AKS add-on into the cluster that will be controlled (or audited) by policy:
   - From the portal, locate and select the Kubernetes Service.
   - Select any of the AKS clusters listed (or create one if there are none).
   - Select **Policies (Preview)** from the navigation menu.
   - Click the **Enable Add-On** button on the main section of the page.

The Policy Add-on will check in on AKS once every five minutes via a full scan of enabled clusters. Once this scan completes the details of the scan and the data collected will be returned to Azure Policy and included in the compliance details reporting provided.

Implementing Azure Blueprint

Azure Blueprint is a way to create repeatability within a cloud environment that sticks to standards the organization has configured. Azure Blueprint is a declarative orchestration resource to help build better Azure environments.

> ***NOTE*** **BETTER DOESN'T MEAN BETTER**
>
> **In this case, better was intended to specify more organized and repeatable. Blueprint is not required to keep things repeatable. Azure is very accommodating to any method of automation and build-out.**

One of the advantages of Blueprint is the Cosmos DB back end. This makes the objects used within Blueprint available across regions due to the globally distributed operation of Cosmos DB. Keeping objects available across Azure ensures low latency deployment of the resources regardless of the region where they get deployed. If an organization keeps resources local to them within West US 2, Blueprint will be there and not need to be reached from a different region for use.

To get started and configure Blueprint, complete the following steps (shown in Figure 2-72 below):

1. Log in to the Azure portal and select **Blueprints** from the services list (or search if that is faster).
2. Select **Blueprint Definitions** from the navigation list on the left.
3. On the main screen, select **Create Blueprint**.
4. There are some pre-defined Blueprints available to choose from including, but not limited to:
   - HIPAA Policies
   - Resource Groups with RBAC
   - Basic Networking

5. Select a built-in Blueprint or choose to start with a blank one.

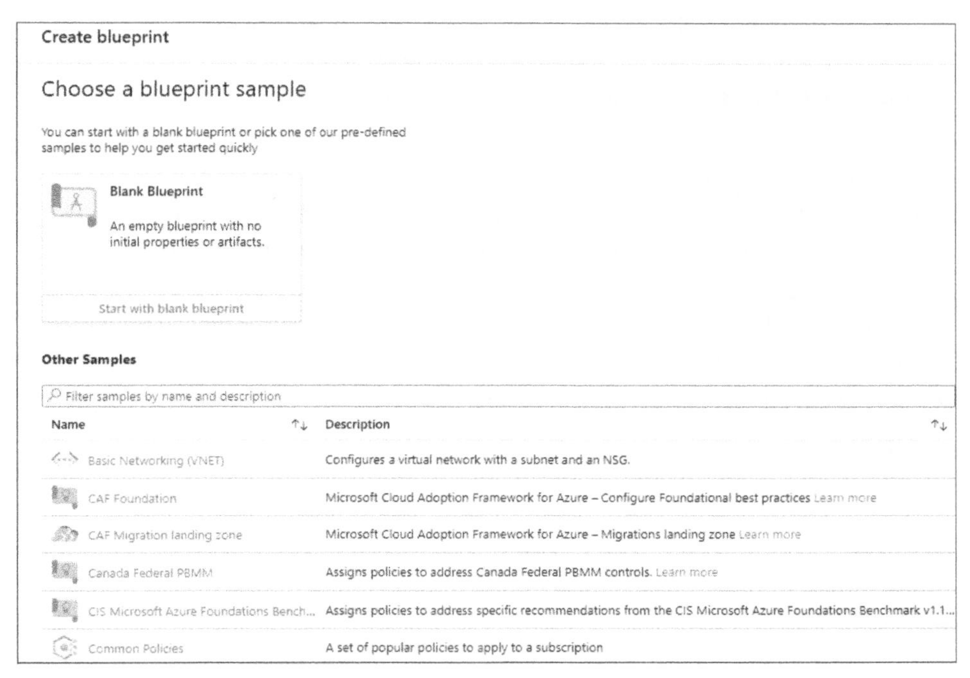

FIGURE 2-72 Configure Azure Blueprint

6. Provide the following for the Blueprint resource (shown in Figure 2-73):
   - **Blueprint Name.** A name for the Blueprint resource
   - **Blueprint Description.** What does this Blueprint do
   - **Definition Location.** Where the Blueprint will be saved/scoped
7. Add the artifacts that this Blueprint will create; available resource types include:
   - **Resource groups.** For organization and RBAC at build time
   - **ARM Templates.** The configuration files and variables used to build resources
   - **Policies.** The control policies assigned to resources created by this Blueprint
   - **RBAC Roles.** Roles assigned to resources created by this Blueprint
8. Save the Blueprint draft.
9. Click the saved draft and then click **Publish** to make the Blueprint available for assignment.
10. When things are ready for use, click the newly published Blueprint and click **Assign Blueprint**, and then provide the following:
    - **Assignment Name.** The name of the assignment
    - **Location.** Choose the default location

- **Blueprint definition version.** The version number of this Blueprint
- **Lock assignment.** Should this Blueprint be locked? If not, users or service principals with appropriate permission can modify the Blueprint
- **Managed Identity.** The identity used by the Blueprint

11. Click **Assign**.

When deciding if a Blueprint assignment should be locked, consider where the resources are destined to end up. If this will target production level resources, then locking the assignment might make sense to ensure that resources do not get deleted either intentionally or by accident.

If the assignment process cannot collect default values from the resource templates provided in the Blueprint, it might ask you (with some red ink) to assist in providing variables for the assignment. If that happens, provide the needed information, and click **Assign** to continue.

Once the assignment succeeds, resources requested as part of the Blueprint will be provisioned.

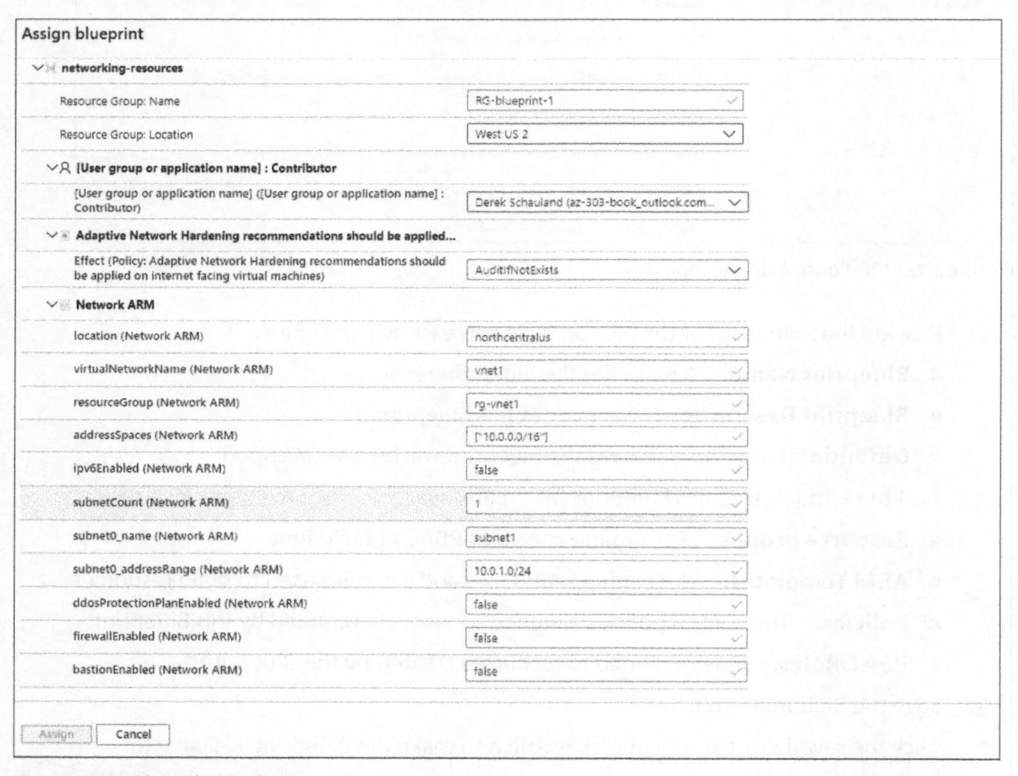

FIGURE 2-73 Blueprint Assignment

> ***NOTE*** **JSON IS VALIDATED DURING CREATION**
>
> **When saving the Blueprint definition, the JSON of any template files included will be validated; if it does not pass, the save will fail.**

Should Blueprint be used instead of Resource Manager Templates?

The use of Blueprint includes resource deployment with ARM templates to build or rebuild items in Azure. In addition, the security aspects of Azure Policy and configuration of access control using management groups or RBAC can be included as well. This allows Azure Blueprint to cover the whole deployment of an environment all in one overarching configuration.

For example, if my organization is planning to build an application that will leverage things like service bus, Azure DNS, App Services, and APIM, I can certainly handle those resources with ARM templates and automation pipelines. However, I will need to account for security and access configuration as well. Rather than relying on separate templates and configurations, creating an Azure Blueprint of the entire configuration will not only bring all of the needed solutions under one configuration, but it will allow the entire thing to be repeated without needing to reassemble all the necessary individual ARM template files.

If some of the ARM templates already exist, these can be leveraged by Blueprints to reduce reinvention of the resources needed.

Remember, in the end, an assigned Blueprint will deploy (or update) all of the associated resources defined within it. If multiple related items will be managed together and deployed together, a Blueprint might be the logical choice. For smaller, or one-off deployments, an ARM template could be a better fit.

Implementing and leveraging management groups

A management group in Azure is a resource that can cross subscription boundaries and allow a single point of management across subscriptions.

If an organization has multiple subscriptions, they can use management groups to control access to subscriptions that may have similar access needs. For example, if there are three projects going on within an organization that have distinctly different billing needs—each managed by different departments—access to these subscriptions can be handled by management groups, allowing all three subscriptions to be managed together with less effort and administrative overhead.

Management groups allow RBAC configurations to cross subscription boundaries. Using the scope of a management group for high-level administrative access will consolidate visibility of multiple subscriptions without needing to configure RBAC settings in each of many subscriptions. This way, the admins group can be assigned owner access in a management group that contains all the subscriptions for an organization, simplifying the configuration a bit further as shown in Figure 2-74.

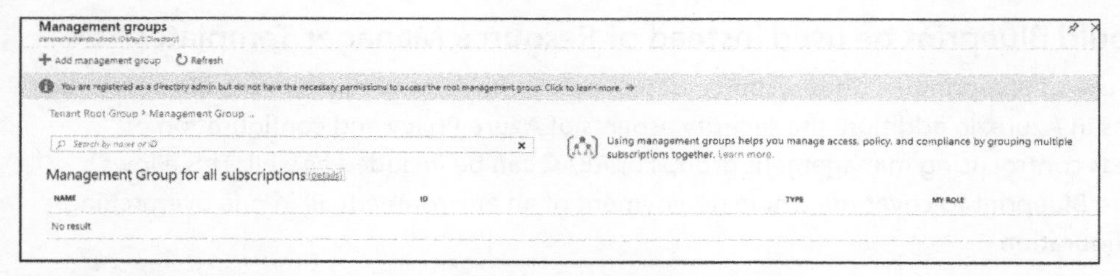

FIGURE 2-74 Management groups can be used across subscriptions for access

Top-level access management groups have a top-level root group scoped to the Azure AD tenant. Administrative users can't see this with usual administrative or owner RBAC permissions. To allow this visibility, assign the User Access Administrator role to the group that will be working with management groups.

To add subscriptions or management groups to a management group, complete the following steps:

1. Log in to the Azure portal.
2. Select **Management Groups** from the **All Services** list on the navigation pane.
3. If no management group exists, click **Add Management Group**.
   - Enter the ID for the new management group. (This cannot be changed.)
   - Enter the display name for the management group.
4. Click **Save**.
5. Click the name of the management group to which items will be added. There will likely be very little information visible when viewing a management group. Click the **Details** link next to the name of the group to see more information and take action on the management group, including adding management groups and subscriptions.
6. For subscriptions, click **Add Subscription**.
7. Select the subscription to be managed by this group.
8. Click **Save**.
9. For management groups, click **Add Management Group**.
10. Select to create a new management group or use an existing group.

Management groups can be nested to consolidate resource management. This should be used carefully because doing so can complicate management of subscriptions and resources further than necessary.

11. Select a management group to include and click **Save**.

IMPORTANT **CHANGING MANAGEMENT GROUPS MAY REQUIRE PERMISSION REVIEW**

When moving items from one management group to another, permissions can be affected negatively. Be sure to understand the effect of any changes before they are made to avoid removing necessary access to Azure resources.

NEED MORE REVIEW? **ADDITIONAL RESOURCES FOR GOVERNANCE OPTIONS**

Check out the articles at the following URLs for additional information:

- "What is Azure Policy?" at *https://docs.microsoft.com/en-us/azure/governance/policy/overview*
- "Understand Azure Policy for Kubernetes clusters" at *https://docs.microsoft.com/en-us/azure/governance/policy/concepts/rego-for-aks*
- "What are Azure management groups?" at *https://docs.microsoft.com/en-us/azure/governance/management-groups/overview*
- "What is Azure Blueprints?" at *https://docs.microsoft.com/en-us/azure/governance/Blueprints/overview*

You also can review the Azure CLI documentation at *https://docs.microsoft.com/en-us/cli/azure/get-started-with-azure-cli?view=azure-cli-latest.*

Skill 2.8: Manage Role-Based Access Control (RBAC)

Role-Based Access Control (RBAC) provides a manageable way to assign access to resources in Azure by allowing permissions to be assigned across job roles. If you're a server operator, you may be able to start and restart VMs but not power off or delete them. Because every resource in Azure is permissible and requires access, the consolidation of permissions into roles can help keep things organized.

This skill covers how to:

- Create a custom role
- Configure access to resources by assigning roles
- Configure Management Access to Azure
- Troubleshoot RBAC

Create a custom role

While Azure provides roles for certain activities—like contributor and reader, which provide edit and read access respectively—there may be job roles within an organization that don't fit nicely into these predefined items. Custom roles can be built to best suit the needs of an organization. To create a custom role, complete the following steps:

1. Log in to the Azure portal and select the resource group containing the items for which access will be customized.
2. In the navigation list for the resource group, select **Access Control (IAM)**.
3. The **IAM** blade appears as shown in Figure 2-75 with the **Check Access** tab selected.

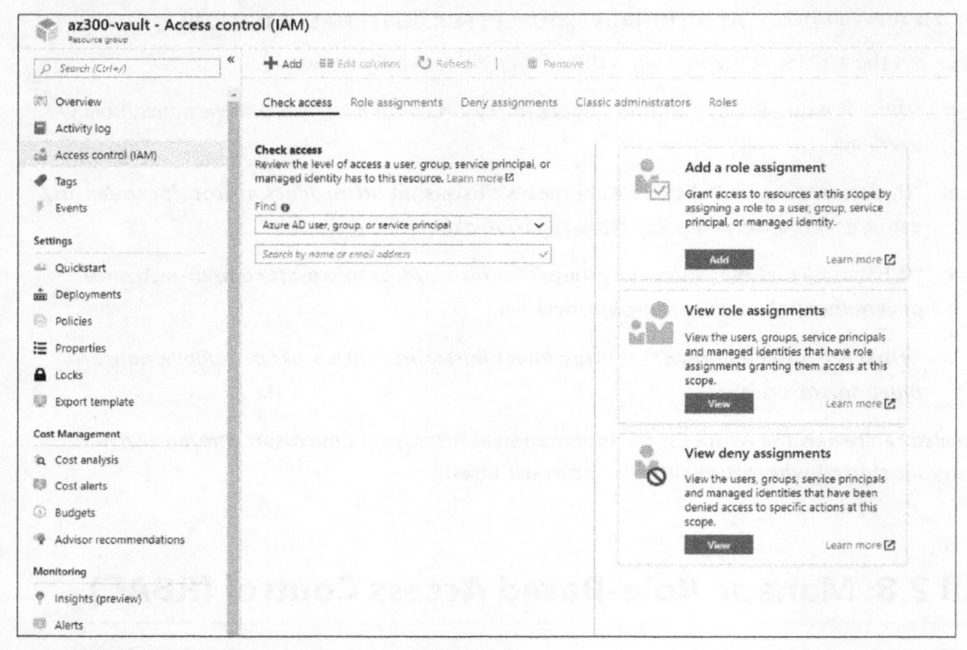

FIGURE 2-75 Check access to Azure resources

4. Before creating a custom role, it's a good idea to check the access for the user or group the custom role will include. In addition to determining the need for a custom role, this check helps ensure existing access is known and can be updated after custom roles are created.
5. In the **IAM** blade, select **Roles** at the top right to view a list of the access a predefined role already has.
6. Click a role that might have some of the access your custom role will need to review its permissions.

The creation of custom roles happens through the Azure CLI or Azure PowerShell because there's no portal-based method to build roles as of this writing. To create a custom role using PowerShell, complete the following steps:

1. Open a PowerShell console and connect to your Azure Subscription.

2. Use the following PowerShell command to collect the role you will start with:

```
$CustomRole = Get-AZRoleDefinition | where {$_.name -eq "Virtual Machine
Contributor"}
```

3. To view the actions this role has already, display the `Actions` property:

```
$CustomRole.Actions
```

To keep the custom role creation fairly simple, create a role for VM operators that can manage and access virtual machines. The role called out earlier is allowed to manage but not access machines. The Virtual Machine Administrator Log in role allows log in but no management of the machine.

```
$AdminRole = get-azroledefinition | where {$_.name -eq "Virtual Machine
Administrator Log in"}
```

At this point, the `$CustomRole` variable should contain an object for the Virtual Machine Contributor role, and `$AdminRole` should contain an object for the Virtual Machine Administrator Log in role.

As you can see from Figure 2-76, the actions allowing access to the VMs are missing from the Virtual Machine Contributor Role.

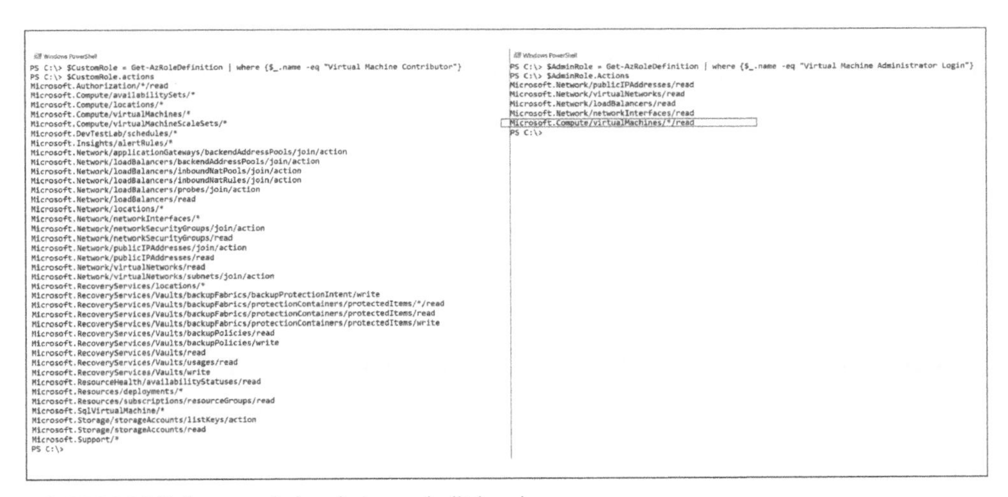

FIGURE 2-76 Missing permissions between built-in roles

4. To complete the custom role, add the missing admin permission to the $customRole object:

```
$customRole = get-azroledefinition | where { $_.name -eq "Virtual Machine
Contributor" }
$customRole.id = $null
$customRole.name = "Custom - Virtual Machine Administrator"
$Customrole.Description = "Can manage and access virtual machines"
$customRole.Actions.Add("Microsoft.Compute/VirtualMachines/*/read")
$customRole.AssignableScopes.Clear()
```

```
$CustomRole.AssignableScopes = "/subscriptions/<your subscription id>/
resourceGroups/<Resource Group for role>"
New-AzRoleDefinition -role $CustomRole
```

This will create a custom role called Custom - Virtual Machine Administrator and assign all the roles from the Virtual Machine Contributor Role plus the ability to log in to Azure Virtual Machines.

The role will be scoped to the supplied resource ID for the resource group chosen. This way, the added permissions are applicable only to the resource group(s) that need them—perhaps the Servers resource group.

Figure 2-77 shows the output of the command to create this custom role, with sensitive information redacted.

```
PS C:\> $customRole.id = $null
PS C:\> $customRole.name = "Custom - Virtual Machine Administrator"
PS C:\> $Customrole.Description = "Can manage and access virtual machines"
PS C:\> $customRole.Actions.Add("Microsoft.Compute/VirtualMachines/*/read")
PS C:\> $customRole.AssignableScopes.Clear()
PS C:\> #$CustomRole.AssignableScopes = "/subscriptions/<your subscription id>/resoureGroups/<Resource Group for role>"
PS C:\> $CustomRole.AssignableScopes = "/subscriptions/38b97161-b529-4733-969d-61f1aeaefac4/resourceGroups/az300-vault"
PS C:\>
PS C:\> New-AzRoleDefinition -role $CustomRole

Name             : Custom - Virtual Machine Administrator
Id               : 0c41319c-7e7b-4ac9-8c4c-010a691a47b2
IsCustom         : True
Description      : Can manage and access virtual machines
Actions          : {Microsoft.Authorization/*/read, Microsoft.Compute/availabilitySets/*, Microsoft.Compute/locations/*,
                   Microsoft.Compute/virtualMachines/*...}
NotActions       : {}
DataActions      : {}
NotDataActions   : {}
AssignableScopes : {/subscriptions/3                              4/resourceGroups/a          }


PS C:\>
```

FIGURE 2-77 Newly created custom role

Configure access to resources by assigning roles

Previously, a custom role was created to allow management of and access to virtual machines within an Azure Resource Group. Because the custom role was scoped at the resource group level, it will only be assignable to resource groups.

To make use of the custom role and any built-in roles, the roles need to be assigned to users or groups, which makes them able to leverage these access rights.

To assign the newly created custom role to a group, complete the following steps:

1. In the Azure portal, locate the resource group to which the custom role was scoped.
2. Click the **Access Control (IAM)** link in the navigation pane.
3. Click **Add** and select **Add Role Assignment**.
4. In the **Select A Role** box, enter the name of the custom role "**Custom** –" and click the name of the role.

NOTE CUSTOM ROLE NAMING

Although the type of any custom roles is set to CustomRole when roles are added, we've found prepending the word "Custom –" to the beginning of the name or following a naming standard predefined by your organization may make custom roles easier to find when searching for them at a later time.

5. The **Assign Access To** drop-down menu displays the types of identities that access can be assigned to:
   - Azure AD user, group, or service principal
   - User Assigned Managed Identity
   - System Assigned Managed Identity
     - App Service
     - Container Instance
     - Function App
     - Logic App
     - Virtual Machine
     - Virtual Machine Scale Set

   Because virtual machine administrators are generally people, keep the Azure AD user, group, or service principal selected.

6. In the **Select** box, enter the name of the user or group to which this new role should be assigned.
7. Click the resultant username or group to select them.

IMPORTANT ABOUT GROUPS

Keep in mind that using a group for role assignments is much lower maintenance than individually assigning users to roles.

8. Click **Save** to complete the role assignment.

The user (or users if a group was assigned) was assigned new access and might need to log out of the portal or PowerShell and log back in or reconnect to see the new access rights.

Configure Management Access to Azure

Like access to resources running in Azure, access to the platform itself is controlled using RBAC. There are some roles dedicated to the management of Azure resources at a very high level—think management groups and subscriptions.

When you use RBAC roles, the method of assigning access to subscriptions or management groups is the same as other resources, but the roles specific to management and where they're assigned are different. These would be set at the subscription or management group level.

> ***IMPORTANT*** **CUMULATIVE BY DEFAULT**
>
> **RBAC access is cumulative by default, meaning contributor access at the subscription level is inherited by resource groups and resources housed within a subscription. Inheritance is not required because permission can be granted at lower levels within a subscription all the way down to the specific resource level. In addition, permission can also be denied at any level; doing so prevents access to resources where permission was denied. If denial of permissions happens at a parent resource level, any resources underneath the parent will inherit the denial.**

There will always be an entity in Azure that is the overall subscription admin or owner. Usually this is the account that created the subscription but can (and should) be changed to a group to ensure that more than one person has top-level access to the subscription. In addition, this change will account for job changes, staff turnover, and reduce the likelihood that someone forgets about access to Azure during these situations.

To configure access to Azure at the subscription level, complete the following steps:

1. Log in to the Azure portal and select **Subscriptions**.
2. Click the subscription to be managed.
3. Click the **Access Control (IAM)** navigation item.
4. On the **IAM** blade, select **Role Assignments**.

The users or groups who have specific roles assigned are displayed. At the subscription level there should be few roles assigned, as shown in Figure 2-78. Most access happens at the resource group or resource level.

5. Click **Add** at the top of the **IAM** blade.
6. Select **Add Role Assignment**.
7. Choose the **Owner Role**.
8. Leave the **Assign Access To** drop-down menu set to **Azure AD User**, **Group**, or **Service Principal**.
9. Select a group to assign to the owner role by searching for the group and then clicking it in the results.
10. Click **Save**.

The group has owner access at the subscription level. This access allows members of the group to create, modify, and remove any resources within the selected subscription.

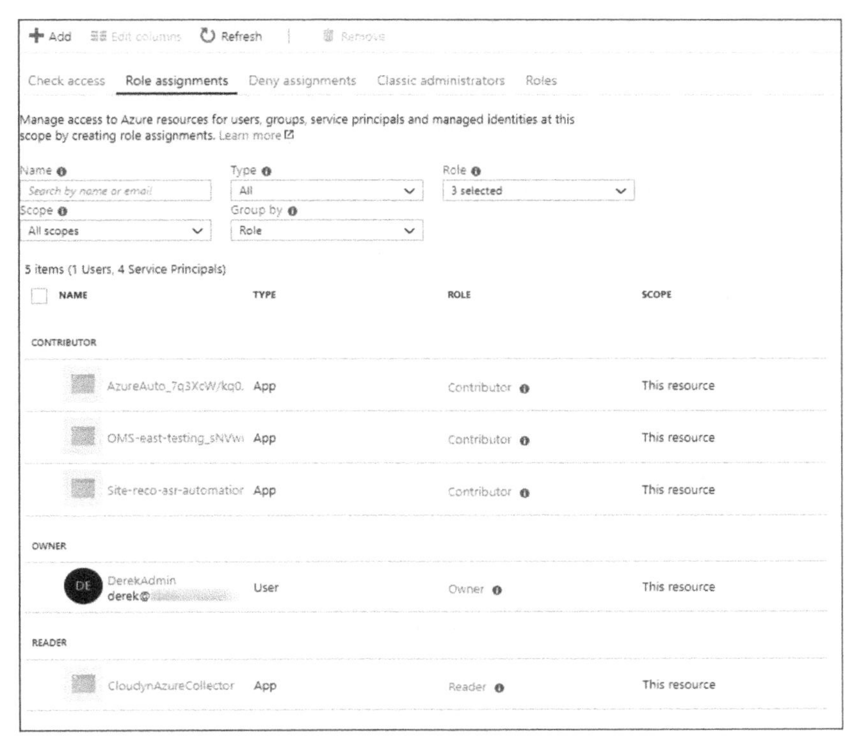

FIGURE 2-78 Roles assigned at the subscription level

> ***NOTE*** **ADDING A COADMINISTRATOR**
>
> **This is only necessary if Classic deployments are being used (the Classic portal). Assigning Owner RBAC rights in the Resource Management portal achieves the same result.**

Troubleshoot RBAC

Identifying the cause of problems with RBAC may require some digging to understand why a user is unable to perform an action. When you're assigning access through RBAC, be sure to keep a group of users configured for owner access. In addition to a group, consider enabling an online-only user as an owner as well. This way, if there is an issue with Active Directory, not all user accounts will be unable to access Azure.

Because Role-Based Access Control (RBAC) is central to resource access in Azure, using RBAC carefully is paramount in working with Azure. Like permissions in Windows before it, Azure RBAC brings a fair amount of trial and error to the table when assigning access. Also, because Azure is constantly evolving, there may be times when a permission just doesn't work as stated.

The main panel of the **IAM** blade has improved considerably in recent time by providing a quick way to check access up front. If someone is questioning their access, an administrator or other team member can easily enter the username or group name where access is being questioned and see which role assignments are currently held. No more sifting through the role assignments list to determine if Fred has contributor or viewer access to the new resource group. This is one of the key tools in troubleshooting—being able to see who has what level of access.

During the times when Fred should have access to a particular resource, but claims to be missing access while Azure shows the correct role assignments, the **Roles** tab on the **IAM** blade shown in Figure 2-79 can help determine whether all the needed permissions are available. Sometimes they won't be.

Looking at the list of roles is only somewhat helpful. If Fred claims that he can't read a resource, but he's listed as having the reader role for the resource, there will likely be something going on behind the role. To see the permissions assigned to the listed role, click on the name of the role.

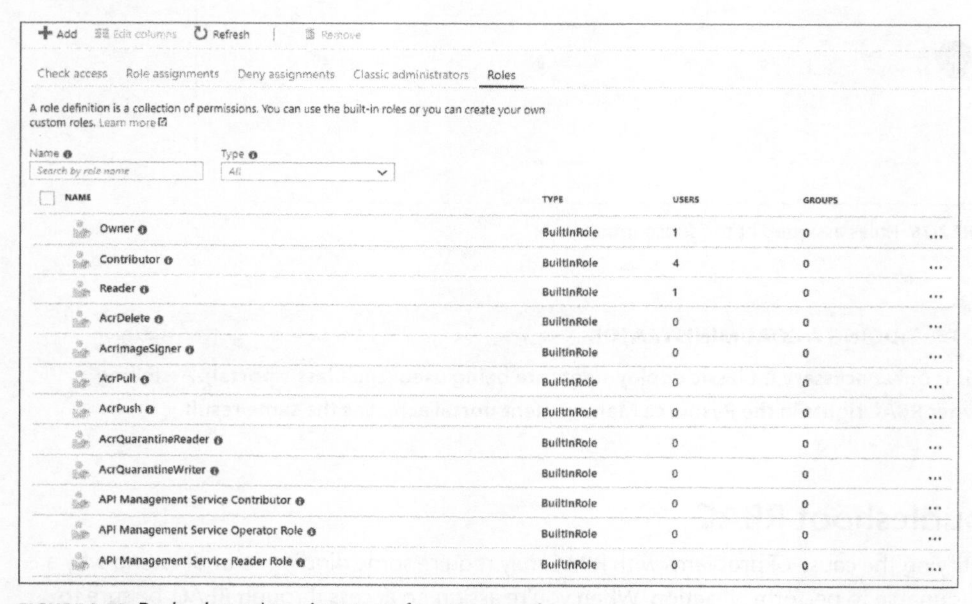

FIGURE 2-79 Reviewing role assignments for groups and users

On the top of the listed assignments page for the role, click **Permissions** to see the list of permissions that make up the role.

You will see, as shown in Figure 2-80, the list of resource providers that the role meets and whether they have partial access or all access to the provider as well as what data access for a provider the role has.

Permissions (preview)
Reader

RESOURCE PROVIDER	MANAGEMENT	DATA
84codes.CloudAMQP	Partial	--
Azure Data Box	Partial	--
Azure Database Migration Service	Partial	--
Azure IoT Central	Partial	--
Azure Log Analytics	Partial	--
Azure Stack Resource Provider	Partial	--
Bot Service Resource Provider	Partial	--
CloudSimple Private Cloud IAAS	Partial	--
Conexlink MyCloudIT	Partial	--
Crypteron DataSecurity	Partial	--
Domain Services Resource Provider	Partial	--
FriendlyRpNamespace	Partial	--
LiveArena.Broadcast	Partial	--
Machine Learning Services Resource Provider	Partial	None

FIGURE 2-80 Resource provider permissions within a role

Selecting a provider name from this view displays the components used by this role within a given provider and the permissions assigned, as shown for the Azure Data Box provider in Figure 2-81.

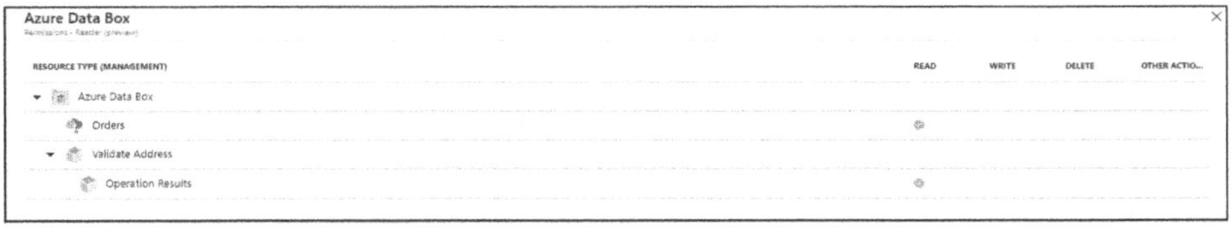

Azure Data Box
Permissions - Reader (preview)

RESOURCE TYPE (MANAGEMENT)	READ	WRITE	DELETE	OTHER ACTIO...
Azure Data Box				
Orders	●			
Validate Address				
Operation Results	●			

FIGURE 2-81 Permissions within the reader role for Azure Data Box

In addition to investigating which permissions get assigned with certain roles, changing roles for certain users or groups to see how access changes is another method that's useful in working through access issues.

There also can be times when changes to RBAC are being cached—when settings changes just aren't appearing once they've been made. In the Azure portal, changes made can take up to 30 minutes to be reflected. In Azure CLI or a PowerShell console, the process of signing out and signing in again will force settings to refresh when making changes to RBAC. Similarly, when using Rest APIs to manage permissions, updating the current access token will refresh permissions.

There are also times when certain resources may require permissions that are higher than the stated need—for example, working in an App Service may require write permission to the underlying storage account to ensure performance monitoring is visible; otherwise, it returns an error. In cases like this, perhaps elevated access (contributor in this case) might be preferable for a time to allow monitoring. This way, the developers get access to the items they need, but maybe the access doesn't remain assigned long term.

Chapter summary

- Virtual machines from on-premises datacenters or other cloud environments as well as physical servers can be migrated to Azure.
- Azure Bastion removes the need for dedicated IaaS resources used to manage machines within a virtual network. In addition, since Bastion is a Platform-as-a-Service offering, there is no patching or updating that needs to be performed by the user.
- Application load balancing and network load balancing work in tandem to ensure an all-around solution.
- Serverless compute and Platform-as-a-Service resources move infrastructure management more to the cloud provider than having all the resources managed by an organization's IT staff. This can save money in the long term.
- Azure Traffic Manager can be used to route traffic between regions to help improve high availability for resources running in Azure and elsewhere.
- Logic Apps perform custom integrations between applications and services both inside and outside of Azure.
- Virtual network peering allows communication between networks in Azure without need for a VPN, whereas Site-to-Site VPNs connect Azure to existing on-premises networks and ExpressRoute provides completely private connections to Microsoft services from an on-premises environment.
- Azure Firewall is a cloud-native firewall solution that currently exists per virtual network. Firewall policies can be pushed to multiple Azure Firewall instances for more uniform configuration.
- Role-Based Access Control aligns user access to Azure resources more closely with job roles. Keep in mind that this alignment is not always perfect and multiple roles may be necessary to provide the correct access.
- Policies in Azure help to ensure that resources can be audited for compliance and deployment controlled as required by the organization.
- Managed Identity Services will allow applications to register within Azure Active Directory. Using fully managed tokens for these applications keeps the credentials out of application code and seamlessly provides access to other Azure resources.
- Azure Key Vault allows managed identity access for secure access to secrets, keys, and certificates with very little overhead.
- Azure Blueprint provides fully templated resource creation, including policy and role-based access to the new resources. Leveraging these for repeatable deployment can improve the speed and efficiency of deployment.

Thought experiment

In this thought experiment, demonstrate your skills and knowledge of the topics covered in this chapter. You can find the answers to thought experiment questions in the next section.

You are an Azure architect hired by Fabrikam to help them configure Azure networking and access to resources within their environment as they move from an on-premises datacenter to Azure.

Meetings have been productive for the most part in reviewing what they have in Azure today, but in researching the environment you make the following recommendations/requirements:

Connections between virtual networks are incurring a significant cost: this should be reduced if possible.

IaaS workloads in Azure have open access to RDP to allow maintenance and are exposed to the Internet on public IP addresses. To improve security, the public IP should be removed while still allowing access for server management.

A web application has been called out by others in the organization for issues with high availability. This is something that should be done as soon as possible—there is no need at this time to worry about regional boundaries.

Considering the discovered requirements, answer the following questions:

1. How would you reduce the cost of virtual network connections within Azure?
2. What Azure solution(s) could allow you to remove public IP addresses from virtual machines and still access them for management tasks?
3. What could you use to ensure that the web application is failed over to another site in the event of an outage?

Thought experiment answers

This section contains the solution to the thought experiment for this chapter. Please keep in mind there may be other ways to achieve the desired result. Each answer explains why the answer is correct.

1. Connections between Virtual Networks in Azure can be made using VNet Peering. Creating two one-way peers between two VNets should reduce the cost of the connections because there is no need to pay for Virtual Network Gateway resources in each VNet. Since the peers can also cross region boundaries, they will maintain connections between regions as well.

2. Public IP addresses can be a necessary resource to ensure your customers can reach your applications. There are a number of possible solutions here—since the requirement is for management access to servers and no public IP addresses, the least overhead method would be to configure Azure Bastion on the VNet hosting the server(s) and use that for access. This way the public IP addresses could be removed. If the servers are joined to an Active Directory Domain and available over a Site-to-Site VPN, RDP will still work, and a public IP would not be needed.
3. Ensuring high availability for web applications can also take multiple paths. Leveraging an Application Gateway would provide a regional public endpoint that your customers could access. This would also send the inbound traffic to one or multiple backend resources to provide high availability in the event one resource becomes unavailable or needs maintenance. To work across regions, a duplicate configuration would be needed for the Application Gateway and any app services needed. Then a traffic manager would be deployed in front of the Application Gateways to direct incoming DNS-based traffic to the desired Application Gateway.

CHAPTER 3

Implement Solutions for Apps

Azure App Service is a managed platform used to quickly build, deploy, and scale web apps in the cloud. App Service supports applications built using common frameworks such as .NET, .NET Core, Node.js, Java, PHP, Ruby, or Python. One of the biggest advantages to using App Service is the ability to instantly achieve enterprise-grade performance, security, and compliance without having to worry about routine maintenance and operational tasks.

In this chapter, you learn how to create and deploy web applications that run in the Azure App Service environment, and you'll gain an understanding of modern patterns and practices used to build and deploy containerized applications.

Skills covered in this chapter:

- 3.1: Implement an application infrastructure
- 3.2: Implement container-based applications

Skill 3.1: Implement an Application Infrastructure

Azure App Service gives you the ability to build and host web apps, mobile back ends, and RESTful APIs without getting bogged down in the depths of managing traditional infrastructure. Offloading the heavy lifting of server maintenance, patching, and backups gives you the freedom to concentrate on your application. App Service includes Microsoft's best practices for high availability and load balancing as part of this managed service offering. You can easily enable and configure autoscaling and deploy Windows or Linux-based applications from common deployment sources such as GitHub, Azure DevOps, or any local Git repo.

This skill covers how to:

- Create and configure Azure App Service
- Create an App Service Web App for Containers
- Configure networking for an App Service
- Create and manage deployment slots
- Implement Logic Apps
- Implement Azure Functions

Create and configure Azure App Service

Microsoft offers a variety of methods for deploying web apps in Azure App Service. The term *web app* simply refers to a managed application running in App Service. You can use the Azure portal to create a web app, and you also can use the Azure CLI, PowerShell, and other IDE-based tools such as Visual Studio that provide integration with the Azure platform.

1. To create an Azure App Service web app, start by signing in to the Azure portal and use the following procedure: Navigate to the **App Services** bookmark on the left side of the Azure portal.
2. Click on **Add** to create a new web app.
3. On the **Web App** screen (see Figure 3-1), configure the following options and then click **Review And Create**:
   - **Subscription.** Select the appropriate subscription for the web app resource. You can have different subscriptions in your enterprise that are dedicated to development or production environments or are dedicated for use by specific teams in your organization.
   - **Resource Group.** Select an existing or new resource group where the web app will reside. Remember that you can deploy multiple resources into a group and delegate access control at the resource group level if needed.
   - **Name.** Enter a globally unique host name for your web app under *azurewebsites.net*. This might take several attempts because many host names are already in use. Enter the name for your web app in all lowercase letters. It should have between 3 and 24 characters.
   - **Publish.** Select **Code** as the **Publish** option unless you're deploying a web app that has been packaged into a Docker container image.
   - **Runtime Stack.** Select the appropriate runtime stack for your application. Multiple runtimes are supported in App Service, including .NET Core, ASP.NET, Java, Node, and Python.
   - **Region.** Choose the appropriate region to host your web app. Keep in mind that proximity between users and application infrastructure might be very sensitive, depending on the type of web application you're deploying. It's a common practice to host cloud resources in regions closest to users.
   - **App Service Plan.** Select a new or existing App Service Plan, which is the managed infrastructure hosting your web apps. Various pricing tiers are available that provide everything from basic capability all the way to very advanced capabilities. The Standard S1 plan is the recommended minimum pricing tier for production web apps.

FIGURE 3-1 Creating an App Service Web App

EXAM TIP

You can also use the command line to deploy your web apps. For example, use the `az webapp create` **command with the Azure CLI to perform this task from your local terminal or Azure Cloud Shell instance.**

Create an App Service web app for containers

The ease of Azure App Service makes deploying Windows or Linux container–based web apps a simple process. You can pull Docker container images hosted in the Docker Hub or use your own private Azure Container Registry. One of the greatest benefits to this approach is that you can include all the dependencies you need for your application inside your container images. Microsoft will take care of the patching, high availability, and load balancing that powers the underlying infrastructure.

Creating a web app for containers is a similar process to building a standard web app. Use the following procedure in the Azure portal to create a containerized web app in App Services:

EXAM TIP

Azure PowerShell is a common command-line alternative used to deploy web apps. You can use the `New-AzWebApp` cmdlet to script the deployment of standard or containerized web apps in App Service.

1. Navigate to the **App Services** bookmark on the left side of the Azure Portal.
2. Click **Add** to create a new web app.
3. Provide all the required details for your web app and make sure to set the **Publish** option to **Docker Image**; then click **Next**.
4. Enter the following details for your Docker container image, as shown in Figure 3-2, and then click **Review And Create**:
   - **Options.** Selecting **Single Container** is the most common option. Multi-container support using Docker Compose is currently planned for a future release.
   - **Image Source.** The Docker Hub is the default container registry for public images. You also can select your own private registry or an Azure Container Registry resource.
   - **Access Type.** Public images are the default access type for Docker Hub; however, private images are also supported with App Service web apps. If you select **Private** for your access type, you're prompted to enter your registry credentials.
   - **Image And Tag.** Enter the name of your container image and corresponding tag (optional).
   - **Startup Command.** Optional startup scripts or commands are supported. This is often unnecessary because container images can be built to use a specific startup command by default.

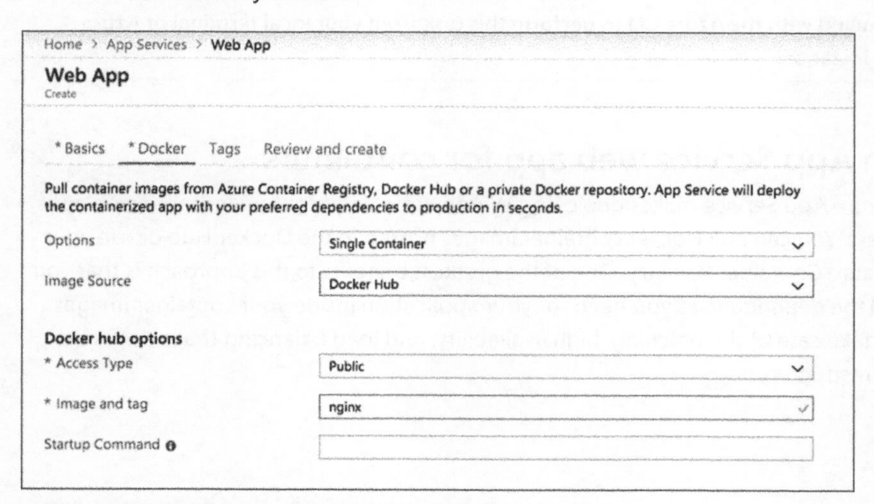

FIGURE 3-2 Configuring the Docker image settings

NEED MORE REVIEW? APP SERVICE OVERVIEW

To review further details about Azure App Service, refer to the Microsoft Azure documentation at *https:// docs.microsoft.com/en-us/azure/app-service/overview.*

Configure networking for an App Service

Azure Virtual Networks (VNets) allow you to place many Azure resources in a private and fully isolated virtual network used to host virtual machines, load balancers, and more. Azure App Service provides a VNet integration feature that allows your apps to access resources inside a VNet.

For example, imagine you were hosting a Microsoft SQL database on an Azure Virtual Machine. You could use VNet integration to allow your App Service to communicate with the SQL server, without sending that traffic over the public Internet.

It's important to note that the VNet integration functionality is a mechanism that allows your apps to access isolated network resources. It doesn't place the App Service inside the VNet.

If you want to enforce private network access for your App Service applications, then you should choose the App Service Environments (ASE) service plan that offers fully isolated and dedicated networking for App Service. ASE places your App Service resources within your Azure VNet.

If you're not using ASE, you can follow the process for giving your App Services access to resources in your VNet requires using the following procedure:

1. Go to the **Networking UI** in the **App Service** portal. Under **VNet Integration**, select **Click Here To Configure**.
2. Select **Add VNet**, as shown in Figure 3-3.

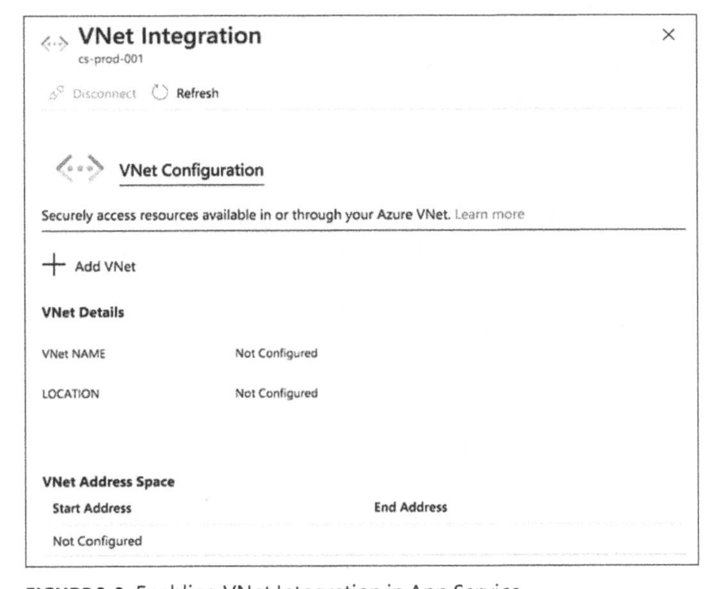

FIGURE 3-3 Enabling VNet Integration in App Service

3. The **Virtual Network** drop-down menu contains all the Azure Resource Manager virtual networks in your subscription in the same region. Select the VNet you want to integrate with, as shown in Figure 3-4.

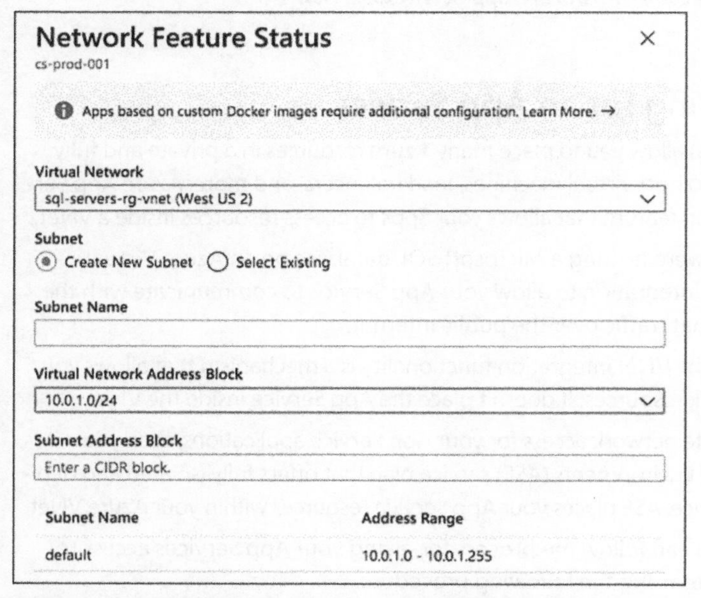

FIGURE 3-4 Selecting a VNet and Subnet for App Service VNet Integration

Create and manage deployment slots

Azure App Services running in the Standard, Premium, or Isolated App Service plan tiers support the concept of deployment slots, which allow you to run different live apps with their own host names. Deployment slots are typically used to stage new versions of your application and ultimately, swap new versions into production.

Each production-grade App Service plan tier supports a different number of deployment slots. There's always an implicit production slot.

Deploying your application to a non-production slot allows you to validate app changes in a staging slot before swapping it into a production slot.

Use the following procedure to add a slot and swap the code into your production environment:

1. Navigate to the properties of an existing web app in the Azure portal.
2. Scroll down on the left-hand side and select **Deployment Slots**.
3. After clicking the **Add Slot** button, give the slot a name and choose the default clone setting in the **Clone Settings From** menu, as shown in Figure 3-5. You can then deploy new versions of your application to this new slot.

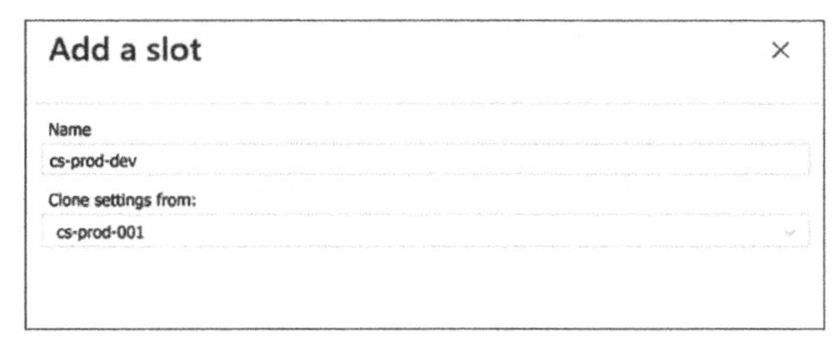

FIGURE 3-5 Creating an App Service Deployment Slot

4. Finally, you can bring a new version of your application into production, as shown in Figure 3-6.

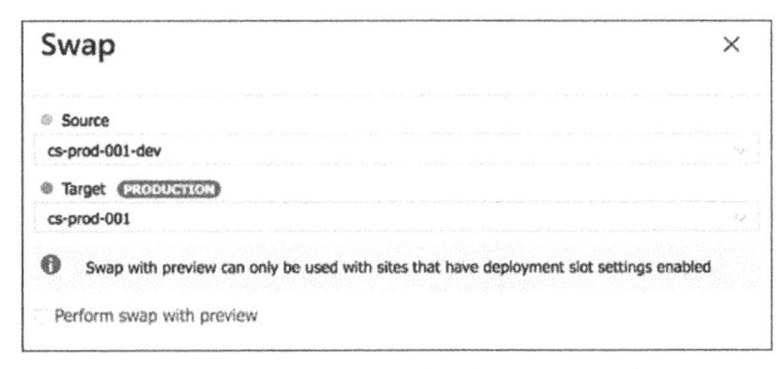

FIGURE 3-6 Creating an App Service deployment slot

When you swap two slots (usually from a staging slot into the production slot), App Service ensures that the target slot doesn't experience downtime.

Implement Logic Apps

Azure Logic Apps help you schedule, automate, and orchestrate tasks, business processes, and workflows. You can use Logic Apps to integrate applications, data, systems, and services across enterprises or organizations.

Every logic app workflow starts with a trigger, which fires when a specific event happens. Each time that the trigger fires, the Logic Apps engine creates a logic app instance that runs the actions in the workflow. These actions can also include data conversions and workflow controls, such as conditional statements, switch statements, loops, and branching.

For example, you can use Logic Apps to send email notifications with Office 365 when events take place in different apps and services. Or you can move files uploaded via SFTP to Azure Storage. Another common workflow pattern would be to monitor social media to analyze the sentiment of tweets and create alerts or tasks for items that need to be reviewed.

Complete the following steps to create your first Azure Logic App:

1. From the Azure portal, in the search box, find and select **Logic Apps**.
2. On the **Logic Apps** page, select **Add**.
3. On the **Logic App** pane, provide details about your logic app. After you're done, select **Create**.

4. After Azure deploys your app, on the Azure toolbar, select **Notifications** > **Go To Resource** for your deployed logic app.
5. The Logic Apps Designer opens and shows a page with an introduction video and commonly used triggers. Under **Templates**, select **Blank Logic App**. This will take you to a blank canvas in the Logic App designer, as shown in Figure 3-7.

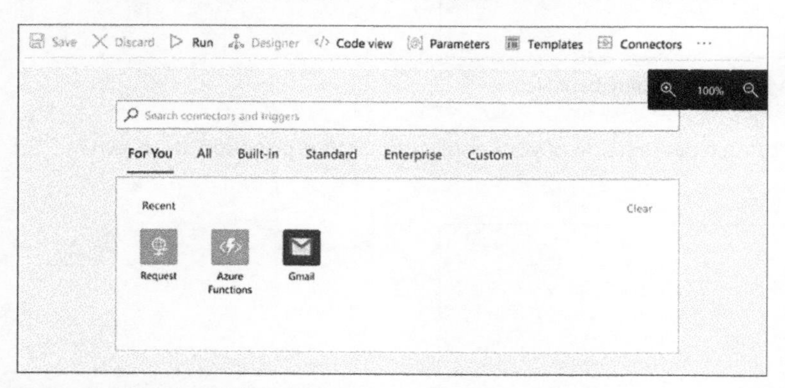

FIGURE 3-7 Creating a blank Logic App

EXAM TIP

Make sure that you understand the process for creating a blank Logic App, along with how to build a trigger and an action to a Logic App, such as sending new RSS items via email.

Once you have a blank Logic App, create a trigger and an action using the following process. This example explains how to send new RSS feed items via email:

6. With the Logic App designer, within the search box, enter **rss** to find the RSS connector. From the **Triggers** list, select the **When A Feed Item Is Published** trigger.
7. Provide the **RSS Feed URL** and define the frequency at which you want to check for new items by setting a value in **How Often Do You Want To Check For Items?**, as shown in Figure 3-8.

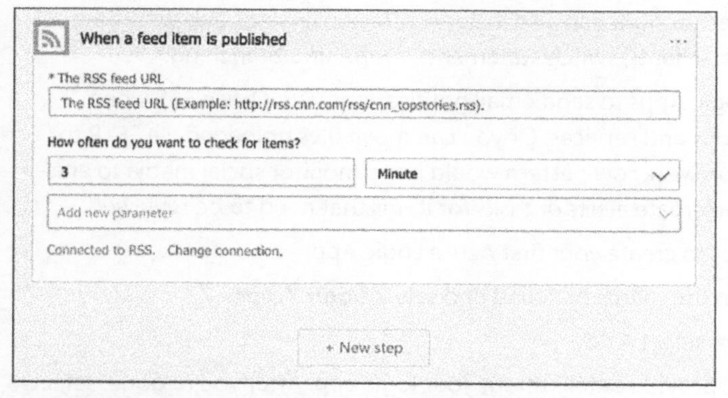

FIGURE 3-8 Creating an RSS trigger for a Logic App

8. Now add an action that sends an email when a new item appears in the RSS feed. Under the **When A Feed Item Is Published** trigger, select **New Step**.
9. Under **Choose An Action** and the search box, select **All**.
10. In the search box, enter send an email to find connectors that offer this action. From the **Actions** list, select the **Send An Email** action for the email service that you want to use, as shown in Figure 3-9.

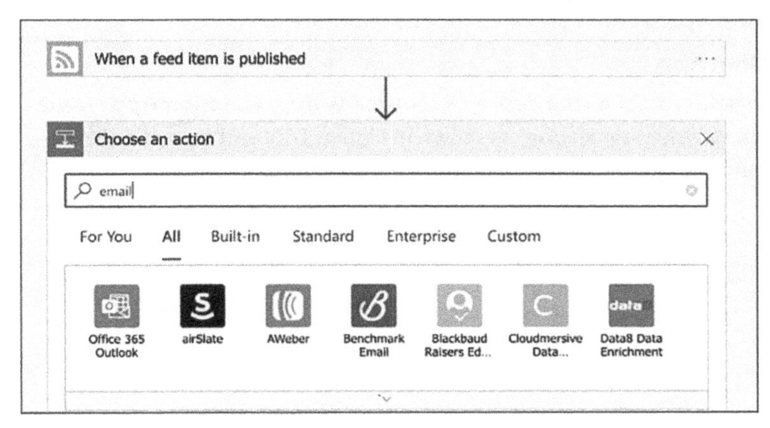

FIGURE 3-9 Creating an email action for a Logic App

11. If your selected email connector prompts you to authenticate your identity, complete that step now to create a connection between your logic app and your email service.
12. Save your logic app. To manually start your logic app, on the designer toolbar bar, select **Run**.

> ***NOTE*** **LOGIC APPS QUICKSTART**
>
> **Learn how to build your first workflow by using Azure Logic Apps, such as creating a blank logic app, adding a trigger and an action, and then testing your logic app at** ***http://docs.microsoft.com/en-us/azure/logic-apps/quickstart-create-first-logic-app-workflow.***

Implement Azure Functions

Azure Functions allows you to focus on code without worrying about application infrastructure. With Azure Functions, the cloud infrastructure provides the compute environment you need to keep your application running at any scale.

Functions are "triggered" by a specific type of event, which includes triggers responding to changes in data, responding to messages, running on a schedule, or as the result of an

HTTP request. Integration with other services is streamlined by using bindings. Bindings give you declarative access to a wide variety of Azure and third-party services.

Functions are a great solution for processing bulk data, integrating systems, working with the Internet of Things (IoT), and building simple APIs and micro-services.

Complete the following steps to create your first Azure Function App and serverless function:

1. Navigate to **Function App** on the left side of the Azure portal.
2. Click **Create Function App**.
3. Complete the form fields to define the desired **Resource Group**, **Function App Name**, and **Runtime Stack** for your application, as shown in Figure 3-10, and then click **Next**. These are the available language frameworks that can be used to develop and run your functions.
   - .NET Core
   - Java
   - Python
   - PowerShell Core

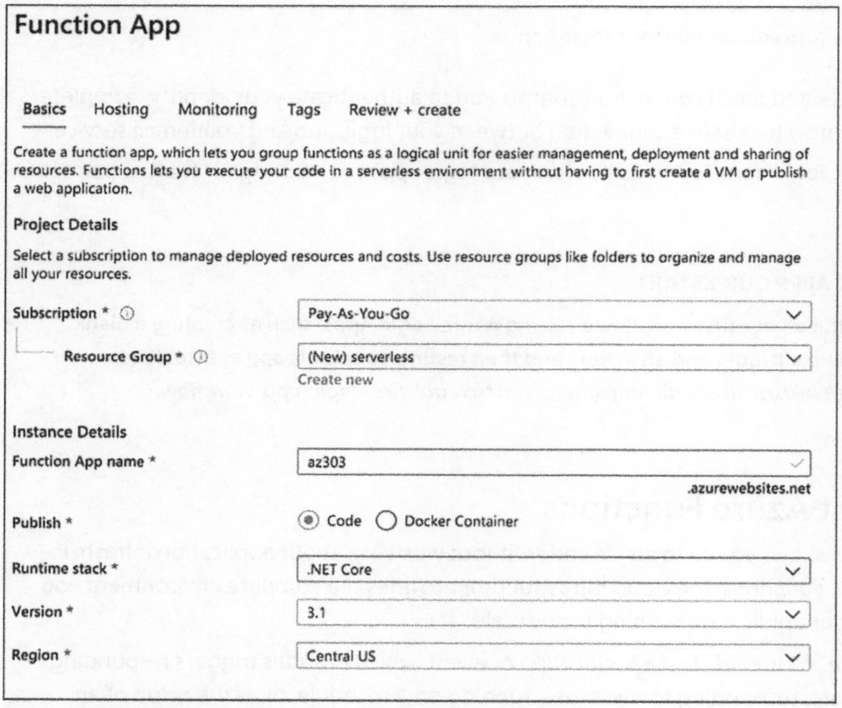

Function App

Basics Hosting Monitoring Tags Review + create

Create a function app, which lets you group functions as a logical unit for easier management, deployment and sharing of resources. Functions lets you execute your code in a serverless environment without having to first create a VM or publish a web application.

Project Details

Select a subscription to manage deployed resources and costs. Use resource groups like folders to organize and manage all your resources.

Subscription * Pay-As-You-Go

Resource Group * (New) serverless

Create new

Instance Details

Function App name * az303

.azurewebsites.net

Publish * Code Docker Container

Runtime stack * .NET Core

Version * 3.1

Region * Central US

FIGURE 3-10 Creating an Azure Function App

4. Select the appropriate pricing **Plan Type** and click **Create** to build your function app, as shown in Figure 3-11. These are the **Plan Type** options:
   - **Consumption Plan.** When you're using the Consumption plan, instances of the Azure Functions host are dynamically added and removed based on the number of incoming events. This serverless plan scales automatically, and you're only charged for compute resources only when your functions are running. On a Consumption plan, a function execution times out after a configurable period of time.
   - **Premium Plan.** When you're using the Premium plan, instances of the Azure Functions host are added and removed based on the number of incoming events just like the Consumption plan.
   - **Dedicated (App Service) Plan.** Your function apps can also run on the same dedicated VMs as other App Service apps (Basic, Standard, Premium, and Isolated SKUs). Consider an App Service plan when you have existing, underutilized VMs that are already running other App Service instances.

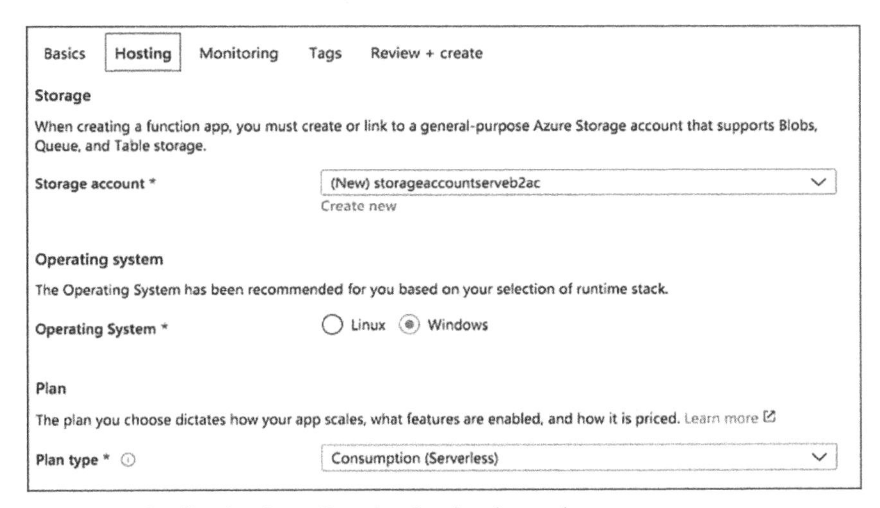

FIGURE 3-11 Configuring Azure Function App hosting options

EXAM TIP

Make sure that you understand that you can publish code directly to a Function App from development tools like Visual Studio Code and Visual Studio, or from continuous delivery systems such as Azure DevOps.

After you have a function app up and running you can complete the following steps to build your first function:

1. Navigate to your Function App in the Azure portal.
2. Click **Functions** > **Add**.
3. Select a template to trigger your function. In this example, we'll select **HTTP Trigger**.

> **NOTE HTTP TRIGGER TEMPLATE**
>
> **The HTTP Trigger template creates a function that accepts input from an HTTP post operation. The function is looking specifically for a "name" key in the query string or in the request body. This code can be replaced with any logic that makes sense for your application.**

4. Give your function a name, set your authorization level, and click **Create Function**.
5. Click the **Code + Test** option to bring up the code editor.
6. Click **Test/Run** to invoke your function with a query string parameter for a "Name" key, as shown in Figure 3-12.

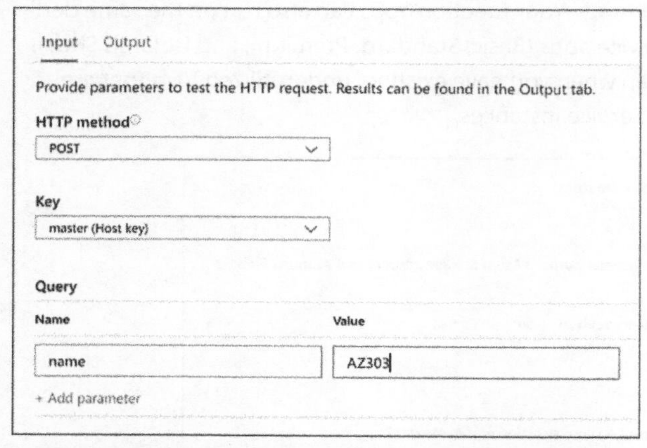

FIGURE 3-12 Configuring test inputs for an Azure Function in the portal

7. Review the output in the portal, as shown in Figure 3-13.

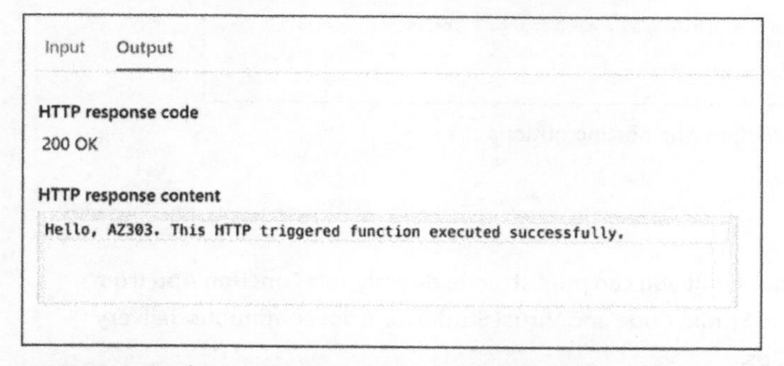

FIGURE 3-13 Reviewing the output from an Azure Function in the portal

> **NOTE CREATE AZURE FUNCTIONS WITH VISUAL STUDIO CODE**
>
> **Learn how to use Visual Studio Code to create a C# class library-based function that responds to HTTP requests at *http://docs.microsoft.com/en-us/azure/azure-functions/functions-create-first-function-vs-code*.**

Skill 3.2: Implement Container-based Applications

Containerization has completely disrupted the IT industry over the past several years, and there's no sign of the trend slowing down. The Azure team understands this and has gone to great lengths to make it incredibly simple to deploy containerized applications in App Service.

This skill covers how to:

- Create a container image
- Publish and automate image deployment to the Azure Container Registry
- Publish a solution on an Azure Container Instance
- Configure Azure Kubernetes Service

Create a container image

Container images are the artifacts that make it possible to deploy modern applications at speeds never seen before. Applications run inside containers, which are launched from container images. Think of container images as templates that can be used to start up containers. We use container images to package up our code and application dependencies, and then we can invoke running instances of these images to create containers. The Docker toolset has become the gold standard for managing this entire process.

You need to be familiar with the following procedure for creating Docker container images:

1. Create a new text file called `Dockerfile` (make sure you do not add a file extension).

```
1 FROM node:alpine
2
3 WORKDIR /usr/app
4
5 COPY . .
6 RUN npm install
7
8 CMD ["npm", "start"]
```

FIGURE 3-14 Writing a Dockerfile

2. Add commands, like those shown in Figure 3-14, to automate the build process for a Node.js application packaged into a container image. Each instruction in the Dockerfile adds a read-only layer to the container image.
   - **FROM.** Create a layer using the official Node.js container image based on Alpine Linux.
   - **WORKDIR.** Set the working directory for the application.

- **COPY.** Add files from the developer machine into the Docker image.
- **RUN.** Install all the required `npm` packages that the application will need.
- **CMD.** Use to specify the command to run when the container is started.

3. The final step is to use the Docker client to build your container image. Docker Desktop, which runs on Mac and Windows, is used by millions of developers to develop apps locally with Docker. You can use the `Docker Build` command after you've installed Docker Desktop to create a container image using your Dockerfile, as shown in Figure 3-15.

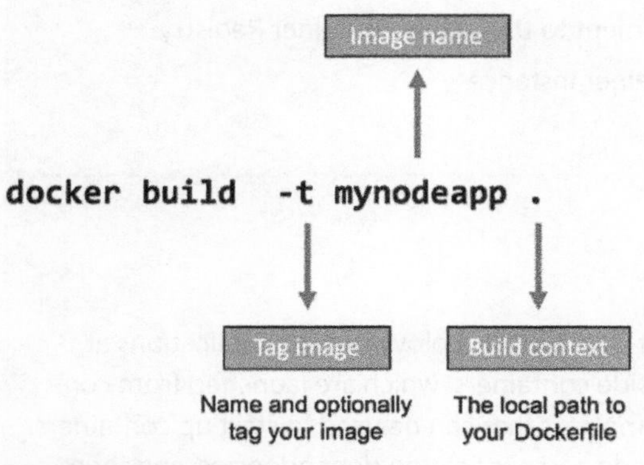

FIGURE 3-15 Running a Docker Build

> ***NOTE*** **DOCKERFILE REFERENCE**
>
> **The Docker image build process is incredibly versatile. To learn more about writing your own Dockerfile, visit the official Docker reference at *https://docs.docker.com/engine/reference/builder/*.**

Publish and automate image deployment to the Azure Container Registry

Container registry services are used as a central location for storing container images. The Azure Container Registry (ACR) is a fully managed Docker registry service based on the open-source Docker Registry. You can build an ACR resource and integrate a variety of Azure services with your container registry. This is useful for keeping images in close proximity to application infrastructure, and you can use native security controls in Azure to permit or deny access to ACR.

After you've built your own container images, you can push them to an ACR instance. Complete the steps in the following procedure to build an ACR resource to store your container images:

1. Log into the Azure portal and click **Create A New Resource**.
2. Select **Containers** from the **Azure Marketplace** and click **Container Registry**.

FIGURE 3-16 Creating an ACR resource

3. Enter the registry details, as shown in Figure 3-16, and click **Create**.
   - **Registry Name.** Enter a globally unique hostname under `azurecr.io`. Follow standard DNS naming rules and use alphanumeric characters only.
   - **Admin User.** Enable to use an ACR-specific username and password to log into the registry using tools like the Docker CLI.
   - **SKU.** Select the pricing tier. The tier you select dictates the performance and scalability of your ACR resource.
4. Navigate to the properties of your ACR resource after provisioning has completed. Click **Access Keys** under **Settings** to retrieve the log-in server details and password for your ACR admin user account.
5. Log in to your ACR instance using the Docker client (for example, `docker login <your ACR name>.azurecr.io`).

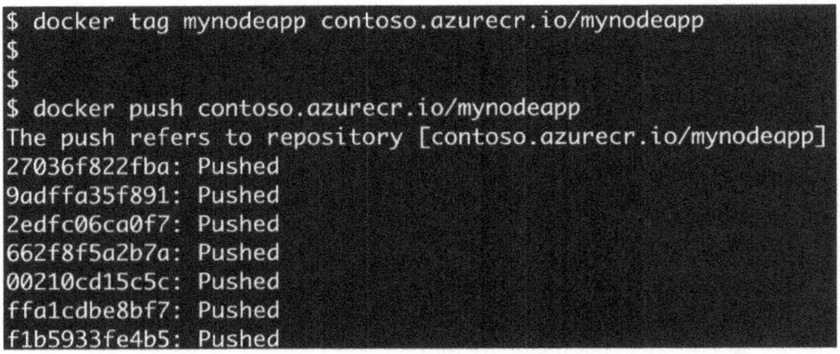

```
$ docker tag mynodeapp contoso.azurecr.io/mynodeapp
$
$
$ docker push contoso.azurecr.io/mynodeapp
The push refers to repository [contoso.azurecr.io/mynodeapp]
27036f822fba: Pushed
9adffa35f891: Pushed
2edfc06ca0f7: Pushed
662f8f5a2b7a: Pushed
00210cd15c5c: Pushed
ffa1cdbe8bf7: Pushed
f1b5933fe4b5: Pushed
```

FIGURE 3-17 Tagging and pushing a container image to ACR

6. After logging into ACR, you can publish images using the Docker CLI, as shown in Figure 3-17.
    - **`docker tag`.** Use the `docker tag` command to tag your image with the ACR name in the format of `<ACR hostname>/<your image name>`. Note that this can also be done during build time when creating the image with docker build.
    - **`docker push`.** Publish the image to ACR using the registry hostname included as part of the image name.

EXAM TIP

You can use an Azure AD service principal to delegate access to your ACR resource in addition to an admin user.

Implement an application that runs on an Azure Container Instance

The ability to quickly spin up applications inside containers opens numerous possibilities. In addition to running containers in App Service, you also can take advantage of a model that provides containers as a service. Azure Container Instances (ACI) are a service offering that allows you to spin up containers on demand, without any existing infrastructure such as virtual machines or even App Service Plans. ACI enables you to design and deploy your applications instead of managing the infrastructure that runs them.

Use the following procedure to create an Azure Container Instance:

1. Log into the Azure portal and click **Create A New Resource**.
2. Select **Containers** from the **Azure Marketplace** and click **Container Instances**.
3. Enter the ACI details, as shown in Figure 3-18, and click **Create**. These inputs provide the details about your container instance, including name, image type, and location.
    - **Container Name.** Enter a meaningful name for your container.
    - **Image Type.** Select **Public** if your image is hosted in a public registry. Otherwise, choose **Private** to enable the options to include your registry log-in details.
    - **Image Name.** Enter the exact name of your container image.
    - **Image Registry Login Server.** Provide the fully qualified domain name of your log-in server. If you're using ACR, this will be your ACR login server name.
    - **Image Registry User Name.** Enter the username for your registry.
    - **Image Registry Password.** Provide your registry password.
    - **OS Type.** ACI supports both Linux and Windows-based containers. Select the appropriate OS type from the list.
    - **Size.** ACI requires that you set resource limits for each instance of your application. This also controls the pricing for the ACI resource, and you can change the size at any time after the ACI resource has been provisioned.

Home > New > Create container instance

Create container instance

Basics Networking Advanced Tags Review + create

Azure Container Instances (ACI) allows you to quickly and easily run containers on Azure without managing servers or having to learn new tools. ACI offers per-second billing to minimize the cost of running containers on the cloud. Learn more about Azure Container Instances

Project details

Select the subscription to manage deployed resources and costs. Use resource groups like folders to organize and manage all your resources.

* Subscription: Microsoft Partner Network

* Resource group: Core-Infrastructure
Create new

Container details

* Container name: mynodeapp

* Region: (US) Central US

* Image type: Public / Private (selected)

* Image name: contoso.azurecr.io/mynodeapp

* Image registry login server: contoso.azurecr.io

* Image registry user name: contoso

* Image registry password: ••••••••••••••••••••••••••••••••

* OS type: Linux (selected) / Windows

* Size: 1 vcpu, 1.5 GiB memory, 0 gpus
Change size

FIGURE 3-18 Creating an Azure Container Instance

EXAM TIP

ACI is a great solution for basic applications and task automation. For production scenarios that require full orchestration, Microsoft recommends running containers on Azure Kubernetes Service (AKS).

Manage container settings by using code

The Azure platform provides access to numerous language-specific SDKs and tools that you can use to programmatically manage your infrastructure. Developers can use .NET, Java, Node.js, PHP, Python, and Go to build applications that interact with your Azure resources.

In addition to the SDKs, Microsoft offers support for PowerShell and the Azure CLI for authoring operational scripts and for running ad-hoc administration commands locally or in the interactive Cloud Shell.

Azure solution architects are expected to understand how to tap into these automation capabilities to manage container settings using code. This is true whether the code is part of a robust application built by developers or used in provisioning scripts created by the DevOps team. Since the SDKs and command-line tools are all leveraging the Azure RESTful APIs behind the scenes, Azure solution architects can leverage any tool of their choice to get the job done.

Use the following procedure with Azure CLI to discover the commands you can use to manage container settings using code:

1. Navigate to *shell.azure.com* in your web browser and start a new Cloud Shell instance.
2. Run the following command to review all the subcommands available to manage your Azure Container Registry (ACR) instances:

```
az acr --help
```

3. Run the following command to review all the subcommands available to manage your Azure Container Instances (ACIs):

```
az container --help
```

4. To create a resource, such as an Azure Container Instance (ACI), use the `az container create` command:

```
az container create \
--resource-group Core-Infrastructure \
--name mynodeapp \
--image mynodeapp:latest \
--cpu 1 \
--memory 1
```

5. Once you have an ACI instance running, you can manage the settings and lifecycle of the instance using code, as shown in the following command that restarts the instance:

```
az container restart --name mynodeapp
```

EXAM TIP

Microsoft might test your knowledge using performance-based, hands-on tasks that need to be completed in the Azure portal. Be prepared to use the Cloud Shell to gain access to Azure CLI or PowerShell, and make sure you understand how to use the help system to discover commands and the appropriate syntax to complete the task.

Configure Azure Kubernetes Service

For production-grade applications, Microsoft recommends running containers using the fully managed Azure Kubernetes Service (AKS), making it quick and easy to deploy and manage containerized applications. AKS eliminates the burden of ongoing operations and maintenance required by managing your own Kubernetes deployment. As a hosted service, Azure handles critical Kubernetes tasks like health monitoring and maintenance, and the AKS is free to use. You pay only for the agent nodes within your clusters, not for master nodes controlling your clusters.

Use the following procedure to create an Azure Kubernetes Service (AKS) cluster using the Azure CLI:

1. Navigate to *shell.azure.com* in your web browser and start a new Cloud Shell instance.
2. Create a new resource group using the following Azure CLI command:

```
az group create \
--name AKS \
--location eastus
```

3. Create a new AKS cluster using the following Azure CLI command:

```
az aks create \
    --resource-group AKS \
    --name AKSCluster01 \
    --node-count 1 \
    --enable-addons monitoring \
    --generate-ssh-keys
```

4. After the AKS cluster has been created, you can connect and manage the cluster from the command line. First, install the AKS CLI inside your cloud shell instance using the following command:

```
az aks install-cli
```

5. Download your AKS credentials and configure the AKS CLI to use them within your shell session:

```
az aks get-credentials \
--resource-group AKS \
--name AKSCluster01
```

6. Verify that your connection to the AKS cluster is working properly by using the kubectl command to retrieve a list of cluster nodes.

```
kubectl get nodes
```

NOTE **AZURE CONTAINER SERVICE (ACS)**

Prior to releasing the Azure Kubernetes Service (AKS), Microsoft offered the Azure Container Service (ACS) as a managed solution that provided multiple orchestration systems as a service, including Kubernetes, Docker Swarm, and DC/OS. ACS has been deprecated, and existing ACS customers will need to migrate to AKS.

Chapter summary

- Azure App Service gives you the ability to build and host web apps, mobile back ends, and RESTful APIs without having to manage server, network, and storage infrastructure.
- App Service supports applications built using common frameworks such as .NET, .NET Core, Node.js, Java, PHP, Ruby, or Python.
- You can deploy web apps using the Azure portal, CLI, PowerShell, or any of the available SDKs provided by Microsoft.
- App Service supports both Windows and Linux applications, including Docker containers.
- Azure web apps are instances of an App Service that run within an App Service Plan.
- Azure Container Instances have no dependencies on an App Service Plan.
- Azure provides rich support for Docker containers and images can be built and stored in the Azure Container Registry (ACR).

- The Azure Kubernetes Service (AKS) is a fully managed container orchestration system that makes it easier for teams to run containers in production.

Thought experiment

In this thought experiment, demonstrate your skills and knowledge of the topics covered in this chapter. You can find answers to this thought experiment in the next section.

You're an Azure architect for Contoso Ltd. You've been asked to design and implement a solution to run a collection of line-of-business applications in the Azure cloud. Answer the following questions about leveraging Azure App Service to deploy your solution for Contoso.

1. You need to move a web application to Azure that the Human Resources department uses to train corporate employees in the Los Angeles branch office. The web app implements an embedded video player that serves video training content to each user. All videos are produced in the highest possible quality. How should you architect the solution to reduce the latency between the users and the application infrastructure?
2. You've been tasked with refactoring an on-premises web application to run inside a Docker container in Azure App Service. You need to ensure that container images can be accessed only by certain members of the IT staff. How can you accomplish this with the least amount of administrative effort?
3. You currently have a nightly task that runs a PowerShell script on an on-premises Windows server. The process generates a report and sends the output to the IT support staff at Contoso headquarters. You need to move this process as part of Contoso's migration to Azure, but you need to do so using the least amount of administrative effort. You already have plans to deploy several websites in Azure App Service. What should you do to run the nightly process in Azure?

Thought experiment answers

This section contains the solution to the thought experiment. Each answer explains why the answer choice is correct.

1. Deploy the App Service infrastructure in a west coast–based Azure region. This will put the infrastructure in close proximity to the users in the Los Angeles branch office. For global applications, consider using the Azure CDN service to distribute static content to edge locations available across the Azure global infrastructure.
2. Deploy an Azure Container Registry (ACR) resource inside your Azure subscription. Disable admin access and delegate control to the ACR resource using Role-Based Access Control (RBAC).
3. Create an Azure WebJob within one of the existing web app resources running in your Azure subscription. Upload the PowerShell script and configure a triggered WebJob that runs on a daily schedule.

CHAPTER 4

Implement and manage data platforms

In today's era of modern application development in the cloud, the strategy for storing application data in the cloud is critical for any application success. Cloud-native applications require you to adapt to new approaches and various modern tools and services to manage data in the cloud securely and efficiently.

Microsoft Azure platform provides a rich set of data storage solutions designed specifically for different data classification requirements of your application in the cloud.

The AZ-303 exam expects you to know the different data platform storage solutions and choose the optimal solution based on the classification of application data, its usage pattern, and performance requirements.

Skills covered in this chapter:

- Skill 4.1: Implement NoSQL Databases.
- Skill 4.2: Implement Azure SQL Databases.

Skill 4.1: Implement NoSQL Databases

Nowadays, the data generated and consumed by applications, including a wide variety of IoT devices, social networking sites, is enormous. Handling such massive data with traditional Relational Database Management Systems (RDBMS) sometimes becomes daunting and inefficient. The heterogeneity and complexity of the data (also known as Big Data) emitted by numerous connected devices is also difficult to manage using traditional database storage solutions.

To efficiently handle such a large volume of data, the concept of NoSQL databases comes in. NoSQL databases are non-relational databases that offer horizontal scalability and are cost-efficient compared to relational database systems. NoSQL databases also provide more flexible data models and data access patterns optimized for large and complex datasets. NoSQL databases offer the following data models:

- **Key-value databases.** A key-value database is a non-relational database that uses a key-value pair method to store data. The key represents a unique identifier for a given collection of data values that allows you to perform simple commands like GET, PUT, or DELETE. Key-value databases are highly partitionable and support horizontal scaling at a massive scale. Microsoft Azure platform provides the following popular key-value database visualizations:

  - Azure Table Storage
  - Azure Cosmos DB Table API
  - Azure Cache for Redis

- **Document databases.** A document database model enables us to store data using a markup language like XML, JSON, and YAML or even use plain text. The document databases are schema-agnostic and do not require all the documents to have the same structure. Azure Cosmos DB is a popular document database that supports a wide variety of powerful and intuitive APIs, software SDKs, and languages to manage a large volume of semi-structured data.
- **Graph databases.** Graph databases are typically designed to store and visualize the relationship between data entities. A graph database has two types of information: nodes and edges. Nodes denote a body, and the edges indicate the relationship between entities.
- **Column family databases.** Column family databases look similar to relational databases, with data stored in rows and columns. Column family databases allow you to group columns based on logically related entities to form a column family, wherein each column holds the data for all grouped entities. Apache HBase is a column family database.

This skill covers how to:

- Configure storage account tables
- Select appropriate Cosmos DB APIs
- Set up replicas in Cosmos DB

Configure storage account tables

Azure Table storage service provides a massively scalable data storage option for structured, NoSQL, and key-value data storage. Azure Table storage is schemaless storage that stores data values in an entity that can change over time as application data evolves. The service provides REST APIs to interact with the data for insert, update, delete, and query operations using the OData protocol and LINQ queries using .NET libraries. The following are some common use cases for Azure Table storage:

- You need cost-effective storage to handle terabytes (TBs) of structured data that scales at-large and on-demand.
- Your application stores a massive dataset, and you need high throughput and low latency.

- Your application data needs to be secured with disaster recovery, reliable backup strategy, load balancing, replication, and high availability.

In the following section, you learn the underlying data model of the Azure Table storage service.

Azure Table storage service underlying data model

As we learned in the previous section, Azure Table storage service lets you store structured, NoSQL datasets using a schemaless design. Figure 4-1 shows the underlying data model of Azure Table storage service.

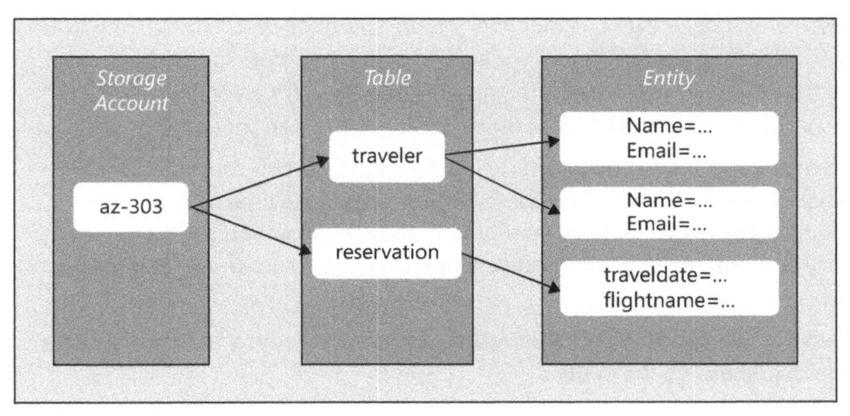

FIGURE 4-1 Azure Table storage data model

The following are the key elements of the Azure Table Storage as you see in the previous figure 4-1.

- **Storage Account.** The storage account name is a globally unique identifier that serves as parent namespace for a Table service. Authentication and authorization on the Table service is done at the storage account level. You can create one or many tables within the storage account. For example, in the previous figure 4-1, we have two separate tables: **traveler** and **reservation** to store the respective information. All tables you create underneath the storage account would get a unique base URI to interact with the service using REST APIs, PowerShell, or Azure CLI. An example of a base URI is *https://<storage-account>.table.core.windows.net/.* Storage account comes with two SKUs as follows:
  - **General-Purpose V2.** Microsoft recommends using General-Purpose V2 to take advantage of Azure storage's latest features.
  - **General-Purpose V1.** This type is the legacy SKU and is kept for backward compatibility with older deployments. General-Purpose V1 does not support the new Hot, Cool, or Archive access tiers or zone-level replication.

- **Table, Entities, and Properties.** Table within the storage account store a collection of entities in rows. Entities have a collection of properties with a key-value pair that is similar to a column. An entity in the storage account can store up to 1MB of data and include up to 252 properties. Each entity has three system-defined properties, as mentioned below.
  - **PartitionKey.** A partition key is a unique identifier for a given partition of data within a table. It is designed to support load balancing across different storage nodes for better performance and throughput. The partition key is the first part of the clustered index, and it is indexed by default for faster lookup. The name of the partition key can be a string up to 1KB in size.
  - **RowKey.** A row key is a unique identifier within a partition and is designed to form a second part of the clustered index for a given entity. You must specify both a row key and a partition key while performing CRUD operation for an entity within a table. Like the partition key, a row key is an index column with a size limit of 1KB.
  - **Timestamp.** The Timestamp property is a date-time system-derived attribute value applied automatically on the server-side to record the time an entity was last modified. The Azure Table storage service does not allow you to set a value externally and uses the previous modified Timestamp (LTM) internally to manage optimistic concurrency.

The REST API lets you interact with the tables within a storage account and perform insert, update, and delete operations on the entities.

```
https://<storage-account>.table.core.windows.net/<tablename>
```

The simple Azure Table storage service design is shown in Figure 4-2. 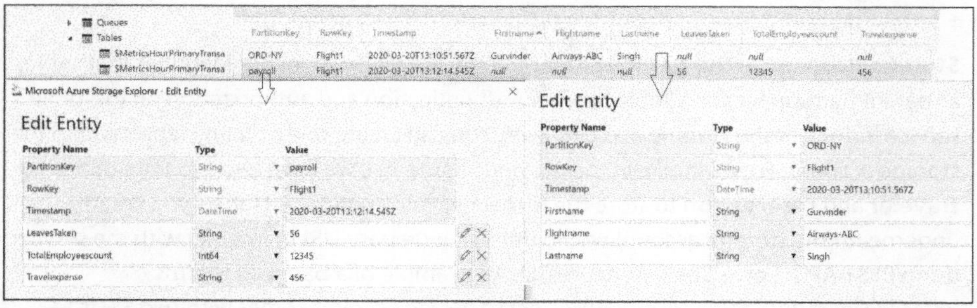

FIGURE 4-2 A simple table design

As you see in Figure 4-2, the schemaless nature of the table allows you to store entities with a different set of properties within the same table.

The custom, user-defined properties for each of the separate entities can have a data type, such as a string or integer. By default, properties have the string data type unless you specify otherwise. The Azure Table storage service also allows storing complex data types in the properties using a different serialized format, such as JSON or XML.

MORE INFORMATION? **DESIGN A SCALABLE PARTITION**

While Azure storage is massively scalable, it is crucial to design table partitions to take advantage of auto-scaling and load balancing across different server nodes. See the comprehensive Microsoft documentation "Design a scalable partitioning strategy for Azure Table storage" at ***https://docs.microsoft.com/en-us/rest/api/storageservices/designing-a-scalable-partitioning-strategy-for-azure-table-storage#gdft.***

Create an Azure Table storage service

As stated in the previous section, before you create an Azure Table storage service, you need a storage account as its base unit. You can accomplish this using the Azure portal, Azure PowerShell, or Azure CLI.

EXAM TIP

The AZ-303 exam expects that you have at least basic knowledge of the PowerShell az module or Azure CLI (cross-platform command-line interface) to interact with Azure services. The comprehensive list of PowerShell and Azure CLI commands to manage Azure Table storage service is published at ***https://docs.microsoft.com/en-us/cli/azure/storage/table?view=azure-cli-latest#az-storage-table-create.***

MORE INFORMATION? **LEARN MORE ABOUT AZURE CLI**

To learn more about the Azure CLI commands and different native thin client SDKs for cross-platform, visit the Microsoft documentation at ***https://docs.microsoft.com/en-us/cli/azure/?view=azure-cli-latest.***

This code snippet is an example of an Azure CLI command to create an Azure Table storage service within an Azure storage account:

```
az storage table create --name    [--account-key] [--account-name]
```

- --**name** The name is a required parameter representing the unique name of the table to be created. It should contain only alphanumeric characters and cannot begin with a numeric character. It is case insensitive and must be from 3 to 63 characters long.
- --**account-key** This is a secure storage account key.
- --**account-name** This represents a storage account name.

Follow these steps to create an Azure Table storage using Azure Cloud Shell. The steps assume that you already have an Azure subscription and a storage account. If not, visit *https://azure.microsoft.com/en-in/free/* to create one.

1. Log in to the Azure portal at *https://portal.azure.com/* with your subscription credentials.

2. On the top right corner, below the user information, click on the Cloud Shell button, as shown in Figure 4-3.

FIGURE 4-3 Azure Portal Icon to Open Cloud Shell

3. Choose the bash runtime and run the following command on the cloud shell, as shown in Figure 4-4.

```
az storage table create --name az303table --account-key cMwq9LmP06vGxxxxxxxxxxxx
xxxxxxxxalUDpKJ7irIjLdZe8o+lH38c8ZKIlsT5pu/y/YCupazeNGgA== --account-name sgaz303
```

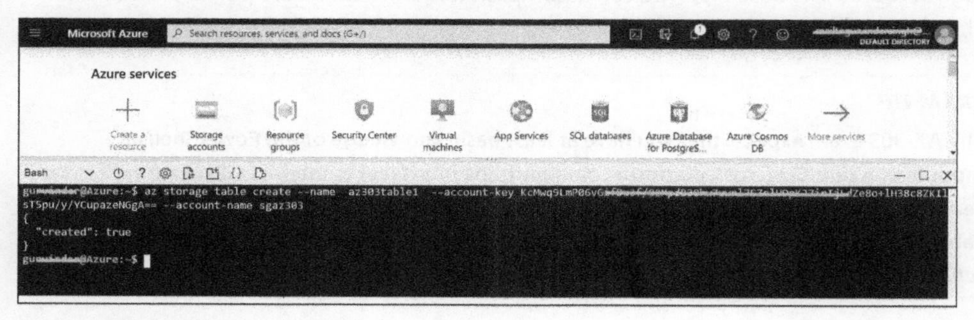

FIGURE 4-4 Azure Cloud shell console

Once the command is executed, you will see a `created: true` message, as shown in Figure 4-4. The message indicates that the table has been created. You can see the table by navigating to the storage account within the Azure portal, as shown in Figure 4-5.

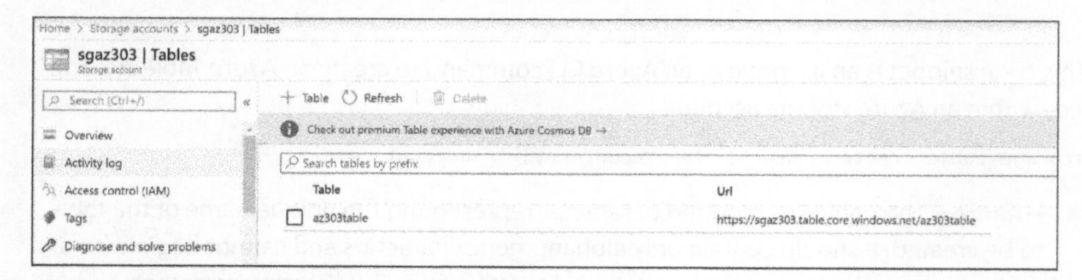

FIGURE 4-5 Azure Table storage blade

Configure Table Storage Data Access

You can use storage account keys that Azure generates when you spin up a storage account. Using the native storage keys or exposing these keys to developers might not be a good practice from a security standpoint. Also, using keys would not give you the ability to configure granular, time-bound access to one or more storage account services or allow you to revoke access on the services when needed. This is where shared access signature (SAS) and stored access policies come in:

- **Shared Access Signature.** Shared access signature (SAS) on the storage account allows you to configure delegated and granular access to the storage account services. A shared access signature is available in the following types:
  - **User delegation SAS.** This kind is secured using Azure AD (AAD) and applies to Blob storage only.
  - **Service SAS.** This is a service SAS that is secured by a storage account key and is typically used to delegate access to only one of the Azure storage services.
  - **Account SAS.** Account SAS is also secured by a storage account key and is used to delegate access to one or more storage account services simultaneously.
- **Stored access policy.** Stored access policy is an additional level of granular control on the service level SAS. When you use a service SAS with a stored access policy, it allows you to revoke or change the SAS access parameters, such as start time, expire time, and permissions on the signature after the SAS has been issued.

The following steps show how you would configure a stored access policy on the Azure Table storage service using Azure CLI.

1. Log in to the Azure portal at *https://portal.azure.com/* using your subscription credentials.
2. Open the browser-based cloud shell and follow the previous set of steps.
3. Run the following CLI command, the components of which are explained following the command:

```
az storage table policy create --name readupdateonly --table-name az303table
--account-name sgaz303 --account-key <account-key goes here> --expiry
2020-12-30'T'16:23:00'Z' --start 2020-3-01'T'16:23:00'Z' --permission ru
```

   - **--name** Specifies the policy name.
   - **--table-name** Specifies the table name on which the policy is created.
   - **--account-name** The storage account name.
   - **--account-key** A secure storage account key.
   - **--expiry** Expiration UTC datetime in (Y-m-d'T'H:M:S'Z').
   - **--start** start time in UTC datetime in (Y-m-d'T'H:M:S'Z')
   - **--permission** Specifies the allowed operations. In this example, we allowed only read and update operations. Allowed values are as follows:
     - (r) for read/query
     - (a) for add
     - (u) for update
     - (d) for delete

After running the command on the cloud shell, you will see a stored access policy created on the Azure Table account service, as shown in Figure 4-6.

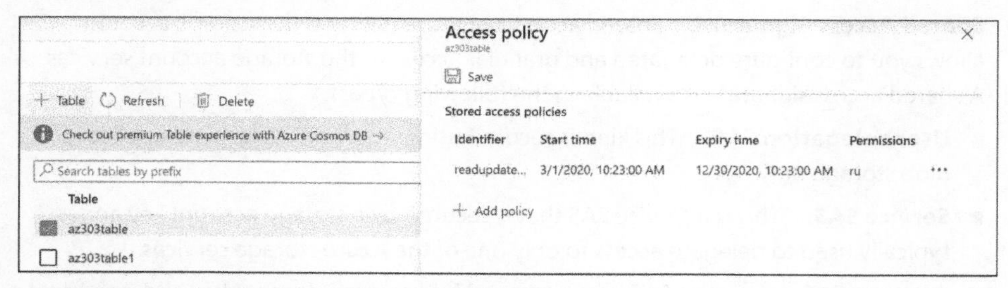

FIGURE 4-6 Stored access policy on Azure Table storage

Choose between Azure Table storage service and Cosmos DB Table API

Azure Cosmos DB Table API is the latest futuristic NoSQL database offering from the Azure Cosmos DB product family. Microsoft recommends that you use Cosmos DB Table API for new applications so that you take advantage of the latest product features, such as multi-model database support, turnkey global distribution, auto-failover, and auto-indexing for better performance.

Cosmos DB Table API and Azure Table storage use the same data model for CRUD operations. Therefore, for existing applications, you can seamlessly migrate from Azure Table storage to Azure Cosmos DB without changing the application code. In the upcoming section, you learn about Azure Cosmos DB and its supported APIs at length.

Azure Cosmos DB

In this section, you learn what Cosmos DB is, why it has been such a popular database for enterprise-grade applications, and what tools, languages, and industry-standard APIs it supports.

What is Cosmos DB?

Azure Cosmos DB is Microsoft's globally distributed, multi-model database. Azure Cosmos DB enables you to elastically and independently scale the throughput and storage across the globe with guaranteed throughput, low latency, and high availability.

The Cosmos DB offers the following benefits:

- **Guaranteed throughput.** Cosmos DB guarantees the throughput and the performance at peak load. The performance level of Cosmos DB can be scaled elastically by setting Request Units (RUs).
- **Global distribution.** With an ability to have multi-master replicas globally and built-in capability to invoke failover, Cosmos DB enables 99.999 percent read/write availability in each data center where Azure has its presence. The Cosmos DB *multi-homing API* is an additional feature to configure the application to point to the closest data center for low latency and better performance.

- **Multiple query model or multi query-API.** The multi-model database support allows you to store data in your desired format, such as document, graph, or a key-value data model.
- **Choices of consistency modes.** The Azure Cosmos DB replication protocol offers five well-defined, practical, and intuitive consistency models. Each model has a trade-off between consistency, performance throughput, and latency.
- **No schema or index management.** The database engine is entirely schema-agnostic. Cosmos DB automatically indexes all data for faster query response.

Understand the Cosmos account

Azure Cosmos account is a logical construct that has a globally unique DNS name. For high availability, you can add or remove regions to your Cosmos account at any time with an ability to set up multiple masters/write replicas across different regions.

You can manage the Cosmos account in an Azure subscription either by using the Azure portal, Azure CLI, AZ PowerShell module, or by different language-specific SDKs. This section describes the essential fundamental concepts and mechanics of an Azure Cosmos account.

As of the writing of this book, you can create a maximum of 100 Azure Cosmos accounts under one Azure subscription. Under the Cosmos account, you can create one or more Cosmos databases, and within the database, you can create one or more containers. In the container, you put your data in the form of documents, key-value entities, column-family data, or graph data by choosing its appropriate APIs. Figure 4-7 gives you the visual view of what we've shared about the Cosmos account thus far.

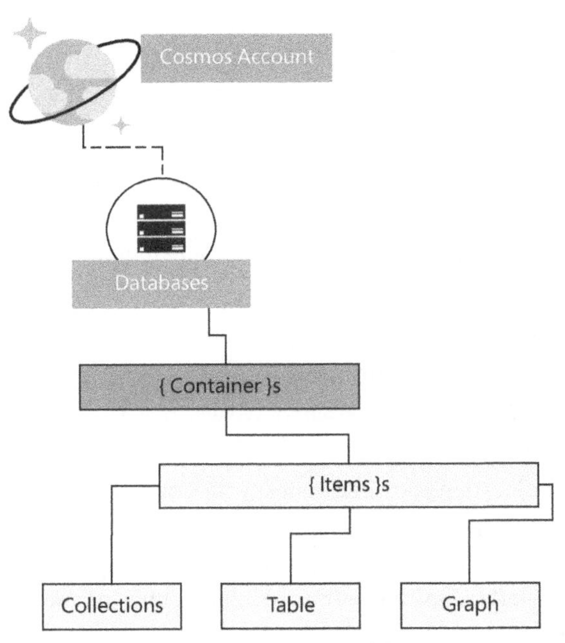

FIGURE 4-7 Azure Cosmos account entities

Create a Cosmos account

To set up a Cosmos account using the Azure portal, use the following steps:

1. Sign in to the Azure portal *https://portal.azure.com*.
2. Under your subscription in the upper-left corner, select **Create A Resource** and search for **Cosmos DB**.
3. Click **Create** (see Figure 4-8).

FIGURE 4-8 Creating an Azure Cosmos account

4. On the **Create Cosmos DB** Account page, supply the basic mandatory information, as shown in Figure 4-9.
   - **Subscription.** The Azure subscription you need to create an account under.
   - **Resource Group.** Select existing or create a new resource group.
   - **Account Name.** Enter the name of the new Cosmos account. Azure appends documents.azure.com to the name to construct a unique URI.
   - **API.** The API determines the type of account to be created. We will look at supported APIs in the coming section.
   - **Location.** Choose the geographic location you need to host your Cosmos account.
   - **Capacity** In the capacity option, keep the default selected capacity as the **Provisioned throughput**, which is in general availability (GA). You can set up throughput at the container level or a database level. The provisioned throughput can be set up upfront, or you can Opt-in for auto-scale.

- **Apply Free Tier:** The tier gives you 5 GB of data storage and the first 400 RUs (Request Units) free forever.
- **Account Type** Pretty understood, you need to select **Production** for production workload and **Non-Production** for stating or Dev/Test workload.
- You can skip the Network and TAG section and click **Review + Create**. It takes a few minutes for the deployment to complete. You can see the Cosmos account created by navigating to the **Resource Group** resources.

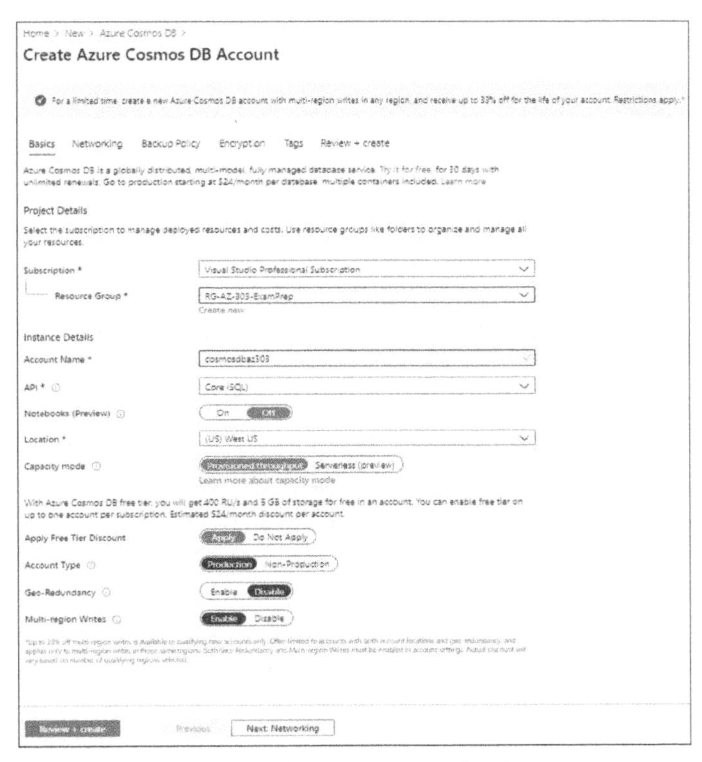

FIGURE 4-9 Create an Azure Cosmos Account wizard

Set appropriate consistency level for operations

In geo-distributed databases, you're likely reading the data that isn't the latest version, which is called a "dirty read." The data consistency, latency, and performance don't seem to show much of a difference within a data center as data replication is much faster and takes only a few milliseconds. However, in the geo-distribution scenario, when data replication takes several hundred milliseconds, the story is different, which increases the chances of dirty reads. The Cosmos DB provides the following data consistency options to choose from with trade-offs between latency, availability, and performance.

- **Strong.** A strong consistency level ensures no dirty reads, and the client always reads the latest version of committed data across the multiple read replicas in single or multi-regions. The trade-off with a strong consistency option is the performance. When you write to a database, everyone waits for Cosmos DB to serve the latest writes after it has been saved across all read replicas.

- **Bounded Staleness.** The bounded staleness option gives you the ability to decide how much stale data an application can tolerate. You can specify the out of date reads that you want to allow either by (X) version of updates of an item or by time interval (T) reads could lag behind by the writes.
- **Session.** Session ensures that there are no dirty reads on the write regions. A session is scoped to a client session, and the client can read what they wrote instead of having to wait for data to be globally committed.
- **Consistent Prefix.** Consistent prefix guarantees that reads are never out of order of the writes. For example, if an item in the database is updated three times with versions V1, V2, and V3, the client would always see V1, V1V2, or V1V2V3. The client would never see them out of order, like V2, V1V3, or V2V1V3.
- **Eventual.** You probably use eventual consistency when you're least worried about the freshness of data across the read replicas and the order of writes over time. All you care about is the highest level of availability and low latency.

To set up a desired consistency on the Cosmos DB, perform the following steps:

1. Log in to the Azure portal and navigate to your Cosmos account under **Resource Group**.
2. On the **Default Consistency** pane (see Figure 4-10), select the desired consistency from the five available consistency levels.
3. For **Bounded Staleness**, define the lag in time or operations an application can tolerate.
4. Click **Save**.

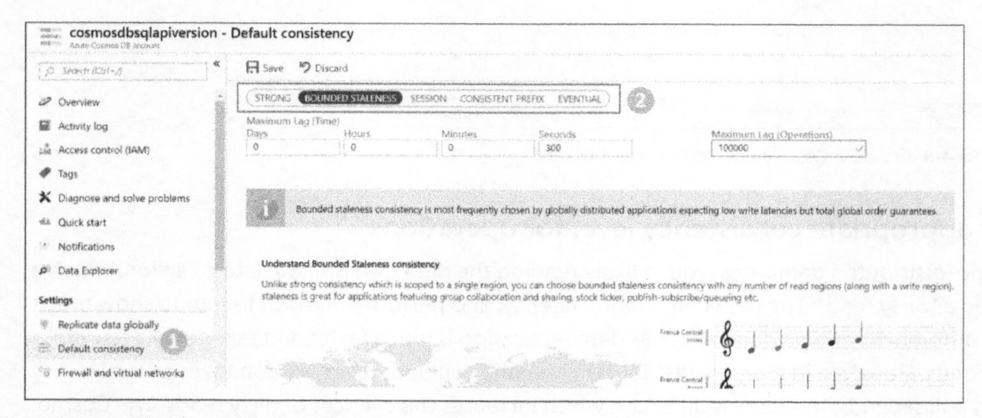

FIGURE 4-10 Setting Cosmos DB consistency

NOTE BUSINESS CONTINUITY AND DISASTER RECOVERY

For high availability, it's recommended that you configure Cosmos DB with multi-region writes (at least two regions). In the event of a regional disruption, the failover is instantaneous, and the application doesn't have to undergo any change; it transparently happens behind the scene. If you're using a default consistency level of Strong, there will not be any data loss before and after the failover. For bounded staleness, you might encounter a potential data loss up to the lag (time or operations) you've set up. For the Session, Consistent Prefix, and Eventual consistency options, the data loss could be up to a maximum of five seconds.

Select appropriate Cosmos DB APIs

Azure Cosmos DB currently provides the following APIs in general availability (GA). See Figure 4-11.

- Core (SQL) API and MongoDB API for JSON document data.
- Cassandra for a columnar or column-family datastore.
- Azure Table API for key-value datastore.
- Gremlin (graph) API for graph data.

EXAM TIP

You can create only one Cosmos DB API per Cosmos account. For example, if you need to create a Cosmos DB that uses SQL API and a Cosmos DB that uses MongoDB API, you will need to create two Cosmos accounts.

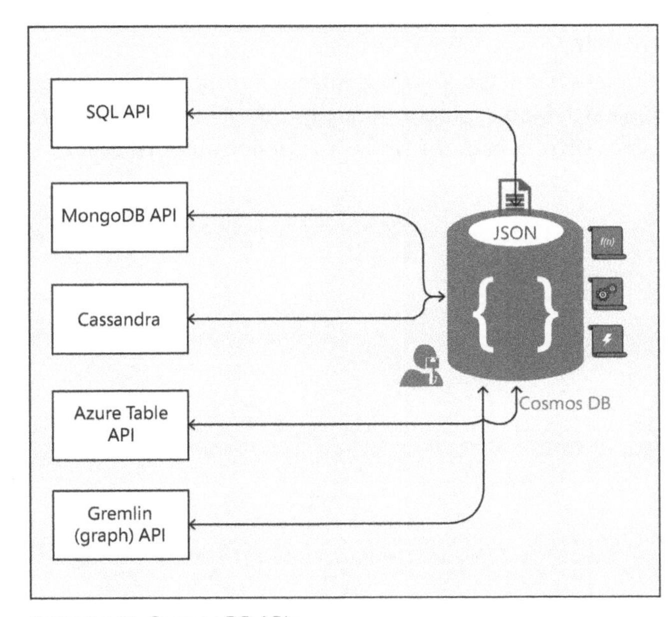

FIGURE 4-11 Cosmos DB APIs

The choice of selecting APIs ultimately depends on your use case. You're probably better off selecting SQL API if your team already has a T-SQL skillset, and you're moving from a relational to a non-relational database. If you're migrating an existing application that uses a MongoDB and you don't want to make any changes in the current application, you must select a MongoDB API; the same is true for the Cassandra API. Similarly, to take advantage of better performance and global scale, use Table API if you're using Azure Table storage. The Gremlin API is used for graph modeling between entities.

SQL API

Structured Query Language (SQL) is the most popular API adopted by the industry to access and interact with Cosmos DB data with existing SQL skills. When using SQL API or Gremlin API, Cosmos DB also gives you an ability to write server-side code using stored procedures, user-defined functions (UDFs), and triggers, as shown in Figure 4-12. These are JavaScript functions written within the Cosmos DB database and scoped at the container level.

Following are the key considerations when you choose writing server-side code with Cosmos DB:

- Stored procedures and triggers are scoped at the partition key and must be supplied with an input parameter for the partition key, whereas UDFs are scoped at the database level.
- Stored procedures and triggers guarantee atomicity ACID (Atomicity, Consistency, Isolation, and Durability) like in any relational database. Transactions are automatically rolled back by Cosmos DB in case of any exception; otherwise, they're committed to the database as a single unit of work.
- Queries using stored procedures and triggers are always executed on the primary replica as these are intended for write operations to guarantee strong consistency for a secondary replica. In contrast, UDFs can be written to the primary or secondary replica as UDFs are for read operations only.
- The server-side code must complete within the specified timeout threshold limit, or you must implement a continuation batch model for long-running code. If the code doesn't complete within the time, Cosmos DB rolls back the whole transaction automatically.

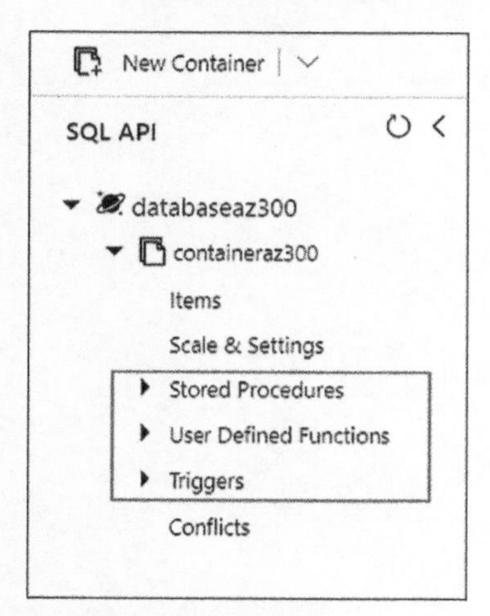

FIGURE 4-12 SQL API

- There are two types of triggers you can set up:
  - **Pre-triggers.** As the name defines, you can invoke some logic on the database containers before the items are created, updated, or deleted.
  - **Post-triggers.** Post-triggers are run after the data is written or updated.

NEED MORE REVIEW? **SQL QUERY REFERENCE GUIDE FOR COSMOS DB**

To learn more about SQL Query examples and operators, visit the Microsoft Doc "Getting started with SQL queries" at *https://docs.microsoft.com/en-us/azure/cosmos-db/sql-query-getting-started#GettingStarted.*

MongoDB API

You can switch from MongoDB to Cosmos DB and take advantage of excellent service features, scalability, turnkey global distribution, various consistency levels, automatic backups, and indexing without having to change your application code. All you need to do is create a Cosmos DB for MongoDB API (see figure 4-13). As of the writing of this book, Cosmos DB's MongoDB API supports the latest MongoDB server version 3.6, and you can use existing tooling, libraries, and open-source client MongoDB drivers to interact with Cosmos DB.

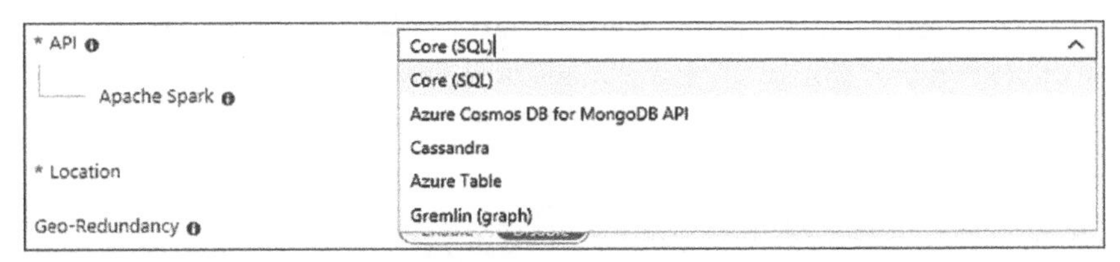

FIGURE 4-13 Cosmos DB supported APIs

Table API

Similar to MongoDB API, applications that are originally written for Azure Table storage can seamlessly be migrated to Cosmos DB without having to change the application code. In this case, you would create a Cosmos DB for Azure Table from the API options.

The client SDKs in .Net, Java, Python, and Node.js are available for Table API. Migrating from Azure Table storage to Cosmos DB provides you the service's premium capabilities, as we've discussed since the start of this chapter.

Cassandra API

You can switch from Apache Cassandra and migrate to Cosmos DB and take advantage of Cosmos DB's best-of-class features without having to change your application code. As of the time of this writing, Cosmos DB's Cassandra API supports Cassandra Query language V4, and you can use existing tooling, libraries, and open-source client Cassandra drivers to communicate with Cosmos DB.

Gremlin API

The Gremlin API is used for generating and visualizing a graph between data entities. The Cosmos DB fully supports an open-source graph computing framework called Apache TinkerPOP. You use this API when you would like to present complex relationships between entities in graphical form. The underlying mechanics of data storage are similar to what you have learned in the previous sections for other APIs, such as SQL or Table. That said, your graph data gets the same level of

- Scalability
- Performance and throughput
- Auto-indexing
- Global distribution with guaranteed high availability

The critical components of any graph database are the following:

- **Vertices.** Vertices denote a discrete object such as a person, a place, or an event. If you think about the analogy of an airline reservation system that we discussed in the SQL API example, a traveler is a vertex.
- **Edges.** Edges denote a relationship between vertices. The relationship could be unidirectional or bidirectional. For instance, in our analogy, an airline carrier is a vertex. The relationship between the traveler and the airline that defines which airline you traveled within a given year is considered an edge.
- **Properties.** Properties include the information between vertices and edges—for example, the properties for a traveler, comprised of his or her name, date of birth, address, and so on. The properties for the edge (airline) could be an airline name, travel routes, and so on.

Gremlin API is widely used in solving problems in a complex business relationship model like social networking, the geospatial, or scientific recommendation in retail and other businesses.

Here's a quick look at the airline reservation analogy and how to create vertices and edges using the Azure portal. You can do this programmatically using SDKs available in .NET and other languages.

Creating Vertices

Use the following steps to create a vertex traveler in the graph database:

1. Log in to the Azure portal and navigate to your Cosmos DB account that you created for Gremlin API.
2. On the **Data Explorer** blade, create a new graph database by specifying the name, storage capacity, throughput, and a partition key for the database. You must provide the

value for the partition key that you define. In our example, the partition key is graphdb, and its value is az303 while creating vertices.

3. After the database is created, navigate to the **Graph Query** window, as shown in Figure 4-14, and run the following commands to create vertices, edges, and several properties for travelers and airlines:

```
g.addV('traveller').property('id', 'thomas').property('firstName', 'Thomas').
property('LastName', 'Joe').property('Address', 'Ohio').property('Travel Year',
2018).property('graphdb', 'az303')

g.addV('traveller').property('id', 'Gurvinder').property('FirstName',
'Gurvinder').property('LastName', 'Singh').property('Address', 'Chicago').
property('Travel Year', 2018).property('graphdb', 'az303')

g.addV('Airline Company').property('id', 'United Airlines').
property('CompanyName', 'United Airlines').property('Route 1', 'Chicago').
property('Route 2', 'Ohio').property('graphdb', 'az303')

g.addV('Airline Company').property('id', 'American Airlines').
property('CompanyName', 'American Airlines').property('Route 1', 'California').
property('Route 2', 'Chicago').property('graphdb', 'az303')

g.addV('Airline Company').property('id', 'Southwest Airlines').
property('CompanyName', 'Southwest Airlines').property('Route 1', 'Chicago').
property('Route 2', 'California').property('graphdb', 'az303')

g.addV('Airline Company').property('id', 'Delta Airlines').property('CompanyName',
'Delta Airlines').property('Route 1', 'Chicago').property('Route 2', 'Ohio').
property('graphdb', 'az303')
```

In the preceding Gremlin commands, `g` represents your graph database, and `g.addV()` is used to add vertices. `Properties ()` is used to associate properties with vertices.

Creating Edges

Now that you've added vertices for travelers and airlines, you need to define the relationship in a way that explains which airline a traveler has traveled within a given year and if travelers know each other.

Create an edge on the vertex 'traveler' that you created previously. Like the vertices you created in step 3 in the preceding section, follow the same method and run the following commands on the graph window to create edges, as shown in Figure 4-14:

```
g.V('thomas').addE('travelyear').to(g.V('Delta Airlines'))
g.V('thomas').addE('travelyear').to(g.V('American Airlines'))
g.V('thomas').addE('travelyear').to(g.V('United Airlines'))
g.V('Gurvinder').addE('travelyear').to(g.V('Delta Airlines'))
g.V('Gurvinder').addE('travelyear').to(g.V('United Airlines'))
g.V('thomas').addE('know').to(g.V('Gurvinder'))
```

In this example, `addE()` defines a relationship with a vertex traveler and an airline using `g.V()`. After you run the preceding commands, you can see the connection between entities on the graph using the Azure portal, as shown in Figure 4-15.

FIGURE 4-14 Gremlin API

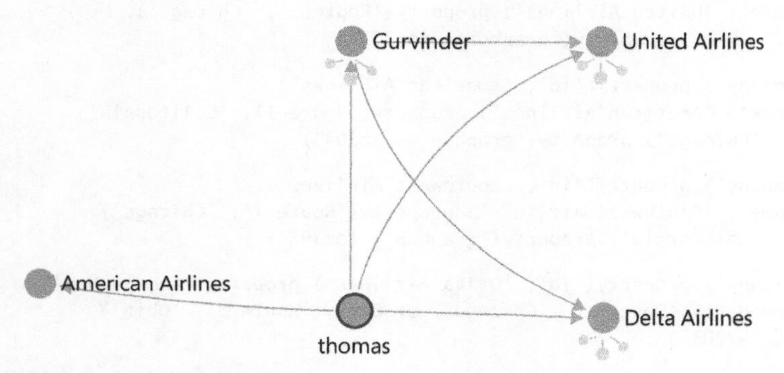

FIGURE 4-15 Gremlin API Graph

You now understand the different industry-standard APIs that are available to choose from, but the question is, how do you make a choice? Table 4.1 outlines the decision criteria, which will help you choose the right API.

TABLE 4-1 API decision criteria

Criteria	CORE SQL	MongoDB	Cassandra	Table API	Gremlin
Are you starting a new project, and does your team have the SQL queries skill set?	X				
Does your current application use MongoDB, and do you want to use existing skills, code, and seamless migration?		X			
Does your application need to drive the relationship between entities and visualize them in a graph?					X
Does your existing application use Table storage and have large volumes of data? Do you want to minimize the migration time and use current application code when switching to Cosmos DB?			X	X	

Set up replicas in Cosmos DB

For globally distributed applications, you might want to distribute your application database in multiple data center—for better performance and low read/write latency. In addition to replicating databases across multiple data center, you might also want to enable active-active patterns using multi-master features. The multi-master allows the application to write to the database closest to the application's region. Azure Cosmos DB has all these capabilities, and it automatically takes care of eventual consistency on cross-region databases to ensure that global consistency and data integrity is maintained.

To set up the global distribution of your Cosmos DBs and enable multiple replicas across regions, use the following steps:

1. In the Azure Portal, navigate to the Cosmos account.
2. Click the **Replicate Data Globally** menu (see Figure 4-16). In the right-side pane, you can add a region by selecting the hexagon icon for your desired region on the map, or you can choose from the drop-down menu after you click **+Add Region**.
3. To remove regions, clear one or more regions from the map by selecting the blue hexagon(s) displayed with checkmarks.

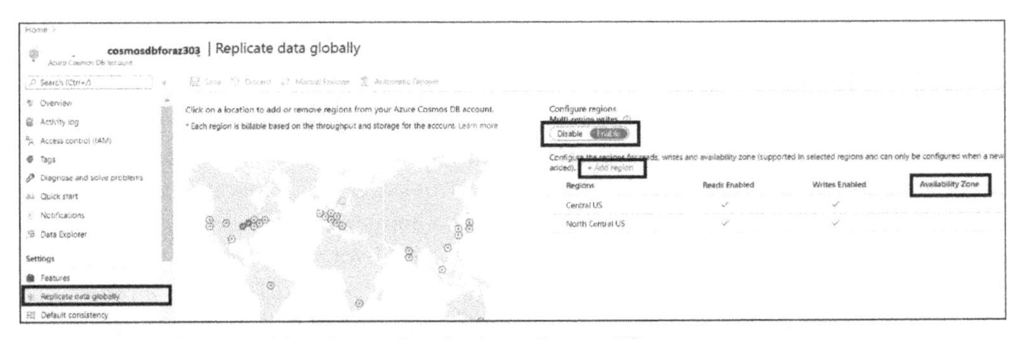

FIGURE 4-16 Setting up multi-region replicas for Azure Cosmos DB

4. Click **Enable Multi-Region Writes**. The multi-master or multi-region writes allow you to take advantage of a supplemental feature called **Availability Zone** recommended for production workloads.
5. Click **Save** to commit the changes.

Table 4-2 provides a fair understanding of different Cosmos account configurations that you can choose from depending upon your application availability and performance requirements.

TABLE 4-2 Cosmos DB account configurations

Single Region	Multi-Region with Single Region Writes	Multi-Region with Multi-Region Writes
Provides SLA of 99.99 percent on read/write operations.	Provides SLA of 99.999 percent on read operations and 99.99 percent on write operations.	Provides SLA of 99.999 percent on read/write operations.

Single Region	Multi-Region with Single Region Writes	Multi-Region with Multi-Region Writes
Availability zone capability is not available in a single region.	Availability zone capability is not available with a single master.	Availability zone support provides additional resilience and high availability within the data center.
Single region account might experience disruption during regional outages.	With multi-region read and single write master, production workloads should have the **Enable Automatic Failover** setting switched to **On** to allow Azure to automatically failover your account when there is a regional disaster. In this configuration, the availability and data loss are subject to the type of consistency level being used.	In multi-region writes, all read regions that you currently have on the account will become read/write regions and hence, this setting provides the highest availability and lowest latency for workload reads and writes.

IMPORTANT **GEO-REDUNDANT PAIRED AZURE REGIONS**

For BCDR, you must choose regions based on Azure-paired regions for a higher degree of fault isolation and improved availability. See Microsoft's documentation at *https://docs.microsoft.com/en-us/azure/best-practices-availability-paired-regions*.

Skill 4.2: Implement Azure SQL Databases

Small, medium and large enterprise companies have been using relational databases for decades as a preferred way to store data for their small or large-scale applications. In a relational database, the data is stored as a collection of data items with a predefined relationship between them. The data in any relational database is stored in rows and columns. Each row of the table has a unique key that represents a collection of values associated with an entity and can be associated with rows of other tables in the database that defines the relationship between entities. Each column of a row holds the values of an entity or object. In addition to it, the relational databases come with built-in capability of managing data integrity, transactional consistency, and ACID (Atomicity, Consistency, Isolation, and Durability) compliance.

As part of the platform as a service (PaaS) offerings, Microsoft provides the following managed databases to choose from for your application needs:

- **Azure SQL Database.** Azure SQL Database is a Microsoft core product and the most popular relational database in the cloud.
- **Azure Synapse Analytics.** Formerly known as Azure SQL Data Warehouse is a relational database for Big Data analytics and enterprise data warehousing.
- **Azure Database for MySQL.** Azure Database for MySQL is a fully managed database-as-a-service where Microsoft runs and manages all mechanics of MySQL Community Edition database in the cloud.
- **Azure Database for PostgreSQL.** Like MySQL, this is a fully managed database-as-a-service offering based on the open-source Postgres database engine.

- **Azure Database for MariaDB.** Azure Database for MariaDB is also a managed, highly available, and scalable database-as-a-service based on the open-source MariaDB server engine.

Regardless of the database you select for your application needs, Microsoft manages the following key characteristics of any cloud-based service offerings:

- High availability and on-demand scale
- Business continuity
- Automated backups
- Enterprise-grade security and compliance

This skill covers how to:

- Configure Azure SQL Database settings
- Implement Azure SQL Database Managed Instances
- Configure HA for an Azure SQL Database
- Publish an Azure SQL Database

Provision and configure relational databases

In this section, we dive into the critical aspects of how you set up a relational database in the cloud and configure the cloud-native features that come with the native service offerings.

Azure SQL Database

Azure SQL Database is the Microsoft core and most popular managed relational database. The service has the following flavors of database offerings.

- **Single database.** With a single database, you assign pre-allocated compute and storage to the database.
- **Elastic pools.** With elastic pools, you create a database inside the pool of databases, and they share the same resources to meet unpredictable usage demand.
- **Managed Instance.** The Managed Instance flavor of the service gives close to 100 percent compatibility with SQL Server Enterprise Edition with additional security features.

NOTE **REGIONAL AVAILABILITY OF SQL AZURE SERVICE TYPES**

Although the AZ-303 exam does not expect you to get into the weeds of regional availability of the Azure SQL Database service, as an architect, you must know this part. See "Products available by region" at *https://azure.microsoft.com/en-us/global-infrastructure/services/?products=sql-database®ions=all.*

It is crucial to understand the available purchasing models, so that you choose the right service tier that meets your application needs. Azure SQL Database comes with the following purchasing models:

- **DTUs (Database Transaction Units) model.** DTUs are the blend of compute, storage, and IO resources that you pre-allocate when creating a database on the logical server. For a single database, the capacity is measured in DTUs; for elastic databases, capacity is measured in eDTUs. Microsoft offers three service tiers, as listed below in this model, which provide the flexibility of choosing compute size with a pre-configured and fixed amount of storage, fixed retention period, and fixed pricing.
  - **Basic.** Suited for dev/test or generic workload, not demanding high-throughput and low-latency. Backed by 99.99 percent SLA and IO latency of 5 ms (read) and 10 ms (write). The maximum point-in-time backup retention for the basic tier is 7 days.
  - **Standard.** Suited for dev/test or generic workload, not demanding high-throughput and low-latency. Backed by 99.99 percent SLA and IO latency of 5 ms (read) and 10 ms (write). The maximum point-in-time backup retention for the standard tier is 35 days.
  - **Premium.** Suited for production workload demanding high-throughput and low-latency. Backed by 99.99 percent SLA and IO latency of 2 ms (read/write). The maximum point-in-time backup retention for the premium tier is 35 days.
- **vCore (Virtual Core) model.** The vCore-based model is the Microsoft recommended purchasing model where you get the flexibility of independently scaling compute and storage to meet your application needs. Additionally, you get an option to use your existing SQL Server license to save up to 55 percent of the cost with Azure Hybrid Benefit (AHB) or take advantage of the significant discount by reserving compute resources with Azure SQL Database reserved instance (RI). The vCore purchasing model provides two service tiers as listed below:
  - **General Purpose.** Suited for dev/test generic workload and backed by 99.99 percent SLA with IO latency of 5-10 ms. The compute and storage in the General Purpose tier has three options:
    - **Provisioned.** Pre-allocated compute and storage and it is billed per hour.
    - **Serverless.** Designed for a single database that needs auto-scaling on demand.
    - **Hyperscale.** Suited for production workload and primarily intended for customers with many databases with scaling needs up to 100 TB.
  - **Business Critical.** Recommended for production workload and backed by 99.99 percent SLA with IO latency of 1-2 ms and a higher degree of fault tolerance. You can also configure Read Scale-Out to offload your read-only workload automatically at no extra cost.

You might choose a vCore model instead of a DTU model for the following reasons:

- You can leverage the hybrid benefit feature and save up to 55 percent of the database cost by using your on-premises SQL server licenses.

- You can independently scale compute, IOPS, and storage.
- You can choose the hardware generation that could improve the performance of your database. The available hardware generation in the vCore model includes Gen4/Gen5, M-series (memory-optimized), and FsV2 series (compute optimized).

Configuring Azure SQL Database settings

In this section, you learn how to use the different features of the Azure SQL Database. We start by creating a database server and a single Azure SQL Database. A database server is a logical construct that acts as a database container. You can add one or more Azure SQL Databases on the container and configure settings such as database logins, firewall rules, auditing, backups, and security policies. The settings applied at the database server level automatically apply to all the databases on the server. You can also overwrite them for individual databases. Follow the steps below to create an Azure SQL Database.

1. Log in to the Azure portal.
2. On the **navigation** blade on the left side of the portal, click **Create A Resource** and search for **SQL Database**; which opens the page shown in Figure 4-17.

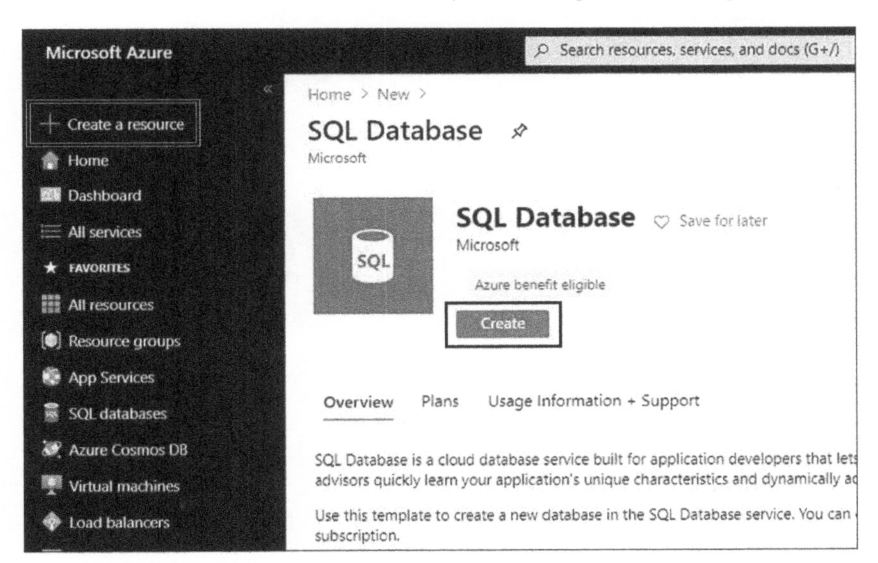

FIGURE 4-17 Create a SQL Database

3. On the **Create SQL Database** screen (see Figure 4-18), fill in the **Database Name** field, and select the **Subscription**, **Resource Group**, and **Server**. If the SQL Server doesn't exist, you can create one by clicking **Create New** (see Figure 4-19).

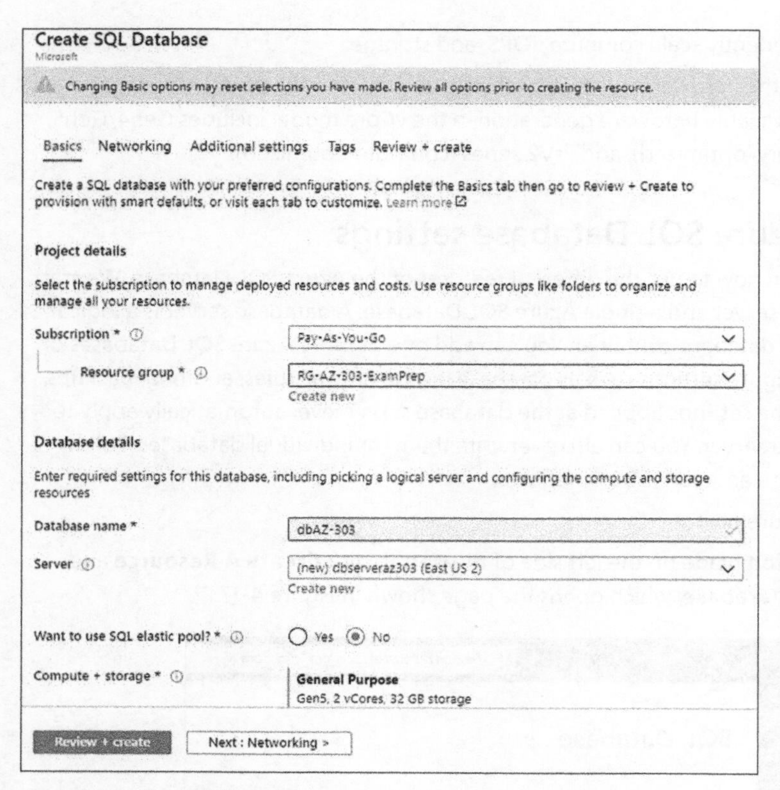

FIGURE 4-18 Create SQL Database

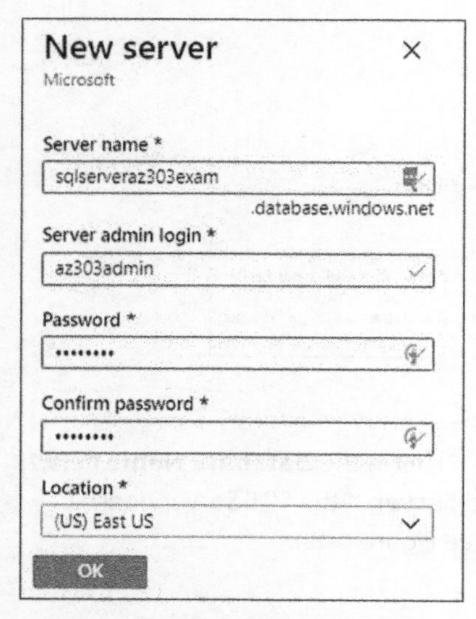

FIGURE 4-19 Create a SQL Server

4. Click **Next Networking** to move on to the **Networking** tab. By default, the database is accessible using public endpoint, but you can restrict access over the public Internet in the **Networking** tab. You can skip this, as we are just creating a database for demonstration purposes.
5. You can also ignore the **Additional Settings** tab that allows you to set up optional settings, such as geo-replication. Click **Next Tags**.
6. The next tab is **Tags**. Tags are used to tag your resources and group them for chargebacks, billing, and governance purposes. You can skip this step and click **Review + Create**.
7. On the review screen, you can review your configuration and click **Create** to initiate database deployment, as shown in Figure 4-20.

FIGURE 4-20 Review and Create

After the database is created, you can navigate to the database in the Azure portal by searching for the SQL database in the **Search Resources, Services, and Docs** search box at the top. The Azure SQL Database blade appears as shown in Figure 4-21.

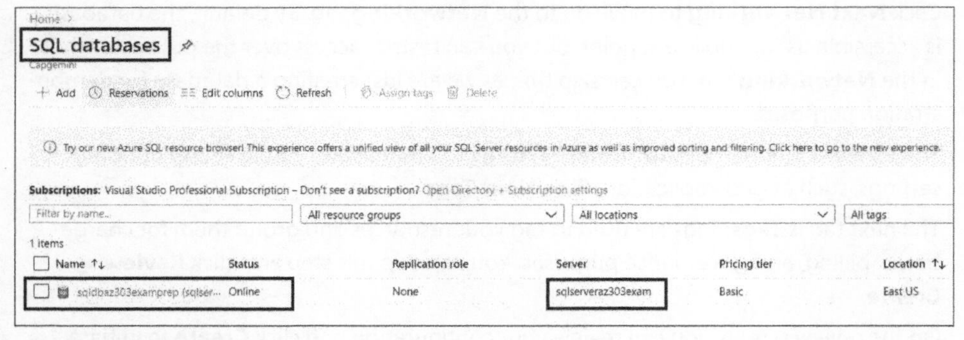

FIGURE 4-21 SQL Databases blade

Now we have Azure SQL Database up and running. In the following section, you will learn about various database settings for the Azure SQL Database that you can configure for your specific business scenarios.

- **Manage backups.** The backup policy is imperative for business continuity and disaster recovery of any line-of-business (LOB) application. The backup strategy protects your database from human errors, such as accidental data deletion or data corruption or data center outages. The backups are automatically encrypted at rest using transparent data encryption (TDE). Azure SQL Database provides you the following options to manage database backups.
    - **Automated Backups.** Regardless of the service tier you choose, the Azure SQL Databases are automatically backed up in read-access-geo-redundant-blob storage (RA-GRS) to facilitate high availability of backups even in the event of a data center outage. The automatic backups are known as a point-in-time restore (PITR). In PITR, the full backup is taken weekly, a differential backup is taken every hour, and a transactional log backup is taken every 5–10 minutes. The PITR backups are kept for 7 days for the basic tier and up to 35 days for the standard premium tier in the DTU purchasing model. For the vCore purchasing model, the retention period is 7–35 days for the General Purpose and Business Critical tiers and 7 days for the Hyperscale tier.
    - **Long-Term Backup Retention.** The **Long-Term Backup Retention** option, also known as **LTR**, keeps the full database backup and is used to retain the database backups beyond 35 days, up to 10 years. LTR can be enabled for single or pooled databases. At the time this book was written, LTRs are not available for managed-instance databases.

Follow these steps to set up long-term backup retention using the Azure portal:

1. Log in to the Azure portal at *https://portal.azure.com* with your subscription credentials and search for **SQL Server** in the search box.
2. In the **SQL Server** blade, choose **Manage Backups**, as shown in Figure 4-22.

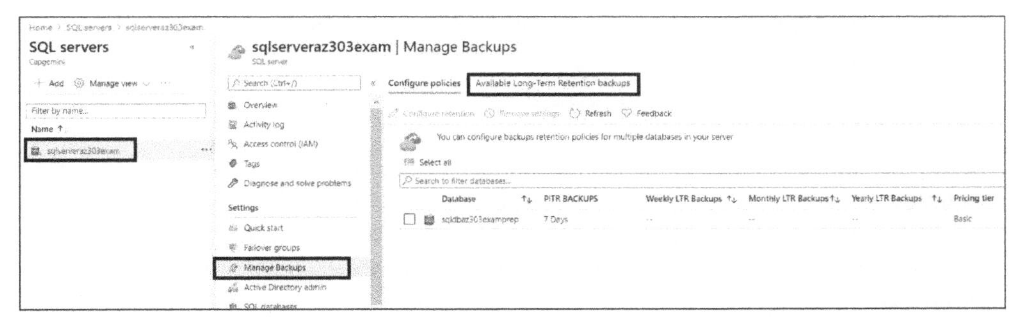

FIGURE 4-22 Setting up backup policies

3. Choose the database for which you want to configure a backup policy and click **Configure Policies**. See Figure 4-23.

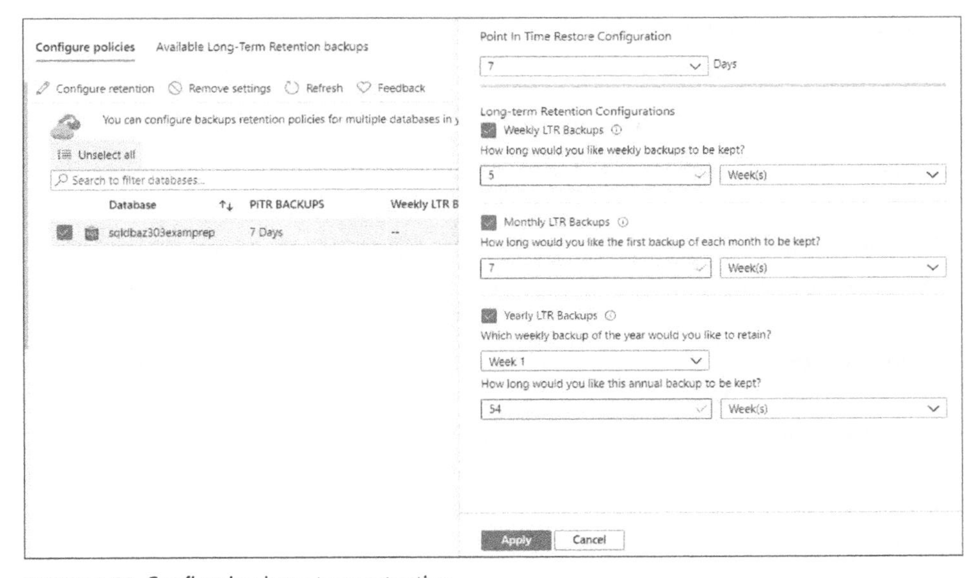

FIGURE 4-23 Configuring long-term retention

As you see, PITR backup policies are automatically created, and you can modify the retention period between 7 and 35 days. Long-term retention policies can be set to days, weeks, months, or years. The LTR policy shown in Figure 4-23 is set as follows:

- **Weekly LTR Backups.** Every backup is retained for 5 weeks.
- **Monthly LTR Backups.** The first backup is made each month and is retained for 7 weeks.
- **Yearly LTR Backups.** The first backup is made on week 1 of the year and is retained for 54 weeks.

4. Finally, click **Apply** at the bottom for policy to apply. The LTR backups might take up to 7 days to become visible and available for restoration.

EXAM TIP

At the time this book was written, the Azure portal did not support restoring LTRs to servers within the same subscription as the primary database, and it only supported restoring the database on the same server as the primary database. Therefore, for such cases, you must use Azure PowerShell or Azure CLI. It is recommended you go through the list of AZ SQL (Azure CLI) and AZ.sql commands given at the links below:

- ***https://docs.microsoft.com/en-us/cli/azure/sql?view=azure-cli-latest***
- ***https://docs.microsoft.com/en-us/powershell/module/az.sql/?view=azps-3.6.1***

Use the following AZ PowerShell script to create and restore LTRs, use the following scripts.

To create an LTR, use this command:

```
Set-AzSqlDatabaseBackupLongTermRetentionPolicy -ServerName {serverName} -DatabaseName
{dbName}  -ResourceGroupName {resourceGroup} -WeeklyRetention P1W  -MonthlyRetention
P4M -YearlyRetention P10Y -WeekOfYear 11
```

- **-ServerName.** This is the name of the SQL server on which you want to configure the LTR policy.
- **-DatabaseName.** This is the name of the Azure SQL Database you want to back up.
- **-WeeklyRetention.** This is the retention period for the weekly backup taken every 7 days for up to 10 years.
- **-MonthlyRetention.** This is the retention period for the monthly backup taken every 30 days for up to 10 years.
- **-YearlyRetention.** This is the retention period for the yearly backup taken every 365 days up to 10 years.
- **-WeekOfYear.** This is the week defined for yearly backup; you can choose a value of 1 to 52.

To restore an LTR, use this command:

```
Restore-AzSqlDatabase -FromLongTermRetentionBackup -ResourceId $ltrBackup.ResourceId
-ServerName $serverName -ResourceGroupName $resourceGroup -TargetDatabaseName $dbName
-ServiceObjectiveName P1
```

- **FromLongTermRetentionBackup.** This indicates that the backup be restored from long term retention.
- **ResourceId.** This is the ID of the resource that will be restored.
- **ServerName.** This specifies the name of the SQL Server.
- **ResourceGroupName.** This specifies the name of the resource group.

- **TargetDatabaseName.** This specifies the name of the target database that will be restored.
- **ServiceObjectiveName.** This specifies the name of the service tier.

> ***NOTE*** **HOW TO SET UP LONG TERM RETENTION FOR MANAGED INSTANCE**
>
> **You cannot configure LTR for databases on Managed Instances. Instead, you can use an SQL Agent Server job to schedule copy-only database backups. To learn more, visit the Microsoft documentation at** ***https://docs.microsoft.com/en-us/sql/relational-databases/backup-restore/copy-only-backups-sql-server?view=sql-server-ver15.***

Manual backups

You can generate an on-demand manual backup of existing databases and store them on Azure Blob storage. The backup created manually is stored in Blob storage in the form of a **BACPAC** zip file that contains both data and schema. You can use the file to restore a database when required. To initiate an export to a BACPAC file using the Azure portal, go to the Azure SQL Database blade and click **Export** on the top, as shown in Figure 4-24. Once initiated, you can see the export status by navigating to the SQL server that contains the database. The exported BACPAC files can be used to restore the database using SSMS, Azure portal, or PowerShell.

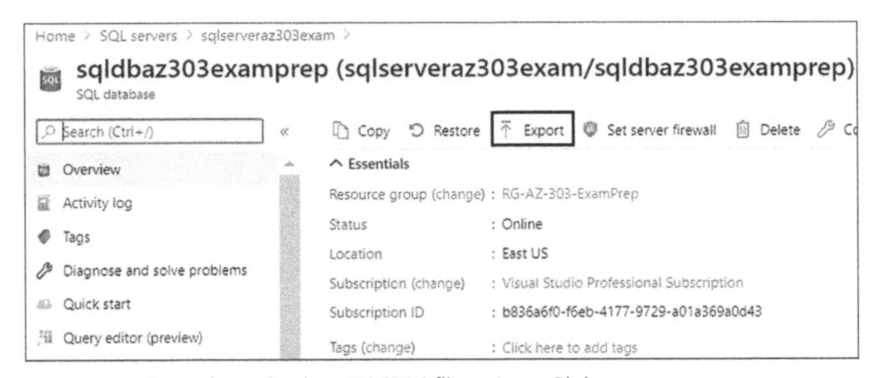

FIGURE 4-24 Exporting a database BACPAC file to Azure Blob storage

Scaling an Azure SQL Database

The SQL Azure database can be scaled up or down (vertical scaling) by adding more compute, storage, or switching to higher or lower service tiers. SQL Azure does not provide horizontal scaling out of the box.

Follow the below-mentioned steps below to scale your database using the Azure portal.

1. Log in to the Azure portal at *https://portal.azure.com* with your subscription.

2. Navigate to your Azure SQL Database blade and click **Configure,** as shown in Figure 4-25.

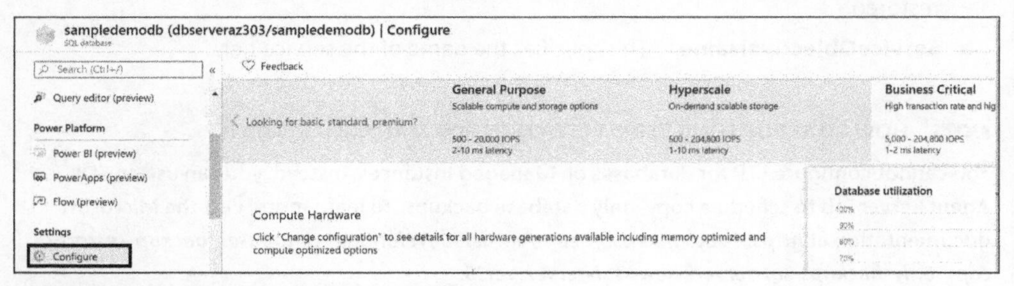

FIGURE 4-25 Scaling Azure SQL Database service tiers

As shown in Figure 4-25, the horizontal blade displays the different service tiers for DTU and vCore model that allow you to change the service tier to scale up or down without affecting the database performance. In this example, we have selected the **Business Critical** tier.

3. Scroll down and choose other scaling parameters, such as **Hardware Generation**, **vCores**, and Storage Size. Opt-in for hybrid benefits if you own the SQL server license already and **click** Apply, as shown in Figure 4-26, for the scaling to take effect.

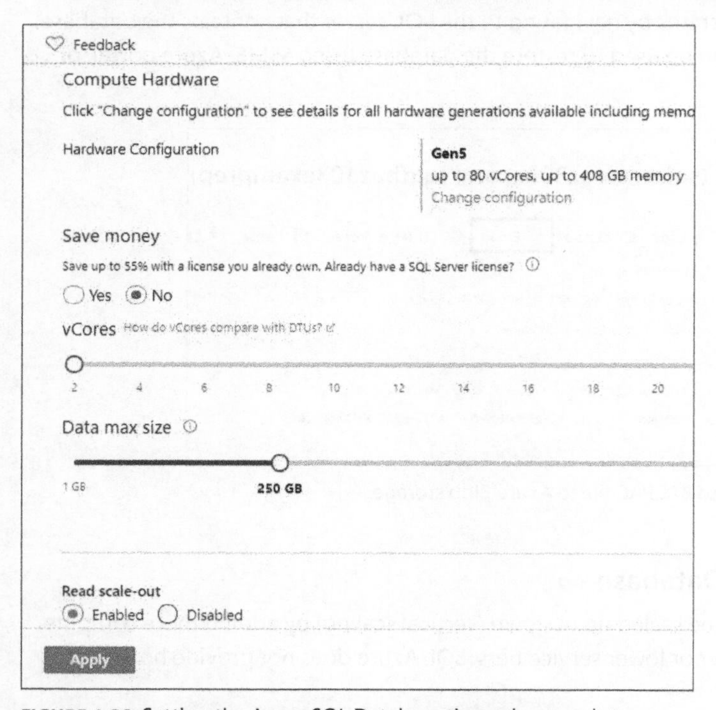

FIGURE 4-26 Setting the Azure SQL Database throughput and storage

Read scale-out

Read scale-out is a promising feature to load balance the read and write for improved performance. The feature is available for Premium, Hyperscale, and Business Critical tiers at no extra cost. Read scale-out is enabled by default for available service tiers when you create a new database. After you enable it, you get a read-only replica of your database to offload the read workload, such as reports, by specifying the ApplicationIntent=ReadOnly in the connection string.

> ***NOTE*** **USING READ-SCALE-OUT WITH GEO-REDUNDANT DATABASES**
>
> **If the Azure SQL Database is Geo-replicated for HADR, ensure that read scale-out is enabled on both the primary and the geo-replicated secondary databases. This configuration will ensure that the same load-balancing experience continues when your application connects to the new primary after failover.**

Azure SQL Database security

For any organization using the cloud, the security and the privacy of customer data is always the first and foremost priority. The Azure SQL Database has a built-in multi-layer defense-in-depth strategy to protect your data at multiple layers, including physical, logical, and data in transit and at rest. Because the Azure SQL Database is a managed service, securing the database becomes a shared responsibility.

You can use the following defense-in-depth layers to set up a robust security posture for your database:

- **Network security.** When you create a new database server (single or pooled), the database gets a public endpoint by default. For example, a database server named `mydbAZ303` would be named **`mydbAZ303.database.windows.net`**, and it would be accessible on TCP port 1433. The database firewall is the first level of defense against unauthorized access; by default, the database firewall blocks all incoming requests to the SQL server public endpoint. The network security settings allow you to set up the firewall rules, as described in the next bullet.
- **Server-level firewall rules.** Server-level firewall rules enable clients to access all the databases on the server if the originating client IP address is present in the allow rule. Server-level rules can be configured at a virtual network level or for a specific IP address or IP range.
- **Database-level firewall rules.** Database firewall rules allow a particular IP address or IP ranges to connect to the individual database. You can only configure IP addresses and not the virtual network on the database-level rules.

As far as best practices go, you should configure a database-level firewall unless the access requirements are the same for all the databases on the server. Regardless of the firewall rules, the connection toward the database always traverses over the public Internet. Though SQL Azure encrypts the data in transit and at rest, a connection over the public Internet might not be aligned with the security requirements of your organization. You can leverage a new offering known as Azure private link, which allows you to eliminate the exposure over the public Internet and keep traffic toward the Azure SQL Database from the Azure VNet/Subnet over the Microsoft backbone network.

You can use the Azure portal, PowerShell, TSQL, or Azure CLI to configure network firewall rules. In this example, we will look at a few examples using the Azure portal. You must have at least the SQL DB Contributor or the SQL Server Contributor RBAC role to manage database-level or server-level firewall rules.

> ***NOTE*** **NETWORK SECURITY IN MANAGED AZURE SQL DATABASE INSTANCE**
>
> **Unlike the Azure SQL Database, the Managed-Instance Azure SQL Database connectivity architecture works differently. By default, the database endpoint is exposed through a private IP address from Azure or hybrid networks. Refer to the connectivity architecture of the Managed-Instance database later in this chapter.**

Follow these steps to configure server-level firewall rules using the Azure portal.

1. Log in to the Azure portal.
2. Navigate to Azure SQL Database blade and click **Set Server Firewall**, as shown in Figure 4-27.

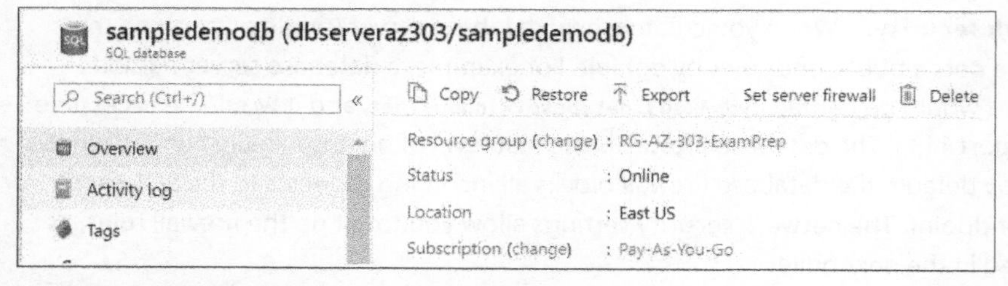

FIGURE 4-27 Setting up SQL server firewall rules

Figure 4-28 shows a variety of settings in addition to firewall rules:

- **Deny Public Network Access.** The default is **No**, which means a client can connect to the database via a private and public endpoint. Switching it to **Yes** will allow a connection only via private endpoints.
- **Connection Policy.** Azure SQL Database supports the following three connection policies:
- **Redirect.** This is the recommended policy for low latency and better performance and throughput. Redirect enables clients to connect to the database host directly. All connections originating within Azure use the Redirect connection policy by default.

From outside Azure, if you enforce a Redirect policy, make sure you enable outbound connections in addition to default TCP port 1433 from the client network for Azure IP addresses in the region on port range 11000-11999.

- **Proxy.** In this mode, the connections to the database host go via a database gateway. All connections outside Azure default to Proxy policy.
- **Allow Access To Azure Services.** This enables connectivity from IPs within Azure services to access the database.

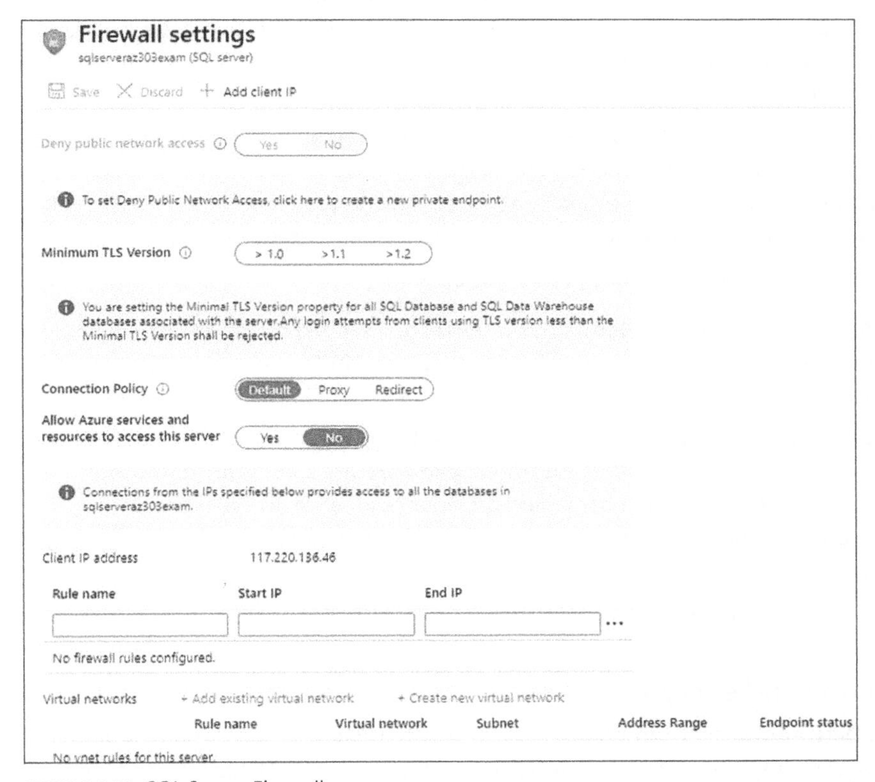

FIGURE 4-28 SQL Server Firewall pane

3. As shown in Figure 4-28, click **Add Client IP** to add the IP address of your network and then click **Save**. You can update the IP addresses at any point, or you can delete them by clicking the ellipsis on the IP rule. If you want to enable access from the subnet from within an Azure virtual network, click **Add Existing Virtual Network**.
4. Click **Save**.

Azure SQL Database also gives you leeway to configure the database-level firewall using the TSQL commands. The sample code snippet is shown below:

```
EXECUTE sp_set_database_firewall_rule N'Allow Rule, '{0.0.0.0}', '{0.0.0.0}'; Go;
```

In the command above, you must specify `Go` for the command to execute. You can view the database level rules by using the view `sys.database_firewall_rules` option with the following TSQL command:

```
SELECT * FROM  sys.database_firewall_rules
```

Access control

The firewall rules enable the client to connect to the Azure SQL Database. The next layer of protection is access control, which requires the client to go through the authentication and authorization process. Let us look at the authentication process first. Azure SQL Database supports two types of authentication methods:

- **SQL Authentication.** In this process of authentication, you create a database user, also called a contained user, either on the master database or on the individual database. Log in with your SQL Server admin account, the one you created while setting up SQL server, and use the following TSQL command to create database users:

  ```
  CREATE USER dbUser WITH PASSWORD = 'strongpassword';  GO
  ```

- **Azure AD (AAD) authentication.** This is the recommended method to connect to the Azure SQL Database using the identities managed in Azure Active Directory a.k.a (AAD).

Authenticated users, by default, do not get any access to the data. The access to the data is further controlled by the database roles/permission groups, such as db_datawriter and db_datareader. The db_datawriter command provides read/write access, while the db_datareader command provides the read access to the database. Use the following TSQL command to add a user to the groups:

```
ALTER ROLE db_datareader ADD MEMBER dbUser;
```

Data protection and encryption

The Azure SQL Database protects your data at rest and in-transit using transparent data encryption (TDE). Security is enforced for any newly created Azure SQL Database and Managed Instance, which means TDE is enabled by default. If TDE is enabled, the data encryption and decryption happens in real-time and transparently for all database operations within Azure. The default encryption key is a managed key within Azure, but you have an option to bring in your encryption key with a popularly known concept: Bring Your Own Key (BYOK).

In addition to TDE, you can further protect your sensitive information, such as personally identifiable information (PII), by enabling Dynamic Data Masking. You can use the Azure portal to configure Dynamic Data Masking and transparent data encryption by navigating to the **Azure SQL Database** blade and selecting the corresponding security setting, as shown in Figure 4-29.

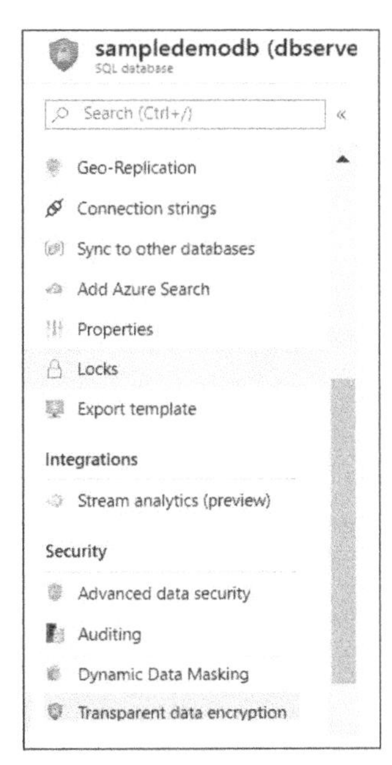

FIGURE 4-29 SQL Azure Database security settings

Advanced threat protection

Azure SQL Database provides advanced threat protection through its advanced data security (ADS) capabilities, including data discovery and data classification for sensitive data and vulnerability assessment. ADS helps discover potential database security loopholes, such as an unencrypted database, anonymous and unusual activities, and suspicious data access patterns that could lead to data exploitation.

ADS also provides smart alerts for potential database vulnerabilities, SQL injection and brute force attacks, suspicious actions, and data exfiltration, and it provides recommendations to investigate and mitigate threats.

You can enable the ADS feature for single, pooled, or managed-instance databases using Azure Portal or Azure CLI. Follow the steps below to configure ADS.

1. Log in to the Azure portal and navigate to the **SQL Server Database** blade.
2. Click **Advanced-Data Security** under the **Security Settings** pane, as shown in Figure 4-30.
3. Specify the email addresses for alerts on vulnerability reports.
4. In the **Advanced Threat Protection Types** section, opt out or in for security scan configuration.
5. Click **Save**.

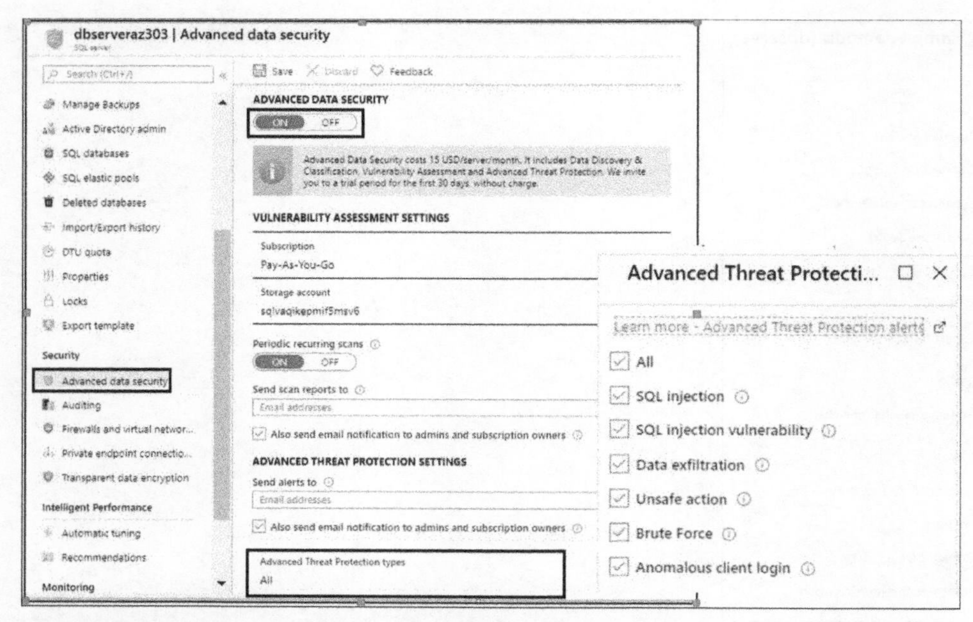

FIGURE 4-30 Configuring Azure SQL Database Advanced Threat Protection

Auditing

Auditing is an essential aspect of database monitoring that helps investigate database security breaches such as suspicious activities or unauthorized access. When auditing is enabled, you can configure all database operations to be recorded in Azure Storage or Log Analytics workspace, or Event Hubs. It is recommended that you enable auditing at the database server level that is automatically inherited for all the databases on the server unless you have a specific need to allow database-level auditing. Follow the steps below to enable database server-level auditing:

1. Log in to the Azure portal and navigate to the **SQL Server** blade.
2. Under the **Security** heading in the left menu, click **Auditing**, as shown in Figure 4-31.
3. In the right-hand menu, toggle **Auditing** to **ON** and specify your preferred storage service.
4. Click **Save**.

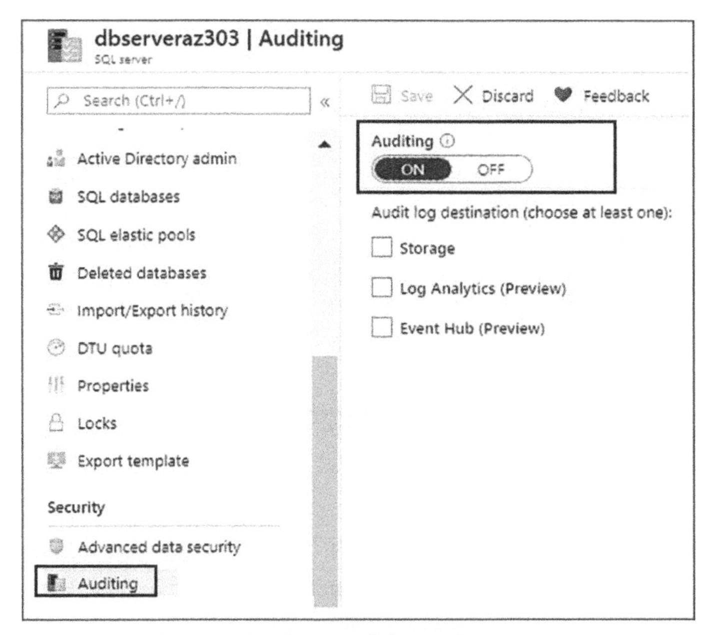

FIGURE 4-31 SQL Azure Database Auditing settings

Implement Azure SQL Database Managed Instance

Azure SQL Database Managed Instance is another flavor in the Azure SQL Database product family that provides nearly 100 percent compatibility with an on-premises SQL Server (Enterprise Edition) database engine. It is exposed only through a private IP address that allows connectivity only from the peered virtual networks or on-premises network using Azure VPN Gateway or ExpressRoute.

Managed Instance is provisioned on a single tenant with dedicated infrastructure (compute and storage) under the vCore purchasing model. Figure 4-32 shows the high-level connectivity architecture of the Azure SQL Managed Instance Database.

As you can see in **figure 4-32**, Azure SQL Managed Instance Database is hosted inside its dedicated subnet. In the dedicated virtual network subnet, Azure automatically creates isolated virtual machines that form a virtual cluster to host one or multiple Managed Instances. You cannot host any other service inside the Managed Instance's dedicated subnet. The virtual cluster and virtual machines are entirely transparent and managed by Azure.

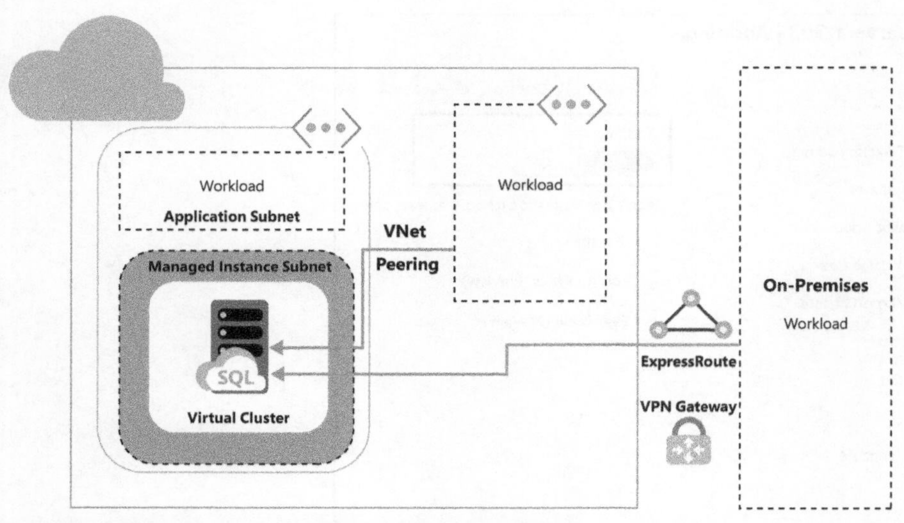

FIGURE 4-32 SQL Azure Database Managed Instance connectivity architecture

Client applications can connect to a Managed Instance via a peered virtual network, VPN, ExpressRoute connections, or from a subnet within the same VNet as a Managed Instance. You use the hostname **<databasename.dns_name.database.windows.net>**, which automatically resolves to the private IP address that belongs to the Managed Instance internal load balancer. The traffic is then redirected to the Managed Instance gateway, facilitating the connection to the specific database instance within a virtual cluster.

Follow these to create an Azure SQL Database Managed Instance using the Azure Portal.

1. Log in to Azure using your Azure subscription credentials.
2. On the left menu, click **Create A Resource** and search for **Azure SQL Managed Instance**. You will see the screen shown in Figure 4-33.
3. Next, click **Create**.

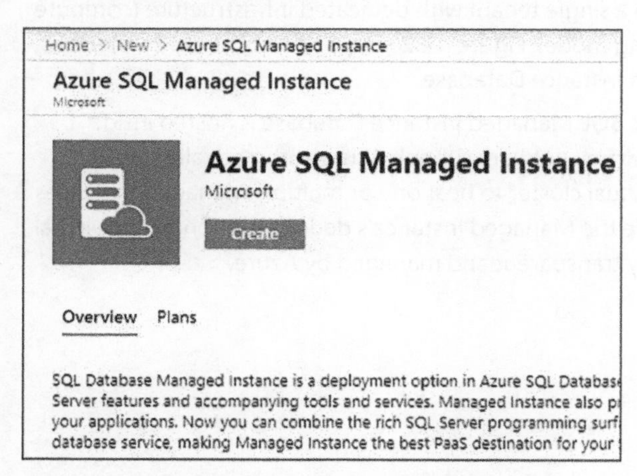

FIGURE 4-33 Creating an Azure SQL Managed Instance

4. On the **Create Azure SQL Database Managed Instance** screen, as shown in Figure 4-34, provide the mandatory information, such as a **Unique Database Name**, **Resource Group**, **Region**, **SKU**, and **Administrator Username** and **Password**.
5. Click **Next: Networking**.
6. On the **Networking** tab (see Figure 4-35), create a mandatory virtual network and dedicated subnet for the Managed Instance; if you do not do so, Azure automatically creates one for you.

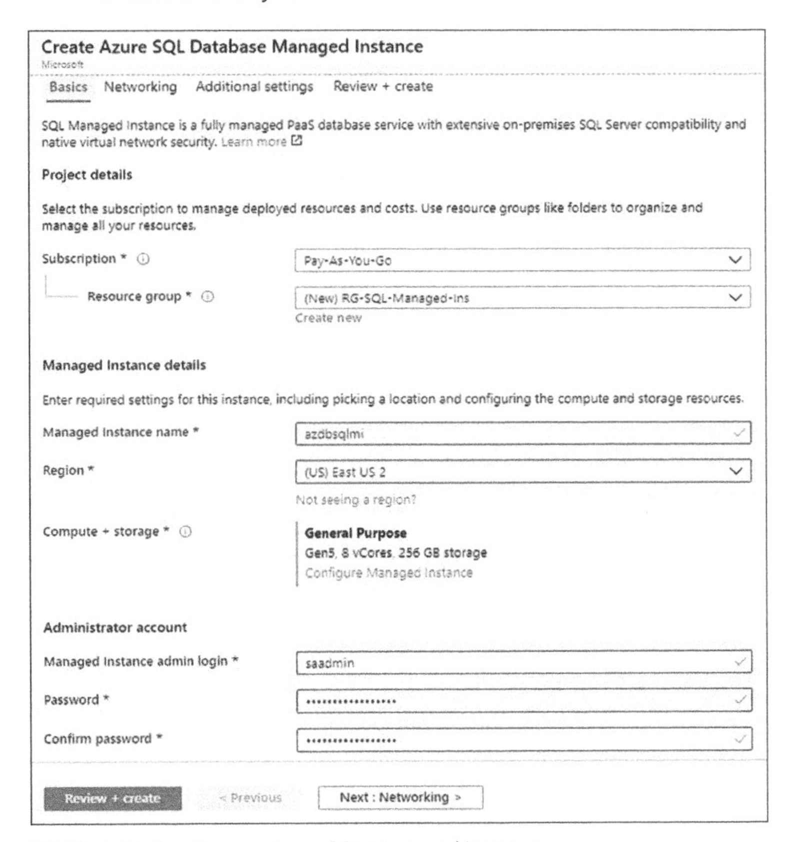

FIGURE 4-34 Creating an Azure SQL Managed Instance

The next step is to specify the **Connection Type** (see Figure 4-35).

- **Proxy (Default).** The proxy connection enables connectivity to a Managed Instance via a gateway component (GW). It uses port 1433 for a private connection and port 3342 for a public connection.
- **Redirect.** The redirect mode provides low latency and better performance because it connects to the database directly. You can only use this mode for private connections. You must enable the firewall and NSGs to allow connections on port 1433 and ports 11000–11999.

7. Next, we have the public endpoint. Switch the toggle button to **Enable** if you want to allow public endpoints.

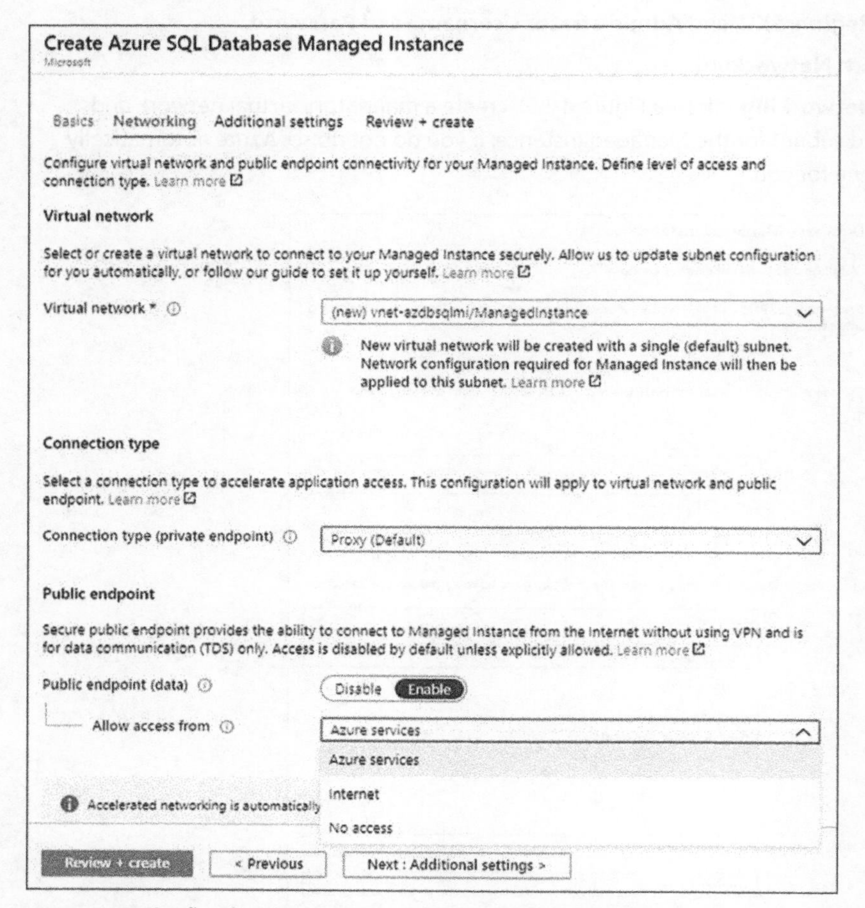

FIGURE 4-35 Configuring the network configuration for a Managed Instance

8. Next, select **Azure Services**, **Internet**, or **No Access** for your connectivity requirements. See the previous **Figure 4-35**.
9. You may skip the optional settings such as **Database Timezone, Geo-Replication**, and **Collation** on the **Additional Settings** tab. If you skip them, Azure will automatically apply the default settings. Next, click the **Review + Create** button (See Figure 4-36). As you can see in the notification at the top, unlike the single/pooled database, the Managed Instance Database deployment takes up to 6 hours on average, especially when you are creating a virtual network along with it. Changing the service tier on the existing Instances takes up to 2.5 hours, and deleting a database takes up to 1.5 hours.
10. Review the configuration and click **Create** (see Figure 4-36).

FIGURE 4-36 SQL Database Managed Instance review screen

Configure HA for an Azure SQL Database

The Azure SQL Database has build-in robust high availability architecture that guarantees an SLA of 99.99 percent uptime, even during the maintenance operations or underlying hardware or network failure. In this section, you learn the key features you get out of the box for the high availability of Azure SQL Database and recommendations for you to implement business continuity and disaster recovery procedures. Before we go deeper, let us look at the basics to understand the terms High Availability (HA), Business Continuity, and Disaster Recovery (BCDR).

- **High availability.** The phrase "high availability" refers to key characteristics that is intended to keep the system up and running as per the defined service level agreement (SLA) regardless of the underlying hardware, network failures, or planned maintenance operations.
- **Business continuity.** The phrase "business continuity" refers to the set of procedures and policies that you put together to keep your applications and businesses operational in the event of adverse impact on the data center that may cause a data center outage or data loss. Although the Azure SQL Database provides an SLA of 99.99 percent, specific disruptive scenarios such as data deletion by a human error, regional data center outages, etc., are not automatically handled by the Azure SQL Database. You will have

to do exclusive planning and implement procedures to achieve the desired state of business continuity. We will talk about these procedures later in this chapter.

- **Disaster recovery.** The phrase "disaster recovery" refers to the procedures that we implement to recover from an outage, data loss, and downtime caused by a disaster such as regional data center outages or human errors.

Designing a business continuity and disaster recovery strategy requires immense planning, end-to-end understanding of application workload, application infrastructure, and dependencies. There are two key factors you must consider when designing a BCDR:

- **Recovery Point Objective (RPO).** RPO defines the maximum data loss a business can afford before the application is restored to its normal state. RPO is measured in units of time, not the volume of data; for example, if your application can afford to lose up to one hour of uncommitted transactional data, then your RPO is one hour.
- **Recovery Time Objective (RTO).** RTO is a maximum duration of acceptable downtime an application can afford before the restoration. For example, if your application database takes eight hours to restore, you may define acceptable downtime to be nine hours considering an additional one hour for validation and fail-fast testing; thus your RTO becomes nine hours.

As stated earlier, the default built-in high availability architecture of Azure SQL Database gives you an SLA of 99.99 percent uptime regardless of the different service tiers you choose. The availability architecture has two models:

- **Standard availability model** Basic, Standard, and General Purpose tiers use the standard model, where the compute and storage are managed separately. The availability of compute is managed by a Service Fabric controller that triggers the failover to another physical node in the same region in case of failure of the current node. The data layer that contains the data files `(.mdf/.ldf)` is managed on the highly redundant Azure Blob storage. When the failover happens, the persistent storage of data and log files stored on the Azure storage is automatically attached to the new physical node.
- **Premium availability model** This model works on the similar principle of the SQL Server Always On feature. The Premium and Business critical tier uses the premium availability model to opt-in for zone-redundancy that further enhances availability and fault tolerance by spreading the replicas across the availability zone within the region. The data files `(.mdf/.ldf)` in this mode are managed on the same local attached SSD storage, thus providing low latency and high throughput. This mode is typically for business-critical applications.

Additionally, the premium model maintains the three secondary replicas and the primary node in the same region. At least one secondary replica is always synchronized before committing the transactions. The failover is managed by a Service Fabric that initializes the failover to the synchronized secondary replica when needed.

With the additional three secondary replicas, you also get a feature called Read Scale-Out (at no extra cost) to separate read workload to one of the secondary replicas within a primary region, which seems like a promising feature for improved performance.

Azure SQL Database provides the following options that you can leverage to design your business continuity, disaster recovery, and high availability strategy:

- **Automated Backups.** As we saw earlier in this chapter, the built-in automated backups and point-in-time restore (PITR) help you restore the database in the event of a failure.
- **Long-Term Backup Retention.** Allows you to retain the backups for up to 10 years.
- **Active Geo-Replication.** Enables you to create up to four read-only replicas of your database within the same or different regions so that you can manually failover to any secondary replica in case of failure of the primary database. Active geo-replication is not supported for Azure SQL Managed Instance Database. You would use the Auto-failover group instead.
- **Auto-Failover Group.** Works on the similar principle of active geo-replication that helps you automatically perform the failover in case of a catastrophic event that can cause a data center outage. With auto-failover enabled, you cannot create secondary replicas in the same region as a primary database.

The geo-replication strategy does not form a complete BCDR solution and requires you to think through all potential failure scenarios and design a robust plan. For example, in the event of human error, such as data deletion or data corruption, the replication would synchronize the data to all secondary databases that result in secondary databases being in the same state as the primary database. In this case, you would have to restore the data from the available backups such as point-in-time restore (PITR) or long-term retention (LTR) backups.

If you are using LTR and geo-replication or a failover group as a BCDR solution, you need to make sure you configure the LTR on all secondary replicas so that LTR backup continues when failover happens, and your secondary replica becomes primary.

Configure an auto-failover group

As we learned earlier, the auto-failover group is the recommended method for a high degree of fault tolerance and disaster recovery. The failover group feature in the Azure SQL Database product family uses the same underlying technology as geo-replication. It allows you to seamlessly manage auto-failover of databases (single, pooled, or Managed Instance) configured on the primary and secondary server in different Azure regions. The failover can be configured to trigger automatically, or you can also do it manually when an outage occurs.

Auto-failover supports only one secondary server that must be in a different Azure region from the primary server. If you need multiple secondary replicas, consider using active geo-replication to create four replicas in the same region as the primary server or in the different Azure regions from a primary server.

The following are the steps to configure the failover group for Azure SQL Databases. We will look at a single database in our example. (The steps are the same for the elastic pool databases.)

1. Log in to Azure using your Azure subscription credentials.
2. Navigate to the **Azure SQL Database Server** blade, and under the **Settings** menu, choose **Failover Groups** > **Add Group** at the top (see Figure 4-37).

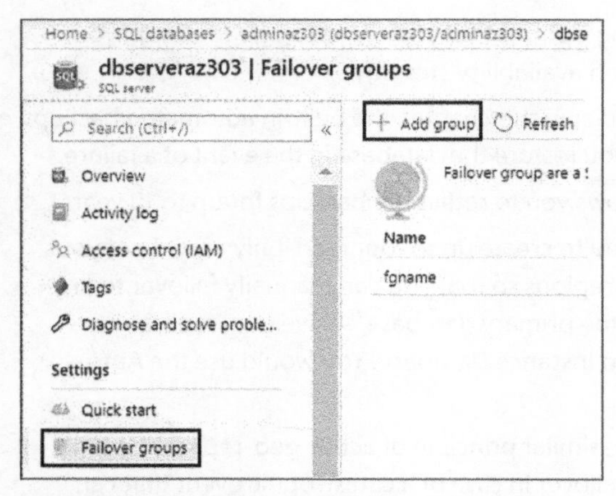

FIGURE 4-37 Failover Groups settings

The database server dbserveraz303 is our primary server in the East US, on which we want to set up a failover group.

3. Click **Add group**, and the screen shown in Figure 4-38 appears. Fill in the following required information:
   - Provide the name of failover group.
   - Select or create the secondary server in a **different region** from the primary.
   - Specify the failover policy that defines the grace period before the failover is triggered upon outage on the primary server. The default is 1 hour.
   - Select the databases on the primary server to be part of the failover group as you see them on the **Databases** blade in Figure 4-38.
4. Click **Create**.

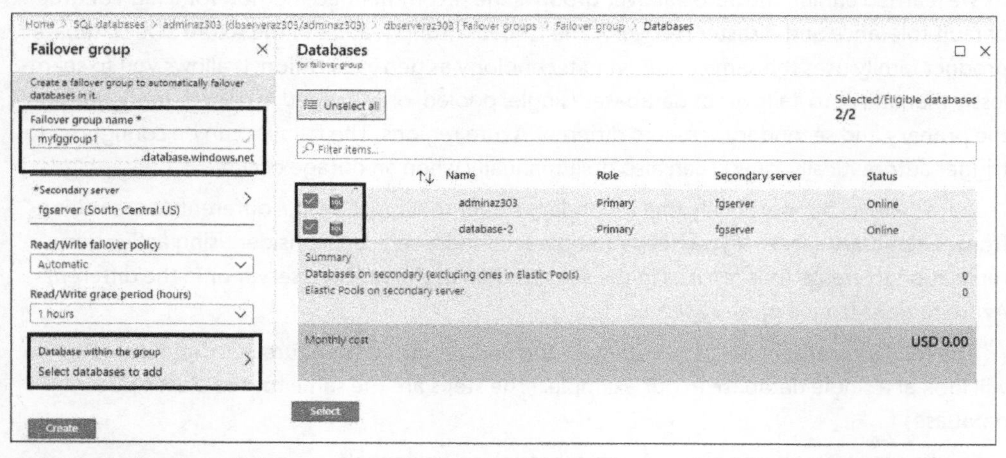

FIGURE 4-38 Creating a Failover group

> ***NOTE*** **SECONDARY SQL SERVER IN THE FAILOVER GROUP**
>
> **The secondary server you create in the different regions for the failover group should not have a database with the same name as the primary server unless it is an existing secondary database.**

Adding databases to the failover group automatically triggers the geo-replication for all the databases in the failover group to the selected secondary region; see Figure 4-39. As you can see, when a failover group is created, Azure forms the two `CNAME` records:

- Read/Write Listener (Primary Server), which is formed as `<fgname.database.windows.net>`
- Read-Only Listener (Secondary Server), which is formed as `<fgname.secondary.database.windows.net>`

To connect to a geo-replicated database on the secondary server, use the secondary listener endpoint to perform functions such as offload the read queries. By default, the failover on the secondary listener is not enabled. You must allow it by explicitly using the `AllowReadOnlyFailoverToPrimary` property to automatically redirect the read traffic to the primary server if the secondary server is offline.

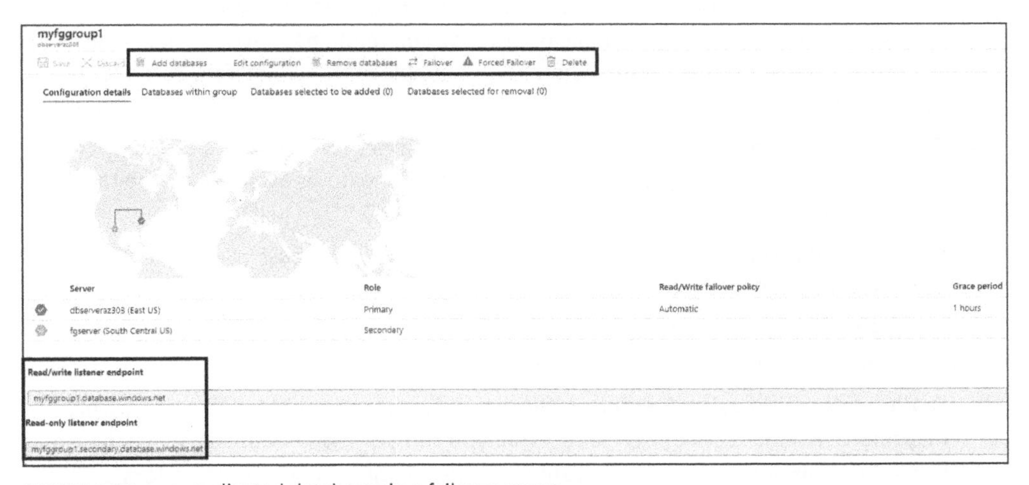

FIGURE 4-39 geo-replicated databases in a failover group

> ***NOTE*** **READ SCALE-OUT VERSUS FAILOVER GROUP**
>
> **The failover group gives you a geo-replicated secondary read-only database in the different regions with a cost equal to 100 percent of the primary database cost. The read scale-out, when enabled on the geo-replicated database, provides another pair of read-only replicas at no additional cost.**

IMPORTANT **DELETING A DATABASE THAT IS PART OF THE FAILOVER GROUP**

You must remove the secondary database from the failover group if you want to delete it. Deleting a secondary database before removing it from the failover group is not permitted.

Publish an Azure SQL Database

Migrating on-premises SQL Server databases to Azure SQL Database (single, pooled, or Managed Instance) requires immense planning and assessment to develop the robust migration strategy using the appropriate methods that are deemed fit for a given workload type. In this section, you learn how to select the appropriate migration strategy to publish an existing on-premises SQL Database to the Azure SQL Database.

The database migration process typically consists of the following methods.

- **Discovery.** Discovery mode starts with identifying your existing database workload, usage scenarios, and database version compatibility level and exploring the right target database and service tier available on the target platform.
- **Assessment.** In the assessment phase, you discover any compatibility issues between the source and target platform. For example, if you migrate from on-premises SQL Server to Azure SQL Database (single or pooled), you might need to look at SQL server features such as cross-database queries as an example and validate if the target database supports it.
- **Transform.** In the transform phase, you make changes to the existing SQL script to resolve any incompatibility issues or adapt to the new features available on the target platform instead.
- **Migrate and Monitor.** In this phase, you migrate your database to the selected Azure SQL Database, validate your migration, monitor remediation, and optimize cost.

Microsoft Azure provides the following database migration methods for the on-premises SQL Server database to the Azure SQL Database.

- **Offline migration using Database Migration Assistant (DMA).** The Azure Data migration assistant (DMA) is a free tool that you can download on the local machine and use for assessment to identify compatibility issues before you attempt to migrate. This method does not support the Managed Instance. They are typically used for supported databases when an application can afford to have more extended downtime.
- **Online migration using Azure Database Migration Service (DMS).** The Azure Database Migration Service (DMS) is the recommended way to migrate databases at scale with minimal downtime. The DMS supports both online and offline migration for

single, pooled, and Managed Instance databases. In the offline migration, the application downtime begins when you initiate the migration. With the online migration, the downtime is minimal and is limited to the time required to perform actual cutover.

MORE INFORMATION? **SQL AZURE DATABASE MIGRATION TIPS**

When you migrate your database, you want to see comparatively improved performance on the Azure SQL Database. It requires you to carefully evaluate your on-premises SQL server usage scenario, workload, and source and target database compatibility. The blog post on cloudskills.io has a comprehensive guide on key considerations that you must take before you migrate. Learn more by visiting *https://cloudskills.io/blog/azure-sql-database-performance*.

The overall migration process consists of the migration of the two elements, the schema and data. In the assessment phase of the migration, you start with determining the compatibility issues between the source SQL Server and the target Azure SQL Database using a database migration assistant (DMA) tool followed by fixing the reported issues if there are any. After you have fixed all the identified compatibility issues, you must deploy the script generated by DMA on the target pre-created Azure SQL Database. After the schema has been migrated, you start with the next step of data migration.

The following step-by-step instructions describe the end-to-end process for publishing your on-premises SQL Server database to the Azure SQL Database using the Azure database migration service (DMS).

1. Download and install the Azure Database migration assistant from **https://www.microsoft.com/en-us/download/details.aspx?id=53595**.
2. Using the DMA tool, create an assessment project by clicking the + icon on the left blade and providing the project name. Select an SQL server as a source, select an Azure SQL Database as the target, and click **Create**.
3. In this example, because we are accessing the on-premises SQL Server database with Azure SQL Database for any incompatibility, you must choose **Check Database Compatibility** and **Check Feature Parity** (see Figure 4-40). Click **Next**.
4. Connect to the source SQL Server database by using database credentials and start an assessment. Note that the credential used to connect to the SQL server must be a member of the sysadmin server role.
5. After the assessment results are ready, the next step is to resolve the issues or any migration blockers that might affect the migration. Repeat the assessment steps until all the issues are fixed.

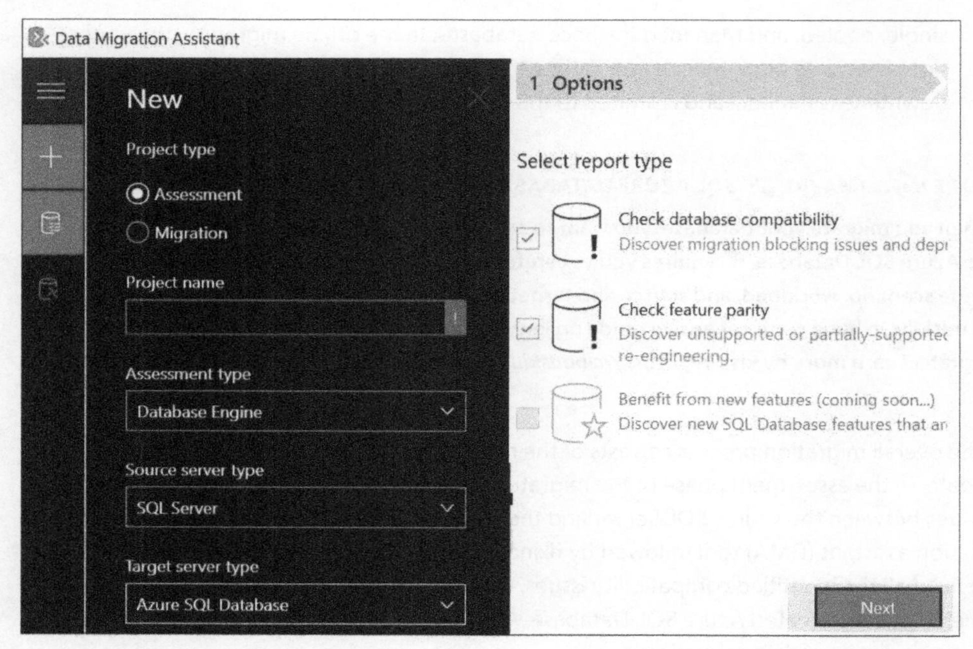

FIGURE 4-40 Database migration assistant

After you are confident that all issues have been addressed and the on-premises SQL Server database has become a good candidate for migration, continue with the following steps to deploy a schema on Azure SQL Database:

1. Log in to Azure Portal and create a blank Azure SQL Database.
2. Once the database is ready, navigate to its blade and create a firewall allow rule on Azure SQL Database for a source machine outbound IP address where you are running your DMA tool.
3. Next, in the DMA tool, create a new migration project by selecting the **Migration** option, as shown in Figure 4-40. The wizards on the DMA tool will guide you to provide a source and target database details. You must use a credential with control server permission to connect to the source database and control database permission to connect to the target database.
4. Using the DMA tool, select the database schema objects to generate a script. After the script is ready, use the deploy schema feature of DMA to deploy the schema to the target database.

Now that we have successfully deployed the schema of the on-premises SQL database on the Azure SQL Database, we will create an Azure Database Migration Service for data migration. Follow these steps:

1. In the Azure portal, search for **Azure Database Migration Service** resource and click **Add** (see Figure 4-41).

Home > Azure Database Migration Services
Azure Database Migration Services
Default Directory
+ Add   Edit columns   Refresh   Assign tags
Subscriptions: Pay-As-You-Go – Don't see a subscription? Open Dire
Filter by name...   All resource g
1 items
Name   Status

FIGURE 4-41 Azure Database Migration Services

2. Consider the following critical points while creating a database migration service (DMS):
   - The DMS requires a virtual network that facilitates connectivity to the source server. That said, you must either create a new virtual network along with the setup of a DMS or choose from the existing one. You would use either site-to-site VPN or ExpressRoute for on-premises connectivity. The service endpoint, `Microsoft.Sql` must be added on the VNet to allow outbound connection to the Azure SQL Database.
   - Ensure the NSGs on the Azure virtual network allow inbound connectivity for DMS on TCP ports 443, 53, 1433, 9354, 445, and 12000.
   - You must choose the location of the DMS service closest to your source database data center for low latency and faster migration. It is recommended you select higher SKUs on the target database to speed up the data migration process. You can scale down the database SKU after the migration is complete.
3. Now that the DMS has been created, navigate to the overview blade of DMS and click **New Migration Project**, as shown in Figure 4-42.

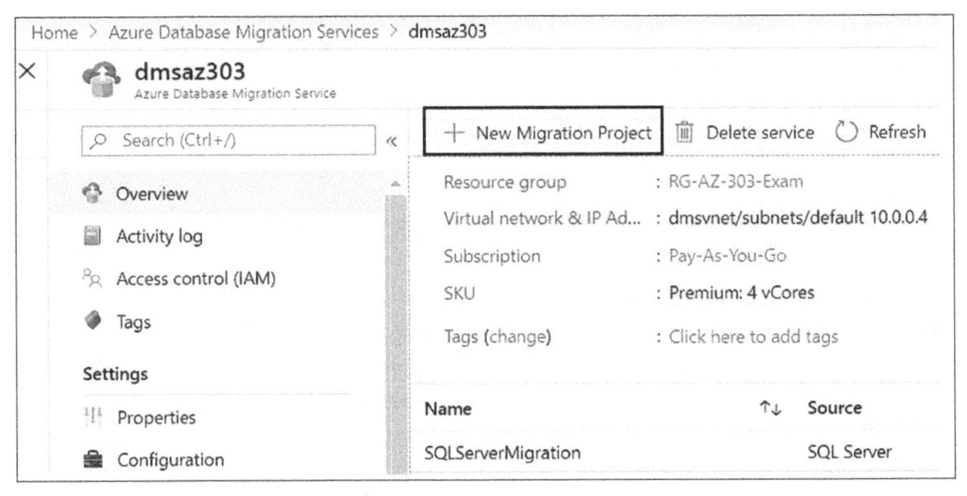

FIGURE 4-42 Adding a new migration project in DMS

4. Fill in the required fields, as shown in Figure 4-43. Set **Source Server Type** to **SQL Server** and set **Target Server Type** to **Azure SQL Database**. Under **Type Of Migration/Activity**, choose **Online Data Migration**, and click **Save**.

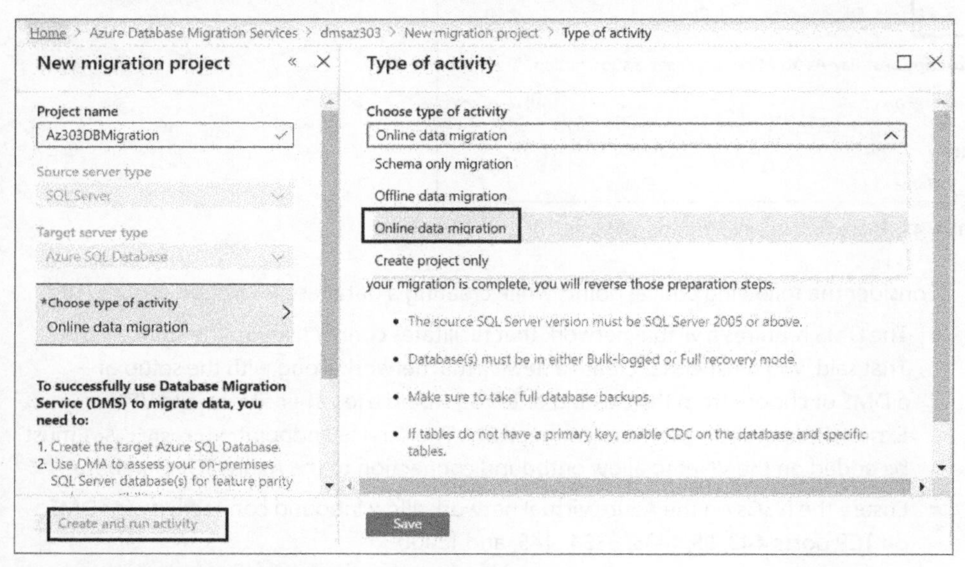

FIGURE 4-43 Configuring a database migration project

For online migration, continuous data replication is required. Therefore, you must do the following configurations on the source database for replication.

1. The replication feature must be installed on the source SQL server. Use the following TSQL commands to check whether the replication component is installed. You will see an error if it isn't:

```
USE master; DECLARE @installed int; EXEC @installed = sys.
sp_MS_replication_installed;
SELECT @installed as installed;
```

2. Use the following TSQL to enable replication:

```
USE master
EXEC sp_replicationdboption @dbname = <databasename>,  @optname = 'publish', @
value = 'true' GO
```

3. After the replication is enabled, configure the distributor role for the source SQL Server. The steps for publishing SQL server distribution are given on the Microsoft documentation at *https://docs.microsoft.com/en-us/sql/relational-databases/replication/configure-publishing-and-distribution?view=sql-server-ver15*.

4. The database must be in full recovery mode. Use the following TSQL commands to check for and enable full recovery mode:

```
USE master;
SELECT name, recovery_model_desc   FROM sys.databases   WHERE name =
<databasename>
ALTER DATABASE <databasename>  SET RECOVERY FULL;
```

5. Ensure all the tables on the source database have a clustered index (primary key). Use the TSQL commands below to find tables without a clustered index and create them accordingly:

```
USE <databasename>; go
SELECT is_tracked_by_cdc, name AS TableName FROM sys.tables WHERE type = 'U' and
is_ms_shipped = 0 AND
OBJECTPROPERTY(OBJECT_ID, 'TableHasPrimaryKey') = 0;
```

6. Ensure the full backup of the source database is taken.
7. Ensure you configure a Windows firewall rule to allow the Azure Database Migration Service to access the source SQL Server; by default, this is TCP port 1433.
8. Ensure the TCP/IP protocol is enabled on the source SQL server.

IMPORTANT **ONLINE MIGRATION LIMITATIONS AND WORKAROUND FOR A SINGLE DATABASE**

The DMS service has some limitations at the writing of this book, and workarounds for such limitations are detailed on the Microsoft document posted at *https://docs.microsoft.com/en-us/azure/dms/known-issues-azure-sql-online*. Make sure you evaluate all of them before you adapt to on-line migration.

9. In the migration wizard shown in Figure 4-44, select the source and the target database, as shown in steps 1 and 2 on the **Migration Wizard** pane.
10. On the source database pane, **Migration Source Detail**, provide the connection details for the source database. It is recommended that you use the trusted certificate on the source server to encrypt the connection credentials. In case you do not have it installed, you can use a self-signed certificate created by DMS by selecting a trust server certificate.
11. Click **Save**.
12. On the target database pane, under **Migration Target Detail**, specify the connection details for the Azure SQL Database that you created in step 6. It is recommended that you encrypt the connection between source and target databases by selecting **Encrypt Connection** (see Figure 4-44).
13. Click **Save**.

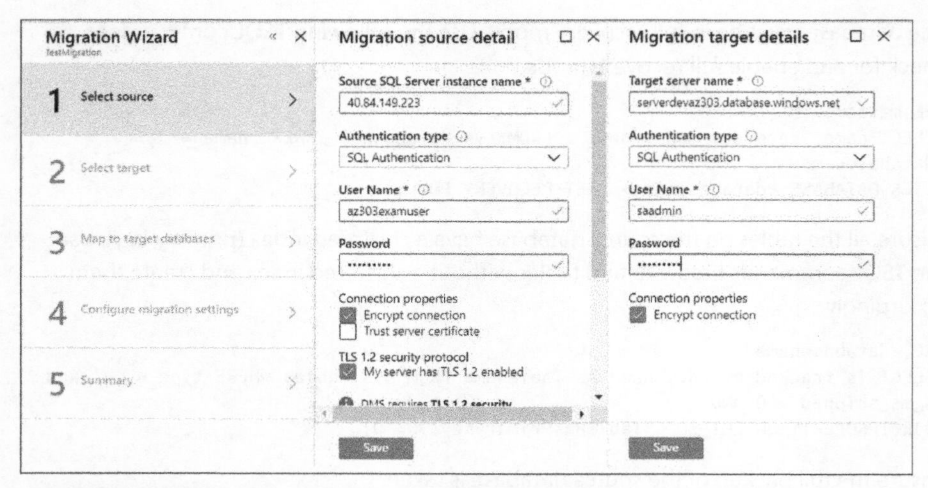

FIGURE 4-44 Configuring source and target database connectivity details

14. Under **Map To Target Databases**, map the source and target databases unless the name of the target database is the same as the source database.
15. Under **Configure migration settings,** select the tables on the source database to be migrated.
16. Lastly, on the summary screen, click **Run Migration,** as shown in Figure 4-45.

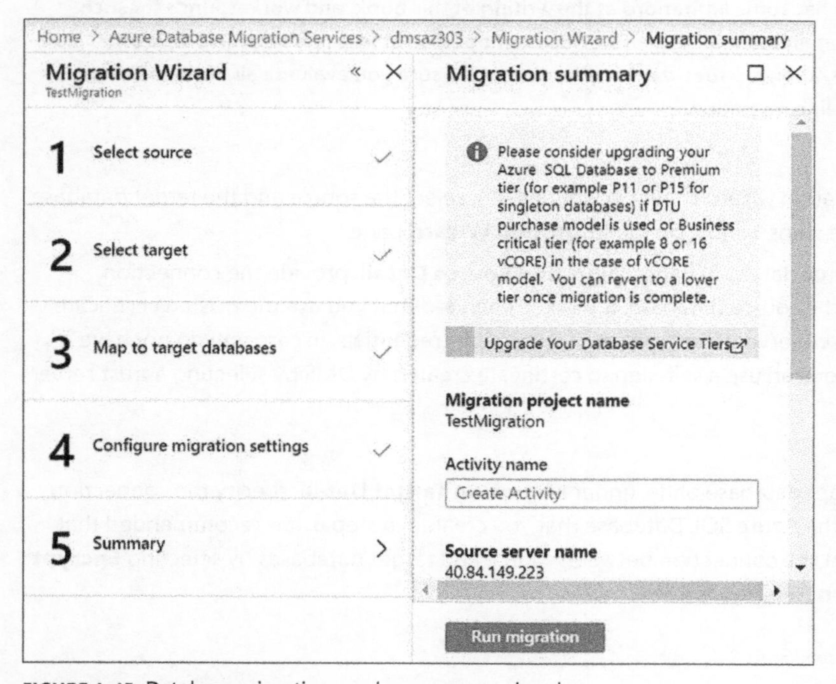

FIGURE 4-45 Database migration service summary wizard

17. Figure 4-46 shows the migration activity. From here, you can monitor the migration status. Once it is completed, you can plan for the final cutover by clicking the **Start Cutover** button. Before you plan to cutover, make sure you stop new transactions on the source database or wait for existing pending transactions to complete. After the migration is done, perform data validation on the target Azure SQL Database and connect the application to the new Azure SQL Database.

FIGURE 4-46 A database migration status wizard

Chapter summary

- NoSQL databases are non-relational databases designed to provide a flexible data model and access patterns for various complex datasets.
- Typical types of NoSQL database include key-value data store, document databases, graph databases, and column-family databases.
- Azure Table storage is a highly scalable key-value data storage for structured data.
- Azure Cosmos DB is a globally distributed, multi-master database that enables you to independently scale throughput and storage across the globe with guaranteed throughput and performance.
- Azure Cosmos DB supports five programming APIs: SQL API, Mongo API, Cassandra API, Gremlin Graph API, and Table API.
- Azure Cosmos DB allows you to set up multi-master replicas across regions to facilitate failover and high availability in case of a disruptive event in the primary region.
- Azure SQL Database is one of the most popular managed relational databases. The service has different tiers to choose from based upon your application performance needs.
- Database transactional units (DTUs) are a blended measure of compute, storage, and IO resource that you pre-allocate when you create a database on the logical server.
- The vCore-based model is the Microsoft recommended purchasing model where you get the flexibility of independently scaling compute and storage to meet your application needs.

- Point-in-time restore backups in the Azure SQL Database are stored up to 35 days in geo-replicated Blob storage. If you need backup to be retained beyond 35 days, you can configure long-term backup retention policies.
- Azure SQL Managed Instance Database provides close to 100 percent compatibility with on-premises SQL Server. The database can only be created within a dedicated VNet and exposed over a private endpoint by default.
- Azure database migration service supports both online and offline database migration. The service uses the database migration assistant tool for schema migration and synchronous replication between source and target database for data migration.

Thought experiment

In this thought experiment, demonstrate your knowledge and skills that you have learned throughout the chapter. The answers to the thought experiment are given in the next section.

You're an architect of an online education institution. The institution has its own IT and software development department. The institution has its student base across the world and provides online study courses on various subjects, conducts exams, and provides online degrees upon successful completion of the course. The course content is made available online during weekdays, and instructor-led training is held over the weekend. The online web portal used by the institution is built-in .NET core, and the backend is an SQL server for storing details of available courses and MongoDB NoSQL for application custom auditing. The application is hosted in the U.S. The institution is facing several challenges and getting complaints from students around the world that application for online courses and practice exams work very slowly at times. The management of the institution wants to leverage cloud technologies to address slowness challenges and approaches you to answer the following questions:

1. The institution has a limited budget and cannot afford to rewrite the application code to adopt the cloud. The management does not want to change the bunch of batch jobs written in the SQL server.
2. The institution management has security concerns using the cloud databases in terms of keeping databases outside of the private network in the cloud.

Thought experiment answers

This section contains solutions to the thought experiment.

1. Because the application is built on Microsoft technology stack, you can host it on Azure App Services and configure autoscaling. Regarding SQL server backend, Azure SQL Database Managed Instance provides you close to 100 percent SQL Server compatibility. Therefore, you will not have to change the application code when you migrate from SQL Server to Azure SQL Managed Instance.

2. For the NoSQL backend, MongoDB, you can use Cosmos DB MongoDB API and migrate without changing any application code.
3. To address security concerns, the security posture of Azure SQL Managed Instance provides native integration with Azure virtual network where your application traffic does not go over the public Internet and remains in the Microsoft backbone network.

Index

A

B

C

D

E

F

G

H

I

J-K

L

M

N

O-P

Q-R

S

T

U

V

W-X-Y-Z